HAMLET
PRINCE OF DENMARK

EDITED BY

ROBERT HAPGOOD

Professor Emeritus of English, University of New Hampshire

CAMBRIDGE
UNIVERSITY PRESS

PUBLISHED BY THE PRESS SYNDICATE OF THE UNIVERSITY OF CAMBRIDGE
The Pitt Building, Trumpington Street, Cambridge CB2 1RP, United Kingdom

CAMBRIDGE UNIVERSITY PRESS
The Edinburgh Building, Cambridge CB2 2RU, UK   http://www.cup.cam.ac.uk
40 West 20th Street, New York, NY 10011–4211, USA   http://www.cup.org
10 Stamford Road, Oakleigh, Melbourne 3166, Australia

First published 1999

Printed in the United Kingdom at the University Press, Cambridge

Typeset in Monotype Ehrhardt 10/12.5pt, in QuarkXPress™ [SE]

A catalogue record for this book is available from the British Library

Library of Congress Cataloguing in Publication data

Shakespeare, William, 1564–1616.
Hamlet / edited by Robert Hapgood
p.   cm. – (Shakespeare in production)

ISBN 0 521 44438 1 hardback
ISBN 0 521 64635 9 paperback

CONTENTS

ILLUSTRATIONS

SERIES EDITORS' PREFACE

It is no longer necessary to stress that the text of a play is only its starting-point, and that only in production is its potential realized and capable of being appreciated fully. Since the coming-of-age of Theatre Studies as an academic discipline, we now understand that even Shakespeare is only one collaborator in the creation and infinite recreation of his play upon the stage. And just as we now agree that no play is complete until it is produced, so we have become interested in the way in which plays often produced – and pre-eminently the plays of the national Bard, William Shakespeare – acquire a life history of their own, after they leave the hands of their first maker.

Since the eighteenth century Shakespeare has become a cultural con-struct: sometimes the guarantor of nationhood, heritage and the status quo, sometimes seized and transformed to be its critic and antidote. This latter role has been particularly evident in countries where Shakespeare has to be translated. The irony is that while his status as national icon grows in the English-speaking world, his language is both lost and renewed, so that for good or ill, Shakespeare can be made to seem more urgently 'relevant' than in England or America, and may become the one dissenting voice that the censors mistake as harmless.

'Shakespeare in Production' gives the reader, the student and the scholar a comprehensive dossier of materials – eye-witness accounts, contemporary criticism, promptbook marginalia, stage business, cuts, additions and rewrit-ings – from which to construct an understanding of the many meanings that the plays have carried down the ages and across the world. These materials are organized alongside the New Cambridge Shakespeare text of the play, line by line and scene by scene, while a substantial introduction in each volume offers a guide to their interpretation. One may trace an argument about, for example, the many ways of playing Queen Gertrude, or the politi-cal transmutations of the text of *Henry V*; or take a scene, an act or a whole play, and work out how it has succeeded or failed in presentation over four hundred years.

For, despite our insistence that the plays are endlessly made and remade by history, Shakespeare is not a blank, scribbled upon by the age. Theatre history charts changes, but also registers something in spite of those changes. Some productions work and others do not. Two interpretations may be entirely different, and yet both will bring the play to life. Why? Without setting out to give absolute answers, the history of a play in the theatre can often show where the energy and shape of it lie, what has made it tick, through many permutations. In this way theatre history can find common ground with literary criticism. Both will find suggestive directions in the introductions to these volumes, while the commentaries provide raw material for readers to recreate the living experience of theatre, and become their own eye-witnesses.

J. S. Bratton
Julie Hankey

This series was originated by Jeremy Treglown and published by Junction Books, and later by Bristol Classical Press, as 'Plays in Performance'. Four titles were published; all are now out of print.

ACKNOWLEDGEMENTS

The historical record of *Hamlet*-in-production through the centuries is richer than for any other play. Its extent is all but overwhelming. This is true even when, as in this edition, the focus is largely on live performances as reported by eye-witnesses. (Since the numerous *Hamlet* motion pictures and recordings are readily available, they will – with the exception of the land-mark films by Laurence Olivier and Kenneth Branagh – receive relatively light treatment here.) Of stage productions, there are reviews in abundance and a number of extraordinarily detailed accounts of full performances. Back-stage lore also abounds, including scores of promptbooks, a host of memoirs and biographies by and about leading actors and directors, and – in recent years – several logs of rehearsals kept by cast-members.

Drawing together these resources, the Introduction offers a chronological survey of the main productions of *Hamlet* from Burbage to Branagh. Even more than for most plays, contemporary accounts of these productions have emphasized the interpretation of the title-role, and my survey reflects this emphasis. But the historical record is full enough to give as well a sense of whole productions, including the work of supporting players, directors, and designers. And these productions are best understood in a cultural context that includes developments in theatre history and literary analysis. The survey incorporates these larger perspectives.

As extensive as the data encompassed in this edition may seem, its coverage of available information is by no means exhaustive; on the contrary, space considerations have made it necessary to be highly selective. There is a need for a full-scale performance history of *Hamlet*. In its absence the interested reader will find especially helpful, as I have, certain standard references. Useful supplements to my chronology of 'Productions' are Harold Child's concise survey of noteworthy English stage performances in an appendix of Dover Wilson's edition of *Hamlet* and J. C. Trewin's detailed listing of productions in the West End, at the Old Vic, and at Stratford-upon-Avon in the appendix of *Shakespeare on the English Stage, 1900–1964*. Outside of England, Robert Speaight has chapters on Continental productions in *Shakespeare on the Stage*, while Charles Shattuck devotes two volumes to *Shakespeare on the American Stage*. Both studies give extensive attention to *Hamlet*. For a selection of pictures of stage productions, see *Hamlet through the Ages* by Raymond Mander and Joe Mitchenson. For motion picture versions, Jack Jorgens's *Shakespeare on Film* remains the best place to start.

Two recent studies are especially useful. Readers who wish larger backgrounds for the portraits of the English and American Prince Hamlets profiled in my Introduction will find them in John Mills's *Hamlet on Stage: The Great Tradition*; each of his portraits begins with a knowing section on the general style and career of each actor. Those who wish more instances of stage business and readings than are provided in my Commentary will find them in Marvin Rosenberg's *The Masks of Hamlet*; his work is especially valuable for its details about foreign-language productions and for its particulars about the many English and American productions he has himself seen. With respect to documentation, Mills provides precise and reliable citations of contemporary reviews in periodicals, Rosenberg, a broadly inclusive bibliography of pertinent books and articles.

Of course, my greatest resource has been archival data. Gathering it has taken me to the Harvard Theatre Collection and the Athenaeum Library in Boston, the Hampden/Booth Library at the Players Club and the Billy Rose Theatre Collection at the Lincoln Center in New York, the National Film Archive and the National Sound Archive in London, the Shakespeare Centre Library in Stratford-upon-Avon, and the Special Collections of the University of Southern California. All these institutions have been just as forthcoming as one could wish. Special thanks are due to the patient staffs of the Colindale Newspaper Collection of the British Library, the Shakespeare Collection of the Birmingham (England) Central Library, and the Folger Shakespeare Library, where I made more extended but very intense visits that put heavy stress on their retrieval systems. This travel and other research expenditure was supported by a summer fellowship from the National Endowment for the Humanities and by grants from the Graduate School, College of Liberal Arts, Research Council, and Humanities Center of the University of New Hampshire.

John Mills and Alan Hughes handed on microfilms, xeroxes, and other materials surviving from their own researches. Miriam Gilbert permitted me to use her unpublished accounts of the Jonathan Pryce and Mark Rylance *Hamlet*s. Donald Foster let me inspect his statistical findings while still in progress. Russell Jackson gave me a timely and very fruitful suggestion. William Alexander transcribed the musical items. Julie Hankey was a stimulating general editor. I was privileged to sit in on rehearsals of a production of *Hamlet* at Ashland, Oregon, in 1961, directed by Robert Loper, with Richard Risso as Hamlet.

As always my greatest debt is to my wife Marilyn, who has been especially supportive of this project.

ABBREVIATIONS

Boaden	James Boaden. *Memoirs of the Life of John Philip Kemble*, I, London, 1825.
Clarke	Charles Clarke. Unpublished columns of commentary on Edwin Booth's *Hamlet* in the Folger Shakespeare Library.
Davies	Thomas Davies. *Dramatic Mi[s]cellanies*, London, vol. III, 1784.
F	*The Tragedie of Hamlet, Prince of Denmarke*, 1623 (First Folio).
Field	Kate Field. *Charles Albert Fechter*, Boston, 1882.
G. I. Hamlet	*Maurice Evans' G. I. Production of Hamlet*, acting edition, Garden City, NY, 1947.
Gilder	Rosamund Gilder. *John Gielgud's Hamlet; A Record of Performance*, Oxford, 1937.
Gould	Thomas R. Gould. *The Tragedian: An Essay on the Histrionic Genius of Junius Brutus Booth*, New York, 1868.
Phelps	Henry P. Phelps. *Hamlet from the Actor's Standpoint*, Brooklyn, 1977.
Q1	*The Tragicall Historie of Hamlet Prince of Denmarke*, 1603 (First Quarto).
Q2	*The Tragedie of Hamlet, Prince of Denmarke*, 1604–5 (Second Quarto).
Rosenberg	Marvin Rosenberg. *The Masks of Hamlet*, Newark, Del., 1992.
Rossi	Alfred Rossi. *Minneapolis Rehearsals: Tyrone Guthrie Directs Hamlet*, Los Angeles, 1970.
Russell	Edward R. Russell. *Irving as Hamlet*, London, 1875.
SD	stage direction.
Senelick	Laurence Senelick. *Gordon Craig's Moscow Hamlet*, Westport, Conn., 1982.
Shattuck	Charles H. Shattuck. *The Hamlet of Edwin Booth*, Chicago, 1969.
South Bank Show	'Hamlet', South Bank Show, televised 2 April 1989, prod. M. Bragg; available on video from Iambic Productions.

Sterne   Richard L. Sterne. *John Gielgud Directs Richard Burton in Hamlet: A Journal of Rehearsals*, New York, 1967.

Stone   *Edwin Booth's Performance: The Mary Isabella Stone Commentaries*, ed. D. Watermeier, Ann Arbor, Mich., 1990.

Terry   Ellen Terry. *Ellen Terry's Memoirs*, ed. E. Craig and C. St. John, 1932; rpt. Westport, Conn., 1970.

PRODUCTIONS

This table presents a select chronological list of the principal productions of *Hamlet* referred to in this edition. Dates of less noteworthy performances are given in passing in the text. A span of years indicates the first and last known dates of performance. Occasionally, the first date indicated is that of the first major performance (Macready, for instance, gave 'benefit' performances before his full-scale London debut in 1823). A name on its own indicates the actor of the title-role. The name of the theatre shown first is the site of the first performance date given. Further theatres listed housed subsequent performances; additional dates are indented for distinct later productions by the same performer of special importance. All theatres are in London unless otherwise indicated.

Date(s)	Actor(s), Director	Venue(s)
?1601–1618	Richard Burbage	Globe/Blackfriars
1607, 1608	Captain William Keeling's crew	HMS Dragon on the high seas
1619/20–1642	Joseph Taylor	at Court Globe/Blackfriars
1661–1709	Thomas Betterton	Opera Lincoln's Inn Fields Drury Lane
1706–8?–1732	Robert Wilks	Drury Lane
1742–1776	David Garrick	Drury Lane
1777–1784	John Henderson	Haymarket Drury Lane Covent Garden
1783–1817	John Philip Kemble	Drury Lane After 1803: Covent Garden
1803	François Joseph Talma	Comédie Française, Paris
1807–1832	Charles Mayne Young	Covent Garden
1814–1832	Edmund Kean	Drury Lane
1823–1851	William Charles Macready	Drury Lane Covent Garden

Date(s)	Actor(s), Director	Venue(s)
1837	Pavel Mochalov	Petrovski, Moscow
1838	Charles Kean	Drury Lane
		Haymarket
1850		Princess's
1860	Edwin Booth	Winter Garden (NY)
1864		Winter Garden
1870		Booth's (NY)
1880		Princess's
1891	Ophelia: Helena Modjeska (1889–90)	touring
1861	Charles Fechter	Princess's
1864		Lyceum
1870		Niblo's Garden (NY)
1874	Henry Irving	Lyceum
1878	Ophelia: Ellen Terry	
1885		
1875	Thomasso Salvini	Drury Lane
1881	William Poel	St. George's Hall
1884	Wilson Barrett	Princess's
	Claudius: E. S. Willard	
1886	Jean Mounet Sully	Comédie Française, Paris
1892	Herbert Beerbohm Tree	Haymarket
1897	Johnston Forbes-Robertson	Lyceum
	Polonius: J. H. Barnes	
1899	Sarah Bernhardt	Théâtre de la Renaissance, Paris
1900	William Poel, dir.	Carpenter's Hall
1900	Claudius: Oscar Asche	Lyceum
	(with Frank Benson)	
1905	(with H. B. Irving)	Adelphi
1904	Ophelia: Julia Marlowe	Illinois Theatre, Chicago
	(with E. H. Sothern)	
1907		Waldorf
1905	John Martin-Harvey	Lyric
1912	Vasili Kachalov/Gordon Craig/	Kamergersky
	Konstantin Stanislavsky	(Moscow Art Theatre)
1914	Esme Percy/William Poel	Little Theatre
1922	John Barrymore	Sam H. Harris Theatre (NY)
1925		Haymarket

Date(s)	Actor(s), Director	Venue(s)
1925	Barry Jackson's Birmingham Repertory Claudius: Frank Vosper	Kingsway
1930	John Gielgud	Old Vic, then Queen's
1934		New Theatre
1936		Empire, then St James (NY)
1939		Lyceum, then Kronborg Castle
1944		Haymarket
1937	Laurence Olivier	Old Vic
1948		Two Cities Film
1938	Alec Guinness Dir: Tyrone Guthrie	Old Vic
1951		New Theatre
1948	Paul Scofield	Stratford
1955	Claudius: Alec Clunes	Moscow, then Phoenix
1949	Michael Redgrave	Old Vic
1958		Stratford
1953	Richard Burton	Assembly Hall, Edinburgh, then Old Vic and Kronborg Castle
1964	Dir: John Gielgud	Lunt-Fontanne (NY)
1963	George Grizzard Dir: Tyrone Guthrie	Guthrie, Minneapolis
1964	Dir: Grigori Kozintsev	Lenfilm film
1965	David Warner Dir: Peter Hall Ophelia: Glenda Jackson	Stratford
1969	Nicol Williamson	Round House Woodfall film
1971–1980	Vladimir Vysotsky Dir: Yuri Lyubimov	Taganka Theatre, Moscow
1975	Ben Kingsley Dir: Buzz Goodbody	The Other Place, Stratford, then Roundhouse
1980	Jonathan Pryce Dir: Richard Eyre	Royal Court
1980	Derek Jacobi	BBC-TV
1988	Mark Rylance Dir: Ron Daniels	Stratford

Date(s)	Actor(s), Director	Venue(s)
1988	Kenneth Branagh	Phoenix
1992/3		Barbican then Stratford
1996/7	Claudius: Derek Jacobi	Castle Rock Film
1989	Polonius: Michael Bryant (with Daniel Day Lewis)	National
1990	Mel Gibson Dir: Franco Zeffirelli	Carolco film

than usually open to interpretation. In *Rosencrantz and Guildenstern* (1874), W. S. Gilbert (evidently thinking mostly of Edmund Kean, Charles Fechter, Henry Irving, and Edwin Booth) made sport of the fact that the Prince is

> Alike for no two seasons at a time.
> Sometimes he's tall – sometimes he's very short –
> Now with black hair – now with a flaxen wig –
> Sometimes an English accent – then a French –
> Then English with a strong provincial "burr".
> Once an American, and once a Jew –
> But Danish never, take him how you will!

Yet Kenneth Tynan spoke for many in finding the variability of the role to be a strong point: 'The best acting parts (*Hamlet* is an obvious example) are those which admit of the largest number of different interpretations.'[6] Since Gielgud made a great success as a young actor in the role (he was 26), it has more and more become a diploma-piece in which promising stars, usually now in their thirties, show what they can do. Ben Kingsley calls it 'the greatest part for a young actor': 'there are so many beautiful mysteries locked in there about boyhood becoming manhood' (*Independent*, 17 March 1989).

These acting opportunities can also constitute severe challenges. John Barton lists some requirements for the Prince:

> He must have the capacity to be noble and gentle but also brutal and coarse
> . . . he has to be obviously full of passion but able to stand outside his own
> passion and be objective about it. He has to have a strong sense of irony, wit,
> humour. He has to have a *deep* intellectual energy. He has to have a *very*
> volatile temperament, so that you never know what he's going to be like from
> one moment to the next . . .   (South Bank Show)

'The demands', Barton concludes, 'are huge.' How are these demands to be met? Gielgud reports Harley Granville-Barker's advice to him: 'You must start the next scene where you left off in the last one, even if there is another scene between the two'; and when he directed Burton he passed this advice on: 'The important thing is to tell the story of the play and to make every scene a progression.'[7] He once told Kenneth Branagh that the play describes 'the process of living' (*Birmingham Post*, 18 March 1993).

Hamlets have also learned to pace themselves, for the role demands sheer physical stamina. Michael Pennington has mapped the terrain, finding the

---

6 Tynan, *He that Plays*, p. 31.   7 Gielgud, *Acting*, p. 42.

INTRODUCTION

'*Hamlet* is always going on somewhere.'[1] So director Tyrone Guthrie once remarked, and it is almost literally true. The play has been performed more than any other and has led a virtually continuous life in the theatre since Shakespeare's time. Even during the Puritan interregnum, when all stage performances were banned, a 'droll' excerpted from the gravedigger scene was performed.[2] Since then productions have at times been so numerous as to seem ludicrous; London has more than once had three productions running simultaneously. In April and May of 1905, for instance, H. B. Irving, H. Beerbohm Tree, and John Martin-Harvey all opened West End productions of the play, provoking P. G. Wodehouse's 'Too Much Hamlet':

> It's 'Hamlet' here and 'Hamlet' there
> And 'Hamlet' on next week.
> An actor not in 'Hamlet' is regarded as a freak.   (*Books of Today*, 1905)

What has been the basis of *Hamlet*'s phenomenal record as a theatre-piece? For one thing, it is so eminently performable that performers have simply wanted to do the play. Guthrie points out that it can be rehearsed very quickly: 'There are few scenes involving more than two or three people; the big ensemble scenes are short.'[3] All the scenes, John Gielgud adds, 'are audience-proof . . . if they are played theatrically for all they are worth they will always hold the house' (Gilder, p. 50). As for the play's dialogue, Richard Burton feels that 'there isn't a line in it that isn't infinitely, effortlessly speakable'.[4] For supporting players it offers a range of colourful middle-sized parts, each with a scene or two alone with the Prince, plus a variety of cameos (the Ghost, the First Player, the gravediggers, Osric, Fortinbras), all of which lend themselves to vivid portrayal. In the past the roles matched the standard stock company 'lines': the heavy, the old man, the male and female juveniles, the eccentric and low comedians, the walking gentlemen.[5]

For leading actors, Prince Hamlet is the role of roles, its extraordinary length (it is by far the longest part in Shakespeare) and its exceptional variety providing opportunities for virtuoso acting. The role is also more

1 Guthrie, *Directions*, p. 72.   2 'The Grave-makers' in Kirkman, *Wits*.
3 Guthrie, *Theatre*, p. 65.   4 Richard Burton, 'Interview', p. 54.
5 Donohue, *Character*, pp. 72–3.

first third of the play the easiest because the play carries the Prince rather than the reverse. But 'the great middle arc of the play, from the nunnery through to the departure for England, was the most taxing stretch . . . this is where the part shakes you like a rat, racing you from one crisis to the next with scarcely time to draw breath'.[8] Even the quieter last part will require the fight at Ophelia's grave and the final duel.

Some have thought the demands of the role to exceed any stage fulfilment. Such an attitude was satirized by Dickens in *Nicholas Nickleby* where Mr and Mrs Curdle, those despairing patrons of the drama, ask: 'What man is there, now living, who can present before us all those changing and prismatic colours with which the character of Hamlet is invested?' They conclude: 'Hamlet is gone, perfectly gone' (ch. 24). Despite its daunting challenges, however, there has been no shortage of recent aspirants to the role. The part of the Prince can offer rare rewards. Olivier promises that it 'can give you moments of unknown joy': 'Hamlet just takes you by the hand and either treats you roughly or shows you the way to the stars.'[9] One of its prime attractions, and a major factor in *Hamlet*'s longevity, has been the Prince's extraordinary rapport with the audience, an intimacy that Shakespeare enhances by giving him an unmatched number of opportunities to confide his thoughts and feelings, whether to other characters or to the audience in his soliloquies. To David Warner the rapport he experienced while playing the role at times approached a religious experience: 'A lot of actors say there are moments, maybe just once in a split second in your career, you get next to God. There is this ONENESS – one moment where every single member of the audience is THERE, together with yourself, where you feel everybody is in tune, one split second . . . '[10]

The actors and directors quoted above identify abiding strengths that help to account for *Hamlet*'s unrivalled durability and worldwide popularity. To these should be added its exceptional responsiveness to changing times and places. Whatever the circumstances, it seems, the play can speak to them. During World War II, for example, Maurice Evans found in the cut-down version he presented to American troops a strong parallel between Hamlet's situation and theirs: 'Each of them was in his own way a Hamlet, bewildered by the uninvited circumstances in which he found himself and groping for the moral justification and the physical courage demanded of him' (G. I. *Hamlet*, p. 17). Meanwhile in Nazi Germany *Hamlet* was no less topical. Although Hitler frowned on Hamlet as overly intellectual, Gustaf Gründgens was allowed to play the role, depicting 'a hero that the Third Reich could be proud of: dynamic, a man of action and,

8 Pennington, 'Hamlet', pp. 125–6.   9 Olivier, *Acting*, pp. 89, 77.
10 Maher, *Soliloquies*, p. 62.

most important, a full-blooded Nordic' (*New York Times*, 2 November 1988). In 1989/90 Berlin, Heiner Müller found the play as topical as ever. Taking *Hamlet* to be the tragedy that has most to say about the coming together of Western and Eastern Europe, he saw it as dealing with 'two epochs, and with the fissure between them. This fissure is straddled by an intellectual, who is no longer certain how to behave and what to do: the old things don't work any more, but the new ways aren't to his taste.'[11] The play's relevance need not be so immediate, but its performance history confirms that it can be an 'abstract and brief chronicle' not only of its own place and time but also of many places and times since, including our own.

The story of *Hamlet* in production thus records an ongoing process of discovery, as earlier interpretations lose their currency and new performers seek out what it is in the play and in themselves that will speak most power-fully and immediately to the audiences of their own times. To celebrate the play's multifariousness, however, is not to reduce it to a Rorschach blot from which a series of cultural constructs have been drawn. That would be to leave the playwright out of the encounter between playwright, player, and playgoer that makes a play a play. Indeed the whole production history of *Hamlet* – what has passed and is to come – may be seen as an unfolding of the endlessly fertile potentials for drama latent in Shakespeare's originating imagination.

Furthermore, this unfolding has been marked not only by change but by lines of continuity, large and small. Derek Jacobi has called *Hamlet* 'the greatest of all acting traditions'. Like many other actors he likes to empha-size connections with performers before and since. He recalls how seeing Richard Burton play Hamlet at the Old Vic made up his mind that he wanted to be an actor and how thrilled he was when Burton came to see him play the role at the Old Vic: 'And also there was another visitor at that time who came backstage and told me that seeing the performance had made up *his* mind to go into acting. His name was Kenneth Branagh.'[12] One marvels that there should be a felt line of succession among three such different actors, whose portrayals of Hamlet have proved so different from one another. Perhaps what they share is less a matter of style than of aspiration: the daring to take on the challenges the role presents and the courage to come to terms with them, each in his own way. In a longer perspective Gielgud has commented in detail on the place of his own work within what he calls 'The Hamlet tradition' (Gilder, pp. 29–73) while Olivier has sketched his general line of inheritance from Henry Irving (with a deep bow to John Barrymore) through Edmund Kean and David Garrick to Richard

11 Quoted in Pfister, 'Hamlets', p. 76n.   12 Jacobi, '*Hamlet*' video.

Burbage.[13] No one, though, could feel a deeper affinity for a forebear than must Nicol Williamson for John Barrymore, having played his ghost in Paul Rudnick's *I Hate Hamlet* and recreated his life in the one-man show *Jack*. In the latter, Williamson would begin a *Hamlet* soliloquy in a baritone reminiscent of Barrymore's recordings that soon gave way to his own natural tenor, with nasal intonations familiar from Williamson's stage and film performances; eerily, one could hear in the overlap the mingling of the two perturbed spirits.

The rest of this introduction will fill in the outlines of these patterns of change and continuity.

Scripts

For the stage history of *Hamlet*, five versions of the play may be distinguished. The first three published editions reflect performance of the play during Shakespeare's lifetime; they are the First Quarto (Q1) published in 1603, the Second Quarto (Q2) published in 1604–5, and the First Folio (F) published in 1623. Since there is currently no consensus among textual experts as to the relationships of the three with one another or with Shakespeare's presumed manuscript(s), it seems best simply to assume that each was in some way the basis for performance and to note their main differences.

The First Quarto title-page advertises that 'it hath been diverse times acted by his Highnesse servants in the City of London: as also in the two Universities of Cambridge and Oxford, and elsewhere'. At 2,154 lines it is by far the shortest of the three versions. Structurally it is unique in placing Hamlet's 'to be or not to be' soliloquy and the 'nunnery scene' at the beginning of the sequence of six scenes leading up to Hamlet's instructions to the players rather than at the end, as in Q2 and F. Q1 thus allows the playlet to follow directly from Hamlet's resolve that 'the play's the thing / Wherein I'll catch the conscience of the king' whereas in the other versions the execution of his resolve is interrupted by his 'to be or not to be' soliloquy and the nunnery scene. (Like Q1, a number of films have similarly rearranged these episodes.) Among other differences in characterization, Q1's Leartes (Laertes) does not lead a rebellion but simply seeks revenge for his father's death, and its Queen is decidedly different: she is informed by Hamlet that the King murdered her husband and later by Horatio of the plot to have her son killed in England; and she explicitly changes her loyalty from her husband to her son, vowing to 'conceal, consent, and doe my

13 Olivier, *Acting*, pp. 35–66.

best, / What stratagem soe'er thou shalt deuise'. In the 'to be or not to be' speech it is the 'joyful hope' of a happy life after death that deters Hamlet from killing himself. Although the First Quarto's diction is relatively pedestrian and in places garbled, several productions in this century have shown it to be stage-worthy.[14]

The Second Quarto (3,674 lines) differs from the other two in its inclusion of a number of passages. The most important of these is Hamlet's 'How all occasions do inform against me' soliloquy. Also the ties between the Q2 Hamlet and his mother are strengthened in 5.2 by the unique inclusion of the Lord who confirms Osric's embassage and conveys the Queen's desire that Hamlet 'use some gentle entertainment to Laertes, before you fall to play'; in F this gesture seems altogether Hamlet's own idea.

The First Folio (3,535 lines) is largely similar to Q2. It differs from the other two especially in the extra banter it includes between Hamlet and Rosencrantz and Guildenstern ('Denmark's a prison') and the full account it gives of the boy actors in 2.2. These inclusions, plus the absence of later indications of their knowing involvement in Claudius's plot to execute the Prince in England, make for a more sympathetic treatment of Hamlet's 'excellent good friends' than in Q2. Laertes, too, is in general more sympathetically treated in F than Q2, and Hamlet shown to be somewhat less intuitive.[15] Until recently it was thought that because they are unusually long, Q2 and F must have been heavily cut for performance. Recently, however, that assumption has been cogently called into question.[16]

Although these differences among the three versions are important (further instances will be noted in the Commentary), they should not be exaggerated. Especially between Q2 and F the points of difference are far fewer than those of resemblance. As with popular ballads, the fact that the play exists in more than one version does not mean that its identity is an indeterminate blur. Jacobean playgoers would still have recognized any one of them as *Hamlet*. Nor do the three versions rule out a distinguishable authorial presence; on the contrary, they afford insight into Shakespeare's originating hand at work in multiple manifestations.

What may be called a fourth version of *Hamlet* is delineated by the pattern of abridgements that, with individual variations, prevailed in the theatre from the Restoration to the end of the nineteenth century. Apart from Garrick's short-lived reworking of the last act, the play has not undergone the major textual modifications which helped *Richard III* and *King*

14 Loughrey, 'Q1', pp. 123–36.   15 Werstine, 'Mystery'.
16 Urkowitz, 'Basics', pp. 266–70.

Lear to hold the boards.[17] Surviving promptbooks and published 'players editions' show, however, that *Hamlet* was considerably altered for performance, with cuts of sufficient consistency as to define in rough outline a 'players version' of the play.[18] Regularly left out or severely trimmed in this version are the ambassadors Cornelius and Voltemand, the scene between Polonius and Reynaldo, Hamlet's long speech reflecting on a 'custom more honoured in the breach than the observance', the 'little eyases' passage about the boy actors, the dumb show, much of Hamlet's bawdy talk to Ophelia at the play, his speech about 'the politic convocation of worms', Ophelia's mad song concluding 'By Cock they are to blame', much of the King's plotting with Laertes, Hamlet's graveyard musings about politicians, courtiers, lawyers and their skulls, his account to Horatio of his voyage, and the lord who seconds Osric's invitation to the fencing match.

Now-familiar speeches were unspoken for centuries. Polonius's advice to Laertes was omitted by leading productions from Betterton through Macready. Hamlet's 'Now might I do it pat' monologue was often cut (for example, by Garrick, Kemble, and Irving), as was his 'How all occasions do inform against me' soliloquy. Hamlet's appeal for secrecy about his 'madness' and his mother's vow to keep his secret (3.4.182–218) were rarely heard from 1755 to 1900.[19] In the nineteenth century Fortinbras was most commonly left out altogether; it was a major innovation when, at G. B. Shaw's urging, Forbes-Robertson had him appear at the end. Diction was commonly modernized until Kemble, controversially, restored a large number of original readings. References to God were omitted or altered from Betterton through the eighteenth century and, to a lesser degree, into the first half of the nineteenth century.

In the twentieth century it is the fully 'conflated' (combined) version that constitutes a fifth version of *Hamlet*. In it, the parts of Q2 lacking in F and the parts of F lacking in Q2 are all included, plus occasional readings from Q1. Most modern productions have used a conflated edition as their basis. Occasionally, full-length productions have been mounted. Although these can last four hours or more, there is abundant testimony that the play in its entirety ('in its eternity', goes the old joke) can be less tiring to watch and perform when its easy flow is free from what Margaret Webster termed 'the

---

17 Garrick's adaptation omitted Hamlet's voyage to England, the conspiracy of Claudius and Laertes, the gravediggers, Osric, the fencing match, and the deaths of Laertes, Rosencrantz and Guildenstern, and the Queen, who is reported to have gone mad. Stone, 'Alteration', pp. 890–921.

18 Glick, 'Texts', pp. 17–37. Glick groups the texts in a way that differs from mine. See also Halstead, *Spoken*. 19 O'Brien, 'Revision', pp. 27–35.

compressed tension caused by cutting'.[20] Nevertheless, most productions have trimmed the conflated text to the running-time they desire and the particular interpretive emphases they wish to give.

Most conflated editions vary according to whether in points of overlap they generally follow the Folio or the Second Quarto. The present conflated edition follows verbatim the text prepared by Philip Edwards for the 'New Cambridge Shakespeare' series (1985). In his introduction to that edition Edwards develops an elaborate theory of the history of the *Hamlet* texts, leading up to his postulate of an 'ideal version of the play' that is 'somewhere between' the Second Quarto and the Folio editions. The line-readings he has chosen for the main body of the text therefore favour neither the one nor the other but are eclectic. In the current state of scholarship, Edwards's theory is by necessity highly speculative. As it happens, I do not find it so persuasive as to alter my own conviction that the provenance of the three early texts is at present simply unknowable with any certainty. His text is nonetheless serviceable for my purposes because it includes all the passages that appear in Q2 but not in F (marked off by brackets) and all the passages in F but not in Q2 (the principal ones are identified as such in my Commentary). In the Commentary I have also added readings from Q1 where pertinent. Stage directions that are not in either Q2 or F are bracketed. Readers who wish to make a fuller comparison of the three early editions will find them conveniently paralleled in *The Three-Text Hamlet*.[21]

The first *Hamlets*: Richard Burbage

The very first specific performance of *Hamlet* for which there is a dated record took place off Sierra Leone in 1607 aboard the Dragon, a ship bound for the East Indies. It was performed by the crew as entertainment for a visiting dignitary. The ship's captain William Keeling seems to have been pleased with it because in the following year, as he wrote in his journal: 'I envited Captain Hawkins to a ffishe dinner, and had Hamlet acted abord me: which I permitt to keepe my people from idlenes and unlawful games, or sleepe.'[22] In London and on tour the play had certainly been done a few years before that.

Otherwise relatively little is known for sure about the early performance history of *Hamlet*. A good deal, however, may reasonably be inferred. Richly implicated in the theatrical life of its time, the play is notably self-conscious about its own theatricality, including the play-within-a-play,

20 Webster, *Shakespeare*, pp. 211–12.   21 *Three-Text Hamlet*.
22 Chambers, *Facts*, II, pp. 334–5.

Hamlet's advice to the players and other comments on acting, and references to such current developments in the theatre as ad-libbing comedians and the popularity of boy-companies. Polonius's reference to playing Caesar and being killed 'in the Capitol' (3.2.91) may have been an in-joke if the actor of Polonius had himself played Caesar at the Globe. The reference must be to Shakespeare's *Julius Caesar* (1599) because in all other versions Caesar was killed in the Forum.[23]

In writing a revenge tragedy Shakespeare was reviving a genre that had been in vogue some years before, most notably in Kyd's *Spanish Tragedy* (1587–9) and in an early version of the Hamlet story, now lost, which surviving allusions indicate to have included a ghost crying for revenge. Shakespeare sophisticated this tradition, capitalizing on a deepening in acting styles that had moved from impersonation to 'personation', a term that came into currency at just this time.[24] The latter involved the submergence of self in a role at which Shakespeare's leading actor, Richard Burbage, excelled, 'transforming himself into his part'. With Burbage's personating powers at his disposal, Shakespeare could make an unprecedented exploration of his hero's inner life.

Everything indicates that Richard Burbage did originate the role of the Prince. 'Young Hamlet' is listed as one of his parts in 'A Funerall Ellegye on ye Death of the famous Actor Richard Burbedg'. The elegy goes on: 'Oft have I seen him, leap into the Grave / Suiting the person, which he seem'd to have / Of a sad Lover . . . ' If the 'grave' is that of Ophelia, the lines tell us something about how Burbage performed the graveyard scene. Since the Prince asks 'who plucks off my beard?' and since Burbage wears a beard in his portrait, his Hamlet was evidently bearded. Ophelia's account of his 'doublet all unbraced' confirms that, as was customary, he wore an Elizabethan costume, and the exchanges at the beginning of the second scene, make it clear that he wore black in mourning, including an 'inky cloak'. It seems likely that John Raynold reflected Burbage's business with Yorick's skull: 'He held it still, in his sinister [left] hand, / He turn'd it soft, and stroakt it with the other, / He smil'd on it' (*Dolarnys Primerose*, 1606).

It is tempting but hazardous to try to deduce Burbage's whole interpretive approach from contemporaries' passing references and allusions to the play. Conklin made such an attempt; yet his influential conclusion that the Elizabethan Hamlet was a straightforward avenger and malcontent is patently tendentious. His own examples can be read to indicate a much more deliberative hero (as in the frequent early allusions to Hamlet's 'to be or not to be' soliloquy and his contemplations on a skull).[25] Since evidence

23 Orgel, 'Authentic Shakespeare', p. 10.   24 Gurr, *Stage*, p. 98.
25 Conklin, *History*, p. 9.

of this sort is so fragmentary, it seems best not to speculate, one way or the other.

Tradition has it that Shakespeare himself played the Ghost. In his 1709 edition, Rowe reports as the sole finding of his investigation into Shakespeare's acting career that 'the top of his Performance was the Ghost in his own *Hamlet*' (I, p. vi).[26]

More generally, contemporary theatrical conditions suggest something of the overall impact of the play. At the Globe a number of features must have helped to hold a performance of *Hamlet* together whether or not anyone was deliberately trying to make that happen. Uninterrupted by changes of scenery, the play's action could unfold at a rapid pace, aided by stage conventions (asides, soliloquies, and the like) that made for clear and economical story-telling. Players and playgoers shared the same light of the afternoon sun, and since – without being set apart by a proscenium arch – the platform stage extended into the midst of the audience, they shared the same space and breathed the same air. Taken together these features appear to have provided the nucleus for a richly inclusive unity of impact that, when the features changed, it would take stage practice centuries to approximate.

Hamlets of the Restoration and eighteenth century: Thomas Betterton and David Garrick

Hamlet performances during the Restoration period were decidedly and deliberately distinct from earlier ones. In sharp contrast with the Puritan regime that had prohibited performances altogether, theatre in general under Charles II was much more oriented towards the court and its extravagant, Francophile tastes than ever before. Royal control at first extended to the repertory of the two new patent companies. By royal order the exclusive right to revive the play was assigned to the Duke's Men, headed by William Davenant. *Hamlet* was one of the leftovers after the other patent company, the King's Men, had taken the lion's share of the preferred plays by

---

26 Statistical support for this tradition may come from Donald Foster's ongoing studies of rare words (those that occur fewer than eleven times in the plays). He shows that the rare words spoken by the Ghost appear much more frequently in plays written after *Hamlet* than in plays written before, a difference he attributes to Shakespeare's having memorized these words and spoken them frequently in performance. From Foster's lexicons, one sees that the recurring rare words tend to cluster within a line (as in the Ghost's 'A *couch* for *luxury* and damned *incest*') or a series of lines: 'So lust, thou to a *radiant* angel linked, / Will *sate* itself in a celestial bed / And *prey* on garbage'. There may, of course, be other ways of explaining these clusters.

Beaumont and Fletcher and Jonson, plus several plays by Shakespeare that had already been successfully revived.[27] Ironically, it was partly thanks to *Hamlet* that Davenant's company came to outshine its favoured rival. Downes, the company's prompter, records that 'no succeeding Tragedy for several Years got more Reputation, or Money to the Company than this'.[28]

One of the chief innovations of Restoration theatre was the introduction of movable, perspective scenery, and *Hamlet* was one of the first to be so mounted. Following French fashion, Ophelia and Gertrude were for the first time played by women rather than boy-actresses. In general, the Restoration patentees were directed to expunge all profanity, scurrility, and obscenity, and so Davenant did with *Hamlet*, along with considerable modernization of diction. The play was also involved in some of the competitive shenanigans of rival companies as they struggled to attract audiences.[29]

Compared with other plays, however, the impact of these practices on the performance of *Hamlet* was characteristically moderated. It did not undergo the extensive alterations that were made to *The Tempest*, nor was it subjected to the heavy emphasis on spectacle of Davenant's adaptation of *Macbeth*, although in 1674 it was briefly 'adorned and embellished with very curious dances between the acts'.[30] Mrs Betterton, the first female Ophelia, is said by Davies to have received from Davenant 'such an idea of it as he could catch from the boy-Ophelias he had seen before the civil wars' (p. 226). In Thomas Betterton's portrayal of the Prince too one finds a concern for continuity. Downes reports that Davenant had seen Joseph Taylor act the part before the interregnum and taught Betterton 'in every particle of it'.[31]

Betterton was twenty-six at this time, and from surviving reports he continued throughout his long career to emphasize the Prince's own youth, portraying 'a young man of great expectation, vivacity, and enterprise' ('Mr Greenhat' in Richard Steele's *Tatler*, No. 71, 22 September 1709).

Too much, though, has been made of the omission of some of the lines of self-reproach from the 1676 text that Betterton probably used (2.2.514–527, 532–40). Certainly, McManaway and those who have followed him are mistaken in finding that 'The spectator who saw a

27 Thomas, *Documentary*, pp. 7–20.   28 Downes, *Roscius*, p. 21.
29 Cibber, *Apology*, pp. 113–14.   30 *London Stage*, I, p. 225.
31 Downes, *Roscius*, p. 21. He also claims that Taylor had been instructed by Shakespeare. Although Taylor's instruction can not have been direct from Shakespeare (Shakespeare died in 1616 and Taylor did not join the company until 1619, two months after the death of Burbage, whom he replaced), Taylor may well have continued the original treatment of the role.

performance of this Restoration version would never question the valor of the Prince or suspect that he was tardy in driving to his revenge.'[32] To the contrary Hamlet does in this edition say 'I am pigeon liver'd, and lack gall'. When the King is at prayer, he defers the opportunity to accomplish his revenge and delivers the 'now might I do it pat' speech. The Ghost speaks of whetting his almost blunted purpose, and he himself observes that 'conscience does make cowards of us all'.

Steele's Mr Greenhat singled out certain parts of Betterton's performance 'which dwell strongly upon the minds of the audience, and would certainly affect their behaviour on any parallel occasions in their own lives': Hamlet's 'to be or not to be' soliloquy, his 'expostulation' with his mother, his 'noble ardour' after seeing the Ghost, and his 'generous distress' at the death of Ophelia. These are not the emphases of a single-minded revenge-hero.

When he saw the Ghost Betterton's 'naturally ruddy' face turned 'pale as his Neckcloath' as he trembled all over (*Laureat*, 1740, p. 31). Yet when he spoke, Colley Cibber reports, he did not indulge in the 'straining vociferations' of other Hamlets; in contrast Betterton was 'governed by decency, manly, but not braving; his voice never rising into that seeming outrage, or wild defiance of what he naturally revered'. By such means 'he made the ghost equally terrible to the spectator as to himself'.[33] Betterton had an extraordinary ability to make his auditors feel what his character was feeling. That this power was felt by his fellow performers is humorously confirmed by Barton Booth: 'When I acted the Ghost with Betterton, instead of my awing him, he terrified me' (Davies, p. 32).

Betterton was followed by a number of lesser Hamlets. The royal assignment of exclusive performance rights to a single company having soon broken down, the play was for years regularly in the repertory of all the leading theatres, each of which had its long-standing performer of the role. Not until David Garrick made his spectacular debut, however, did a Hamlet dominate his time as Betterton had dominated his. Garrick made the role his own, not because his company owned the play (like Burbage) or had been given a royal monopoly (like Betterton) but on his own merit in competition with other interpreters.

What were the secrets of Garrick's success? He shared certain characteristics with the succession of actors who have won recognition as *the* Hamlets of their era. Each successful claimant has had virtuoso acting ability; not only has he often been regarded as 'the first actor of his time' but he frequently has managed his own company. Typically, his acting style has

32 McManaway, *Studies*, p. 95.   33 Cibber, *Apology*, p. 61.

differed strikingly from that of his immediate predecessor. In some way, also, he must be felt to be authentically in touch with the play or Shakespeare in general, often through involvement in textual debates or through promotion of worthy causes that establish him as Shakespeare's contemporary spokesman. Certainly a claimant must have it in him to play with conviction some important part of Hamlet's multifaceted personality. Furthermore his address to the role must mesh with the tastes of his audience; for what makes one production of *Hamlet* definitive for one generation and another for the next depends as much upon changes in the generations as upon changes in the productions. Garrick was in all these respects superlative.

A particular qualification for most Prince Hamlets has been that they seem 'princely', as princeliness has been variously defined. This concern comes directly from the play, where Ophelia laments the loss in Hamlet of 'The courtier's, soldier's, scholar's eye, tongue, sword, / Th'expectancy and rose of the fair state, / The glass of fashion and the mould of form' (3.1.145–7) and where Fortinbras eulogizes him as one who 'was likely, had he been put on, / To have proved most royal' (5.2.376–7). Circumstances at the time of *Hamlet*'s composition, gave special interest to the figure of the Prince since England – with its Virgin Queen – lacked a real heir apparent. By imagining a Crown Prince in Prince Hal and then in Hamlet, Shakespeare was helping to fill a cultural vacuum, one that was felt more and more intensely as the Queen grew older without naming a successor, reaching a crisis just when he was writing *Hamlet*. She died in 1603.

As it happens, Garrick is the first Hamlet whose princeliness received much surviving comment. Galt did praise Wilks for showing 'the delicacy of a prince' in his treatment of Ophelia,[34] but in other respects he seemed to the *Prompter* lacking in 'weight' (24 October 1735). Why did princeliness come into prominence with Garrick? Perhaps it was that, as Thackeray was to emphasize in 'The Four Georges' (1860), the Georgian kings were far from being ideal monarchs, reaching a nadir with the Prince Regent. In the absence of a satisfactory real Prince people of their times may well have put a premium on the princeliness of an imaginary one. Whatever the initial reasons, the concern has persisted, extending through the nineteenth century and up to the present. A reviewer celebrated Gielgud's 'gracious bearing, a princely manner and the imperiousness of a young eagle' (*Boston Herald*, 18 October 1936). I myself recall walking up the aisle at the interval of David Warner's 1965 Hamlet and hearing from one cluster of playgoers after another the sibilant verdict: 'Not princely!' On the other hand, others

34 Galt, *Lives*, I, p. 61.

found something lordly in his disregard for custom.[35] In praise of Kenneth Branagh, Benedict Nightingale declared him to be 'the most impressively princely Hamlet I have seen in ages' (*The Times*, 21 December 1992) while Michael Coveney found in his nobility an attempt 'to define and reshape a notion of modern royalty' (*Observer*, 20 December 1992).

Garrick's Prince was energetic and decisive, even more so than Betterton's. He used acting texts through most of his career that cut passages suggesting irresolution, such as the 'How all occasions do inform against me' soliloquy.[36] He was said by Davies to be the first to cut the 'Now might I do it pat' soliloquy (p. 101), thus not only sparing the Prince an excess of ardour in damning his enemy to eternal torment but also removing a concrete opportunity to carry out the act of vengeance – that he declined. Resolve pervaded his portrayal. He was 'vehemently resolute' when following the Ghost[37] and delivered 'smile and smile, and be a villain' with the 'purposeful tone of one bent on immediate action'.[38]

Garrick's Prince was exemplary in his devotion to his father, as manifested not only in his active and determined pursuit of revenge but also in his heartfelt expressions of grief. His emphasis on action was thus balanced by his brilliant portrayal of Hamlet's sensitive *re*actions.[39] This emphasis took part in an 'era of sensibility' then in its heyday that included Richardson's *Pamela* (1740) and *Clarissa* (1747) and Sterne's *Sentimental Journey* (1768). It was Henry Mackenzie, author of *The Man of Feeling* (1771), who would write in 1780 that 'The basis of Hamlet's character seems to be an extreme sensibility of mind, apt to be strongly impressed by its situation, and overpowered by the feelings which that situation excites' (*Mirror*, Edinburgh, No. 99, 17 April). In his reactions Garrick did not, however, seem simply passive; on the contrary his reactions were typically dynamic. Nor were they so 'overpowering' as to impede his ability to act decisively. The drama was in the sometimes contradictory drives compelling a hero who was both a man of action and a man of feeling.

Garrick struck the keynote of mourning at his first appearance. Contemporaries observed how much more he was upset by the loss of his

---

35 See Wells, *Shakespeare*, p. 35.

36 It is true that in the adaptation he devised near the end of his career, this soliloquy was included, yet with a significant difference from the original. Instead of ending 'O from this time forth, / My thoughts be bloody, or be nothing worth', the adapted version reads: 'O from this time forth, / My thoughts be bloody all! The hour is come – / I'll fly my keepers – sweep to my revenge'. (Garrick's first draft had shown less determination: 'My thoughts be bloody: I will fly my keepers / And hie me to Revenge – the game is up –'.)   37 Davies, *Memoirs*, I, p. 63.

38 Lichtenberg, *Visits*, p. 31.   39 Donohue, *Character*.

father than by the disgraceful conduct of his mother. Later subtle pangs of loss were also powerfully projected. In one of the striking transitions for which Garrick was famous, his fulminations against the 'treacherous, lecherous' Claudius were interrupted by the sudden 'tear of anguish' started by '*kindless* villain'. His sorrow was by no means incapacitating, however. It was, in fact, his sense of the terrible wrong done his father by the inhumanness of his uncle that led him, in another transition, to the commanding vigour of 'I have heard, / That guilty creatures, sitting at a play . . . ' (Davies, pp. 68–9).

In keeping with the central concern with filial love, Garrick's most memorable moments came at the Prince's encounters with the Ghost. He was most famous for his stylized 'start' at the first encounter: as Partridge in Fielding's *Tom Jones* put it, 'if that little man there upon the stage is not frightened, I never saw any man frightened in my life' (Bk. XVI, ch. 5). The business of knocking over a chair at the Ghost's appearance in the closet scene was also celebrated. What kept these bits from being mere 'stage trick' was that they were part of a rich complex in which Garrick 'preserves every gradation and transition of the passions'.[40] He was frightened by the apparition, yes – so much so that his terror 'was instantaneously communicated to the audience' – but this terror was mixed with 'filial awe' and 'respect'.[41] In the closet scene Garrick's reaction to seeing the Ghost was again marked by 'The start – the heave – the stagger – and the stare'.[42] Yet when the Queen says the Ghost is but the coinage of his brain, Garrick made it the occasion for yet another transition, 'turning short from looking after the apparition with wildness of terror, and viewing his mother with pathetic concern'.[43]

The manners of Garrick's Prince were a concern to his contemporaries. Davies complained that in giving his advice to the players Garrick was too much the stage manager, lacking the 'condescending quality' expected from a 'princely monitor' (pp. 88–9, 79). In Smollett's original version of *Peregrine Pickle*, too, Garrick's Hamlet is taken to task for shaking 'his fist with all the demonstrations of wrath at his mistress' and is said to 'behave like a ruffian to his own mother' (ch. 55). Perhaps Garrick's Prince grew more mannerly in the course of his career, or perhaps standards of decorum changed. For at a farewell performance, admiring Hannah More averred that 'he never once forgot he was a prince; and in every variety of situation, and transition of feeling, you discovered the highest polish of fine breeding and courtly manners'.[44]

40 More, *Letters*, p. 47.   41 Davies, *Memoirs*, I, p. 63.
42 Kelley, 'Prologue', p. 665.   43 Gentleman, *Censor*, I, p. 56.
44 More, *Letters*, p. 46.

1 David Garrick first sees the Ghost (1.4). As part of his famous 'start' Garrick's hat fell
off and his hair may well have been wired to stand on end. Yet amid this dishevelment he
strikes a classic pose, one that closely resembles the style of Betterton (as may be seen in
the illustration of the closet scene in Rowe's edition). Claiming to speak for Betterton,
Gildon describes the decorous posture appropriate for expressing 'Surprise, Admiration,
Abhorence', finding that Nature 'throws the Hands out as Guards to the Eyes on such an
occasion'. He cautions, however, that 'In the lifting up the Hands to preserve the Grace,
you ought not to raise them above the Eyes; to stretch them further might disorder and
distort the body' (*Betterton*, p. 70). Garrick appears to have 'preserved the Grace'. For
Lichtenberg's graphic account of Garrick's start as performed at the very end of his
career, see the Commentary for 1.4.39.

So definitive were Garrick's portrayals of Hamlet and other Shakespearian characters that he became in the eyes of many of his contemporaries the Bard's latter-day embodiment. A 1750 poem has Shakespeare's ghost looking to Garrick, 'my great restorer', 'to vindicate my injur'd song . . . speak my words and do my meaning right' (*London Magazine*, June); a 1752 poem exclaimed 'SHAKESPEARE revives! in GARRICK breathes again!' ('A Poetic Epistle from Shakespear in Elysium to Mr. Garrick'). The identification of the two reached an ultimate in the Stratford Jubilee that Garrick organized in 1769, an event that did much to further the canonization of Shakespeare as the English national poet while elevating Garrick as his prime spokesman.[45]

Most of all Garrick's claim to preeminence rested on his style, whose difference from his rivals was nothing short of revolutionary. In contrast to the prevailing statuesque and ponderous manner that had become conventional, Garrick seemed fresh and dynamic; Walter Scott found him 'impetuous, sudden, striking, and versatile'.[46] Although his performance was highlighted by bold stage business, virtuoso transitions of mood, and many broken sentences and significant pauses, his contemporaries felt that its most remarkable feature was its naturalness. Not only did he avoid altogether the 'titum-ti' sing-song of his predecessors but his words appeared to come forth spontaneously, as 'the instantaneous expression of his feelings, delivered in the most affecting tones of voice, and with gestures that belong only to nature'.[47] Scott hinted that there was something less than probing about Garrick's 'naturalness', finding that he 'made his impression from his skill in seizing and expressing with force and precision the first and most obvious view of his part'.[48] But for most spectators, Mr Partridge, Fielding's naive playgoer in *Tom Jones*, must forever have the last word. Decrying Garrick's reputation as 'the best Player who ever was on the Stage', he protested: 'Why I could act as well as he myself. I am sure if I had seen a Ghost, I should have looked in the very same Manner, and done just as he did' (bk. XVI, ch. 5).

John Philip Kemble's 'Princely Perfection' dethroned by Edmund Kean

After Garrick the next in the line of Hamlets who were definitive for their time was John Philip Kemble. In one sense Kemble's style was distinct from Garrick's because in its formality it was a throwback to that of Garrick's statuesque predecessors. In contrast to Garrick he was seen as the prototype of art as opposed to nature. His style was often castigated as mere

45 Dobson, *National Poet*.   46 Scott, 'Kemble', p. 214.
47 More, *Letters*, p. 47.   48 Scott, 'Kemble', p. 215.

affectation and staginess, artificial ways of seeking applause 'by starting, stamping; by grimace and tricks' (*Morning Chronicle*, 6 October 1783). His sister, Sarah Siddons, saw into the problem more deeply, finding at times in his manner – by Scott's account – 'a sacrifice of energy of action to grace'.[49] Yet to some his stately manner was so eloquent that Gilbert Austin in his book on gesture extolled it as exemplary: 'the perfection and the glory of art, so finished, that every look is a commentary, every tone an illustration, every gesture a model for the statuary, and a study for the painter'.[50] One might expect the resulting performance to be very subdued, yet it could be theatrically compelling and memorable, well-suited to the ever-larger auditoriums then being built. At Kemble's first appearance, one observer attested, 'You could not take your eye' from the 'princely perfection before you' (*Port Folio*, XVI, July 1823, p. 200).

In other respects Kemble was forward-looking. He made a significant advance in dramaturgy. In the Restoration and eighteenth century many of the features which had helped to hold together an Elizabethan production had loosened. The apron stage had receded within the proscenium arch and the flow of the action was interrupted by changes of scenery. Not until Kemble towards the end of the eighteenth century did the English theatre begin deliberately to foster once more the kind of coordination of parts that may well have seemed second nature to Shakespeare and his contemporaries. In the eighteenth century, Garrick and others, for example, customarily used stock sets for *Hamlet*; they were chosen to suit individual scenes but not for overall effect. Kemble introduced scenes especially painted for the play.

For another example, take the performance of the title-role, in all its extraordinary length and fascination surely the single most important unifying factor in any *Hamlet*. In concept, what Fielding in *Tom Jones* saw in Garrick was his truth to the behaviour of generalized human nature, the ability, as Hamlet put it, to 'show virtue her feature'. Similarly, Steele's Mr Greenhat felt that Betterton exemplified for his auditors conduct that 'would certainly affect their behaviour on any parallel occasions in their own lives', serving to introduce the boy who accompanied him into 'the Affections and Passions of Manhood' (*Tatler*, 22 September 1709). In style, commentators in the Restoration and through most of the eighteenth century were primarily concerned with how the leading actor rendered particular speeches and scenes rather than with his overarching interpretive approach. In the latter part of the century, however, literary critics were for the first time extensively engaged in 'character analysis', emphasizing the

49 *Ibid.*, p. 216.   50 Austin, *Chironomia*, p. 279.

careful differentiation of what is individual about Shakespeare's characters and appraising the consistency with which this individuality is rendered. So too on the stage the *Morning Chronicle* was concerned for 'the whole performance' that Kemble delivered (20 September 1799).

To William Hazlitt 'the distinguishing excellence' of Kemble's acting was 'in the seizing upon some one feeling or idea, in insisting upon it, in never letting it go, and in working it up, with a certain graceful consistency'.[51] For Kemble's Hamlet this predominant feeling was by common consent one of princely melancholy. As the German critic Tieck observed: 'What Kemble brought prominently out was the sad, the melancholy, the nobly suffering aspect of the character' while all the while he 'bore himself like a man of high blood and breeding'.[52] This emphasis owed something to Kemble's own personality; Walter Scott describes him as 'the grave, studious, contemplative actor, who personated Hamlet to the life'.[53] Yet – as Scott marvels – he could when he chose play against type and succeed, even with so volatile a role as Hotspur. His Hamlet thus was not only congenial to his temperament but an interpretive choice. Looking back half a century, Mary Russell Mitford struck the right balance: 'John Kemble is the only satisfactory Hamlet I ever saw – owing much to personal grace and beauty – something to a natural melancholy, or rather pensiveness of manner – much, of course, to consummate art.'[54]

Such consistency has characterized Hamlets ever since. Hazlitt rebuked Kemble's successor, Kean, for its absence: he found Kean's style 'too pointed' – too concerned with the impact of isolated moments to the neglect of the whole.[55] In contrast, the portrayal of the Prince by Kean's successor Macready was praised for its 'grandeur of SUSTAINMENT' (*Examiner*, 11 October 1835). By the end of the nineteenth century, it would be customary for reviewers to begin by defining the actor's distinctive concept of the Prince and then appraise the effectiveness of its application in detail.

Ironically, Hazlitt judged that it was Kemble's very consistency that caused him to fail as Hamlet. Where Shakespeare's hero is unique in his 'flexibility', 'quick sensibility,' and 'a perpetual undulation of feeling', Kemble played the role 'in one undeviating straight line'.[56] Actually, Kemble's portrayal was more varied than Hazlitt claims. Lamb much admired his skill with 'pointed and witty dialogue' and 'the playful court-

---

51 Hazlitt, *Theatre*, pp. 129–30.
52 T. Martin, 'Eye-Witness', p. 284. Tieck's comments, in German, were published in 1826.   53 Scott, 'Kemble', p. 219.   54 Mitford, *Life*, II, p. 336.
55 Hazlitt, *Theatre*, p. 12.   56 Hazlitt, *Theatre*, p. 127. See also Galt, *Lives*, II, p. 256.

bred spirit in which he condescended to the players in Hamlet'.[57] Tieck praised the naturalness of his failure to remember the beginning of the Pyrrhus speech.[58] His genteel restraint gave way especially in his scenes with Ophelia and Gertrude. *Le Beau Monde* took exception to Kemble's making Hamlet 'bang a door on one side, half burst a lock on the other' and did not think 'this harsh behaviour to Ophelia gallant or tender enough' (March 1807). In the closet scene the 'smile of exultation' with which he asked 'Is it the king?' was one of his most acclaimed points; the *Morning Chronicle* found in it 'an admirable mixture of hope and anxiety' (20 September 1799). Later in the scene Martin traces the modulations in his exchanges with his mother: 'no rant – it was bitter truth, spoke in indignation, with energy, with irresistible force; but passion did not rise till just before the Ghost again appeared, and it gave a fine contrast to the subdued feeling that followed'.[59] The dominant and distinctive tone of Kemble's Hamlet was thus one of melancholy, but it was set off by a variety of contrasting tones.

In addition to his princely manner, Kemble's claim to authority as a Shakespearian interpreter was strengthened by his pioneering return to a more authentic text. His approach to the text was much more studied than that of his predecessors. His *Hamlet* was filled with what his conservative critics deplored as 'new readings.' A good many of these were in fact *old* readings, from the original texts, that had been displaced by stage tradition. For one example of many, his Hamlet referred to 'the native hue of resolution' instead of its 'healthful face'.

After Kemble's retirement, an admirer looked back nostalgically to his heyday. Suggesting that Hamlet 'should be played as if in moonlight . . . a link between the ethereal and the corporeal', this commentator felt that Kemble played it so: 'Tragedy reigned in solemn grandeur then – for the broken starts and rapid familiarities of the new school were in Kemble's bright time unknown' (*Port Folio*, XVI, July 1823, p. 207). The new school was that of Edmund Kean.

Garrick's widow saw in Kean a throwback to Garrick. But he may better be regarded as usurping the role of Hamlet, interrupting the legitimate line of player princes. A long-time associate compared him to Napoleon: 'reckless, restless, adventurous, intemperate'.[60] Whereas Betterton and Garrick had retired before a full-fledged successor presented himself, upstart Kean wrested the position from Kemble by force majeure. The contrast with Kemble was stark. Where Kemble was neoclassic in temperament, Kean

---

57 Lamb, 'Comedy', *Elia*.   58 T. Martin, 'Eye-Witness', pp. 284–5.
59 H. Martin, *Remarks*, p. 7.   60 Grattan, *Paths*, p. 195.

2 John Philip Kemble in the graveyard scene (5.1). His costume was in the 'stage Elizabethan' style that he originated. His sable-plumed hat later became conventionalized (in *Great Expectations*, Dickens's would-be tragedian Mr Wopsle sported one).

was Romantic. Where Kemble's venue was the Tory Covent Garden, Kean's was the Whig Drury Lane. Where Kemble was consistent and coherent in style, Kean was disordered and fragmented. Kean also set himself apart from other previous Hamlets. At times he scored by under-playing what they had highlighted. His vow to speak to the Ghost 'though hell itself should gape' was given in 'a quick and low tone, which was in total opposition to the manner of every other actor'.[61] When the Ghost does appear, unlike earlier Hamlets who were struck with terror, Kean was remarkable because he was '*not frightened*'.[62] On the contrary, he showed 'filial confidence in following it'.[63]

As revolutionary as Kean was among stage Hamlets, a still larger usurpa-tion in *Hamlet* interpretation was under way, one in which the primacy of the stage itself as an interpretive instrument was challenged by print. In the seventeenth century, published versions were regarded as records of per-formance, comparable to printed film and television scripts. In the course of the eighteenth century *Hamlet* more and more came to be understood through reading as well as playgoing, and a body of critical commentary developed. Usually these commentaries had run in tandem with stage inter-pretations, but with the Romantics came a radical break, in which Lamb and Hazlitt (both of them inveterate playgoers) denied the adequacy of the theatre to Shakespeare's imagination as it may be discerned through reading his words.

The reader's Hamlet that Hazlitt delineated was a character marked not 'by strength of will or even of passion, but by refinement of thought and sentiment'.[64] Coleridge saw in him 'great, enormous, intellectual activity, and a consequent aversion to real action' (*Notes and Lectures upon Shakespeare*, 1808). Both had been anticipated by Mackenzie, who in 1780 had said of Hamlet that Shakespeare 'throws around him, from the begin-ning, the majesty of melancholy, along with that sort of weakness and irresolution which frequently attends it' (*Mirror*, No. 99).

This way of regarding the Prince was reinforced by another development in the enlarging *Hamlet* tradition, for Hamlet had begun his ascent to the pantheon of cultural icons, where like Don Quixote and Faust he would lead a life virtually free of the particular circumstances set forth in the work in which he first appeared. There he was to become the personification of procrastination and overly introspective irresolution, deeply melancholy and forever paralysed by doubts as to whether 'to be or not to be'. Much of the impetus for this view came from Continental Europe, often based on a

61 Phippen, *Kean*, p. 98.   62 Finlay, *Miscellanies*, p. 220.
63 Hazlitt, *Theatre*, p. 13   64 *Ibid.*, p. 10.

3 Edmund Kean in 1818 talking with Polonius (2.2). Kean's most original reference to the book Hamlet is reading was at 'For if the sun breeds maggots in a dead dog' (179–80) which 'Mr. K. gave as a passage from the book he held in his hand, and then, stopping short, asked Polonius, "have you a daughter?"' (a letter to the *Examiner*, 27 March 1814, signed PGP).

translated text. Its most influential formulation was the first one: in Goethe's novel *Wilhelm Meisters Lehrjahr* (written about 1783) Hamlet is seen as a soul unfit for the great action laid upon it, a costly jar shattered by the oaktree of revenge planted in it. In the course of the nineteenth century 'Hamletism' became not only a private malady but a general condition with political implications. In 'The American Scholar' (1837) Emerson felt his generation 'infected with Hamlet's unhappiness.' To Turgenev and others in Russia the affliction applied to the class of liberal intellectuals made up of refined but 'superfluous' men, an idea he developed in his lecture 'Hamlet and Don Quixote' (1860) and many novels. To the revolutionary poet Ferdinand Freiligrath ('Hamlet', 1844) 'Germany is Hamlet', a whole nation too much given to thought in place of action. That such attitudes persist may be seen in Seamus Heaney's 1975 poem on his own 'dithering, blathering' over the troubles in Northern Ireland: 'I am Hamlet the Dane . . . smeller of rot / in the state, infused / with its poisons, pinioned by ghosts / and affections, murders and pieties' ('Viking Dublin' in *North*).

English stage interpretations have stood in complex interrelationship with such conceptions. The Hamlet of the Romantics had been anticipated by Thomas Sheridan, a minor rival of Garrick, who – as he told Boswell – conceived the Prince to be 'a young man of a good heart and fine feelings who had led a studious contemplative life and so become delicate and irresolute', lacking the 'strength of mind to execute what he thinks right and wishes to do'.[65] If this view informed his own portrayal, it did not make a major impact; Sheridan is chiefly remembered for his elocutionary techniques. Certain aspects of the Romantic Hamlet had, however, been portrayed on stage. In his soliloquies Garrick appeared 'to be uttering his thoughts aloud to himself, without regard either to the manner or the spectators',[66] and in the graveyard Kemble too had an introspective air, especially as depicted in Reynold's painting. Kean also made an 'appeal to the mind' (*Examiner*, 20 March 1814) and revealed a 'sadness of soul'.[67]

Yet stage Hamlets, then and since, have largely held back from going all the way with the Romantic readers. It is true that the Romantic view has textual basis in Hamlet's self-castigation of 'my weakness and my melancholy' (2.2.554) and his fault of 'thinking too precisely on th'event' (4.4.41). But in limiting itself to this most distinctive phase of Hamlet's career, it left out of account what no stage Hamlet could omit: the fact that he does not delay forever but in the end accomplishes what he has set out to do; he does kill the King. Coleridge especially exaggerated the protractedness of

65 Boswell, *London Journal*, 6 April 1763.   66 Young, *Memoir*, p. 26.
67 Procter, *Kean*, p. 62.

Hamlet's 'endless' hesitating and 'constant' escape from action ('Lecture XII', 1811–12) and belittled his accomplishment of his goal as 'mere accident' (*Table Talk*, 1827). While finding Hamlet 'incapable of deliberate action', Hazlitt does grant him the ability to act 'on the spur of the occasion, when he has no time to reflect' as in the killing of Polonius; but he significantly makes no mention of the killing of Claudius (*Characters of Shakespeare's Plays*, 1817). The Romantic view of the role was not to enter fully into the main stream of stage interpretation until Edwin Booth, whose Prince – as will be discussed – was so sensitive that he was appalled by the success of his own revenge. With Kean there was no such ambivalence. For the most part, his passionate Prince, famed for his fencing, was the opposite of Hazlitt's restrained figure who was 'as little of the hero as man can well be'.

In style, however, Kean was very much of his period, recalling the Romantic taste for vivid fragments. As Keats put it of his portrayal of Richard III: 'Other actors are continually thinking of their sum-total effect throughout a play. Kean delivers himself up to the instant feeling' (*Champion*, 21 December 1817). 'His mode of delivery is the very opposite of Kemble's', Tieck commented; 'he stares, starts, wheels round, drops his voice, and then raises it to the highest pitch'.[68] The impression of impetuosity thus created was, however, artful. Kean told Garrick's widow that 'There is no such thing as impulsive acting; all is premeditated and studied beforehand.'[69] G. H. Lewes confirms that Kean's roles were exactly repeated throughout his career and that his preparations included counting the steps between speeches.[70] Ordinary spectators, however, would not have been aware of these back-stage techniques. Vandenhoff recalls his youthful response to Kean's 'impulsive, fitful, flashing' style, 'abounding in quick transition . . . carrying you along with his impetuous rush'.[71] For them, seeing Kean act, as Coleridge famously put it, would have been 'like reading Shakespeare by flashes of lightning' (*Table Talk*, 27 April 1823).

Certain discrete moments in Kean's performance were especially telling. His most memorable moment came at the end of his interview with Ophelia where, after screaming 'get thee to a nunnery' he started out

> and has already grasped the handle of the door, when he stops, turns round, and casting back the saddest, almost tearful look, stands lingering for some time, and then, with a slow, almost gliding step, comes back, seizes Ophelia's hand, imprints a lingering kiss upon it with a deep-drawn sigh, and straightway dashes more impetuously than before out of the door, which he slams violently behind him. (T. Martin, 'Eye-Witness', p. 293)

---

68 T. Martin, 'Eye-Witness', p. 292.   69 Hawkins, *Kean*, p. 208.
70 Lewes, *Actors*, p. 18.   71 Vandenhoff, *Leaves*, pp. 22–3.

The effect was electrifying.

Only to a few did it matter that the King then flatly contradicted Kean's mime: 'Love! his affections do not that way tend'. Kean's ability to project Hamlet's inner turmoil carried all before it. Similarly, Kean's naturalistic death by poisoning was much admired, even though 'Laertes and the king, both of whom had been wounded *after* Hamlet, were lying dead before him.'[72]

The play scene was another point of high intensity. Unlike Kemble, Kean did not disguise his surveillance of the King by his attentions to Ophelia; in fact, during most of the playlet he directly turned his back on her. His overt concentration on the King rose towards a climax as he 'crawled upon his belly towards the King' (*Herald*, 14 March 1814) and openly stared at him, as if 'bullying the King into confusion' (*Sun*, 14 March 1814). He thus externalized Hamlet's inner state, irrespective of ordinary prudence. Here as with his loving return to kiss Ophelia's hand and his protracted death agonies, Kean's style anticipated dramatic Expressionism, for the sake of revealing inner truths projecting Hamlet's subtext – how the moment felt to him – and disregarding a literal reading of the play.

Nor were such effects confined to the visual. Kean's verbal projection of Hamlet's inner life could be very subtle. A letter to the editor in the *Examiner* (27 March 1814) signed PGP felt that Kean's 'fie on't! oh fie!' (1.2.135) 'after a pause of meditation, applied to the hasty marriage of his mother and his uncle', even though it is some lines further before Hamlet actually mentions their marriage. Similarly PGP felt that Kean's brooding delivery of 'Very like – very like' (1.2.236), again following 'a profound meditation', applied to his intuition of his uncle's guilt, even though confirmation of that does not come until 1.5.40. (Later commentators, possibly influenced by PGP, drew the same or comparable inferences: *Champion*, 29 September 1821; Hawkins, *Edmund Kean*, p. 192). Whether or not PGP's particular readings of Kean's subtext are valid, they clearly reflect a quality Keats noted in Kean's Richard III: 'we feel that the utterer is thinking of the past and future while speaking the instant' (*Champion*, 21 December 1817).

The composite style of William Charles Macready: Classic/Romantic/Realistic

Kean's reign ended with his death in 1833. It was relatively short, lasting two decades rather than the three of Garrick and Kemble; Betterton's was

---

72 Finlay, *Miscellanies*, p. 224.

nearly four. Although the next dominant Hamlet, Macready, had been acting Hamlet earlier, he did not come into his own until after Kean's death. It was only in 1835 that Forster made the kind of large claims for Macready's Hamlet that herald a definitive portrayal (*Examiner*, 11 October). Even then there was something grudging about the preeminence granted him. In his diary entry for his last performance of the part, Macready comments that 'the press has been slow to acknowledge my realization of the man'.[73] Only in retrospect did Lewes realize that Macready stood at 'an immeasurable height' when 'compared with any one we have seen since upon the stage'.[74]

With Macready, the line of player princes resumed its respectability. Where Garrick had risen to a higher social status than that of previous actors and Kemble had sustained an aristocratic lifestyle, Kean had been notoriously disreputable in his private life, a 'blackguard,' was Macready's word for him. Nor had he become an actor-manager in the tradition of Garrick and Kemble; the stage historian Odell refers to the period of his dominance (1817–37) as 'the leaderless age'.[75] In contrast, Macready was very much a member of the legitimate theatre establishment, heading the patent theatres Covent Garden (1837–9) and Drury Lane (1841–3).[76]

Unlike other definitive Hamlets Macready did not originate a distinctive style. His was composite. To Hackett it compounded 'the classical dignity of John Kemble with the intense earnestness and colloquial familiarity of Edmund Kean'.[77] Macready himself told Coleman of his 'admiration' for Kemble but plainly found Kean more stirring: 'oh my — ! he could act'.[78] At the same time he sought to moderate their excesses (as Hazlitt put it Kean's Hamlet is 'as much too splenetic and rash as Mr. Kemble's is too deliberate and formal'). His praise of the French actor Talma seems to reveal his own aspirations; he found Talma 'not below Kean in his most energetic displays, and far above him in the refinement of his taste and extent of his research, equalling Kemble in his dignity, unfettered by his stiffness and formality'.[79]

In concept, Macready's Hamlet was an optimist turned pessimist, a 'perturbed spirit' who in the end finds a measure of rest and grows patient and trustful. Accordingly, the early acts expressed 'the impetuous rebellion of a generous nature when its trust has been cruelly deceived'. His friend Forster found his 'What a piece of work is man!' unforgettable: 'so earnest in its faith, and so passionate in its sorrow. Here is the true Hamlet. No

---

73 Macready, *Diaries*, 29 January 1851.   74 Lewes, *Actors*, p. 42.
75 Odell, *Shakespeare*, II, p. 117.   76 Bate, 'Romantic', p. 111.
77 Hackett, *Notes*, p. 140.   78 Coleman, *Players*, I, p. 53.
79 Macready, *Reminiscences*, ch. 15.

wonder the shock of this outraged sense of good should drive him nearly mad' (*Examiner*, 11 October 1835). In following scenes his dominant mood was of irony and misanthropy, 'except for a touch of melancholy tenderness for a lost ideal in Ophelia, or of the courtesy which his princely nature prescribed to his inferiors'.[80] In the last act, Macready depicted, as he put it, 'the resignation of a generous nature when the storm has spent itself'.[81]

Along with this unifying conception, a concern for variety was a hallmark of Macready's approach. Lady Pollock found in him 'the flexible, impressionable Hamlet of Shakespeare': 'alternately meditative and impassioned, deliberate and sudden'.[82] He himself said that he sought to bring out the 'striking contrasts' inherent in his guiding interpretation – 'its passion, its imagination, its irony, its colloquial realism'.[83]

For Macready, the greatest of these was passion. Reviewers marvelled at his ability to express and communicate emotion, whether simple or complex, subtle or powerful, 'never losing the original impulse, but avoiding all excess'.[84] Regularly Macready caused the members of his audience to share his feeling, particularly at his first encounter with the Ghost and the climax of the play scene, where he was so intense that he 'wrought up the spectators to an almost equal degree of suspense, which the tremendous burst of horrid triumph when the king rose, fully satisfied' (*New Monthly Magazine*, p. 333).

Macready could also convey subtler progressions of feeling, as in his first soliloquy, where he revealed 'the gentle modulations of the soul' (*Champion*, 19 December 1819): 'thought visibly suggested thought, and one image or regret or indignation grew out of the other' (*New Monthly Magazine*, 1 July 1821). He was no less gifted in conveying sudden transitions of feeling and, most remarkably, could convey two distinct emotions at once. In his diary he confessed that he found it so difficult to render 'the ease and dignified familiarity, the apparent levity of manner, with the deep purpose that lies beneath . . . that I almost despair of moderately satisfying myself'.[85] Others, however, found that he met this challenge admirably. In the play scene, his Hamlet 'feigns a jocular mood, speaks sarcastically, whilst the desire to confirm beyond doubt his father's murder, is welling through every vein' (*Theatrical Journal*, 29 August 1840). In the closet scene, 'he regards his mother as one who still was dear to him but still as one who was about to hear awful truths from his lips' (*Theatrical Journal*, 5 September 1840).

---

80 Marston, *Actors*, I, p. 80. 81 *Ibid.*, I, pp. 80–1.
82 Lady Pollock, *Macready*, p. 107. 83 Marston, *Actors*, I, p. 81.
84 Kirk, 'Tragedies', p. 614. 85 Macready, *Diaries*, p. 242.

4 William Macready in the play scene (3.2). Macready is making the 'crawl' towards the King originated by Kean. Marston describes how 'with body prone, and head erect, and eyes riveted on Claudius, he dragged himself nearer and nearer to him' (*Actors*, 1, p. 82). See the Commentary for 3.2.233a. The staging follows the most common triangular arrangement, with the players upstage, the King, Queen, and Polonius (with staff) on one side, Horatio, Ophelia, and Hamlet on the other.

As powerful as were such points of maximum intensity, reviewers were no less impressed by Macready's quieter moments (*New Monthly Magazine*, 1 July 1821, p. 333). The *Morning Post* found Macready's portrayal deliberately lacking in 'tragic pomp – in those scenes where he is not acting under the immediate impulse of the passions, or of some more than ordinary excitement' and citing his interviews with Guildenstern and Rosencrantz and the advice to the Players as exchanges 'given in the tone and manner of common conversational discourse' (18 October 1823). Marston saw how the combination of passion and what Macready called 'colloquial realism' worked together. He praised both Macready's 'exaltation of passion' and 'his power of contrasting it with familiar touches which added to its reality without lessening its dignity'.[86]

The gentlemanly Prince: Charles Albert Fechter and Edwin Booth

Before his debut in England, Fechter was a highly successful actor in Paris (he originated the role of Armand Duval in *La Dame aux camelias*), and he brought across the Channel a realism that Londoners found revolutionary. As Charles Dickens observed: 'Perhaps no innovation in Art was ever accepted with so much favour by so many intellectual persons pre-committed to, and preoccupied by, another system, as Mr. Fechter's Hamlet' (*Atlantic Monthly*, August 1869). He spoke his lines in an 'easy, natural, and conversational tone' (*Era*, 24 March 1861). The *Sunday Times* spoke for many in describing this Prince as 'a thoroughly human Hamlet . . . as natural as humanity itself' (24 March 1861).

Not that Fechter ever fell short of the 'innate nobility' of a prince, 'all its expressions, grave or gay, having a mingled grace and dignity' (*Weekly Dispatch*, 24 March 1861). Lewes found his appearance 'delicate, handsome, and with his long flaxen curls, quivering, sensitive nostrils, fine eye, and sympathetic voice, perfectly represents the graceful prince'.[87] Clearly there was nothing of Kemble's hauteur about Fechter's nobility. He was praised for 'those qualities of the amiable and polished gentleman which are particularly manifested when Hamlet discourses with his social inferiors' (*Saturday Review*, 6 April 1861). 'He was affectionate towards Horatio, and chatty with the players, without any surrender of the dignity of the Prince or the self-respect of the gentleman' (*Macmillan Magazine*, 31 (1874), p. 240).

Fechter's embodiment of the Victorian ideal of the gentlemanly Prince was a key factor in his claim on the role. In 1836 Serjeant John Adams had written to Charles Kean, the son of Edmund Kean, about his Hamlet:

86 Marston, *Actors*, II, p. 198.   87 Lewes, *Actors*, p. 119.

5 Charles Fechter in the graveyard scene, 5.1. Reviewers were struck by the realistic
informality with which Fechter perched on a gravestone. Earlier he had sat on the
ground while talking with the gravedigger. Addressing Yorick's skull and recalling how
often as a child he had kissed the jester's lips, Fechter almost suited his action to his
words before putting the skull aside 'with a shiver' (Fields, p. 110).

you are not enough of the prince – or somewhat deficient in the mixture of condescension and ease which marks the intercourse of a prince of kind and affable disposition with his inferiors. Those who are born to command, acquire a manner which never deserts them, even in their most familiar moments. You are always the *gentleman*, but not always the *prince* – Hamlet is *both*. (Cole, *Kean*, p. 277)

Evidently Fechter struck a more persuasive balance of the two, although by his time gentlemanliness seems to have been given more weight. Such matters were of immediate concern to Victorians. Gentlemanliness was a prime educational value. At Rugby Thomas Arnold had instituted a programme designed to fulfil the hopes of the hero's father in Thomas Hughes's *Tom Brown's School Days* (1857): 'If he'll only turn out a brave, helpful, truth-telling Englishman and a gentleman and a Christian, that's all I want'. By 1864 a Parliamentary Commission Report found that such public schools 'had the largest share in molding the character of an English gentleman'.[88] In their novels Thackeray and Trollope personified in Colonel Newcome and Plantagenet Palliser their perfect gentlemen while the nature of a true gentility is a prominent theme in *Great Expectations* and other novels by Dickens.[89] Fechter's Hamlet put a 'polished gentleman' and 'graceful prince' on the stage.

For some Fechter's Prince was refined to a fault: 'it wants manliness . . . philosophic fortitude and high resolve'; for Fechter clearly emphasized Hamlet's softer side: 'There is nothing of the soldier about him. His manner is soft and winning, and he is sentimental rather than philosophic; and gently pensive rather than profoundly meditative. Of tempestuous emotion he shows but little sign, and of fierce passion, still less' (*Morning Post*, 22 March 1861). Thus far had the stage Hamlet come towards the weak and ineffectual figure of the Romantics, less the future king 'born to command' than a genteel royal, expert in politesse.

This is not the whole truth, however, about Fechter's Hamlet. In the latter part of the play his mild manner changed dramatically. According to Field, 'Fechter's Hamlet was restrained by reasonable doubt, not vacillation of purpose, and no sooner caught "the conscience of the King" than he could drink hot blood' (pp. 92–3). After the killing of Polonius it seemed to Dutton Cook that 'if Fechter's Hamlet had not been well guarded, he would have killed the King then and there', and it was in that fierce spirit that he finally accomplished his revenge.[90]

More than anything else, it was Fechter's realism that was seen by most

88 Castronovo, *Gentleman*, p. 61.   89 Cf. Castronovo, *Gentleman*; Mason, *Gentleman*.
90 Cook, *Hours*, II, p. 263.

forced to some act at which his soul revolts' (*New York World*, 9 January 1876), thus subverting the impact of the Ghost's call to arms. And when he actually does kill Claudius, after a moment of 'mad exultation' he looks at the King with a 'stare of horror, then reels and falters down the steps of the throne' (col. 199); as Clarke concludes: 'his conscientiousness was outraged. His will was appalled, for it had overdone itself' (col. 202).[93] Thus did Booth find a way to include Hamlet's violently decisive actions yet show them to be contrary to his true Romantic nature. He spoke 'O cursed spite / That ever I was born to set it right' as to himself, emphasizing 'cursed', 'I', and 'born': he explained that 'Tis the groan of his overburthened soul' (Shattuck, p. 158).

Booth's Hamlet was 'every inch the noble Prince and true-born gentleman; strong, pure, and refined, in soul and senses'. So judged Mary Isabella Stone, who wrote full accounts of performances by Booth in Boston in 1881 and after (p. 2). Consistently, Booth found ways to soften the sharp edges of Hamlet's scorn for Rosencrantz and Guildenstern, Polonius, his mother, Osric. The gravediggers' lack of refinement contrasted with his gentility.

The social decorum of Booth's student prince was matched by the artistic decorum of his impersonation. Edwin Forrest, his immediate American predecessor in the role, seemed crude by comparison. His assumed madness was conveyed 'more by insinuation . . . than through intense outbreak' (Clarke, col. 73). Stone discerns the artistry by which Booth gave full value to the early scenes yet held himself 'within bounds' in order to build a 'reserve power' for more intense moments to come (pp. 18–19). The expression of this power could be quite subtle. She remarks on how Booth conveys a 'tension of nerves' when Hamlet is with other people and the subsequent relaxation when left alone, or with Horatio (p. 136). She points out how with Horatio in the graveyard scene 'The appearance of anguish of soul is *intensified*, and this is done not by an increase of demonstrativeness, but by an increase of *restrainedness*' (p. 121). Repeatedly, Garland compares Booth to a marble statue, even with the gravediggers.

Occasional lapses in restraint on Booth's part were deplored, which he as a consequence toned down.[94] On the other hand, some felt that Booth was too tame. In 1883 a German critic commented that Booth 'stirs us in many a moment of moving pathos, but he never sweeps us off our feet with tragic passion' (Shattuck, p. 298). While acknowledging a general 'want of fire and *electricity*', a more sympathetic observer found in Booth's interpretation not 'flashes of lightning' but 'a steady light' (Shattuck, p. 91). Clarke's meticulous record of Booth's speech and movement confirms this impression: few

---

93 In 1885 Hamlin Garland recorded a much less-conflicted Hamlet: 'a somber philosopher, a student of life and a man burdened with doubt' ('Lecture', p. 14).

94 Stedman, 'Booth', p. 589.

of his contemporaries as his most radical innovation. The change was not welcomed in all quarters. Earlier, Marston had seen the new style as a lowering of the modern actor's sights, from 'the actor of passions' who must 'display the very soul of the character' and 'general humanity' to 'the actor of sentiment and comedy' who 'has but to display the fit conjunction of feelings with the manners of the time'. He looked back to Macready who combined both kinds of acting, finding that Fechter 'had the familiar, the colloquial side of Macready; but this, with sentiment and refinement, formed his stock-in-trade. He wanted Macready's exaltation of passion.'[91] To Marston Fechter thus represented a partial survival of a past greatness. But for most, Fechter's Hamlet sounded the keynote for the future, and indeed it proved to be the style of acting Shakespeare that would characterize the rest of the century, one in which, as Odell summed it up: 'His poetry was to be read more like prose than verse; action was to be toned down; everything was to be refined and gentle.'[92]

No Hamlet has been more 'refined and gentle' than America's Edwin Booth. He was not the first Hamlet to inherit the part from his father (Junius Brutus) – Charles Kean had given a notable portrayal. Nor was he to be the last – H. B. and Laurence Irving would also follow their father, Henry. But Edwin Booth is the only Hamlet to have surpassed his father in the role. His father might well have agreed. 'You look like Hamlet', he told his son at 19 and urged him to play the part (Shattuck, p. 3).

Booth put his own touch on the general Romantic reading of the character (he had read both Goethe and Hazlitt). He portrayed a Prince 'of a reflective, sensitive, gentle, generous nature, tormented, borne down and made miserable by an occasion . . . to which it is not equal' (*New York Herald*, 28 November 1864). Amid the corrupt materialism of the gilded age in America, he may well have seemed to contemporaries the very reverse of the vulgar and reckless yet strong-willed and all-conquering robber barons of industry and business. To Charles Clarke, whose handwritten columns provide an extraordinarily detailed manuscript account of Booth's 1870 production, Booth's prince was 'a man of first-class intellect but second-class will' (col. 129), resolute in minor matters yet irresolute in major ones. Clarke finds these traits illustrated again and again in the performance. For instance, Booth skilfully mousetraps the king with the play-within-a-play, yet is so overcome by his success that he fails to capitalize on his advantage and follow through to the fulfilment of his revenge. When the Ghost appears in the closet scene, Booth combined 'doubt, anxiety, apprehension, and awe' with 'a new and agonizing fear that he will now be

91 Marston, *Actors*, II, pp. 194, 398.   92 Odell, *Shakespeare*, II, p. 414.

forced to some act at which his soul revolts' (*New York World*, 9 January 1876), thus subverting the impact of the Ghost's call to arms. And when he actually does kill Claudius, after a moment of 'mad exultation' he looks at the King with a 'stare of horror, then reels and falters down the steps of the throne' (col. 199); as Clarke concludes: 'his conscientiousness was out-raged. His will was appalled, for it had overdone itself' (col. 202).[93] Thus did Booth find a way to include Hamlet's violently decisive actions yet show them to be contrary to his true Romantic nature. He spoke 'O cursed spite / That ever I was born to set it right' as to himself, emphasizing 'cursed', 'I', and 'born': he explained that 'Tis the groan of his overburthened soul' (Shattuck, p. 158).

Booth's Hamlet was 'every inch the noble Prince and true-born gentle-man; strong, pure, and refined, in soul and senses'. So judged Mary Isabella Stone, who wrote full accounts of performances by Booth in Boston in 1881 and after (p. 2). Consistently, Booth found ways to soften the sharp edges of Hamlet's scorn for Rosencrantz and Guildenstern, Polonius, his mother, Osric. The gravediggers' lack of refinement contrasted with his gentility.

The social decorum of Booth's student prince was matched by the artis-tic decorum of his impersonation. Edwin Forrest, his immediate American predecessor in the role, seemed crude by comparison. His assumed madness was conveyed 'more by insinuation . . . than through intense out-break' (Clarke, col. 73). Stone discerns the artistry by which Booth gave full value to the early scenes yet held himself 'within bounds' in order to build a 'reserve power' for more intense moments to come (pp. 18–19). The expres-sion of this power could be quite subtle. She remarks on how Booth conveys a 'tension of nerves' when Hamlet is with other people and the subsequent relaxation when left alone, or with Horatio (p. 136). She points out how with Horatio in the graveyard scene 'The appearance of anguish of soul is *intensified*, and this is done not by an increase of demonstrativeness, but by an increase of *restrainedness*' (p. 121). Repeatedly, Garland compares Booth to a marble statue, even with the gravediggers.

Occasional lapses in restraint on Booth's part were deplored, which he as a consequence toned down.[94] On the other hand, some felt that Booth was too tame. In 1883 a German critic commented that Booth 'stirs us in many a moment of moving pathos, but he never sweeps us off our feet with tragic passion' (Shattuck, p. 298). While acknowledging a general 'want of fire and *electricity*', a more sympathetic observer found in Booth's interpretation not 'flashes of lightning' but 'a steady light' (Shattuck, p. 91). Clarke's meticu-lous record of Booth's speech and movement confirms this impression: few

93 In 1885 Hamlin Garland recorded a much less-conflicted Hamlet: 'a somber
   philosopher, a student of life and a man burdened with doubt' ('Lecture', p. 14).
94 Stedman, 'Booth', p. 589.

of his contemporaries as his most radical innovation. The change was not welcomed in all quarters. Earlier, Marston had seen the new style as a lowering of the modern actor's sights, from 'the actor of passions' who must 'display the very soul of the character' and 'general humanity' to 'the actor of sentiment and comedy' who 'has but to display the fit conjunction of feelings with the manners of the time'. He looked back to Macready who combined both kinds of acting, finding that Fechter 'had the familiar, the colloquial side of Macready; but this, with sentiment and refinement, formed his stock-in-trade. He wanted Macready's exaltation of passion.'[91] To Marston Fechter thus represented a partial survival of a past greatness. But for most, Fechter's Hamlet sounded the keynote for the future, and indeed it proved to be the style of acting Shakespeare that would characterize the rest of the century, one in which, as Odell summed it up: 'His poetry was to be read more like prose than verse; action was to be toned down; everything was to be refined and gentle.'[92]

No Hamlet has been more 'refined and gentle' than America's Edwin Booth. He was not the first Hamlet to inherit the part from his father (Junius Brutus) – Charles Kean had given a notable portrayal. Nor was he to be the last – H. B. and Laurence Irving would also follow their father, Henry. But Edwin Booth is the only Hamlet to have surpassed his father in the role. His father might well have agreed. 'You look like Hamlet', he told his son at 19 and urged him to play the part (Shattuck, p. 3).

Booth put his own touch on the general Romantic reading of the character (he had read both Goethe and Hazlitt). He portrayed a Prince 'of a reflective, sensitive, gentle, generous nature, tormented, borne down and made miserable by an occasion . . . to which it is not equal' (New York *Herald*, 28 November 1864). Amid the corrupt materialism of the gilded age in America, he may well have seemed to contemporaries the very reverse of the vulgar and reckless yet strong-willed and all-conquering robber barons of industry and business. To Charles Clarke, whose handwritten columns provide an extraordinarily detailed manuscript account of Booth's 1870 production, Booth's prince was 'a man of first-class intellect but second-class will' (col. 129), resolute in minor matters yet irresolute in major ones. Clarke finds these traits illustrated again and again in the performance. For instance, Booth skilfully mousetraps the king with the play-within-a-play, yet is so overcome by his success that he fails to capitalize on his advantage and follow through to the fulfilment of his revenge. When the Ghost appears in the closet scene, Booth combined 'doubt, anxiety, apprehension, and awe' with 'a new and agonizing fear that he will now be

91 Marston, *Actors*, II, pp. 194, 398.   92 Odell, *Shakespeare*, II, p. 414.

6 Edwin Booth in the 'To be or not to be' soliloquy (3.1). Booth began the speech sitting
down. As depicted, his promptbooks show him rising at 'there's the rub' (65). Clarke
describes him at this point as resting his right hand on the post of the chair, his left hand
at his breast. Perhaps the thought of the afterlife has prompted Hamlet to grasp the
picture of the dead King on the steel chain around his neck (the picture was of Booth's
real-life father Junius Brutus Booth). The cross-gartering was of dark pink cloth, a style
– like the decor – suggestive of the tenth and eleventh century in northern Europe.
Ophelia reads in the side alcove while Polonius and the King spy from the gallery
(Shattuck, pp. 188, 124n.)

intriguing original 'readings' emerge, but his emphases constantly clarify meaning, providing 'a continual elucidation of Shakespere' (*New York Herald*, 28 November 1864). In addition, contemporaries found a certain kind of poetry. In contrast to the prosaic and overly realistic Fechter, Clarke felt that Booth appealed to our sense of the ideal, 'of what might be' (col. 21).

Various commentators found affinities between Booth himself and Hamlet. Stedman saw in Booth 'the gentleman and scholar' that he saw in Hamlet.[95] What is remarkable is that Booth (who grew up as a barn-stormer) was by no means to the manner born. His gentlemanly manner and accomplishments were acquired, through the tutelage of his wife and an early mentor, Adam Badeau. All the same Booth revealingly wrote to Badeau around this time that to play the role 'I shall be called upon to be genteel & gentle – or rather pale & polite'.[96]

It was in his devotion to his father that Booth was most deeply kin to Prince Hamlet. When his wife died in 1863, he took up spiritualism and received messages not only from her but from his father. It was a miniature of his own father that as Hamlet he wore on a neck-chain, and he sometimes fancied he could hear his father's voice in that of the Ghost (Shattuck, p. 7).

By 1870, Booth was acclaimed 'the accepted Hamlet of the American stage' (*New York Herald*, 6 January 1870). Partly his success was personal. Partly it came from favouring cultural trends. Booth's approach was in accord with the general 'feminization' of American culture, as clergy and women writers and readers celebrated such sentimental values as gentleness and a depth and delicacy of feeling.[97] Booth wrote of Hamlet to critic William Winter in 1882, distinguishing between effeminacy and femininity: 'I doubt if ever a robust and masculine treatment of the character will be accepted so generally as the more womanly and refined interpretation' (Shattuck, p. 64). Especially in the 1870 production in Booth Theatre, Booth's *Hamlet* also took part in the 'sacralization' of the arts (opera, classical music, and the fine arts as well as drama and literature) that was separating high brow from low brow culture in America at this time.[98] The souvenir brochure for the new theatre promised that the play would glorify 'our too mundane souls with some of its higher, more heavenly attributes' (Shattuck, p. 72).

In England, however, Booth was felt – in comparison with Henry Irving – to be 'of the old school'.

---

95 *Ibid.*   96 Quoted by Carlisle, *Greenroom*, p. 79.
97 Douglas, *Feminization*.   98 Levine, *Highbrow*.

'An overruling authority': Henry Irving and Ellen Terry

It was in Henry Irving's revelation of Hamlet's inner life that he was most convincing. He introduced a 'psychological Hamlet' (*Academy*, 18 September 1897). It was characteristic of Irving's approach that the 'counterfeit presentments' of King Hamlet and Claudius should be in the mind's eye rather than pictures on a wall or in lockets.[99] The intellectuality of Irving's Hamlet was much remarked upon. W. B. Yeats, who as a boy was indelibly impressed by Irving, would recall his 'lean image of hungry speculation' (*The Trembling of the Veil*, Bk I).

Nonetheless, *The Times* felt that Irving's Hamlet 'is essentially tender, loving, and merciful . . . a fine genial creature, who would willingly have clasped all the world to his bosom' (2 November 1874). In his study book Irving himself commented on Hamlet's remark about having 'Lost all my mirth': 'Hamlet has been a very lively *fellow*.'

Irving rarely gave direct expression to Hamlet's stronger feelings. Indeed, he was faulted for 'the entire absence of tragic passion'.[100] For his Victorian audience, however, the indirectness of Irving's expression of suppressed feelings may have added to their impact. In Hamlet's scene with his mother, 'a regretful tenderness mingles with his wrathful denunciations' (*Theatre*, 1 February 1879, pp. 20–1). With Ophelia, Irving held that 'through all his bitter ravings there is visible the anguish of a lover forced to be cruel'.[101] Especially when Ellen Terry played Ophelia, his audiences were moved by the conflict he projected between love and duty, with duty, in high Victorian fashion, prevailing in the end.

The inner conflicts in Irving's portrayal of the nunnery scene are so intense that for Russell they cross the border between pretended lunacy to 'real frenzy' (p. 39). Among other such crises, his delivery of the 'Hold, hold my heart' speech revealed Hamlet's way of 'fostering and aggravating his own excitements' (Russell, p. 13). Some also found him roused to frenzy by the climax of the play scene and 'the sudden tidings of Ophelia's death' in the graveyard scene (*Punch*, 11 January 1879). Recalling Irving's performance fifty-five years later, Eden Phillpotts was able to see three-way connections between his insanity, his intellectuality, and his failure to act. To this 'man of rare intellect confronted with just those problems that his supreme order of intelligence is powerless to solve', the 'psychical torment' of his inaction brings 'the threat of madness hovering nearer and nearer'.[102]

In his emphasis on this threat Irving was very much of his cultural

---

99 Irving, 'Notes . . . no. 3', pp. 260–3.   100 Towse, 'Irving', p. 666.
101 Irving, 'Notes . . . no. 2', p. 530.   102 Phillpotts, 'Irving', p. 85.

7 Henry Irving and Ellen Terry in the nunnery scene (3.1). Terry writes that Irving was here 'the lover above the prince and the poet. With what passionate longing his hands hovered over Ophelia' (*Memoirs*, p. 104). Irving pictured how Ophelia as she reads Hamlet's pale face, 'gazes into his sleepless eyes, notes the deep-shaded hollows of his cheeks' ('Notes . . . no. 2', p. 526).

moment. His focus on the private life of a man of pronounced individuality (accentuated by Irving's idiosyncratic pronunciations and eccentric way of walking, 'between a stagger and a slouch' – *Macmillan's Magazine*, 1874, p. 240) may be seen as an extreme extension of Romantic subjectivity. But the question of Hamlet's insanity was a special concern of Irving's own time.[103] The section devoted to it in the Variorum edition (1877) shows a growing preoccupation with the issue, by medical as well as literary authorities: a third of the items date from the eighteen seventies. By placing his Prince on the borderline of madness, Irving was able to accommodate this interest while retaining enough of Hamlet's heroic fibre to make the finale a triumph not only over the King – whom he slew with 'contemptuous brutality' (*Daily News*, 2 November 1874) – but also over his own mental weakness.

Adding further to Irving's emphasis on Hamlet's mental condition was Ellen Terry's portrayal of Ophelia. In her view Ophelia from the beginning suffers from 'an incipient insanity': 'there is something queer about her, something which explains her wits going astray later on'. The keynote of her tragedy is that she is afraid, scared of Hamlet, her father, and 'life itself when things go wrong' (p. 110). Terry sees her as 'Shakespeare's only timid heroine . . . her brain, her soul and her body are all pathetically weak.'[104] What she deplored as 'weak', her male reviewers praised as 'maidenly' submissiveness, although Martin-Harvey, who acted with her, recalled 'a poise so frail that one trembled for her sanity, even before she went mad'.[105]

Showalter has outlined how the portrayal of Ophelia's madness has often reflected and influenced changing views of madwomen in society at large.[106] But Terry put her own touch on conventional views. Two factors especially shaped her concept. One was textual – the Gentleman's description of her mad winks and nods (4.5.4–13). The other was a visit Terry made to a madhouse. For the most part, she discovered, the inmates were 'too theatrical to teach me anything'. The exception was a girl – 'very thin, very pathetic, very young' – who was gazing at a wall, her face vacant but her body expressing that she was 'waiting, waiting': 'Suddenly she threw up her hands and sped across the room like a swallow' in a movement 'as poignant as it was beautiful' (p. 122). Terry's strong emphasis on pathos

103 Such intense debates, concerning Irving in particular, were satirized by W. S. Gilbert in *Rosencrantz and Guildenstern* (1874):

> Some [hold] that he's really sane, but shamming mad –
> Some that he's really mad, but shamming sane –
> Some that he will be mad, some that he *was* –
> Some that he couldn't be. But on the whole
> (As far as I can make out what they mean)
> The favourite theory's somewhat like this:
> Hamlet is idiotically sane
> With lucid intervals of lunacy.

104 Terry, *Lectures*, pp. 165–6.   105 Martin-Harvey, *Autobiography*, p. 29.
106 Showalter, 'Ophelia', pp. 77ff.

may derive from this experience. Also Clement Scott observed her 'vacant expression in the eye' and her 'grace of movement'.[107] Further the notes in Terry's studybook stress the suddenness of her mad changes – from quick to slow, bright to sad, laughter to tears.

To Dutton Cook Terry's 'power of depicting intensity of feeling' was another key feature of her success.[108] By her own analysis, however, she was

> not capable of *sustained* effort, but can perhaps manage a *cumulative* effort better than most actresses. I have been told that Ophelia had 'nothing to do' at first. I found so much to do! Little bits of business which, slight in themselves, contributed to a definite result, and kept me always in the picture.
>
> (Terry, p. 122)

These small touches were not lost on her reviewers, who devotedly recorded the details shown in the Commentary of this edition. In the mad scenes, Terry herself marvelled at (and revelled in) the theatrical power of 'This frail wraith, this poor demented thing' (p. 215). One observer remarked on how the flowers she carried were 'one moment heedlessly crushed, and the next smothered with kisses' (*Daily Chronicle*, 31 December 1878). Another noted her 'trick of wiping away her tears with a finger' (*Vanity Fair*, 18 January 1879). Throughout, 'every broken phrase and strange image is suggested by some recollection of the time before she was distraught' (*Toronto Globe*, 13 October 1884). For her son Gordon Craig the cumulative effect was overwhelming: 'I could not compare my notions with hers, because mine were all scattered and she hadn't any – she had no notions – she was the thing itself . . . When the curtain came down, the thought left with us was not "That's the way to do it," but "it is the only way to do it"'.[109]

Inclusion of Ellen Terry was just one of the ways in which Irving in 1878 clinched the strong claim he had made in 1874 to a place in the succession of player princes. In 1870 Booth had secured his position as *the* American Hamlet, with a sumptuously mounted production in his own, richly appointed, new theatre. In 1878 Irving did the same at the renovated Lyceum. The production ran for 200 consecutive nights (by now the length of a long run had become the measure of a Hamlet's impact more than the span of years he successfully played the role in repertory – Booth's 1864 production had run for 100 nights). In their own theatres Irving and Booth were able to crystallize methods of creating an overall unified effect that had been evolving in the course of the nineteenth century.

At its centre was the role of Hamlet, which both Irving and Booth

107 Scott, *Hamlets*, p. 181.   108 Cook, *Nights*, II, p. 143.
109 Craig, *Terry*, p. 172.

treated as a star-part, where the dominant position of Shakespeare's Prince is pushed to something close to total dominance, resulting in a virtual monodrama. Concern for a unifying coherence in the performance of supporting roles was slow to emerge. In his time Garrick was exceptional in his attempts to impart his own style of acting to his supporting casts.[110] That his success was less than total, however, may be seen in the disparities in style between his 'natural' approach to the Prince and the twice-too-loud, conventional portrayal of the King that so impressed Mr Partridge in *Tom Jones*. Kemble and Macready had done their best to rehearse their casts but encountered stubborn resistance by the actors, and their efforts accomplished little. In this, as in many other respects, Fechter was far ahead of common English practice, especially in crowd-scenes where each person seemed 'to take up his position as it were by accident' (*Herald*, 23 May 1864). Irving did rehearse the cast of his Hamlet (Booth made no special efforts in that way), but his instruction was always in how he himself would act the part (Terry, p. 121). Even in 1884 it would be a matter for comment that Wilson Barrett's decision to play Hamlet as very young was accompanied by his casting an appropriately younger Claudius and Gertrude.[111]

If ensemble was only beginning to be a concern in England, the appropriateness of scenery, costumes, and lighting was well advanced. The original dominance of the acted word, with its address to the active imaginations of the auditors, had more and more given place to literal, visual appeals. By the middle of the nineteenth century the various archeological mountings of Macready and Charles Kean had introduced an emphasis upon overall effect, although the consistency was most often to the historical period depicted rather than to the special atmosphere of a given play. With *Hamlet* it was Fechter's elaborate production that had the greatest impact, 'with massive architecture of the Norman style, and the dresses of the medieval Danish period', creating an atmosphere of 'rugged strength' (*Lloyd's Weekly*, 28 May 1864). Rosencrantz and Guildenstern are 'bluff fellows, with thick beards, coarse leggings, and cross garters – and the other personages are after the same model' (*The Times*, 23 May 1864). Entering into the Scandinavian atmosphere, Fechter himself was famous for his flowing blond wig, but the chief effect must have been one of contrast, as his soft style of acting stood out against his Viking-like surroundings.

As actor-managers in their own theatres, Booth and Irving were able to provide for their *Hamlet*s just the surroundings that they wished, employ-

---

110 Burnim, *Garrick*, pp. 50–61.   111 Goddard, *Players*, pp. 258–9.

ing set designers who were making names for themselves in their own right, Charles Witham for Booth, Hawes Craven for Irving, artists whose emphasis was more on the picturesque than on strict archeology. Of Booth's 1870 *Hamlet*, Nym Crinkle (ordinarily no enthusiast) had to praise 'the harmony . . . the interdependencies . . . of the whole work . . . the most amazing combination of all arts that our stage has ever seen' (*World*, 9 January 1870).

In his review of Irving's 1878 *Hamlet*, Moy Thomas argued that 'what is wanted on our stage is . . . an overruling authority, capable of reducing the whole representation to just proportions' (*Academy*, 4 January 1879, p. 17). Like the other actor-managers who would follow him, Irving exercised just such 'an overruling authority' – rehearsing its actors, over-seeing its costumes, sets, and music. But his concern was, like Booth's, less for 'the whole representation' as such than with providing a setting for his own performance of the starring role, an approach that held sway until the mid-twentieth century.

Although Irving's preeminence was further established by his own status in society (he was to become the first English actor to be knighted), his portrayal of Hamlet was not generally regarded as aristocratic. On the contrary, the *Daily News* objected, instead of 'princely ease' he showed 'bourgeois cordiality': he 'habitually takes persons of high and low degree, leans on their shoulders, or clasps them around the neck, and is generally rather familiarly confidential than affable and condescending' (2 November 1874). The *Sporting Times* compared him to a contemporary 'swell' lounging in the drawing-rooms of London (7 November 1874). *The Times* put a more positive construction on the matter: 'Dignity in his Hamlet is not a predominating quality. His heart is too large and too kindly to attach much importance to social distinction' (2 November 1874). But clearly Irving's definitiveness rested on grounds other than its princeliness. It was Irving's successor who embodied the essence of princely manners for their time: Johnston Forbes-Robertson.

'A great gentleman doing his gentlest and bravest and noblest with sad smile and gay humour': Johnston Forbes-Robertson

Certain of the style-setting Hamlets have had successors who carried on their styles. So Garrick had John Henderson, Kemble had Charles Mayne Young. But only Forbes-Robertson achieved anything like the stature of his forebear, Henry Irving, who put at the disposal of his chosen successor his theatre, designer, and composer.

Forbes-Robertson was by no means merely a copy of Irving. His natural attributes were much better suited to the role. Max Beerbohm observed that 'In face, and in voice, and in manner, Mr. Robertson is a heaven-born Hamlet.'[112] His audiences loved to hear him speak, comparing his voice to a cello – G. B. Shaw compared it to a bass clarinet. Like Irving there was nothing declamatory about his delivery, but he was largely free of Irving's idiosyncracies; his verse (and prose) speaking was said to be 'various and delicate, free from the sound-destroying pauses and jerks of Mr. Irving (whose tones he is gradually unlearning), best in the quieter and more limpid passages, easy . . .' (*Manchester Guardian*, 24 May, 1898). In implicit contrast to Irving, G. B. Shaw extolled the fact that Forbes-Robertson 'does not utter half a line; then stop to act; then go on with another half line . . . he plays as Shakespear should be played, on the line and to the line, with the utterance and acting simultaneous, inseparable and in fact identical'.[113] Unlike Irving's, there was no suggestion of genuine madness about Forbes-Robertson's Hamlet, who was 'eminently sane' (*Illustrated Sporting and Dramatic News*, 18 September 1897) and 'never loses his head, no more than he loses his wits' (*Dramatic World*, 1 October 1897, p. 2). Even his pre-tended madness was too 'obviously put-on' to deceive anyone (*St. James Gazette*, 13 September 1897, p. 6).

The most distinctive quality of Forbes-Robertson's Hamlet was its cheerfulness. Reviews are filled with such terms as 'genial', 'lighthearted', 'affable', 'joie de vivre'. Delighting in the life of the mind, whether with the players, the gravediggers, or Osric, Forbes-Robertson seized on 'every opportunity for a bit of philosophic discussion or artistic recreation to escape from the "cursed spite" of revenge and love'. Shaw's term for the result was 'celestial gaiety'.[114]

In contrast was a frequent tone of 'gentle melancholy': the *Daily News* found Forbes-Robertson, 'the most pathetic Hamlet of our time' (13 September 1897). Besides predictable expressions of sorrow his injunction to his mother 'O throw away the worser part' was given 'with tears in the voice'; he brushed away a tear after the First Player's recitation, and, William Archer observed, even 'Aha, boy, art thou there!' was spoken to the Ghost with 'respectful melancholy' instead of 'feverish freakishness' (*World*, 15 September 1897).

Drawing a comparison with other 'gentlemanly Princes of Denmark', the *Court Journal* found 'none so gentle as Forbes- Robertson' (18 September 1897). Madge Kendal remembered how at his first entrance, he 'kissed his mother's hand with reverence and then he paid attention to the elder ladies gathered round. That was what only a real prince would do'.[115] In his 1913

112 Beerbohm, *More Theatres*, p. 487.   113 Shaw, *Shakespeare*, p. 91.
114 *Ibid.*, pp. 93, 87.   115 *Dame Madge*, p. 134.

silent film he also bows the ladies out. At the finale he courteously informed Osric 'in apologetic tones and with a return of the well-known smile that he cannot live to hear the news from England.'[116] 'Lovable' is a term often applied to Forbes-Robertson's Hamlet – 'a great gentleman doing his gentlest and bravest and noblest with sad smile and gay humor'.[117]

To a good many viewers, however, so much 'sweetness and light' was too much. Where, one wondered, was the 'phlegmatic, dubious, morbid, wildly whirling Northman that Shakespeare drew?' (*Clarion*, 18 September 1897). But these criticisms were far outweighed by praise. The finale was particularly admired, especially the sight of the dying prince at last, however briefly, taking his rightful place on the throne, thus elevating Hamlet's revenge from 'brutal murder' to a transcendent beauty in which Robertson's expression was said to be 'beatific'. Genteel to the end, he made 'The rest is silence' 'a touchingly humorous apology for not being able to finish his business'.[118]

As for the revolutionary inclusion of Fortinbras at the end, opinion was divided. Most found it anticlimactic, especially since earlier references to Fortinbras had, as usual, been cut; they missed 'the impressive gloom of the *tableau* which follows Hamlet's last utterance' (*Court Journal*, 18 September 1897). But Shaw, who had suggested the innovation to Robertson, was not alone in finding it praiseworthy. His only reservation was the wish that Fortinbras should 'make straight for the throne like a man who intended to keep it against all comers.'[119]

Continental star Hamlets: François Joseph Talma, Pavel Mochalov, Tomasso Salvini, Jean Mounet Sully, Sarah Bernhardt, Josef Kainz

Like English and American *Hamlet*s, Continental productions were until the twentieth century dominated by star performers of the title-role. Space permits only sketches of the most prominent of them. In France FRANÇOIS JOSEPH TALMA was praised by Madame De Stael in a letter to him in 1809 for the 'poetry of looks, intonations, gestures' that she saw in his Hamlet.[120] The Ghost did not physically walk the French stage, yet as De Staël testifies in *De l'Allemagne* it manifested itself on Talma's face, where terrifyingly one could follow the movement of the Ghost in his eyes.[121] The intensity of Talma's 'pantomime' is suggested by a critic's attack on 'his contorted face,

---

116 Crosse, *Diaries*, I, p. 143.   117 Le Gallienne, 'Forbes Robertson', p. 513.

118 Shaw, *Shakespeare*, p. 88.   119 *Ibid.*, p. 91.

120 Madame De Staël quoted in *Revue D'Histoire du Théâtre*, October–December 1964, p. 338.   121 De Staël, *De l'Allemagne*, III, pp. 236–7.

his wild eyes, his changing voice, his somber and gloomy tones, his taut muscles, his trembling and convulsions'.[122]

Talma could convey subtler impressions as well. An English observer remarked upon Talma's 'capacity to express the *impatience* of suffering' and his restraint towards 'minor and passing sentiments', which English Hamlets gave undue emphasis.[123] Indeed, as De Staël reports, Talma could be totally immobile in his 'to be or not to be' soliloquy as his 'meditation absorbed his whole being' – he 'turned his head only to question the earth and heaven what death is'.[124]

In Moscow in 1837 PAVEL MOCHALOV's portrayal radiated raw energy in an explosive style comparable to that of Edmund Kean and contrasting with his Kemble-like St Petersburg rival, decorous Vasily Karatygin. At 'man delights not me' (2.2.290) he threw 'both arms away from his body, as though he were heaving humanity from the breast to which he had once so strongly clasped it'.[125] Indeed the influential critic Vissarion Belinsky felt that in his first performances Mochalov was too powerful, giving Hamlet far more strength and energy than is possible for 'a man struggling with himself and dispirited by an unbearable burden of calamities', an inbalance later corrected.[126]

Conceptually Mochalov's performance inspired Belinsky to see in Hamlet not Goethe's fragile prince, lacking in nerve, but a strong man, weakened by disillusionment with a lying world and consequent self-doubt, yet full of bitter and unconcealed abhorrence towards his enemies and his own inaction. Belinsky's formulation had a strong political implication, resonating with the suppressed dissatisfaction with Tsarist rule then current. Film director Grigori Kozintsev would look back to the production as one that broke through this 'enforced muteness'.[127]

At the end of the nineteenth century came a concentration of stellar Hamlets. The overwhelming presence that Mochalov acquired by his art (he was small in stature yet 'his gigantic shadow scaled the very ceiling of the auditorium'[128]), the Italian TOMASSO SALVINI had by nature and physique, strengths that made his Othello one of the greatest of all Shakespearian performances. For his Hamlet in 1875, however, he chose to play against type, presenting a prince who by his own formulation showed 'the power of thought over action' (*Putnam's*, December 1907, p. 355), thus seeking to put on the stage the morbidly thoughtful Prince of the Romantics ('his ruling passion is to think, not to act', Hazlitt, *Characters of*

---

122 Geoffroy, *Journal de l'Empire* (27 May 1807).
123 Quoted in Speaight, *Stage*, p. 88.   124 De Staël, *De l'Allemagne*, III, pp. 236–7.
125 Kozintsev, *Shakespeare*, p. 121.   126 *Ibid.*
127 Kozintsev, *Shakespeare*, p. 123.   128 *Ibid.*

Shakespear's Plays, 1817). In contrast to his fiery compatriot Ernesto Rossi, in only a few places did Salvini allow his full strength to show itself: at 'unhand me gentlemen' (1.4.84) he did not – like other Hamlets – need a weapon to free himself from those who would restrain him but did so with a single, explosive wrench of his body.[129] Emma Lazarus was able to see in his portrayal 'the purely intellectual and poetic side of Salvini's genius', his delivery of the 'to be or not to be' soliloquy being 'that of a poet who thinks aloud' – compare Hazlitt's description of Hamlet as one who is 'wrapped up in his reflections, and only *thinks aloud*' (*Century*, November 1881, p. 115). But this quality was lost on most, including G. H. Lewes, who was unable to recognize signs of 'intellectual over-activity'.[130]

It was to a subsidiary aspect of Salvini's intention that reviewers most responded. Salvini felt that Hamlet 'has only three strong affections: for his poor father, for Ophelia and for his friend Horatio' (*Putnam's*, December 1907, p. 354). To Clement Scott his tender way of speaking '*padre*' to the Ghost 'made music' (*Daily Telegraph*, 6 January 1875). It is because of Ophelia's death, Salvini thought, that he himself 'longs for death' (*Putnam's*, p. 355). At the finale, Lewes reports, he had 'dying Hamlet draw down the head of Horatio to kiss him before sinking into silence: which reminds one of the "Kiss me, Hardy," of the dying Nelson'.[131]

In France in 1896, Mallarmé saw in the Hamlet of JEAN MOUNET SULLY *the* summing up of the *fin de siècle*.[132] In his own notes Mounet succinctly described the 'good and tender' prince as a being who was 'born to love but devoted to hatred and scorn'.[133] Monomaniacally devoted to revenging his father's murder and compelled as well to hate his uncle, despise his mother, and suspect Ophelia, he had become a misanthrope. Yet his earlier essential self survived, and, as Mallarmé discerned, it is the resulting duality that distinguished Mounet's interpretation:

> mad, yes, in outward appearance, whipped as he is in both directions by his duty; but oh! nonetheless, his eyes are still upon an image of himself within, and this he keeps intact – like an Ophelia still undrowned! – always prepared to get his balance back again. Jewel intact in the midst of chaos.
>
> (*Essays*, p. 60)

Mounet projected this basic conception throughout his portrayal. His attitudes towards the Ghost were especially mixed. His initial invocations moved from tender to imperative while at the Ghost's departure he stretched his arms out in agonized entreaty and farewell, only then to faint with fear at the dangerous task imposed upon him. The strain of these inner

129 Winter, *Shakespeare*, p. 416.   130 Lewes, *Actors*, p. 230.   131 *Ibid*, p. 232.
132 Mallarmé, *Essays*, p. 60.   133 Quoted in Jacquot, 'Mounet-Sully', pp. 423, 421.

conflicts was reflected in frequent outbursts of wild laughter (as at 'O my prophetic soul') and an unusual amount of weeping.[134] Behind Mounet's outbursts Lemaître recognized that the extreme effort it took the Prince to act at all made him incapable of self-control.[135]

In 1899 SARAH BERNHARDT first played Hamlet in Paris. A long line of women has essayed the role, extending from Mrs Siddons through Charlotte Cushman to Asta Nielsen (in the silent film) and Eva LeGallienne, plus scores of others. In recent years, Judith Anderson, Diane Venora, and Frances de la Tour have carried on the line. There may be something intrinsic in the part that has made it seem possible for a woman to play it (Romeo is another) whereas more 'masculine' roles like Othello and Macbeth seem out of the question. At the time he directed Daniel Day Lewis as Hamlet, Richard Eyre saw the play as a war between the feminine and the masculine within a man, 'the tragedy being that in order to deal with a male-dominated world, Hamlet has to drive out the woman in him' (South Bank Show). For her part, Bernhardt cleverly argued that the role was better played by a mature woman than by a man since Hamlet is a youth of twenty with the mind of a man of forty. An actor of twenty cannot understand Hamlet's philosophy while an older actor does not look young enough. 'The woman more readily looks the part, yet has the maturity of mind to grasp it' (*Harper's Bazaar*, 15 December 1900).

To Bernhardt the prince was 'not a weak or languid person' but 'manly and resolute'. He spares the King at prayer 'not because he is vacillating and weak, but because he is firm and logical', wanting to send him not to heaven but to hell.[136] Yet for contrast she could also depict 'a pleasant humorous, very gay prince' (*London Times*, 13 June 1899). What actress Elizabeth Robins saw portrayed was 'a high spirited, somewhat malicious boy' (*North American Review*, December 1900, p. 909).

In Paris Bernhardt's performance was generally acclaimed. She was the first Hamlet anywhere to appear on screen. In England and the United States, her reception was polarized. Some reviewers simply could not accept the idea of a fifty-four-year-old woman playing Hamlet as a twenty year old and the whole spectacle seemed ludicrous: 'an elderly lady encased in black silk tights'.[137] To those who could suspend their disbelief, however, Bernhardt's performance had many rewards. MacCarthy provides a close-up of the moment when Hamlet kills Polonius behind the arras but jumps to the conclusion that it is the King: 'she stood suddenly tiptoe, like a great

134 Speaight, *Stage*, p. 95.   135 Quoted in Jacquot, 'Mounet-Sully', pp. 420–1.

136 Winter, *Shakespeare*, p. 339.

137 Howells, *Literature*, disparaged 'She Hamlet', Beerbohm, *Around Theatres*, 'The Princess of Denmark'.

black exclamation mark, her sword glittering above her head, and a cry, "C'est le Roi!" rang in our ears, so expressive of final triumph and relief, that for a tingling second it seemed the play itself must be over'.[138]

In Germany and Austria, the Hungarian JOSEF KAINZ was the leading Hamlet of his time, playing the role in Berlin and Vienna between 1891 and 1909. A visiting English reviewer found him a 'brilliant, really princely creature, with the vehemence of his purpose swayed by shifting moods',[139] oscillating 'between the poles of artistic graciousness and a passionate Viking-like fury to revenge his father's murder' (*Shakespeare Survey*, 35, 1982, p. 28). When Hamlet learns of his uncle's guilt from the Ghost, Kainz's first reaction was a shout of 'wild joy' to have the intuition of his 'prophetic soul' confirmed, his gleaming sword swung high toward heaven and remaining there for some while: 'Then his arm drops, as he realizes the awesome consequences of this shocking discovery, he bursts forth, "my uncle", the sword slips from his hand and falls.'[140]

And so Kainz's performance went through an extraordinary range of moods, each heightened to an ultimate degree and expressed with 'febrile energy' – a furious outburst at Rosencrantz and Guildenstern, a corrosively harsh edge to his exchanges with Polonius, a tearful response to the First Player, a dreamy delivery of 'To be or not to be', a feral stalking of the King at the play, and a dancing, shouting, jubilant, orgiastic celebration of its confirmation of the King's guilt. Even Kainz's flickering smiles reflected Hamlet's mercurial feelings – from the 'phantom of a smile' that accompanied his 'perchance to dream', to the malevolently gleeful smile with which he decided to spare praying Claudius until a more damning occasion, to the final 'beatific smile' that followed 'the rest is silence'.[141]

Supporting roles and players: Ophelia, Claudius, Gertrude, Polonius

By the beginning of the twentieth century in the English-speaking theatre, the roles of Ophelia, Claudius, Gertrude, and Polonius had started to achieve a certain autonomy. Through most of *Hamlet*'s post-Restoration life, these characters had been regarded as scarcely more than foils for the Prince: as early as 1710 Shaftesbury had declared that the play 'has only ONE *character* or *principal* part'.[142] Often indeed the other characters were

138 MacCarthy, *Theatre*, p. 155.
139 *Illustrated London News*, 31 October 1891. Unless indicated otherwise, all details
       about Kainz are from this source.   140 Falke, *Kainz*, pp. 25, 49.
141 Richter, *Kainz*, p. 292; quoted by Speaight, *Stage*, p. 112.
142 Shaftesbury, *Characteristics*, I, p. 275.

played in accord with the biased way that Hamlet sees them rather than as they would see themselves. Continental productions were more enlightened. In 1886 an English observer in Paris made the contrast explicit, marvelling at how Mounet Sully's *Hamlet* was far from being a 'one-character piece': 'Nearly all the subordinate characters were admirably acted'; they 'actually succeeded in inspiring an interest in themselves, which, instead of diminishing, greatly enhanced all that is interesting in the character and position of Hamlet'.[143]

In a less concerted way, English practice too had at this time begun to change. On an individual basis certain exceptional players made the principal characters around Hamlet much more than foils. Often these players had been accustomed to performing leading roles in other plays, and commonly they made their mark with Hamlets who were not of the very highest quality. Thanks to their efforts and the growing use of fuller texts in performance, the four characters began to 'inspire an interest in themselves'.

OPHELIA led the way. The role began to be important when Edmund Kean and subsequent Hamlets began to mingle desire for her with the repulsion that had hitherto dominated his treatment of her (sometimes so rough in the nunnery scene – as with Garrick and Kemble – as to be rebuked by reviewers). Of her earlier career in the theatre, not much is recorded. Davies lauded the portrayal of 'sensibility deranged' by Mrs Susannah Cibber, who played Ophelia for Garrick, and shortly after her death the *St. James Chronicle* recalled 'her Expression of Grief mixed with Terror at the Behaviour of Hamlet' (3–5 March 1772).

There then followed a series of 'singing ladies' with whom the melodious delivery of Ophelia's mad songs was the defining qualification. A phase in the breakdown of this custom and a return to more dramatic values may be traced in reviewers' comments on two of Kean's Ophelias. In 1814 Miss Eliza Smith was admonished that 'Ophelia requires musical talents' (*St. James Chronicle*, 15 March). In 1819 Miss Carew, although much admired for her singing ability, was not thought of as a 'songstress' but praised for speaking 'with a most crisp and uncloying sweetness' (*Champion*, 19 December).

The next step was for Ophelia to become a featured role, and now the scene shifts to Paris where in 1827 Harriet Smithson, an Irish actress playing in Charles Kemble's touring company, made a phenomenal success. Much influenced by Kean, with whom she had acted, she brought a reality to Ophelia's grieving madness that was revolutionary in French theatre, emphasized by Smithson's expert mime and broken bits of song.[144] In 1844

143 Lytton, *Personal and Literary Letters* in Williamson, *Readings*, p. 171.
144 Raby, 'Ophelia', p. 66.

Helena Faucit also scored a Parisian success, playing opposite Macready, portraying Ophelia as a child of nature, raised among country people (hence her knowledge of folk songs). Her husband declared that hitherto the role was one 'which no English manager would ever have dreamed of asking a leading actress to play'.[145]

Back in London Mrs Charles Kean was in 1849 playing Ophelia to her husband's Hamlet: in her madness 'even while crouched upon the ground she sings her snatches of song to herself' (*Morning Chronicle*, 16 January 1849). So much for the singing-ladies tradition! By 1864, when Kate Terry triumphed as Ophelia with Fechter, the *Orchestra* reviewer observed that 'Ophelia is generally affected by a star' (28 May 1864).

The star of stars in the role was of course Kate's younger sister Ellen Terry who, as discussed, first played Ophelia opposite Irving in 1878. The other star Ophelia for whom we have the fullest account is Julia Marlowe, whose Hamlet was Edward Sothern. She regarded Ophelia as the high-placed daughter of the Lord Chamberlain, in the eyes of the royal family a suitable bride for the Prince whatever fears her brother and father may have had. As such, her biographer C. E. Russell found, 'she suggested dignity, worth, a self-respect, without loss of sweetness and innocence', her mature poise being shown in tragically unsuccessful efforts to 'protect Polonius and to spare Hamlet'.[146] 'Accustomed to a conventionally passive Ophelia, the *Sunday Times* found Marlowe to have 'almost too much forcefulness of character for Ophelia' (5 May 1907); the *New York Herald* was more perceptive: 'Here was not a gentle lady going daft to slow music, but a woman of strong passions and fine intelligence who succumbs to a terrible catastrophe' (1904).

Why did Ophelia achieve starring status at this particular time? No doubt it was partly because fascination with the play's love interest was at a peak – Terry felt it necessary to defend Irving against the charge that he 'only makes Hamlet a love poem!' (p. 104). Terry's discreet sex appeal was no small part of her success. Henry James responded to her 'embodiment of sumptuous sweetness', finding her Ophelia particularly 'lovely': 'a somewhat angular maiden of the Gothic ages, with her hair cropped short, like a boy's, and a straight and clinging robe'.[147] Martin-Harvey wrote of her 'absolutely irresistible physical attractiveness': 'her long, virginal limbs, her husky voice, her crown of short flaxen hair, her great red mouth' – ample reason he felt for the anxiety about Ophelia's honour expressed by brother and father.[148] Marlowe's 'womanliness' also came in for comment (*Chicago Daily Tribune*, 5 October 1904). When he transcribed the promptbook (143)

145 T. Martin, *Faucit*, p. 131.   146 Russell, *Marlowe*, p. 362.
147 James, *Scenic Art*, p. 143.   148 Martin-Harvey, *Autobiography*, p. 29.

8 Julia Marlowe in Ophelia's mad scene (4.5). No longer the girl who was 'entranced by Hamlet's wooing', her wistfulness, a reviewer remarked, has here 'grown apprehensive'. When an interviewer commented that she had never before seen Ophelia wear a cloak, Marlowe matter of factly replied that 'She had been gathering flowers outside the castle. It was cold' (Russell, *Marlowe*, p. 361).

for one of Marlowe's performances, Lark Taylor seems to have been responding to the latent passion in Ophelia's feeling for Hamlet. When she enters, she is reading a scroll containing Hamlet's love-poems: she 'presses it to her breast, looks at it again, presses it to lips'; later she 'fondles' the pearls he gave her; before 'ha! ha! are you honest?' she 'extends arms tenderly' towards Hamlet. Pictures of Marlowe in the role have a distinctly sensuous quality. Then too both Terry and Marlowe were already stars when they undertook the role. When they retired, Ophelia reverted to the featured but less prominent status that still prevails.

CLAUDIUS has had to be rediscovered as a major role. Although after the Restoration principal actors played the part, by Garrick's time and through most of the nineteenth century, the King's lines were so heavily cut that it was regarded as 'truly wretched for an actor'.[149] All this was changed by Wilson Barrett, who in 1884 restored many of the King's lines and played the Prince as a very young man with Claudius and Gertrude appropriately younger and more amorous than before. These innovations provided fresh opportunities for Barrett's Claudius, E. S. Willard, who had previously portrayed 'gentlemanly scoundrelism' in modern melodramas. His Claudius at first came across as a totally self-assured and pleasure-loving king, 'all lies and lust . . . contemptuous of the loyal, loving student-soul which he could not even understand'.[150] The contrast with Hamlet, wearing black and white, was pointed by the King's garish costume: 'a blue and yellow mantle over a red and yellow tunic with silver edging, red tights, and yellow cross-garters'.[151] In the course of the play, Willard portrayed a variety of facets: 'whether he was fawning on his wife, or plotting fresh villany, trying to deceive Polonius [see the Commentary at 3.1.163], uttering remorse, or watching with anxiety the result of his diabolical duel scheme' (*Sunday Times*, 19 October 1884). But what most impressed reviewers was his depiction of Claudius's growing fear of Hamlet. The *Stage* pointed out how 'the triumphant bearing of Claudius in the first act is a fine contrast to the dismay pictured so vividly by the actor when the King hears of Hamlet's return to Denmark' (24 October 1884).

Later reviewers often looked back to Willard's Claudius as the precursor in impressiveness and sensuality to that of Oscar Asche, whose sheer physical size and presence made understandable his dominance over Gertrude. 'Virile', 'rugged', 'burly', 'brutal', 'barbaric', Asche depicted 'a militant King instead of one on the defensive': in the play scene 'the drama centres in the King, not in Hamlet' (*Sunday Times*, 9 April 1905). Yet Asche was far

---

149 Davies, p. 99; Cook, *Stage*, II, p. 175.   150 Goddard, *Players*, p. 241.
151 Jackson, 'Designer', p. 193.

from muscle-bound. In his diary, Gordon Crosse saw in his performance opposite Frank Benson a complex mixture of traits: 'the sensuous nature of the man, the savageness mingled with cunning, and withal a sufficient measure of dignity and royal bearing'.[152] When Asche played the role opposite H. B. Irving, he was also praised for his rendering of 'the writhing of a murderer's heart' (*Stage*, 6 April 1905) in his 'my offense is rank' soliloquy (3.3.36). His 'resonant' verse-speaking throughout was often commended.[153]

GERTRUDE ('Gertred' in Q1, 'Gertrard' in Q2) is a more important supporting role than her relatively few lines might suggest; for she appears in more than half the scenes and is treasured by all the men in her family. Early performers of the part were valued most for their queenliness, Hannah Pritchard, with Garrick, being singled out for special praise. When the Ghost appeared in her closet, she turned her head slowly around 'with a certain Glare in her Eyes, which looked everywhere, and saw nothing' (*St. James Chronicle*, 20–2 February 1772). After her, however, 'present eminent actresses reject the part, as if it were beneath them' (Davies, p. 116).

Mrs Charles Kean emphasized the Queen's sense of wrong-doing, shown by 'a quick, averted look' early in the closet scene and 'the mechanical way in which her one or two phrases of resistance were urged'.[154] For the most part, though, the Queen's role during this period was commonly 'left to any one who looks matronly enough, and is slurred over', a practice that made Fechter's Queen, Miss Elsworthy, remarkable for her 'haughty, impulsive, and perfectly regal' manner (*Orchestra*, 18 May 1864, p. 551). She is exceptional among Gertrudes, too, in being played as Claudius's accomplice in the murder of her husband.[155]

Later performers have been much concerned with why the scandalous liaison between Gertrude and Claudius occurred in the first place. The sexual attraction between Willard and his 'exceedingly handsome' Queen, Margaret Leighton was palpable (*Truth*, 23 October 1884, pp. 631–2); her voice was described as 'purring' (*Shakespeariana*, IV, 1887, p. 30). So must it have been between Asche and Maud Milton, who played Gertrude in 1905 with H. B. Irving as a matron in her mid-forties 'of opulent Titianesque charms' (*Sunday Times*, 9 April). Fanny Morant, with Edwin Booth, indicated 'delicately but unmistakably that strong under current of voluptuousness' that 'bewitched Claudius to crime no less than his ambition' (*New York Times*, 9 January 1870).

In Gertrude's relations with Hamlet, the chief focus during this period

---

152 Crosse, *Diaries*, II, p. 122.   153 Beerbohm, *Last Theatres*, p. 148.
154 Marston, *Actors*, I, p. 229.   155 Cook, *Hours*, II, p. 261.

was on the propriety of the harsh rebukes that the severe son delivers to his erring mother. Nineteenth-century acting editions regularly ended the closet scene with the couplet: 'I must be cruel only to be kind / Thus bad begins, and worse remains behind' (3.4.179–80), thus cutting Hamlet's charge that Gertrude keep it secret that he is 'But mad in craft' and her promise to do so. This cut and others prevented Gertrudes of that period from showing the transfer of the Queen's loyalties from Claudius to the Prince in the latter part of the play that the original texts invite.[156] Indeed, Hamlets of the time often graphically rejected reconciliation. At the end of their exchange, when Elsworthy, Fechter's guilty Queen, 'outstretched her arm and would embrace her son, he held up sternly the portrait of his father; the wretched woman recoiled and staggered from the stage'.[157] It was an innovation when Irving did not shrink from the blessing of Georgina Pauncefort's 'weak, sensuous, affectionate' Queen (*Academy*, 7 November 1874) but instead lifted her up when she knelt at his 'I'll blessing beg of you'. At his 'So again, goodnight' (3.4.178) his studybook directs: 'Queen kisses him'.

During the Restoration and most of the eighteenth century, POLONIUS was played by low comedians.[158] They were aided by the customary cutting of his advice to Laertes. Since then the role has been in a constant state of reclamation from simple buffoonery. So strong was this tradition that when, at Garrick's urging, Henry Woodward attempted a more serious interpretation, dressed in a costume 'grave and rich, cloth of scarlet and gold', it failed: 'The character, divested of his ridiculous vivacity, appeared to the audience flat and insipid' (Davies, p. 42). Woodward never attempted the role again.

Clearly, simple elimination of the buffoonery was not enough. One recourse was to develop more positive qualities, as when in 1750–1 Macklin 'shewed oddity, grafted upon the man of sense'.[159] Another recourse was to modify Polonius's folly; so in 1772 Baddeley 'never sports with propriety, or through wantonness, degrades this loquacious old Courtier into a buffoon' (*Theatrical Review*, 1772, II, p. 18). Charles Lamb's favourite impersonator of old men, Joseph Munden, combined what is silly about Polonius with what is serious. He saw Polonius as a 'pliant and supple courtier and man of the world, ready to accord with any one's opinion whom he deemed it expedient to flatter'. His son reports that Munden's 'venerable and dignified demeanour' was imitated from old Lord Mansfield, known as 'Murray the Polite'.[160] At the same time he 'contrives to do our hearts good

156 O'Brien, 'Revision'.   157 Cook, *Hours*, II, p. 262.
158 Davies lists them by name (p. 41).   159 Gentleman, *Censor*, p. 571.
160 Munden, *Memoirs*, p. 48

with the most refreshing touches of the humorous. The little delighted chuckles with which he delivers his supposed profundities and courtly jests, quite endears to us the prince of prosers (*Champion*, 19 December 1819). However, with Brougham, Fechter's Polonius, the wheel came full circle. He was commended for refusing to reduce the chamberlain to 'a comic old man' yet like Woodward he 'squeezed the fun out of it', leaving 'not a scintilla of drollery' (*Morning Post*, 23 May 1864).

Most performers of Polonius have been lucky to receive a one-sentence notice. Of the earlier players J. H. Barnes, playing opposite Forbes-Robertson, received the most comment, perhaps because he had earlier been a leading man. By his own account his Polonius was

> the *acting* Lord Chamberlain of the court, a splendid father, with a keen eye for the main chance, and a never-failing solicitude for the welfare of his son and daughter; far too wise and prudent to make an enemy of the prince whom he firmly believes to be mad – or very nearly so . . . On these lines I played him; I venture to assert he was as amusing as he had ever been without losing a particle of his dignity.   (*Forty Years*, p. 216)

He appears to have accomplished his purposes. The *Dramatic World* concluded that Barnes 'presented the two sides of this very complex character most successfully . . . whether as fool or sage, Mr. Barnes is quite at home' (October 1897). Perhaps he was too sagacious for Robertson's Hamlet, whose assumption of an 'antic disposition' was half-hearted: 'A Polonius so shrewd and far-seeing . . . would hardly have experienced any difficulty in plucking out the heart of so thinly veiled a mystery' (*St. James Gazette*, 13 September 1897).

It is significant of the autonomy emerging among supporting players that Barnes, honoured as he was to be asked to play the part by Robertson, should have made the condition that he be allowed to interpret Polonius according to his own conception. Not only did Barnes, like the other players just mentioned, give his character an individual identity, but like them he understood his role in relation to characters in addition to the Prince, especially to his own children. These exceptional performers thus made a start towards the delineation of interrelationships among all the characters that would be an interpretive accomplishment of the century to come.

Enter the director and designer: William Poel's experimental *Hamlets* and the Moscow Art Theatre Production

Overlapping with the prevailing actor-manager style of staging, in which everything was designed to set off the star, was an emerging approach based on a still more encompassing definition of unity. As star Hamlets deployed more and more of the arts of the theatre (costume, scenery, lighting) in their support, these arts grew increasingly important in their own right. Ironically, their growing importance contributed, at the beginning of the twentieth century, to the rise of the director and designer, who today may have as much or more to say about the staging of *Hamlet* as does the actor of the Prince. For as the total dominance of the Prince and the actor who plays him diminished, the ideal of a fully unified production addressed to the whole play gained in importance. Such a production was characterized by a conscious concern for overall impact, in which direction, design of sets and costumes, and interpretation of roles by the leading actor and the supporting cast were fully coordinated. By 1977 the *Sunday Times* was confidently dismissing the Derek Jacobi stage Hamlet as 'nothing but bits of "business"' whereas 'a Shakespeare production today must be a coherent whole' (5 June 1977).

In these developments William Poel's four experimental productions of *Hamlet* played a key part. He insisted that 'It is the play as an epitome of life which is interesting the mind of Shakespeare, and not the career of one individual, even though the whole play be influenced by the actions of that individual.'[161] Poel also led the way towards modern 'high concept' productions, where the hand of the director was especially evident. At first this was shown in the Elizabethan style of staging he employed (no scenery, a thrust platform, a boy-Ophelia, Elizabethan-style costumes, the First Quarto text). The 1914 version, a frank adaptation, emphasized the historical allusions Poel thought Elizabethans would have seen to Queen Bess and old Polonius-Burleigh, and Raleigh and Essex (*Daily Chronicle*, 27 January 1914).

During this period, Gordon Craig led the rise of the designers of sets and costumes. Reacting against the pictorial approach – whether archeological or picturesque – Craig's abstract designs would revolutionize twentieth-century staging. Like his father E. W. Godwin, who designed Wilson Barrett's *Hamlet* in the older archeological style, Craig saw his role as extending beyond mounting a production to an interpretive authority usually reserved for the director.[162]

In the last part of the nineteenth century and the first half of the twentieth, the Continent, headed by the Saxe Meiningen company's concern for ensemble and Wagner's idea of *Gesamtkunstwerk*, had in general led England and the United States in the movement towards fully integrated performances. Yet as it happens there was only one top-quality production

161 Lundstrom, *Poel's Hamlets*, p. 33.   162 Jackson, 'Designer'.

of *Hamlet* of this sort during that time, at the MOSCOW ART THEATRE in 1912. It was the product of the stormy collaboration between Craig and Konstantin Stanislavsky, the exponent of psychological realism and practical man of the theatre, with Vasili Kachalov's portrayal of Hamlet torn between the two approaches. It is customary currently to emphasize the shortcomings and lack of integration in their work, and it is true that the three men were not themselves wholly satisfied with the final result. Yet, as Grigori Kozintsev observes, they were united by a common aspiration towards a new, higher, more complete truth than had hitherto been achieved in a theatre.[163] What they produced was a success at the box-office, it excited thoughtful critical controversy at the time and ever since, and has had an incalculable impact on the style of subsequent productions.

To read the reconstructions of their *Hamlet* by Senelick and Morgan is to realize how much of what was most original about Craig's conception was in fact put on stage.[164] His vision of the falsity and corruption of the Danish court was effectively conveyed by the tarnished gold costumes and decor. It is true that his intended effects were not always accomplished in exactly the way he envisaged. He had pictured the entire court covered by a single golden cape, with the characters' heads protruding through holes in it. When this proved impracticable, Stanislavsky had individual mantles made that, when spread, gave 'the impression of a monolithic golden pyramid'. The sense of cosmic scope that Craig wanted – where the key conflict he saw between the spirit and the material world could be suggested – was achieved by the use of mood lighting and the tall, movable screens that were his most original contribution. He had wanted the action to be continuous, with the screens repositioned by invisible stagehands before the audience's eyes; but after much experiment and a disastrous crashing of the screens, Stanislavky had to abandon this idea and have a curtain drawn for scene changes. The three most powerful scenes in this production – the first court scene, the Mousetrap, and the finale – were all performed very much as Craig had directed.

No doubt the differences in approach could be drawbacks, as in the misplaced realism with which Stanislavsky treated Laertes's rebellion and the gravediggers. In general, the supporting players were weak. Yet for a play that is itself as varied as *Hamlet* is and in a production where design is, like Craig's, seen more as a metaphor than a setting, some creative tension among its parts can be enriching. Kachalov's Hamlet is a case in point. All concerned accepted Craig's vision of the play as a 'monodrama', largely controlled by the point-of-view of an unusually strong Hamlet, who

163 Kozintsev, *Shakespeare*, p. 167.   164 Morgan, *Encounter*.

embodies the mystical powers of the spirit. Differences arose, however, as to how this vision would be realized in performance. Craig, for example, speculated about keeping the Prince on stage throughout the performance and dreamed of an alluring, muse-like spirit of death with whom Hamlet would at times commune, especially in the 'to be or not to be' soliloquy. Neither of these ideas prevailed. Where Craig compared Hamlet to a mountain 'almost motionless', Stanislavsky saw him as much more active and demonstrative. To illustrate a point in rehearsal, he would occasionally act the part; of his rendering of the 'advice to the players' scene, a cast-member wrote: 'This was not Craig's abstract Hamlet, striving to overcome his despised earthly existence . . . Stanislavsky showed Hamlet to be virile, full of human nobility and restrained passion' (Senelick, p. 143).

Kachalov's portrayal, however, was ultimately his own. With Stanislavky's help he stripped away convention and false emotionalism to find a convincing psychological truth. The inwardness, stillness, spirituality, and strength that Craig saw in Hamlet (his costume was like that of a monk) became in Kachalov the extreme reserve of a determined man of principle, who suffered deeply and was exactingly demanding of himself. Even when not soliloquizing he often spoke as if to himself. Only at moments of highest intensity was this restraint abandoned. Craig rightly held that Kachalov's portrayal 'was not *my* Hamlet, not at all what I wanted!' But he had to concede that 'It was interesting, even brilliant' (Senelick, p. 188). The same might be said of the whole production.

Strangely enough, there were no other preeminent *Hamlet*s produced on the Continent during the first half of the century. Max Reinhardt directed Alexander Moissi in 1910, but it did not result in a production of the very highest quality. Meyerhold did not direct the play, although he dreamed of doing so.[165] In 1923 Adolphe Appia did some characteristic designs (projecting the inner life of the Prince and the play), but the production in

---

165 Meyerhold, *Theatre*, p. 118. In a 1934 lecture he envisaged the Prince's encounter with the Ghost in a way that seems more cinematic than theatrical. On a seashore, Hamlet in a black cloak sees through the mist the Ghost of his Father amid the breakers, 'dragging his feet with difficulty from the clinging sandy bottom of the sea. He is clad from head to foot in silver . . . Water is frozen on to the chain-mail and on to his beard.' Hamlet runs to meet him, wrapping his father in his black cloak, revealing his own silver chain-mail. Thus, 'we see the father in silver and Hamlet in black, then the father in black and Hamlet in silver'. They embrace. To Meyerhold it was important that the Ghost be shown to be 'capable of shivering and of displaying affection, of breathing heavily from exhaustion and of embracing tenderly. The ghost might respond with a smile when his son wraps him in the cloak. He is a ghost on whose cheek a tear of gratitude freezes' (pp. 279–80).

which his concepts were employed was not otherwise notable.[166] Leopold Jessner's 1926 *Hamlet* in Berlin converted the play into a coherent political attack on Kaiser Wilhelm II, but it seems to have been little more than that. Brecht gave a reductive reading of the play in the *Short Organum* (section 68) and devised some acting exercises based on it for his unfinished *Der Messingkauf* but never directed a production of *Hamlet*.[167]

In England too the first quarter of the century lacked outstanding new Hamlets. The play was no less popular than before; almost every year saw a production on the West End, at the Old Vic, or at Stratford-upon-Avon. Frank Benson, H. Beerbohm Tree, H. B. Irving, Matheson Lang, John Martin-Harvey, and Ernest Milton are among the actors who played the role repeatedly. But apart from the experiments of William Poel, *Hamlet* happens not to have been on the main line of Shakespearian development during those years. Most notably, it was not among the plays presented by H. Granville Barker in his epoch-making seasons at the Savoy Theatre (1912–14). In 1925, however, came two productions of major importance.

John Barrymore's Hamlet: 'A man of genius who happened to be a Prince'

Robert Edmond Jones's single set for Barrymore's *Hamlet* (first seen in New York in 1922 and at the Haymarket in 1925) continued Craig's tradition, supplemented by Leopold Jessner's trademark steps. Although the set was awkward from a practical point of view, James Agate declared its extended flight of stairs with an arch at the top 'the most beautiful thing I have ever seen on the stage'.[168] In other respects, however, Barrymore followed the star-with-supporting-cast pattern, boldly seizing for himself the mantle of Edwin Booth as America's preeminent Hamlet. After a delegation of Booth admirers had asked him to shorten his New York run out of respect for the memory of Booth's record 100 nights, Barrymore deliberately prolonged his engagement to 101. He is also the only American Hamlet, before or since, to have enjoyed real success in London.

Although Barrymore, who was easily bored, found Hamlet always fresh – 'a stark, blazing, glorious part' – he professed to find the Prince's personality amazingly simple and in no need of explanation beyond Goethe's formulation of 'a great deed laid upon a soul unequal to the performance of it'.[169] The viewers of his Hamlet, however, saw much more in it than that.

---

166 Beacham, *Appia*, pp. 100–4.
167 Cole, *Playwrights*, pp. 100–1. See also Dort, 'Brecht', p. 81.
168 Agate, *Chronicles*, p. 249.   169 Barrymore, *Confessions*, ch. 1.

Perhaps what is perplexing about Hamlet's character seemed self-evident to Barrymore because of a personal affinity. He saw Hamlet as 'a great gentleman . . . full of consideration for others' (*New York Tribune*, 14 January 1923), and he certainly looked the part of 'a gracious and handsome prince' (*Star*, 20 February 1925). More deeply, Ludwig Lewisohn saw between the actor and the character the 'inner kinship' of 'men who live with their nerves and woes in narrow rooms' (*Nation*, 6 December 1922).

Far from seeming simple, Barrymore's Hamlet came across as multifaceted. To Agate it was 'nearer to Shakespeare's whole creation than any other I have seen'.[170] Jotting his first impressions at the time, twenty-year-old John Gielgud praised Barrymore's 'tenderness, remoteness, and neurosis'.[171] Stark Young counted among his accomplishments 'the shy and humorous mystery, the proud irony, the terrible storms of pain' (*New Republic*, 6 December 1922). Many years later Orson Welles, who must have been a boy when he saw him, recalled him as 'tender and virile and witty and dangerous' (South Bank Show). Margaret Webster thought he brought to the part a 'tragic yearning, a terrible sense of waste and despair, and moments, especially with Ophelia, of great tenderness'.[172]

Above all, Barrymore's Hamlet was intelligent. Anything but the mindless ham-actor of his later 'great profile' days in Hollywood, he had studied the part carefully with voice-coach Margaret Carrington. Like the consensus of reviewers, Agate found the result 'informed – and here is the key – by intellectual capacity of a rare order'.[173] Barrymore himself saw Hamlet as a man of 'extraordinary intellect' (*New York Tribune*, 14 January 1923). Welles, indeed, pronounced him 'a man of genius, who happened to be a prince' (South Bank Show). Herbert Farjeon, however, was not completely won over, judging him 'very intelligent' yet laborious: 'He does not merely think things, he thinks them out.'[174]

Others found Barrymore's delivery too slow on other scores. To Gordon Crosse, a devotee of the rapid pace introduced by Granville-Barker's productions, he seemed 'dull'.[175] In a letter Shaw advised Barrymore that 'Shakespeare is the worst of bores' unless played 'on the line and not between the lines' with no pauses or miming of the sort in which Barrymore indulged.[176] His pauses could be extreme. When Hamlet welcomes Horatio to Elsinore and learns of the Ghost, his promptbook (154) indicates pauses in 19 of his first 33 lines. Perhaps the performance seemed slow because of a more basic reason. In one of his imaginary letters from dead actors, Young

170 Agate, *Chronicles*, p. 247.   171 Gielgud, *Notes*, p. 98.
172 Webster, *The Same*, p. 302.   173 Agate, *Chronicles*, p. 247.
174 Farjeon, *Scene*, p. 147.   175 Crosse, Diaries, IX, p. 70.
176 Shaw, *Shakespeare*, pp. 95–7.

has Garrick remark to Barrymore on 'your power to create on the stage not so much the action of a drama as the air of a compelling mood'.[177] For all its energy and variety Barrymore's Hamlet seems not to have undergone significant character development in the course of the play. However that may be, those who felt Barrymore to be overly deliberate were vastly outnumbered by those who like Agate appreciated 'the unexampled clarity' of his delivery and its address to 'the intelligence of the spectator rather than to his susceptibility to "thrills"' (*London Times*, 20 February 1925).

To some, Barrymore's portrayal was too reasonable. Young's imaginary Garrick calls it 'too easy to understand'.[178] *Time and Tide* objects that in seeking to make Hamlet seem 'plausible, natural, and credible to the modern mind' Barrymore 'subdues all its unreasonable elements' (27 February 1925). Similarly, the *Saturday Review* missed the 'earthy Hamlet, the Hamlet of smutty jest . . . tortured and torturing, at once allured and revolted by sensuality, capable of cruelty and mouthing terrible words' (28 February 1925). Others, however, sensed a darker side in Barrymore beneath 'the glass of fashion' surface. Margaret Webster, who played a small role in the London production, wrote later that a 'glittering, lithe, demonic quality shone through like flashing steel'.[179] This quality is evident in the screen-test Barrymore made much later, where, in delivering the 'Now might I do it pat' soliloquy, he contemplates the king's damnation with a satanic gleam in his eye.

Several observers detected an oedipal aspect to Barrymore's portrayal of Hamlet's relation to his mother.[180] Although at the time he did not say that that was his intention, his treatment of the relationship clearly had a powerful sexual subtext. He later told his biographer Gene Fowler what was going through his mind when denouncing Claudius in the 'rogue and peasant slave' soliloquy (2.2.502): 'That bastard puts his prick in my mother's cunt every night.'[181] In the closet scene 'he would lay his head in her lap, against her breasts, would caress her cheeks, touch her breasts and thigh' (p. 178). Seduced by his stepmother at fifteen, Barrymore near the end of his life described Hamlet to Ben Hecht as a 'mother-loving . . . pervert', adding: 'How I loved to play him. The dear boy and I were made for each other' (p. 441). To Blanche Yurka (his American Gertrude) he inscribed a portrait of himself: 'To my mother from her wildly incestuous son' (p. 191).

Barrymore emphasized Hamlet's masculinity. He told his director

---

177 Young, *Glamour*, p. 136.   178 *Ibid.*, p. 131.   179 Webster, *The Same*, p. 301.
180 Shaw, *Shakespeare*, p. 97. MacCarthy, *Theatre*, p. 58. Broun, *New York World*, 18 November 1922.
181 Kobler, *Damned*, p. 180. The page references in the rest of this paragraph are all to Kobler.

Arthur Hopkins, 'I want him to be so male that when I come out on the stage they can hear my balls clank' (p. 174). It was especially his athleticism that reviewers commented upon, comparing him to Douglas Fairbanks, who had in fact helped to choreograph the fencing match. One Laertes after another left the show because of the violence with which Barrymore would be carried away when they fought. Even hockey pads were not enough! To seventeen-year-old Laurence Olivier, Barrymore was 'amazing': 'Everything about him was exciting. He was athletic, he had charisma and, to my young mind, he played the part to perfection.'[182] Olivier also admired Barrymore's approach to the verse, especially singling out his 'way of choosing a word and then exploding it in a moment of passion'. For one instance among many, in 'villain, villain, smiling damned villain!' (1.5.106) 'damned' is underlined in his promptbook, at which he stands up 'shrieking in rage'. Most reviewers deplored such explosions.[183] Yet there is something to be said for each of them.

For the most part, Barrymore's delivery of his lines was dedicated to clarifying their meaning. For example, in his recorded version of his instructions to the players (3.2.1), Barrymore himself 'mouths' his warning against those who 'mouth their words'. Such careful elucidation of meaning is very reminiscent of Edwin Booth. Olivier indeed saw in Barrymore 'the direct link with Edwin Booth': and since Edwin's father Junius Brutus had acted with Edmund Kean, Olivier concluded that thus 'The hand stretching down from Burbage finally crossed the Atlantic'.[184]

Hamlet 'as a modern play': the Birmingham Repertory 'plus fours' production

Later in 1925 the Birmingham Repertory Theatre brought to London another landmark production of *Hamlet*. Nicknamed 'Hamlet in plus fours' (knickerbockers), it was well ahead of its time, not only in its controversial use of modern dress but in its concern for an overall unity, balancing and

---

182 Olivier, *Acting*, pp. 60–1.
183 Young thought his stress too heavy on '*hang* on him as if increase of appetite' (1.2.143 – *New Republic*, 6 December 1922); in his studybook Barrymore underlined the last word in 'Would the night were come' (1.2.255); MacCarthy thought unnecessary his emphasis on '*dreamt of* in our philosophy' (1.5.167 – *Theatre*, p. 62); in 'might his quietus make with a bare bodkin', the last word was shot out fortissimo (3.1.76 – *Sunday Express*, 22 February 1925); in Hamlet's refusal to kill the King at prayer, Agate found 'without meaning' his explosive accent on 'passage' in 'When he is fit and season'd for his passage' (*Chronicles*, p. 248).
184 Olivier, *Acting*, p. 62.

integrating the work of director H. K. Ayliff, designer Paul Shelving, Colin Keith-Johnston, who played Prince Hamlet, and a strong supporting ensemble. Its sponsor (today he might be called as well the 'artistic director' of the company) was Barry Jackson, who was directly in the line of William Poel. The project indeed received Poel's explicit blessing, particularly its avoidance of the 'star' tradition.[185] One of its most ardent supporters went so far as to claim that this *Hamlet* was 'not a play about one person nor a play about six of them, but a play about twenty people, each as vitally interesting as the other'.[186] This, though, was to exaggerate the levelling of roles. Keith-Johnston was not the star yet certainly the 'leading man', with a distinctive interpretive slant that made the Prince 'morose rather than melancholy' (*Spectator*, 5 September 1925). Contrasting the new Hamlet with traditional portrayals, the *Manchester Guardian* judged that the earlier ones had 'missed the actuality of youth at odds with the universe and turned ugly in its anger' (26 August 1925). Entering into the spirit of post-World War I disillusionment, Keith-Johnston was anything but a sweet prince. Recalling the disenchanted mood of Shaw's *Heartbreak House*, Ivor Brown felt that this 'snarling prince' was 'the first heart-break Hamlet I have seen'.[187]

The other role that especially stood out was that of Claudius, played as a suave sophisticate by Frank Vosper in a way that threw fresh light not only on the role but on the whole play. When a personable Claudius is portrayed not as the monster Hamlet hates but as a much more attractive figure, then Hamlet's hesitancy about killing him is more understandable. As John Palmer observes: 'One can even doubt, as Hamlet was inclined to doubt at times, whether such a pleasant gentleman could be really a murderer after all.'[188]

It was, however, Shelving's costumes that were the talk of London; details were even recounted in fashion magazines.[189] Shockingly, the second scene resembled the throne-room of a pre-war Balkan court, with the King in white tie and waistcoat, the courtiers wearing monocles and smoking cigarettes, the ladies overdressed, with one short, stout, tired dowager conspicuous in her magenta velvet and tiara, and Hamlet, 'a sullen little figure' in a lounge suit and wearing a wrist-watch. At this point, as Vosper testifies, 'the house simply sizzles with surprise and criticism' (*Theatre World*, October 1925). Some reviewers especially felt a disparity between the modern clothing and the Elizabethan language.

185 Cochrane, *Shakespeare*, p. 118.   186 Griffith, *Iconoclastes*, p. 62.
187 Quoted in Cochrane, *Shakespeare*, p. 119.
188 Palmer, 'Hamlet', p. 682.   189 Cochrane, *Shakespeare*, p. 109.

But soon, Vosper continues, the 'sizzling' stopped. A few die-hards maintained their resistance to the end. Young John Gielgud dismissed it in a word, 'Unspeakable'.[190] But of the many who came to scoff, most were converted to the production concept. Such conversions exactly fulfilled Jackson's hope. As he explained in the programme, his intention was not novelty for novelty's sake but to clear away the strange costumes and acting conventions in order to make Shakespeare's play available to all as 'a real conflict of credible human beings' (*Sunday Times*, 30 August 1925).

The use of modern dress was thus only the most obvious feature of the unifying approach that governed every aspect of the production: to treat *Hamlet* 'as a modern play.' As such it was felt to appeal especially to the young. Palmer rejoiced at hearing 'the younger generation talking of the tragedy as one talks of a play by Pirandello or Mr Galsworthy.[191] Other commentators pointed out a direct parallel to the finale of Noel Coward's *The Vortex*. Appreciation, however, was by no means confined to the young. The *Sunday Times* judiciously summed up the overall impact: 'A certain matter-of-factness of diction, combined with the absence of gesture and pose, do give a certain added humanity and life, even if sometimes at the expense of majesty' (30 August 1925).

As novel as the modern dress seemed then, in the long view it could be seen as a throw-back to the costuming principle that prevailed from Burbage to Garrick. In the same way still another important production of this time, J. B. Fagan's 1924 Oxford University Drama Society *Hamlet*, set in the early sixteenth century with costumes based on Durer, could be seen as a throw-back to Poel's Elizabethan-style costuming. Yet in the light of subsequent developments both may be regarded as transitional instances of an encompassing trend which still prevails, in which costumes and set may suggest any time and place that enhance the interpretive statement being made by the director and designer. So the play has been set in the eleventh century (Leslie Howard, 1937), 1520 (Gielgud, 1934), 1620 (Gielgud, 1936), Regency (Richard Pasco, 1966), early Victorian (Paul Scofield, 1948), Edwardian (Branagh, 1993), modern 'Ruritanian' (Guthrie, 1938).

John Gielgud's Hamlets

Gielgud played Hamlet in six different productions over a period of sixteen years. A number of other leading Hamlets played the role over an extended period, Betterton for nearly fifty years, Garrick for thirty-four. And often their portrayals changed significantly. Tennyson thought that Irving's

---

190 Gielgud, *Notes*.   191 Palmer, 'Hamlet', p. 678.

second version had not only improved on the earlier one but 'lifted it to heaven'.[192] At the end Edwin Booth was – by Hamlin Garland's account – much more the grey-haired philosopher than before.[193] But none has made as fresh an approach to the role each time as has Gielgud, reflecting not only his own growing maturity but changing times and interpretive emphases.

Of the leading Hamlets profiled thus far, Gielgud stands with Betterton in making his mark at the youngest age. He was twenty-six when he first played the role at the Old Vic in 1930. Reviewers also found Gielgud remarkable for the anger and disgust he showed towards the rottenness of humanity, his own included. Like Barrymore with his veiled demonic streak and Keith-Johnston with his open hostility, Gielgud brought out the darker side of Hamlet's nature. He was, as he later characterized himself, an 'angry young man of the twenties'.[194] He was praised for 'never seeking to nobilify, never understressing the quick bitterness and brutality of this crawler between heaven and earth' (*Graphic*, 14 June 1930). The result was a Prince 'who has bad dreams' (*Sunday Pictorial*, 1 June 1930).

Before the twenties, almost all English and American interpreters, on stage and off, had shared Horatio's high estimation of the 'sweet Prince', even while acknowledging certain faults. In contrast, Mallarmé in *Hamlet et Fortinbras* (1896) had already gone to the other extreme, observing how 'The black presence of the doubter spreads poison, so that all the principal characters die, without his always taking the trouble to stab them behind the arras'. In 1916 D. H. Lawrence had expressed his aversion for Hamlet as a character 'repulsive in its conception, based on self-dislike and a spirit of disintegration' – even Forbes-Robertson seemed to him 'a creeping, unclean thing' ('The Theatre', *Twilight in Italy*). In the same year as Gielgud's performance, G. Wilson Knight in his book *The Wheel of Fire* (1930) presented Hamlet as a sickly and destructive Prince, embodying the death principle, in contrast to the 'healthy and robust life' of Claudius and his court. Knight later modified his interpretation somewhat, but a similar approach was resumed in 1950 by L. C. Knights who saw Hamlet as fixated on himself, infatuated by revenge, nauseated by sex, disgusted by the sullied world around him, and himself tainted by its corruption.[195] The stage has resisted so negative a view. Alec Guinness acknowledges the total failure of his 1951 attempt to play Hamlet as a ruthlessly Machiavellian Prince – Hobson recalled him as 'everything morbid and evil' (*Sydney Morning Herald*, 28 May 1966) – an approach heavily influenced by still another literary interpreter, Salvador de Madariaga (*On Hamlet* (1948)).

192 Alfred Tennyson, quoted in L. Irving, *Irving*, p. 316.
193 Garland, 'Lecture', p. 14.   194 Gielgud, *Stage*, p. 57.
195 Knights, *Approach*.

Gielgud did not go to such extremes; because of his youth and sensitivity his Prince remained a sympathetic figure. Yet his bitterness was felt to be distinctive, its novelty enhanced at times by a conflated script that was unabridged, so that previously cut passages such as Hamlet's bawdy talk to Ophelia and his mother were included. Furthermore, the extended version was felt to confer a special authenticity, consistent with the Old Vic's poor-but-pure reputation. When the production transferred to commercial management in the West End, only a cut text was used.

Gielgud's next portrayal was in 1934, under his own direction. Although this production was a huge success with the public, reviewers felt that Gielgud's objective 'to penetrate the soul by way of the intellect' (*The Times*, 15 November 1934) was too rarefied, lacking in asperity, and emphasizing what is poetic about the character and the play at the expense of theatrical excitements. The 1936 American production, directed by Guthrie McClintic, seems to have reverted to his original approach (Gilder, p. 20).

Ivor Brown liked best the 1939 production, directed by Gielgud for performance at Elsinore Castle and shown briefly in London. This was inspired by Harley Granville-Barker, whose 'Preface' to the play reinvigorated Gielgud's interest in it. (*Observer*, 25 June 1939). Barker also gave notes to Gielgud at a run-through portrayal which resulted in the elimination of such excrescences as breaking the recorder and taking the King's sword when he is trying to pray. Brown found Gielgud's Hamlet 'not only a prince with a vein of poetry; he was a cynic, railer, coarse jester.' In consequence, 'The play itself gains in excitement by the earthy vigour of the prince, who seems not so much a moody creature hampered in his task by delicate sensibilities, as a man of strong conflicting passions whose irresolution depends not on lack of will but on the clash of powerful motives' (*Observer*, 2 July 1939).

To James Agate it was the 1944 production that was the triumph culminating Gielgud's sequence of Hamlets. The 1930 performance had lacked pathos, he felt; the 1934 one had sufficient pathos but lacked theatricality and still represented 'Everest Half Scaled'; the 1939 one made 'an immense advance'[196] yet still lacked the 'ultimate definitiveness' achieved in 1944 (*Sunday Times*, 22 October 1944). Another enthusiast, W. A. Darlington, saw a progression from the beginning to the end of Gielgud's career in the role, as his Hamlet matured from 'a sensitive youth, aghast at the wickedness of the world which he had just discovered, to a sophisticated man to whom that wickedness is no surprise'.[197] With the horrors of World War II still in progress, such awareness of the prevalence of human wickedness

---

196 Agate, *Chronicles*, pp. 257ff.   197 Quoted in Findlater, *Kings*, p. 201.

must have been widely shared. Not everyone agreed with these favourable judgements. Concerning the production as a whole, directed by George Rylands, Tyrone Guthrie thought that 'it lacks courage'.[198] And concerning Gielgud's own performance, Kenneth Tynan felt that his 'acting lacks stomach and heart'.[199] Gielgud himself felt that it was too much in the line of his previous work with the role. He prefers the 1945 version that toured the Far East, with makeshift staging and audiences who had never encountered the play before.[200]

For all the differences in emphasis of these various portrayals, certain general characteristics may be seen in them. From the outset Gielgud was greatly concerned with the continuity of the part, to make sure as he moved from scene to scene that a clear, true line of feeling ran throughout. In several remarkable pages in his *Early Stages*, he recalls in stream-of-consciousness style the concerns that ran through his mind as he first played the role. As the 'To be or not to be' soliloquy approaches, for example:

> one must concentrate, take care not to anticipate, not begin worrying beforehand how one is going to say it, take time, but don't lose time, don't break the verse up, don't succumb to the temptation of a big melodramatic effect for the sake of getting applause at the curtain . . .   (p. 173)

During the play scene: 'remember that Hamlet is not yet sure of Claudius, delay the climax, then carry it (and it needs all the control and breath in the world to keep the pitch at the right level) . . . ' (p. 174). In these two excerpts can also be seen the qualities his mother praised in a letter to him: an 'exquisite sense of rhythm and proportion' and a constant care to keep himself 'in due relation to the play. You can dominate but I have never seen you step out of the canvas to distort the picture'.[201]

No account of Gielgud's Hamlet could omit his verse-speaking, the feature with which his Shakespearian acting has been most identified. From the beginning his speech was praised for its clarity, rapidity, and audibility, even in quiet passages. Its musicality was often mentioned, along with appreciation that 'behind the music was an acute intelligence' (*Era*, 30 April 1930); he 'seems to have pondered each line for its meaning' (*Manchester Guardian*, 29 May 1930). 'When Gielgud speaks the verse,' Lee Strasberg reportedly said, 'I can hear Shakespeare *thinking*.'[202] Not until the latter part of his career did Gielgud begin to be charged with 'singing' the lines, putting musical effect above meaning. Today his recordings of *Hamlet*, with their tremolo and calculated climaxes, sound dated and self-conscious, the

198 Hayman, *Gielgud*, p. 146.   199 Tynan, *He that Plays*, p. 37.
200 Gielgud, *Stage*, pp. 58–9.   201 Quoted in Hayman, *Gielgud*, p. 65.
202 Quoted in Findlater, *Kings*, p. 202.

later ones (where his virtuoso technique is full blown) more than the early ones. But as late as 1944, Tynan still found that 'The voice is thrilling and bears witness to great suffering; an east wind has blown through it.'[203]

Olivier's film *Hamlet* and other screen versions

Of the numerous motion picture and television versions of *Hamlet* to date (there are more of them than of any other play), LAURENCE OLIVIER's film (1948) has made the greatest impact. A great popular success, it received the Academy Award for best picture as did Olivier himself for best actor.

Other *Hamlet* films have had special points of interest. The Nicol Williamson film records his remarkable stage performance, narrow in range but forceful in expressing Hamlet's sneering outrage and self-torment – a man at the very end of his tether. His antic style of fencing has been echoed by later Hamlets, including Mel Gibson and Ralph Fiennes. Grigori Kozintsev's film is less an enactment of Shakespeare's play than a lyric meditation upon it, rendered in visual symbols of stone, iron, fire, sea, earth; but certain scenes in it are unforgettable, especially Ophelia's formal dancing lesson, where the constraints of her social role are made visible – and audible, to Shostakovich's haunting music. Later we see her in an iron corset. The Zeffirelli/Gibson film has a strong cast but the limitation by contract to two hours and a quarter did not give them time to show what they could do nor did it allow Zeffirelli to give his own inventiveness full play. For comment on the 1996/7 Kenneth Branagh film, see pp. 93–6.

Although Olivier's film has dated badly, there remains something compellingly mysterious about it. Its brooding mood and baroque style give Elsinore a dark glamour. Full of Gothic atmosphere, the castle has huge rooms, winding staircases, dark corridors and long vistas through receding archways; its towering battlements look dizzyingly down on a beating tide; and through its mists a spectral ghost appears, its sepulchral voice seemingly muffled by cerements. It is a haunted place where secrets are concealed yet gradually revealed, although the reasons for the Prince's inaction remain a puzzle. It is as if he were under a spell. The ready-for-use rational explanations Olivier himself provides are not much help. The tragic flaw formulation – with the 'dram of e'il' quotation at the beginning and the summary 'This is the tragedy of a man who could not make up his mind' – does not work because Olivier seems quite decisive and the soliloquies in which he berates himself for his inaction were cut. The oedipal suggestions

203 Tynan, *He that Plays*, p. 37.

are not developed beyond enigmatically recurring shots of the Queen's bed and several prolonged kisses.

There is something withheld as well about Olivier's performance. His face is at times mask-like. It is true that voice-overs reveal his inmost thoughts. But he does not confide them to us; the audience is placed in the position of eavesdroppers, overhearing what he is thinking and feeling. The unfolding of his story is much like a dream, its flow smoothed by long shots, with little quick cutting, and with mood-music to bridge the scenes. Hamlet's mimed visit to Ophelia when she is sewing and the hypnotic dumb show epitomize this quality.

Today, the film is chiefly of historical interest. It drew extensively on stage tradition. The by-play between Ophelia and Laertes behind Polonius's back while he gives his precepts, Hamlet's carrying his sword hilt like a cross and falling down flat when the Ghost departs, placing 'to be or not to be' after rather than before the nunnery episode, Gertrude's rejection of Claudius after the closet scene, the omission of 'how all occasions inform against me' and of Fortinbras – these are just a few of the features that derive from past stage productions. The whole way of playing the supporting characters as Hamlet sees them rather than as they see themselves is in direct line from stage tradition.

In particular, the film drew on Olivier's own 1937 stage performance, directed by Tyrone Guthrie. His dangerous jump from a balcony in the film to kill Claudius was anticipated in the stage version by the Queen's dying fall from a platform. In general, however, Olivier's stage Hamlet was much more forceful and energetic and volatile than his subdued film Hamlet, whose victories come easily and gracefully. In the film it is the camera itself that is restlessly roving.

Through the film, easily the most influential production of the play since World War II, a great deal of stage tradition was transmitted to subsequent productions, on and off the screen. So were features that the film originated. For Hamlet's first soliloquy, for example, Kozintsev took over Olivier's voice-over delivery, with the improvement that the Russian actor was not isolated but passing among the courtiers. That its influence is still active may be seen in the many echoes of it in the plot structure and blocking of Zeffirelli's 1990 film. That it retains its preeminence in the general culture was evidenced in the 1993 film *The Last Action Hero*, where Joan Plowright – Olivier's widow – plays the part of a teacher presenting the Prince to her class as 'the *first* action hero' and uses clips from the film to make her point. Anthony Davies is probably right in surmising that 'over the years more people will form an idea of *Romeo and Juliet* or *Hamlet* from the respective films of Zeffirelli and Olivier than will do so from any

9 In the 1948 film Laurence Olivier leaps down on the King before killing him (5.2). The
1937 stage production was even more gymnastic. Celebrating the success of the playlet
(3.2), Olivier made a double leap from the throne-level to the players' level below and
then to the footlights (*Sunday Times*, 10 January 1937); at the finale, it was the Queen
(Dorothy Dix) who made what Ivor Brown called a 'dying fall': 'And what a fall –
backwards from a high rostrum on to the ladies of the court!' (*Observer*, 10 January 1937).
Inspired by Barrymore's ten-foot leap at Claudius (Morrison, *Barrymore*, p. 212),
Olivier's film leap was from a fifteen-foot height; the King's burly stuntman was knocked
unconscious and lost two teeth (Spoto, *Olivier*, p. 207).

encounter with the printed text'.[204] Just as print supplanted the stage as the
most widely influential medium for *Hamlet*, so film (while following stage
traditions) is in the process of supplanting print. A current case in point
may be seen in the 1995 film *Clueless*, where Cher, the Beverly Hills high-
school heroine, challenges a college girl who has mistakenly attributed 'to
thine own self be true' to Hamlet. Cher insists it was 'that Polonius guy'

204 Davies, *Filming*, p. 4.

who said it, and is unfazed by her antagonist's pompously understated claim, 'I think I remember *Hamlet* accurately.' She retorts, 'Well I remember Mel Gibson accurately.'

'A Prince of Decision': Richard Burton

Richard Burton started playing Hamlet with one view of the role and ended with another. At first he portrayed a 'Prince of Decision', sure of purpose and waiting only for the most opportune moment to take his revenge, a view derived from his adoptive father Philip Burton.[205] When he first played the part in Edinburgh, critics found him angry, sturdy, athletic, unsubtle, 'with no gentleness or introspection and little melancholy' (*Daily Sketch*, 25 August 1953). Yet already there were intimations of the portrayal to come in 'the fierce, faraway look, the desolate ring in the voice, the tortured tension of a man at war within himself' (*Daily Mail*, 25 August 1953).

When the same production moved to the Old Vic, Burton's interpretation had already developed. He still depicted 'an uncomplicated prince' rendered 'with dash, attack, and verve, not pausing to worry about psychology' (*Daily Express*, 15 September 1953). Winston Churchill called it 'as exciting and virile as any I can remember' (quoted in *Playboy*, September 1963, p. 54). Yet in addition, the *Times* reviewer found a new 'charm' and 'power' in his manner that pervaded not only the soliloquies but the whole role in all its variety – his 'sullen reserve' towards the King, 'shock' at the Ghost, 'repressed tenderness' towards Ophelia, 'sudden gaiety' with the players, 'fierce animation' in the play scene.[206]

The 1964 production in New York continued the progression. Burton's Hamlet remained a prince of 'tempestuous manliness', played with 'all the stops out' (*New York Times*, 19 April 1964). But the influence of John Gielgud, Burton's choice to direct this production, added richness and – as Elizabeth Taylor put it – 'ease' (Sterne, p. 71). Chiefly Gielgud sought to bring Burton's hyper-intensity under control, helping him to pace himself and by exercising timely restraint to add contrast and variety.[207] Gielgud never tried to impose his more melodious style of speaking on Burton. His suggestions were in the direction of clarity, of not rushing, of letting the words come naturally forth from thought and feeling. Burton's own style was highly praised for his roaring, rasping, howling, moaning delivery and flawless timing. Indeed, the *Time* reviewer felt that while his Hamlet was 'clever, lucid, fresh, contemporary and vivid' he had 'put his passion into Hamlet's language rather than his character' (Sterne, p. 148).

205 Richard Burton, 'Tragedy'. Philip Burton, *Richard*, pp. 43–4.
206 Quoted in Buell, *Hamlets*, p. 157.   207 Gielgud, *Actor*, p. 85.

In general the *Time* reviewer found Burton 'cool' and 'seldom emotion-ally affecting'. As the Electronovision film of his performance reveals, Burton physically closes himself in: he rarely looks at anyone for more than a glance (his absorption with the First Player is exceptional) and regularly stands in a partial crouch with his hands clasped before him. His most open and expansive gesture comes when he raises his hand high at 'O vengeance' – and that immediately becomes the object of his own mockery: 'What an ass am I!' Verbally, in contrast, he seems always to be on the offensive: only with the First Gravedigger is he warmly receptive to someone else's words.

The other main shortcoming found in Burton's performance was that it lacked overall coherence. It had 'flashes of intensity . . . but there were other passages that seemed loosely related to a central concept' (Sterne, p. 121). The Prince of Decision approach provided a strong core for the scenes immediately related to Hamlet's pursuit of vengeance. With Burton the issue was 'not *whether* Hamlet will revenge himself . . . but *when*' (*New Yorker*, 18 April 1964). But less closely related scenes, instead of being inte-gral consequences of Hamlet's inner conflicts, seemed incidental distrac-tions or interruptions to the course of his revenge.

At the same time, such scenes provided opportunities for Burton to explore what he had come to see as the distinctive characteristic of the role, that Shakespeare 'actually put on the stage in one character virtually every emotion of which a man is capable; pity, terror, fear, love, lust, obscenity, virtue, courage, cowardice' (Sterne, p. 291). Clearly Burton was not depict-ing Hamlet as a developing character of the sort Gielgud was urging on him, a maturing prince who discovers a new resolve at 'My thoughts be bloody or nothing worth' and a new serenity at 'let be'. Nor in the event was he confined to Philip Burton's 'Prince of Decision' formula. Instead Burton was spinning a kaleidoscope that revealed the dazzling range of Hamlet's feelings, an approach that was at once distinctively Burton's own and very much of his time. In contrast to an eighteenth-century view of Hamlet as a representative Man and a nineteenth-century view of him as a consistent individual with a few identifying character traits, Burton's Prince was so variable as to suggest a twentieth-century dissolution of self, in which per-sonal identity was intrinsically unstable and beyond individual control.

Such variability extended to Burton's own performance from one night to the next. The Electronovision version differs in a number of particulars from John Mills's detailed account of an earlier performance.[208] For instance, Mills found Burton's 'My thoughts be bloody or nothing worth' to be full of the resolve Gielgud had advocated whereas on Electronovision

208 Mills, *Hamlet*, pp. 254–61.

Burton reverted to his earlier less resolute and more rueful approach. In general the filmed version was less freewheeling than before. In an interview with Sterne at the close of the New York run, Burton explained that much depended on his own mood, his rapport with another actor, the responsiveness of the audience (Sterne, p. 290). The resulting spontaneity of Burton's performance was of the essence. Much of its excitement came from its hair-trigger volatility, the sense Burton conveyed of latent powers, in Hamlet and in himself, which might at any moment be given unexpected expression.

Hamlet politicized: East Germany, Stratford-Upon-Avon, Moscow

Looking at the last half of the twentieth century, Tice Miller estimates that there is 'not a single important city in continental Europe where *Hamlet* has not been revived since World War II'.[209] In Western Europe, the play was treated either as standard fare for consumers of high culture or as material for inventive directors to adapt to their own purposes. In 1964, in Rome and later on a tour that included London, Franco Zeffirelli designed and directed a production whose unmistakable point was to present Hamlet as a modern man, wearing jeans and a charcoal sweater, in a set whose cyclorama stretched the eye 'to an infinity of nothingness' – 'a blank universe in which man can rely on nothing but himself' (*The Times*, 16 September 1964). As trendy as this sounds, the production was praised also for its solid character-development: the Queen ages visibly; Laertes 'grows up before our eyes' (*Financial Times*, 25 September 1964).

In Eastern Europe, the play's political implications were the principal basis of its appeal, often obliquely reflecting local conditions.[210] All productions manoeuvred in an ambiguous and dangerous no-man's-land between what the Soviet authorities would permit and what their audiences, on the lookout for subversive hints, would infer. After Stalin's death in 1953 (regarding Hamlet as 'a miserable weakling', he had banned performance of the play in the Soviet Union), Nikolai Okhlopov's 'iron curtain' production in 1954 was ambiguous enough to be allowed a run in Moscow. On the one hand, its prince was as strong and optimistic a twenty-year-old activist as the most orthodox Party ideologue might wish,[211] while Laertes's rebellion was staged in such a way as to suggest serf and proletarian uprisings against past tyrants.[212] On the other hand, this Hamlet was engaged in an inner struggle against the indecisive 'hamletism' that Russians had long felt

209 Leiter, *Shakespeare*, p. 118. 210 Hattaway, *Europe*.
211 Leiter, *Shakespeare*, p. 132. 212 Rowe, *Hamlet*, p. 137.

themselves prone to and which current authorities deplored. And the set, with its massive iron gate and cell-like cubicles, graphically embodied Hamlet's feeling that 'Denmark is a prison,' making it easy for young spectators to identify the Prince's disillusionments with their own (Rosenberg, p. 143). Soon the authorities cut the run short.

In 1964 in East Germany what had been ambiguous was made clear and explicit. At the Shakespeare Quatercentenary celebrations in Weimar, the Deputy Prime Minister expounded the Party line: that in *Hamlet* Shakespeare upheld ideals that were ahead of his time and were only to be realized through the evolution of socialist society. In the same year Dieter Made's production in Karl-Marx-Stadt exactly followed this concept. The scenes involving the feudal and corrupt court were played in the back part of the stage: it was here that Hamlet, who could not escape the bloody imperatives of his own early era, stabbed Polonius and killed Laertes. In contrast, Hamlet's moments of prophetic introspection took place on an apron extending into the auditorium: it was here that he shared his ideals with the contemporary East German audience. The hopeful message, in the words of the production's dramaturg, was that although the Prince's insights were tragically premature 'What was once a yearning in Shakespeare . . . reaches our audiences today as a modern aim in life.'[213]

A contrasting East German *Hamlet* in that same year, directed by Adolf Dresen, was taken by authorities to be subversive and suppressed after a dozen performances. To Lawrence Guntner the subversiveness was deliberate and provocative, but Maik Hamburger, who collaborated on the translation, calls it 'naively subversive', the product simply of Dresen's direct reading of the play. In any case, the conceptual starting-point for the production could be seen as calling into question the too-easy optimism of the official formulation. Summing up his approach in the slogan 'Buchenwald is near Weimar', Dresen wanted to drive home how destructive high ideals can be when, as with cultured Nazis, they are not accompanied by principled practices. In the event, Hamburger reports, the production in rehearsal soon outgrew Dresen's theoretical scaffolding. The play resisted so critical a treatment of its hero, and it became apparent – to the immense enrichment of the production – that 'the play is not a parable but a tragedy'.

In England *Hamlet*'s political implications had traditionally been minimized. Since Restoration times the Fortinbras story had been drastically reduced if not cut altogether. *Hamlet* had sailed serenely past the sort of involvements with contemporary politics experienced by other

213 Guntner, 'Shakespeare'; Hamburger, 'Consolidation'.

Shakespearian plays. For example, it was not one of the half-dozen that were adapted to capitalize on the Jacobite scare in the early 1720s.[214] Nor has its performance been suspended for political reasons, as was *King Lear* because of the madness of George III. The nearest *Hamlet* came to such involvement was the 1849 Astor Place Riot in New York City. The riot was the outcome of bad feelings towards Macready nursed by the American actor Edwin Forrest, who several years before had conspicuously hissed Macready's handkerchief-waving business in *Hamlet* (see 3.2.80). By the time of the Riot, jingoistic and lower vs upper-class hostilities had been added to the personal rivalry. But they had nothing intrinsic to do with the politics of Shakespeare's Elsinore: the Riot, in fact, occurred during Macready's performance of *Macbeth*.

Yet by 1959 G. K. Hunter was concluding his survey of twentieth-century literary interpretation: 'in *Hamlet* we are face-to-face with an oppressively true picture of social breakdown' (*Critical Quarterly*, I, p. 32), and in 1989 Michael Billington would declare in his round-up of recent productions that '*Hamlet* is a profoundly political play, one that deals . . . with the whole question of the governance of society' (*Guardian*, 21 November). A milestone in this development was the 1965 Royal Shakespeare Company *Hamlet*, directed by Peter Hall. In his talk to the cast, printed in the programme, Hall summed up his initial production concept:

> For our decade I think the play will be about the disillusionment which produces an apathy of the will so deep that commitment to politics, to religion or to life is impossible . . . [Hamlet] is always on the brink of action, but something inside him, this disease of disillusionment, stops the final, committed action.

Hall thus applied to Shakespeare's play the critique of student apathy often voiced by editorial writers in the 1950s and early 1960s, who wished like Hall for 'the ordinary, predictable radical impulses which the young in all generations have had'.

By this time it was expected that the director would thus define the overall concept and atmosphere for a production. Among mid-century directors of *Hamlet*, Tyrone Guthrie had been especially aggressive in doing so, making bold use of oedipal interpretations with both Olivier and Guinness. He also did much to further the subtle development by which the hero's surroundings were seen not merely as background but as milieu. Writing of the Olivier stage Hamlet, W. A. Darlington credits Guthrie's direction with creating 'that unity of atmosphere which builds itself up,

---

214 Branam, *Adaptations*, pp. 62–3.

touch by subtle and original touch' (*Daily Telegraph*, 6 January 1937).[215] In performing these functions Guthrie and other stage-directors paralleled the contemporary concern of literary critics like Spurgeon and Mack to identify those recurring images in *Hamlet* (such as those of hidden disease) and other patterns (such as insistent questions) that contributed to 'themes' with philosophical implications and together comprised a surrounding 'world'.[216] In the study as on the stage, interpreters were thus looking beyond the individual experiences of the characters towards larger unifying features. In his 1989 article, Billington would go so far as to say that 'Elsinore itself, rather than the character of Hamlet, has now come to seem the play's determining factor' (*Guardian*, 21 November 1989).

The director's responsibilities in satisfying these concerns were specified in 1949 by Muriel St Clare Byrne, who presented it as an already accomplished fact that it is the director:

> who will decide what it is he believes the play has to say and how he believes
> the dramatist tried to say it – who will, in fact, decipher and then make
> explicit by his control and coordination of casting, setting, costuming,
> balance, proportion and tempo that emotional-cum-intellectual statement
> and atmosphere which is real 'unity'.   (*Shakespeare Survey*, 2, 1949, p. 17)

Although Hall exercised the director's authority in these areas vigorously, he did not become dictatorial. The play itself resisted a simple working-out of Hall's concept (after all, the Prince at long last does kill the King), as did the actors as they lived their roles and the audience members who responded not as recipients of a directorial statement but as witnesses to larger human values. Hall himself seems to have had a productive ambivalence about his own concept. On the one hand, he spoke in his statement about the play as a 'clinical dissection' of the failures of the younger generation. On the other hand, he seems – like Dresen in East Germany – to have treated this concept as no more than a starting-point in the production process, for his Prince Hamlet, embodying that failure, proved to be immensely sympathetic. At twenty-four, David Warner, although very much under the direction of Hall, seems to have had a more precise feeling

215 When that same production travelled to Elsinore and was forced by a storm to be
performed on an improvised platform in a hotel ballroom, the exciting rapport with
the audience that resulted inspired the new kind of 'thrust stage' theatres which
Guthrie oversaw at Stratford, Ontario, and Minneapolis and which has been
followed by Chichester and a number of chamber theatres (*Theatre*, p. 291). He felt
that the new arrangement succeeded because it 'approximated the Elizabethan
manner' of relating the audience to the stage (p. 318).
216 Spurgeon, *Imagery*; Mack, 'Hamlet'.

than did the director for the real attitudes of his generation. He showed a potential for action that was prophetic of the student uprisings to come at the end of the decade. In 1993 Hall reflected that Warner's performance 'completely expressed the spirit of the young of that period, gentle but dangerous'.[217] Harold Hobson acknowledged that Warner did at times 'wave his arms like a scythe, howl to the moon, and go after the king at a most unrefined gallop'; yet at the final duel, he shows 'an obvious superiority of nerve and skill': 'He is spare, controlled, deadly, and most royally confident . . . in a word, most princely, most exalted, judging as well as being judged' (*Sunday Times*, 22 August 1965). Clearly it was more than Warner's long red scarf and Oxford-style half-gown that won the production a cult status among the young.

Many of their elders appreciated it as well, despite early negative reviews protesting Warner's lack of princeliness. Its admirers testified to the production's power to make them see the play as if for the first time. Ronald Bryden put his finger on the reason for the audience's involvement, observing excitedly that Warner plays the Prince 'as a real student, learning as he goes along' (*New Statesman*, 27 August 1965). Warner, for example, spoke his soliloquies directly to the audience, seeking understanding from the front rows.

It was in its anti-establishment attitudes that the production most directly reflected Hall's original concept. Brewster Mason's smooth, bland Claudius was an able, though corrupt, administrator and diplomat, 'his oversize white hands turned palm upwards in a continual gesture of "political" reconciliation'.[218] In public he remained self-possessed at the showdown when he calls for lights, stopping the performance 'with angry impatience – not startled guilt – when its continuation becomes an impertinence' (*Daily Mail*, 20 October 1965). Tony Church's Polonius was the 'shrewd, tough, establishment figure' Hall called for, complete with 'a clubland drawl' (*The Times*, 20 August 1965). Adding greatly to his gravitas as councillor was 'the intense concentration with which Claudius listened to his every word'.[219] Church told Stanley Wells that 'he had in mind both Lord Burleigh and Mr. Macmillan, chief ministers of the two Elizabeths'.[220] John Bury's set, with its huge spaces, ebony-like walls and grey and black marble-like floors suggested 'a busy centre of Government and social glitter' (*The Times*, 20 August 1965), but not overtly suspect. 'Much better', Speaight remarked, 'for Hamlet to scent the corruption under a facade of sobriety' (*Shakespeare Quarterly*, 16, 1965, p. 320). Only later did the wall panels revolve to reveal a collection of nude paintings.

217 Hall, *Exhibition*, p. 188.   218 Leiter, *Shakespeare*, p. 140.
219 Church, 'Polonius', p. 108.   220 Wells, *Shakespeare*, p. 32.

But it was the Prince's relationship with his father that provided the most intriguing ambivalences. Clearly, Hall wanted to emphasize the Prince's inadequacies. The player king's crown proves too big for him and slides down his nose. He is far from being the king his father was. Yet is this a bad thing? To *The Times* 'the Ghost's call for vengeance is an invitation to involve himself in the life of action from which lies originate' (20 August 1965) and to L. C. Knights 'he is drawn more and more into the world of blood and revenge – a kind of regress' (quoted in *the Observer*, 19 December 1965). He was at his best when scared, Gilliatt felt, as when he 'prayed softly before he wheels round to face his father's ghost' (*Observer*, 22 August 1965).

Warner's laughter during his last speech was variously interpreted. Beyond Jan Kott's idea of general absurdity, commentators discerned differing ironies: that circumstances had allowed him to carry out his father's mission without his having to commit himself to it;[221] that 'it was over at last, that action had been forced upon him';[222] that he 'has finally achieved the princeliness he aspired to by dying' (*New Statesman*, 27 August 1965); that Hamlet has bequeathed such a 'muckup' to his successor (*Birmingham Evening Mail*, 20 August 1965); that it should be young Fortinbras of Norway who – of all people – should end up ruling Denmark (*Shakespeare Quarterly*, 16, 1965, p. 320).

To return to Eastern Europe, the portrayal of the Prince was undergoing a change that reflected the general loss of hope. In the first years after the war, a number of the leading Hamlets – in Warsaw (1947), Budapest (1952), Cracow (1956), Prague (1959) – had been men of strong action, in fatal conflict with corrupt regimes. Later Hamlets, however, were often seen as helpless against an all-powerful state, less confident about the efficacy of action in general, more caught up in their doubts and inner struggles. In 1962 in Hungary, for example, Miklos Gabor was 'active only up to that very point where the truth gets revealed, since his objective is not so much to take revenge, but rather to know'.[223] By 1978 the tragi-farce version of *Hamlet* done by Vaclav Havel's Balustrade Theatre in Prague had gone beyond hopelessness to absurdity. At the very end, for example, the Gravediggers were in charge. They were made up as white-faced clowns with red noses and wearing the black rubber boots, gloves, and aprons of a sanitation unit. Whistling and humming, with evident relish, they added the bodies of Ophelia and Polonius to the heap of corpses already on stage, spread over them a camouflage net, and sprinkled them with chlorine.

---

221 Mills, *Hamlet*, p. 266.   222 Trewin, *Five & Eighty*, p. 133.
223 Leiter, *Shakespeare*, p. 137.

Stříbrný describes the paradoxical impact of this 'image of a disinfected mass grave': 'There was no upward turn, no hope. Shattered as we left the performance, we were still feeling a strange relief, some kind of modern absurd catharsis.' He adds that he later gained insight into this catharsis from a 1990 comment by Havel after he had become President: 'Who knows whether . . . without experiencing the absurdity of the world one can anticipate, look for and find its sense?'[224]

During its long run in repertory (1971–80), THE TAGANKA *HAMLET* in Moscow spanned the general change from early confidence to later doubt. As directed by Yuri Lyubimov, it struck its keynotes in its prologue. Designer David Borovsky's stage was bare. On the exposed, whitewashed backwall leaned metal swords and gauntlets while hanging from it was a large, rough-hewn, weathered, asymmetrical cross. Downstage was an open grave, containing real dirt and real skulls; silhouetted as they worked in it were two obviously Russian gravediggers, drinking vodka with hard-boiled eggs and greasing with garlic the heels of their brown bread. Hamlet stood at the back, strumming his guitar; like the rest of the cast, he wore slacks and a heavy turtle-neck sweater. The role was played by Vladimir Vysotsky, best known as a balladier whose underground protest songs and poems had made him the conscience of his time.[225] Soon he rushed forward and, accompanying himself on his guitar, sang the poem 'Hamlet' from banned *Doctor Zhivago* by Boris Pasternak. It begins:

> The buzz subsides. I have come on stage.
> Leaning in an open door
> I try to detect from the echo
> What the future has in store.
> (Pasternak, *Poems*, p. 125)

After the song the entire cast came on and a huge, coarsely woven hemp curtain fell from the ceiling. Mounted on an elaborate pivot and tracking system that allowed it to move in many directions about the set, the curtain swept the cast, reeling and falling, from the stage, and the action began.

The initial inspiration for this production came from Pasternak, whose 1940 prose translation of *Hamlet* was used. Indeed Lyubimov in part based his idea for the whole Taganka Theatre on the first stanza of the 'Hamlet' poem, with its hope to read the signs of the times and detect what the future has in store.[226] Pasternak's view of the tragedy may be summarized in a speech by an actor in his unfinished play *The Blind Beauty*: 'The false role

---

224 Stříbrný, 'Rates', p. 167.   225 Gershkovich, *Lyubimov*, p. 129.
226 Golub, 'Curtain', p. 160.

of avenger is imposed on Hamlet by the play of fate. The tragedy shows how he plays this role.'[227] Elsewhere, Pasternak affirms his belief that spiritual victory comes only through self-sacrifice, however reluctant, and draws a parallel between Hamlet and Christ;[228] hence the cross in the set.

Vysotsky's way of intuiting his own destiny, with the Ghost holding few surprises, was in Pasternak's spirit. Vysotsky, however, identified himself very closely with Hamlet, and his interpretation of the prince mostly followed the progression of his own thought. Before he played the role he had written the song 'I don't like . . . ' in which he rejected 'chilling cynicism, things done half-way . . . impotence'.[229] In the first years of the run, his Hamlet struck Hedrick Smith as 'an enraged young man struggling against an evil ruler in an evil time' (*New York Times*, 29 February 1972).

Over the ten years Vysotsky played the part, his approach turned to a 'mystical irrationalism', which was 'more aware of life as an unanswerable proposition'.[230] The poem, 'My Hamlet', which Vysotsky wrote in the course of the run, points in the direction of this change:

I'm Hamlet . . .
I could care less about the Danish crown,
   ***

But what's the point of thoughts and science, what's the need,
When everywhere they simply are disproved
   ***

We all just give a tricky, double-dealing answer
And cannot find the necessary question.
        (Gershkovich, *Lyubimov*, p. 129)

Apparently, Vysotsky's final hope was to inspire his Soviet audience to ask 'the necessary question' by pondering such long-suppressed imponderables as the value of human life and justice.[231] Lyubimov also sought to stir 'problems and questions for the audience': 'if it does not make people think about themselves, there is no point in playing it'.[232] His instructions to his designer reflect a concern for ultimates that went far beyond immediate social and political concerns: he called 'for something that had no borders, something wider than desire, a limitless space' but with a strong sense of time and decay,[233] one that chimed with his own use of shortened scenes and a rapid, hurried pace.

Attempts by Western commentators to nail down the precise political implications of the production, as a post-Stalin, Brezhnev-era piece, thus

---

227 Rowe, *Window*, p. 160.   228 *Ibid.*   229 Gershkovich, *Lyubimov*, p. 128.
230 Golub, 'Curtain', p. 164.   231 *Ibid.*   232 Smith, *Russians*, p. 389.
233 Levy, 'Borovsky', p. 37.

seem to limit its larger ambitions. This is especially true of the curtain, which Margaret Croyden simplistically sees as

> a giant monster . . . holding within its folds the symbols and tools of power – black armbands, swords, goblets, thrones edged with knives. It envelopes Ophelia, intimidates Polonius, protects Gertrude, supports Claudius and threatens Hamlet. Finally it sweeps the stage clean and moves toward the audience as though to destroy it, too. (*New York Times*, 31 October 1976)

Felicia Londre, too, sees it as 'an accomplice on the side of political oppression'.[234] Certainly, the curtain had this aspect at times. But by Micky Levy's account of Borovsky's work, the curtain served many other functions: 'it became a wall, a screen, a net . . . a throne . . . a shawl that gave warmth to Ophelia, a tapestry to strike a knife through . . . At times the actors raised the curtain and crawled under it, wrapped themselves in it, climbed up it'.[235] In a split-screen effect, parallel actions were at times performed on either side of it. Golub's paragraph-long fantasia on the symbolism of the curtain suggests the wide range of its possible import – including God, fate, 'the breathing of unsolved mysteries', 'the wind against which the Prince bent his fragile figure and the cloak which protected him from it', and many other implications.[236] In short the curtain became a member of the cast and at the end was appropriately applauded in its own right.

Director's *Hamlet*: rampant in Western Europe, on the wane in England

Meanwhile in Western Europe director's theatre prevailed. In Bochum (1977) Peter Zadek concocted a deliberate travesty of the play, mixing, as Werner Habicht put it, 'variety show, operetta, and circus, combined with pop art and slapstick' (*Shakespeare Quarterly*, 29, 1978). In it Hamlet, fat and zestful if overbearing, put on a butcher's apron to cut up Polonius's corpse, throwing the pieces out the window. To admiring Dennis Kennedy, the production encompassed 'the chaos, obscenity, and joy of contemporary life'. To Zadek's rival, Peter Stein, he had merely shown 'Shakespeare with his trousers down'.[237] If Zadek's work seems absurdist, Hansgunther Heyme's 'media' *Hamlet* (1979) seems surreal. It featured eighteen television monitors on stage, the hanging carcass of a stuffed horse, audibly dripping blood into a chalice, and a schizoid hero – all designed to convey the director's view that 'individual tragedy . . . is no longer possible in a world where electronic phantasms are more compelling than human life'. In

234 Leiter, *Shakespeare*, p. 144.   235 Levy, 'Borovsky', pp. 57–8.
236 Golub, 'Curtain', p. 173.   237 Kennedy, *Looking*, pp. 270, 277.

Stockholm in 1986 (and later on tour) Ingmar Bergman made his own reworking of *Hamlet* raw materials. His drunkard King must be the grossest to date – he is introduced entering his queen from the rear, clapped to his climax by the row of bewigged courtiers in stocking-masks and red judicial robes that witness many of the play's events (*TLS*, 26 June 1987). No less heavy-handed was Bergman's treatment of Ophelia: first seen as a barefoot country-girl with flowers in her hair, she is sent by Gertrude into the nunnery scene, lip-sticked, with red high-heels and fallen shoulder-straps; she is virtually raped by Hamlet in the play scene; and in her mad scene she distributes eight-inch nails instead of flowers. More interestingly, however, she was made by Bergman to witness – as well as sometimes participate in – all of the scenes between 2.2 and her funeral, thus 'absorbing the full weight and meaning of the catastrophe, until, of course, it breaks her' (*Observer*, 4 January 1987).

England has been quicker than the Continent to recognize the limitations of an all-controlling directorial concept. By 1974, Peter Brook had come to see that 'the overall unifying image was much less than the play itself'.[238] In his 1976 *Hamlet* Peter Hall, too, was trying to break free from the expectation that a 'simple thesis' should govern all.[239] By 1985 Roger Warren was praising the Roger Rees/Ron Daniels production precisely because it was 'the least slanted' *Hamlet* he had seen, one that left 'any larger significance to emerge from the telling of the story itself' (*Shakespeare Quarterly*, 36, 1985, p. 79). Yet an altogether neutral directorial approach may not be best either; there can be dramatic value in an overall interpretive line as long as it is not too insistent. In the 1965 RSC *Hamlet*, as in the 1912 and 1972 Moscow *Hamlet*s, a broadening enrichment happened quite spontaneously, where a strong director, a strong designer, a strong leading actor, and a strong supporting ensemble have interacted. Their interplay cancelled out what was reductive about them individually, leaving room for more of Shakespeare to come through.

'Disjoint and out of frame': the 1989 Royal Shakespeare Company production

The three productions just named had a loose unity that may be distinguished from the tighter unity exemplified by the 1925 modern-dress *Hamlet* and by the 1989 Royal Shakespeare Company touring production, directed by Ron Daniels with Mark Rylance as Hamlet. Designer Antony McDonald's set focused boldly on its two thematic emphases. The dizzy-

238 Brook, *Shifting Point*, pp. 78–9. 239 Hall, *Diaries*, p. 239.

ingly out-of-kilter window and walls suggested a world that was danger-ously 'disjoint and out of frame'; Rylance likened it to 'a palace tilting into the ocean'.[240] In particular, it expressionistically projected the Prince's deranged sense of surroundings that were radically 'out of joint'; reviewers felt strongly the atmosphere of a mental institution, an effect heightened when Rylance appeared in stained, striped pyjamas and stockings to deliver the 'to be or not to be' soliloquy.

As Daniels explained to interviewers, the other thematic emphasis saw the play 'as an inter-personal set of reactions within the family' (*Newcastle upon Tyne Evening Chronicle*, 26 September 1988). Hence the prominence of a large bed, not only in the closet scene but in the whole play-within-a-play sequence: Claudius's attempt to pray took place on the bed; he glanced at it when he spoke there of 'my queen'.

The two themes of course intertwine. King Hamlet is depicted as a loving husband – his Ghost protectively cradles Gertrude's unresponding shoulders. But as a father he is stern and remote. When the Prince seeks to comfort the grieving Ghost, he pulls away, then takes his son by the collar to demand 'if thou hast nature in thee . . . '. Clearly, it is with his mother, played by Clare Higgins, that Hamlet has had a loving relationship – the closet scene will climax in an oedipal kiss that takes them both by surprise. But at first her affections are very much directed towards her new husband, who dotes on her. In denial about her son's condition – 'we don't have mental illness in the royal family'[241] – she does not admit the truth about her son until at 4.1.7 she screams it out: '*Mad* as the sea and wind' (*Shakespeare Quarterly*, 41, Spring 1990, p. 107). As for Peter Wight's Claudius he was at first patient with his difficult stepson but is more and more appalled as he realizes the risk that Hamlet poses and the enormity of what he himself has done. This family situation leaves Rylance's Hamlet very much alone. Desperate to escape, he is first seen, isolated and small, slumped, wearing a black overcoat, looking out the large askew window, shabby suitcase packed, and ready for departure to Wittenberg.

From this first appearance on, Rylance was an appealing figure, a boy surrounded by much taller men. At his first soliloquy, 'as if he cannot bear to look us in the eye as he speaks. . . . He does not turn towards us until he speaks of his father: "So excellent a king," he explains, holding out a photo-graph of his father. He speaks directly to us, his face pleading for us to agree . . . ' (*Plays and Players*, June 1989). Throughout his soliloquies Rylance's complete sincerity created a remarkable rapport with the audience, which he treated as his confidant. His Hamlet was notably sympathetic to others.

240 Gilbert, 'Rylance'.   241 *Ibid*.

He comforted Horatio after his distraught 'wondrous strange' (1.5.164), Ophelia after the nunnery exchange, his mother at the end of the bedroom scene, as he tucked her in bed. Yet the audience's sympathies for Rylance were not unmixed, especially in his outbursts of frenzy in the nunnery scene when Ophelia lies to him and in the bedroom scene when he repeatedly stabs the eavesdropper. Covered with blood, he gloats 'A bloody deed', putting the phrase 'in inverted commas' (*TLS*, 5 May 1989). Reviewers felt it a prime strength of the production that it refused to over-simplify, gaining through its even-handedness a 'hard emotional authenticity' (*Shakespeare Quarterly*, 41, 1990, p. 105).

Rylance's Hamlet was clearly not simply assuming an 'antic disposition'. At 'It hath made me mad' he sometimes banged his head on the wall or clutched his head with terrifying self-awareness (*Manchester Guardian*, 28 April 1989). After the touring production visited Broadmoor Hospital for the criminally insane the authenticity of his portrayal was confirmed by a patient there, who wrote to the *Manchester Guardian* that Rylance 'was able to capture every aspect of a person's slip into the world of psychopathic, manipulative paranoia . . . Many of us here in Broadmoor are able to understand Hamlet's disturbed state of mind because we have experienced such traumas' (28 December 1989).[242]

Hamlet's brief departure from Elsinore and sea adventure decisively mark his return to sanity and growth to maturity. No longer stooped over, he stands up straight. For the fencing match, the court is in black (still in mourning for Polonius and Ophelia). When Hamlet has put on his fencing jacket, he is all in white. At the end Rylance addresses 'You that look pale and tremble' to the off-stage spectators, and thus 'once again' – Gilbert observes – 'establishes that rapport with the audience which so marks this performance'.[243] In the South Bank Show, Rylance explained his final view of Hamlet thus: 'He comes to some kind of peace, and I guess that's part of the reason that makes it a tragedy. He's actually reached the state of a prince at the time that he dies, and you should feel he would make a wonderful king.'

Hamlet personalized

Rylance has confessed to a love–hate relationship with the part of the Prince: 'you have to touch on certain things inside you that are very difficult – it's got to be gone through from innocence to consciousness every night' (*Independent*, 17 March 1989). Such interpenetration of actor and role is

242 See also Cox, *Broadmoor*.   243 Gilbert, 'Rylance'.

10 Mark Rylance sponges off Polonius's blood (4.2). Note the striped pyjama-trousers (he had donned pyjamas before entering to deliver the 'to be or not to be' soliloquy). Before this episode is over Rylance will have climbed into the tub and poured water over his head. Frustrated and infuriated, Claudius tries to extort the whereabouts of Polonius's corpse by dunking his nephew's head in the water, but Rylance, choking, remains insouciant; as he makes his exit he gets back into the tub and makes rowing motions while crying 'For England' (Gilbert, 'Rylance').

not, of course, without precedent. Vyzotsky, Booth, and Kemble were thought to have something Hamlet-like in their off-stage selves while Barrymore saw himself and the Prince as a pair of 'mother-loving perverts'. Gordon Craig so identified himself with Hamlet that in his notebook he wrote 'I. D.' beside many of Ophelia's lines in the nunnery scene, referring to his rejected lover Isadora Duncan.[244] Critics too have felt, like Coleridge, that 'I have a smack of Hamlet myself' (*Table Talk*, 24 June 1827). Hazlitt is another: 'it is *we* who are Hamlet' (*Characters of Shakespeare's Plays*, 1817).

Nonetheless, recent decades are remarkable for the number of English Hamlets who have testified to the unique claim that the role makes on the actor's own personality. Michael Pennington has written that playing the Prince 'will take the actor further down into his psyche, memory and imagination' than ever before.[245] Olivier has warned that the role of Hamlet can 'cast you into the depths of despair. Once you have played it, it will devour you and obsess you for the rest of your life. It has me. I think each day about it.'[246] Such obsessions have sometimes exacted a high price. To Mel Gibson, 'It's more than a part – it's an assault on your personality. Every passing day his doubts become more your doubts.'[247] Such assaults proved more than Daniel Day Lewis could bear, and he withdrew from the part in mid-run. Even before his withdrawal he predicted: 'I think this is the year of my nervous collapse. Hamlet's a hard part to live with. It conjures up demons in you . . . This has certainly taken me closer to the abyss than anything else. And I've discovered fears in myself, or generated fears, I never knew before – and once they're there, they're very difficult to put away again' (*Daily Mail*, 13 September 1989).

An actor may fear the difficulties of the role and doubt whether he has the ability to deal with them. Ben Kingsley was so daunted that he felt physically sick: 'At the centre of the play when you're exhausted, battling with it physically and intellectually, sweat pouring into your eyes and you're wondering if anything is achieved, the "to be or not to be" soliloquy coincides with your sensibilities . . .' (*Independent*, 17 March 1989). Young actors may also feel keenly the challenge of great predecessors. For his 1988 portrayal Kenneth Branagh felt 'crushingly the weight of the ghosts of other performances' (*Shakespeare Bulletin*, Fall, 1994, p. 6).

In some instances the actors' anxieties have remained submerged, with no evident consequences in their interpretations. Gibson's Hamlet did not strike me as doubt-ridden, nor Day Lewis's as fearful. Hamlets who have straddled the boundaries between sanity and insanity, however, have more

244 Craig's notations are cited in Payne, 'Craig', p. 319.
245 Pennington, 'Hamlet', p. 117.   246 Olivier, *Acting*, p. 77.
247 Gibson, HBO.

clearly fed their personal involvements back into the role. Rylance is a case in point. Another is Jonathan Pryce, whose intensity was at times so overwrought as to seem barely under control. He has disclosed how his portrayal was influenced by a skinhead's fatal assault with a hammer on his father (*Over 21*, September 1980) and by his experience of seeing

> visions of his father after his death: 'Whether I had seen him, or whether I wanted to see him so much that I'd conjured him up, I don't know. But that's how I approached Hamlet, as someone who had seen his own father's ghost'.
> (*New York Times*, 5 November 1995).

Hamlet's recurring encounters with mortality have come especially close to home. Michael Pennington recalls how 'The death of an old friend over Christmas naturally pulled my centre of gravity over to the scene with the skulls' (*Manchester Guardian*, 17 September 1981). The overlap of performer and role where death is concerned reached an ultimate with Ian Charleson (Day Lewis's replacement), who played the role while afflicted with AIDS. His director Richard Eyre recalls how his last performance 'was like watching a man who had been rehearsing for playing Hamlet all his life. He wasn't playing the part, he became it. By the end of the play he was visibly exhausted, each line of his final scene painfully wrung from him, his farewell and the character's agonizingly merged'.[248] Hamlet's suicidally searching interrogation of life's values has also taken its real-life toll. Commenting on the 'raw' and 'exposed' commitment the play requires, Kingsley paid tribute to director Buzz Goodbody, who killed herself shortly after their production started its previews: 'Buzz got me through *Hamlet*. For some reason, having examined all the implications of it at a high emotional and intellectual level, she didn't get herself through *Hamlet*' (*Time-Out*, 30 January 1976).

All these hazards are integral to the role and have thus presented themselves to Hamlets through the centuries. Why have recent actors of the role been so inclined to emphasize their own vulnerability? One reason may be that where earlier Hamlets tended to emphasize a few salient traits, twentieth-century portrayals have sought to encompass in a single interpretation more of Hamlet's multifaceted personality, Richard Burton being a notable example (see p. 72). Moreover, the facets of Hamlet's personality are particularly disparate. As Stephen Dillane says of the Prince: 'It seems almost impossible to make a coherent, consistent character out of him; he's more like a series of sketches. But you want to take the audience with you, and somehow you have to make them believe in these enormous character shifts'

248 Eyre, *Utopia*, p. 132.

(*What's On*, 2 November 1994). To Gielgud, these shifts are a prime challenge of the role: 'Every new Hamlet must link the strands of the play by an
individual, original attitude.' Supplying these links can put special strains
on the actor's own personality. Branagh calls Hamlet 'one of those x-ray
parts, where you are naked and vulnerable and where you pour out so much
of your self and experience' (*Shakespeare Bulletin*, Fall 1994, p. 7). As
Olivier confided to his son Tarquin, 'It is actually yourself that you have to
reveal'.[249] When he first played the role on stage he was in a quandary about
his adulterous love for Vivien Leigh; he told his director Tyrone Guthrie, 'I
already know what it feels like to be a Hamlet in real life.' Guthrie explains:
'He believed he had a great deal of personal Hamlet-like anguish and spiritual paralysis to bring to the part.'[250]

These strains may be intensified by a distinctly modern anxiety: what if
the individual self proves to be no more than its disparate parts, with no
single, sustained identity to hold them together? Tarquin Olivier disclosed
in a 1993 television interview the insecurity that his father felt about his
own identity, an insecurity that lay behind his compulsive drive to play so
many different roles on stage. This compulsion chimes with Olivier's way of
conceiving the Prince as one who, like himself, 'had to find other people to
be all the time', resulting in a career made up of 'a sporadic collection of
self-dramatizations'.[251] This conception is not prominent in Olivier's film
version. Yet as early as 1937 it was for Raymond Mortimer the hallmark of
his stage portrayal: 'he is not so much one man as a whole troupe of players,
hero, villain, lover, wiseacre and clown' (*New Statesman and Nation*, 16
January 1937).

In a sense the recent impulse to personalize the Prince may be seen as
pushing to the other extreme from the recent impulse to politicize the play:
one heads inwards, the other outwards. Yet the two impulses may also work
in tandem since both have usually reflected the modern feeling that whether
in public life or private an earlier order is going to pieces. Indeed, the akilter
window in the Rylance/Daniels set captures this double implication in a
single image. The 'spirit of disintegration' that Lawrence saw in the title-
character has been extended to the whole play. Yet like so many of the stage
Hamlets before him, Rylance's Prince makes an heroic eleventh hour recovery and comes into his own at the end. It is in adaptations that the disin-
tegrated self of the hero has been pushed to the extreme; there was a spate
of them in the 1960s. In *Hamlet Collage* (1965) Charles Marowitz set out to
ridicule the Prince as 'the supreme prototype of the conscience-stricken but

---

249 T. Olivier, *My Father*, p. 215.   250 Guthrie, *Theatre*, p. 187.
251 Olivier, *Acting*, pp. 79, 77.

paralysed liberal', making him the laughing stock of the other characters; the play ends with their corpses mocking him 'with jeers, whistles, stamping and catcalls'.[252] In Joe Papp's *Naked Hamlet* (1968) the final duel is reduced to a game of Russian roulette; when Hamlet happens to shoot Claudius the moment is played for laughs: his attendants topple over one after the other but the King does not accept that he has been shot dead until Hamlet proves it to him by showing him a copy of the play.[253] In Tom Stoppard's *Rosencrantz and Guildenstern Are Dead* (1967) Shakespeare's conflicted hero is displaced to the sidelines in favour of a totally divided protagonist, a pair out of Beckett, whose identities are confused and whose destinies are completely out of their control and in any case inconsequential. Shakespeare's play does flirt with absurdity, but thus far stage interpretations of the role have not succumbed to it; on the contrary, the threat of utter futility has been seen as part of the sea of troubles against which the Prince must finally take arms. Indeed, such aggressively virile Hamlets as those of Barrymore, Olivier, Burton, Gibson may be seen as reactions against tendencies to exaggerate his weakness.

For post-moderns the lure of chaos has extended to design. As Aronson puts it: whereas modern design tried 'to encompass the world within a unified image', the post-modern world is seen as 'a multiplicity of competing, often incongruous and conflicting elements and images and stage design reflects this perspective'.[254] Accordingly many of the particular features of post-modern design that Aronson identifies run counter to those of modern design (such as their neo-pictorialism and preference for proscenium theatres). They also tend to undo the whole progression towards an overall coordination of elements in a production that I have been tracing. Thus far such productions have not been prepossessing: they seem self-conscious and contrived. For instance, the progression from period-realism to surrealism in Bob Crowley's designs for the 1993 Kenneth Branagh/Adrian Noble *Hamlet* seemed forced and painfully obvious in the 'over-emphatic underlining' of effects.[255] It was all-too predictable, for example, that the piano in Ophelia's bedroom would appear in her mad scene. It may be that discordances in a production are best allowed to happen (having earned their way by the independent vigour of its parts) rather than calculated in advance. Still, these are early days. Perhaps the post-modern discordances can point the way towards a larger, looser, more

252 Marowitz, *Marowitz Shakespeare*, p. 13.
253 Papp, *'Naked' Hamlet*, pp. 154–5.   254 Aronson, 'Design', p. 2.
255 Peter Holland analyses Crowley's 'extravagances' in *Shakespeare Survey*, 47, p. 183. Adrian Noble traces the creation of the design concept for this production in *Shakespeare Bulletin*, 11, Summer 1993, pp. 8–9.

inclusive sense of harmony in a production, one that can incorporate a liberating dissonance among its parts.

Supporting roles and players in the twentieth century

Just such a widening of scope to include autonomous elements may be seen in the recent treatment of *Hamlet*'s supporting roles, as the characters other than Hamlet have more and more emerged as individuals who live out their own destinies as well as participating in the Prince's tragedy. Furthermore, their relations with one another have been more fully developed. In general a feeling for ensemble among the characters and their performers has been an important part of the modern concern for the whole play.

Twentieth-century interpreters of Claudius, literary as well as theatrical, have sought to humanize the King. Critic Wilson Knight saw in him 'a host of good qualities . . . distinguished by creative and wise action, a sense of purpose, benevolence, a faith in himself and those around him, by love of his Queen . . . In short he is very human'.[256] On stage Alec Clunes, who played the role opposite Paul Scofield, presented him as a tragic figure in his own right. Tynan summarized his tragedy as that of 'a man who committed a *crime passionnel* after an internal battle which has left scars on his conscience . . . We watch the slow crumbling of a man of action, who has created through crime a new universe which now falls, stone by stone, about his ears.' Clunes also revealed something pitiable about Claudius and something gallant, when 'To quell Laertes' rebellion he collects himself, weary yet still majestic. This lonely man engages once again in plotting, of which he is still a master, like the gouty Napoleon at Waterloo' (*Observer*, 11 December 1955).

Even Polonius has been shown to have a tragic dimension. One of his most praised recent interpreters was Michael Bryant, who in the Daniel Day Lewis/Richard Eyre production depicted an ageing patriarch who has long dominated his family and the court but now feels his powers to be waning and compensates with bluster. Most notable was the moment when he loses the thread of his instructions to Reynaldo. This was not merely a momentary memory-lapse; during the 'huge panic-stricken pause' (*Independent*, 18 March 1989), Polonius comes to realize 'that age has conquered him' (*Hampstead Highgate Express*, 24 March 1989). Still shaken by this incident, his delivery of 'Or else this brain of mine / Hunts not the trail of policy so sure / As it hath used to do' (2.2.46b–48a) exposed to Rosenberg 'a shadow of real self-doubt' (p. 378). Such nuances contributed

256 Knight, *Wheel of Fire*, pp. 37–8.

to a rounded impersonation, one that allowed the audience 'to view the events at Elsinore through the eyes of Polonius' (*New York Times*, 26 August 1989).

Twentieth-century Ophelias have differed from earlier ones in several ways. Especially in recent productions, Ophelia's sexuality has received much more emphasis than before, most of all in the Richardson/ Williamson film where Marianne Faithfull clearly has an incestuous relationship with Laertes and plays the nunnery episode as a torrid love-scene. In their madness recent Ophelias have especially emphasized strange behaviour. Almost clinical was Susan Fleetwood in the 1976 production at the National, with her 'abrupt, jerky movements and awkward stances as well as the generally unkempt and chewed appearance of an advanced schizophrenic'.[257] In 1982 Dr Jonathan Miller, applying his medical expertise, directed Kathryn Pogson to use 'curious anorectic gestures as she forced her finger down her throat in an attempt to vomit'.[258] Modern Ophelias have also been more assertive than their predecessors, although they all in the end obey male authority. Of these Glenda Jackson is the most remarkable. In the 1965 Royal Shakespeare production she was described as self-possessed, neurotic, tough, fierce, harsh, strident, shrill, bitter, acid, full of rancour – 'a very modern rebellious personality' with the bearing of 'a nurse in a mental hospital' (*Theatre World*, October 1965). With her father, this Ophelia was obedient yet anything but submissive. She stands up to Hamlet in the nunnery scene, yet in the end gives way and reveals 'a highly sexed young woman cracking under the strain of a disintegrating love affair' (*Plays and Players*, October 1965). It was here that her decisive descent into madness began. As Jan Kott explained her plight: 'she cannot find her own way, she will not accept anyone else's . . . she loses her way; and can fall back on madness'. Her suicide, Kott concluded, was 'the final gesture of revolt' (*Sunday Times*, 31 October 1965).

Most modern Gertrudes have been beautiful and highly sexed. In London Barrymore complimented Constance Collier on the 'full-blown provocativeness' of her Queen;[259] Coral Browne, with John Neville in 1957, seemed to Tynan 'maternally voluptuous' (*Observer*, 22 September). Some Gertrudes have been notably young relative to their Hamlets. Opposite Mel Gibson in the Zeffirelli film Glenn Close was played as very youthful; she had clearly borne her son at an early age. Olivier's Queen in the film, Eileen Herlie, was in actuality younger than he was. In the thirties Gertrude's scandalous conduct began to be explained by portraying her as compla-

257 David, *Theatre*, p. 83.   258 Miller, *Performances*, p. 116.
259 Barrymore, *Confessions*, ch. 4.

cently insensitive to moral compunctions. This was the approach of Laura Cowie, Gielgud's Gertrude in 1934 and 1939, who regarded it as a completely new interpretation (*Glasgow Evening Citizen*, 16 April 1935).

Until the twentieth century the emphasis in portraying Gertrude's relationship with her son had been very much upon his attitude towards her. Particularly since World War II more attention than before has been paid to her attitude towards him. In the Branagh/Noble production Jane Lapotaire depicted a motherly Gertrude who in her constant solicitude for her son 'lives almost by his looks' (4.7.12), a concern made graphic by her stage movements: 'She always positions herself, as if subconsciously, where she can best see her son' (*Sunday Times*, 23 December 1992). In the oedipal relationships emphasized in the Olivier and Zeffirelli films, Herlie and Close are the ones who initiate the kissing with their sons. Recent Gertrudes have emphasized her active transfer of loyalty from Claudius to Hamlet in the latter part of the play. Often her withdrawal from the King is projected by her refusal to join him when he repeatedly calls for her to 'Come' with him at the end of a scene as in 4.1 and 4.7 or when they exit separately. By the fencing match there is no doubt that her loyalties lie with Hamlet. The fact of making a choice between husband and son has also provided an opportunity – however brief – for the Queen to discover at last an identity independent of either.

In addition to individualizing the supporting characters in *Hamlet*, the twentieth-century stage has spun a Chekhovian web of interrelationships among all the characters, with the family as an institution the central nexus. The Ghost has come to be seen not just as a spectral or kingly figure but as a father and husband. Various recent productions on screen and stage have suggested marital problems between Gertrude and her first husband – that he was too old for her or too distant. Polonius too has to a greater degree than before come to be seen as a family man as well as a royal counsellor. In the 1980 Pennington/Barton production Tony Church's Polonius was very much a loving father, who knew perfectly well during his parting advice to Laertes that 'his children were smiling behind his back' but 'did not mind'. It was 'the anger of a loving father' at the mistreatment of his daughter that fueled his later hatred of Hamlet.[260]

In the 1965 Warner/Hall production, Church had played Polonius as a wily politician among wily politicians (see p. 77 above). The difference illustrates the way the portrayal of supporting roles may depend on the imagined milieu of a production and the ensemble style of presenting it. Other roles in *Hamlet* have been no less responsive to the prevailing atmosphere of

260 Church, 'Polonius', pp. 109, 112.

the production of which they are a part. This is true even of much smaller roles – such as Rosencrantz and Guildenstern, Reynaldo, Osric; in recent years they have added to the sinister tone of a milieu in which lying and spying are endemic. In general the relative autonomy of the supporting characters, and their interrelation with one another and their surroundings, has often done much to create an Elsinore independent of Hamlet's partial view of it. The resulting sense of an encompassing world has been one of the chief ways in which twentieth-century theatre has expanded its perspective to something like Shakespearian proportions.

Kenneth Branagh's *Hamlets* on stage and screen

Such large-mindedness is a strong point of Kenneth Branagh's film version of *Hamlet*. Its unity lies somewhere between the loose variety of the Moscow Art Theatre and the tighter sort of the Rylance/Daniels production. It is the product of a single, consistent vision of the play (Branagh adapted, directed, and starred in it), yet it is saved from narrowness by the size and variety of this vision. Too often, as many reviewers have felt, Branagh in straining for large effects goes 'over the top'. Yet the inclusiveness of Branagh's approach plus the generally high quality of its execution make it a fitting culmination for this survey of the play's production history to date.

Like his previous Shakespeare films (*Henry V* and *Much Ado about Nothing*) Branagh's *Hamlet* is thoroughly cinematic, with its 70mm sweep, rapid pace, numerous flashbacks, earth-splitting special effects, and extensive use of mood music. Yet in many ways it draws on theatrical resources: in the four-hour version, it is as faithful to the full text as a '*Hamlet* in its entirety' stage version. Its cast is a mix of screen and stage actors. Set in a nineteenth-century military court, it is a 'period' film, yet it is informed by a contemporary sensibility. For example, textual adviser Russell Jackson in his 'Film Diary' explains that Hamlet and Ophelia 'have been to bed together, because we want this relationship to be as serious as possible'.[261]

In an interview on its Website, Branagh describes the film's scope as extending from 'a personal, domestic story about a family and its problems to the epic dimension that reflects the effects of those problems on the nation'. Like most post-World War II directors of *Hamlet*, he gives particular emphasis to matters of state. His Laertes heads a full-scale rebellion and his Fortinbras (with less textual basis) conducts a massive invasion and coup. His Claudius is a skilled politician. Outwardly impressive and

261 Branagh, *Screenplay*, p. 177.

glamorously attractive, Claudius's court is revealed to be corrupt and over-ripe. What is rotten in the state of Denmark leads to 'the end of a dynasty'.[262] The film concludes with the monument to King Hamlet being torn down by Norwegian troops.

As in most twentieth-century productions, design is an integral inter-pretive element. Branagh's Elsinore is not only a setting, it is a milieu – or rather a set of milieus, for each locale within it is distinct. For instance, designer Tim Harvey explains on the Website that on the outside the Winter Palace (Blenheim) is majestic and its public rooms are 'light and airy'; yet a 'murky underside' is revealed in the 'darker and seedier look' behind closed doors. The Palace's glittering hall of mirrors is a place of deception and spying.

Branagh balances public with private concerns. His conception of the title-role has matured through successive stage incarnations. Where reviewers found his 1988 Prince a reckless, impetuous, headstrong, action-man, his 1992 Prince was upright and self-possessed, 'a sober young royal' (*Sunday Times*, 27 December 1992), who is 'aware of his duty and destiny, implacably opposed to the moral laxness of the time' (*Observer*, 20 December 1992). Branagh himself described the style of his 1988 portrayal as 'frenetic' (Website interview); by 1992 it struck me as more varied, inward, and nuanced, with a new authority in his address to the role and a purity in his line-delivery. Many of the 1992 qualities continue into the motion picture, but in it Branagh goes deeper into Hamlet's psyche. He seems desperate to seek out people he can trust. Branagh's acting is at its best when conveying Hamlet's feelings of betrayal by Rosencrantz and Guildenstern and Ophelia and the bitter-sweet satisfaction he feels in fleeting moments of fellow-feeling with Horatio, the players, the grave-digger, and (at the end) his mother.

Again Branagh's approach to Hamlet's characterization is inclusive. At first his princeliness is as pronounced as in 1992, when he was almost as gentlemanly as were his nineteenth-century predecessors.[263] But in the course of the film his characterization takes a modern turn and a new 'demonic' (p. 100), 'unromantic' (p. 145) Hamlet emerges. Accordingly, in his interview with the Ghost Branagh's own eyes eerily take on some of the infernal glow of Brian Blessed's blue eyes. (In places Branagh draws on traditions of the 'horror flick' as well as of the 'movie thriller' and the 'motion picture epic'.) Driven by 'bloodlust' (p. 95), the Prince carries out

---

262 Interview, US National Public Radio, January 1997.
263 Branagh, *Screenplay*, pp. 66, 71. Subsequent page references are all to the screenplay.

his revenge with a ferocity unmatched to date on screen or stage, spearing Claudius with a javelin throw of the poisoned sword, cutting the cord of a chandelier that then swings down on the King, hand-dabbing the poisoned wine in the King's mouth with each word of his final curse. Yet towards the end the Prince is said to become at once 'wiser, harder' (p. 156), ready both to kill and be killed. His new wisdom is effectively conveyed in the 'readiness is all' speech (5.2.196) as he accepts the inevitability of his own death, not without some weeping self-pity, and finds the 'Peace' he has been seeking (p. 162). After Hamlet's death his body is 'held high in the crucifix position' (p. 173). Perhaps it is symbolic that his final costume combines a white undershirt and gloves with black braces and trousers striped in red.

Branagh never loses sight of how the private concerns of the royals have a public aspect. In the 'To be or not to be' soliloquy, the Prince is not only looking at himself in a full-length mirror but also – like Macbeth pondering the assassination of Duncan (1.7) – thinking often of the King, who unbeknownst to Hamlet is watching behind a two-way mirror. Branagh's frequent use of interpolated flash cuts also has this dual, private/public aspect. They show Ophelia's intimate recollections of her love-making with Hamlet and can go so deep inside Hamlet's fantasy life that momentarily he seems actually to have stabbed Claudius while at prayer; we see blood spurt! At the other extreme, the interpolations take cues from the text that widen the context of the action, especially the legendary scenes of Priam's death recalled by the First Player's recitation.

Although Branagh is his own star, his film is by no means a one-man show. Like the best *Hamlet* directors in this century, he treats each of the characters as individuals and in collaboration with an unusually strong cast creates a richly varied set of portraits. Of these the Claudius of Derek Jacobi stands out – without at all calling undue attention to itself – as one of the best in this century. Capitalizing on his volatility as an actor, Jacobi presents Claudius as a complex, self-divided, all-too-human creature, whose ambition to take and hold his crown and his queen is all-compelling. He is not without the milk of human kindness, however. To be sure, he does not have so much of it as to keep him from murdering his brother, but he does have enough to make him, like Macbeth, look with horror on what he has done, both at the time – in a flashback – and thereafter. More companionable to Gertrude than his burly and warlike older brother, he is shown by interpolated shots to be a fun-loving and attentive wooer and a convivial and lusty mate for the vivacious Queen. As a ruler he is decisive and adroit.

Far from being a conventional 'villain', Jacobi's Claudius follows the lifelike kind of zig-zag trajectory that characterizes Shakespeare's tragic heroes. His most defining trait is the strength and resilience that until the very end drive him – whatever his fears and compunctions – to steel himself to meet the successive crises that confront him and take whatever measures are necessary to prevail in them, measures that carry him further and further towards perdition. His characteristic response to the threats that Hamlet presents is one of intense fear followed by mounting anger.

At moments of maximum stress, Jacobi's Claudius can display extraordinary sang froid. Yet he also has a more vulnerable side. No sooner has his growing hatred of Hamlet risen to a ringing 'Do it, England' (4.3.61b) than – in a brilliant transition – he is appalled by his own murderous resolve to take the Prince's life, just as he had been when he killed the King. And he is shattered by his wife's final rejection. Like Macbeth he is finally undone by repercussions from the very acts that for a time allowed him to realize his ambitions.

Like Olivier's film at mid-century, Branagh's film has brought together in a coherent style many of the ways *Hamlet* is understood at the end of the twentieth century. If it has not achieved the 'classic' status that was immediately accorded Olivier's version, definitiveness was not Branagh's aim – indeed he has doubted that a definitive *Hamlet* is achievable (*Boston Globe*, 31 January 1997). In that way too he is of his time.

Hamlet
Prince of Denmark

LIST OF CHARACTERS

HAMLET, *Prince of Denmark*
CLAUDIUS, *King of Denmark, Hamlet's uncle*
GERTRUDE, *Queen of Denmark, Hamlet's mother*
GHOST *of Hamlet's father, the former King of Denmark*
POLONIUS, *counsellor to the king*
LAERTES, *his son*
OPHELIA, *his daughter*
REYNALDO, *his servant*
HORATIO, *Hamlet's friend and fellow-student*
MARCELLUS ⎫
BARNARDO ⎬ *officers of the watch*
FRANCISCO ⎭
VOLTEMAND ⎫ *ambassadors to Norway*
CORNELIUS ⎭
ROSENCRANTZ ⎫ *former schoolfellows of Hamlet*
GUILDENSTERN ⎭
FORTINBRAS, *Prince of Norway*
CAPTAIN *in the Norwegian army*
First PLAYER
Other PLAYERS
OSRIC ⎫
LORD ⎬ *courtiers*
GENTLEMAN ⎭
First CLOWN, *a gravedigger and sexton*
Second CLOWN, *his assistant*
SAILOR
MESSENGER
PRIEST
English AMBASSADOR
LORDS, ATTENDANTS, SAILORS, SOLDIERS, GUARDS

SCENE: *The Danish royal palace at Elsinore*

HAMLET
PRINCE OF DENMARK

1.1 Enter BARNARDO *and* FRANCISCO, *two sentinels*

BARNARDO Who's there?
FRANCISCO Nay answer me. Stand and unfold yourself.
BARNARDO Long live the king!
FRANCISCO Barnardo?
BARNARDO He.   5
FRANCISCO You come most carefully upon your hour.
BARNARDO 'Tis now struck twelve, get thee to bed Francisco.
FRANCISCO For this relief much thanks, 'tis bitter cold
        And I am sick at heart.
BARNARDO Have you had quiet guard?
FRANCISCO   Not a mouse stirring.   10

1.1   This entire scene has sometimes been cut in performance; the missing exposition is supplied by Horatio's account of the visitation in 1.2.

OSD   Often the midnight bell sounds. Tyrone Guthrie directed Francisco to patrol the perimeter of the Minneapolis thrust stage: 'This indicates the shape of the battlements. Look down; that tells a story too' (Rossi, p. 6).

1   Irving 'wanted the first voice to ring out like a pistol shot' (Terry, p. 132). Martin-Harvey thought that Barnardo (usually Bernardo in performance), arriving for guard duty, challenged the sentinel rather than the other way around because he anxiously mistook him for the Ghost (*Autobiography*, p. 299).

2   Wilson Barrett's Francisco corrected Barnardo's error by stressing *me* (*Shakespeariana*, p. 29), Burton's 1964 Francisco, by stressing *self* as well.

4   In Maurice Evans's *G. I. Hamlet* (1944/5) Francisco was unable to recognize Barnardo in the dim light; hence his question.

8   For the 1964 Burton production, Gielgud directed the actors to project the sense of being in the dark, the cold, and the open air (Sterne, p. 24).

9   Lark Taylor, with Barrymore, paused fearfully before saying 'quiet guard' (promptbook 156). To Martin-Harvey, Barnardo is seeking to find out if Francisco has seen the Ghost, whose appearance he and Marcellus have imparted 'in dreadful secrecy' only to Horatio.

BARNARDO Well, good night.
> If you do meet Horatio and Marcellus,
> The rivals of my watch, bid them make haste.
FRANCISCO I think I hear them.

Enter HORATIO *and* MARCELLUS

>   Stand ho! Who is there?
HORATIO Friends to this ground.
MARCELLUS   And liegemen to the Dane.   15
FRANCISCO Give you good night.
MARCELLUS   Oh farewell honest soldier,
> Who hath relieved you?
FRANCISCO   Barnardo hath my place.
> Give you good night.   *Exit Francisco*
MARCELLUS   Holla, Barnardo!
BARNARDO   Say,
> What, is Horatio there?
HORATIO   A piece of him.
BARNARDO Welcome Horatio, welcome good Marcellus.   20
MARCELLUS What, has this thing appeared again tonight?
BARNARDO I have seen nothing.
MARCELLUS Horatio says 'tis but our fantasy,
> And will not let belief take hold of him
> Touching this dreaded sight, twice seen of us.   25
> Therefore I have entreated him along
> With us to watch the minutes of this night,
> That if again this apparition come
> He may approve our eyes, and speak to it.
HORATIO Tush, tush, 'twill not appear.
BARNARDO   Sit down awhile,   30
> And let us once again assail your ears,

---

20 In his studybook Irving wrote 'all shake hands.' To Martin-Harvey it is Barnardo's relief at
not having to encounter the Ghost by himself that prompts Marcellus's next line.

21 In Q2 this speech is assigned to Horatio; 'thing' could go along with his initial scepticism. In
his studybook Booth expresses this thought and calls the tone of the line 'contemptuous', yet
Shattuck believes he always had Marcellus speak it (p. 118). 'Thing' need not carry that tone.
During rehearsals for his 1963 production, Tyrone Guthrie suggested to the men on watch
that they be reluctant to say 'ghost' and thus 'substitute' the other names they use for it –
thing, illusion, image, apparition, spirit, object – creating 'a very slight pause before each of
these substitute references, thereby projecting the characters' fear' (Rossi, p. 7).

> That are so fortified against our story,
> What we two nights have seen.
> HORATIO   Well, sit we down,
> And let us hear Barnardo speak of this.
> BARNARDO Last night of all,   35
> When yond same star that's westward from the pole
> Had made his course t'illume that part of heaven
> Where now it burns, Marcellus and myself,
> The bell then beating one –

Enter GHOST

33B   'Laughingly' (Barrymore promptbook 156).

35–39   Gielgud directed Burton's 1964 Barnardo: 'Each phrase must top the preceding one, as in a
musical crescendo ... Then at that point we hear the bell. *Dong*! And when you hear that
bell you're terrified that the Ghost may come again – and it does ...' (Sterne, p. 24).

39SD   From the first, 'special effects' have been lavished on the appearances and disappearances
of the Ghost. In Shakespeare's time, a trapdoor may well have been used for his descent
into the 'cellarage' (1.5.151). Also Lawrence argued that the Ghost's entrances in the first
scene were through a trap (*Studies*, pp. 105–7). Certainly, in eighteenth-century practice a
trap was used for entrances as well as exits. In *Humphry Clinker* (1771), for example, Mrs
Tabitha Bramble presumes to compliment Quin on his performance 'at Drury Lane, when
you rose up through the stage, with a white face and red eyes'.

   Various spectral lighting devices have been employed. At Shakespeare's Globe with its
natural light, the silent Ghost's power at its first appearance may have come chiefly through
the reactions of the guards and especially by the conversion of Horatio, whose scepticism is
immediately changed to belief. Their faces would have been fully visible, whereas in modern
productions all is often dark and obscure. Harcourt Williams, director of the 1930 Gielgud,
situated the guards around a brazier whose light revealed their faces while the Ghost
remained in the shadows (*Years*, p. 155). With Nicol Williamson the Ghost's presence was
signalled by an intense white light. In the Gielgud/Burton production (1964), the Ghost was
'a great black shadow which suddenly took shape above the stage' (Gielgud, *Acting*, p. 41).
In the 1965 Royal Shakespeare production the Ghost was represented by a ten-foot high
contrivance on wheels, with a large head and movable arms, swathed in a long gown; all but
obscured by shadows and smoke, it seemed to glide, noiselessly, of its own volition. Director
Peter Hall has since thought better of it; he recently spoke of the device to Michael
Pennington – who pushed and steered the mechanism – as a 'folly of his youth'
(*Independent*, 2 November 1994). Yet at the time L. C. Knights compared it to an 'archaic
presence'. In the Kenneth Branagh film, the Ghost took the form of a statue of King Hamlet
that comes to life, gratingly rips his sword from its scabbard and swoops down on the
terrified guards.

MARCELLUS Peace, break thee off. Look where it comes again. 40
BARNARDO In the same figure, like the king that's dead.
MARCELLUS Thou art a scholar, speak to it Horatio.
BARNARDO Looks a not like the king? Mark it Horatio.
HORATIO Most like. It harrows me with fear and wonder.
BARNARDO It would be spoke to.
MARCELLUS   Question it Horatio. 45
HORATIO What art thou that usurp'st this time of night,
          Together with that fair and warlike form
          In which the majesty of buried Denmark
          Did sometimes march? By heaven I charge thee speak.
MARCELLUS It is offended.
BARNARDO   See, it stalks away. 50
HORATIO Stay! Speak, speak, I charge thee speak!

Exit Ghost

MARCELLUS 'Tis gone and will not answer.
BARNARDO How now Horatio? you tremble and look pale.
          Is not this something more than fantasy?
          What think you on't? 55
HORATIO Before my God, I might not this believe
          Without the sensible and true avouch
          Of mine own eyes.

In addition to spooky music, special sound effects have also been deployed. Davies speaks of Barton Booth's 'noiseless tread, as if he had been composed of air' (p. 32), an effect created simply by wearing felt soles. In Olivier's film, an amplified heart-beat signalled the manifestation, an effect he took from Barrault's use of drum-beats.

40–50 With Booth all the speakers emphasized 'speak' or 'spoke' each of the seven times it recurs (promptbook 112). Irving's studybook directs the actors to 'whisper'.

44 With Burton, Gielgud advised Horatio: 'when you see the Ghost, you must be galvanized. *Your* reaction is the most important, because the others have seen it before (Sterne, p. 30).

52SD Gauzes have been artfully employed to simulate the ghost's eery dematerialization. In Fechter's Lyceum production (1864) 'the ghost stood behind a large concealed wheel which, when started, caught up, at each revolution, a fresh piece of some almost transparent stuff, artfully tinted to match the background, until the requisite thickness was obtained. The ghost apparently melted into thin air' (*New York Evening Post Magazine*, 20 December 1919).

Gordon Craig saw the Ghost as offended and frightened, his clothing trembling before quickly vanishing, leaving a slowly fading after-glow (done by lighting). No sooner has the glow disappeared than on successive lines (50–1) a stand-in Ghost appears and disappears at another place and then a second stand-in does the same (Senelick, p. 54–5).

MARCELLUS Is it not like the king?
HORATIO As thou art to thyself.

    Such was the very armour he had on   60
    When he th'ambitious Norway combated;
    So frowned he once, when in an angry parle
    He smote the sledded Polacks on the ice.
    'Tis strange.

MARCELLUS Thus twice before, and jump at this dead hour,   65
    With martial stalk hath he gone by our watch.

HORATIO In what particular thought to work I know not,
    But in the gross and scope of mine opinion
    This bodes some strange eruption to our state.

MARCELLUS Good now sit down, and tell me he that knows,   70
    Why this same strict and most observant watch
    So nightly toils the subject of the land,
    And why such daily cast of brazen cannon,
    And foreign mart for implements of war,
    Why such impress of shipwrights, whose sore task   75
    Does not divide the Sunday from the week.
    What might be toward, that this sweaty haste
    Doth make the night joint-labourer with the day?
    Who is't that can inform me?

HORATIO   That can I –
    At least the whisper goes so. Our last king,   80
    Whose image even but now appeared to us,
    Was as you know by Fortinbras of Norway,
    Thereto pricked on by a most emulate pride,
    Dared to the combat; in which our valiant Hamlet –
    For so this side of our known world esteemed him –   85
    Did slay this Fortinbras; who by a sealed compact,
    Well ratified by law and heraldy,
    Did forfeit (with his life) all those his lands
    Which he stood seized of, to the conqueror;
    Against the which a moiety competent   90
    Was gagèd by our king, which had returned
    To the inheritance of Fortinbras
    Had he been vanquisher; as by the same comart

79–125 Lines 108–25 do not appear in Q1 or F. Gielgud observed that the trimming of this speech
        (which has been customary from Betterton's time) makes 'the second entrance of the Ghost
        far too quick upon the first, which does not therefore take the audience by surprise' (Gilder,
        p. 36). Nevertheless, for the Burton production Gielgud himself cut all but 14 lines. Lines
        80–107 were regularly cut as part of the general excision of Fortinbras.

And carriage of the article design,
His fell to Hamlet. Now sir, young Fortinbras,   95
Of unimprovèd mettle hot and full,
Hath in the skirts of Norway here and there
Sharked up a list of landless resolutes
For food and diet to some enterprise
That hath a stomach in't; which is no other,   100
As it doth well appear unto our state,
But to recover of us by strong hand
And terms compulsatory those foresaid lands
So by his father lost. And this, I take it,
Is the main motive of our preparations,   105
The source of this our watch, and the chief head
Of this post-haste and romage in the land.
[BARNARDO I think it be no other but e'en so.
Well may it sort that this portentous figure
Comes armèd through our watch so like the king   110
That was and is the question of these wars.
HORATIO A mote it is to trouble the mind's eye.
In the most high and palmy state of Rome,
A little ere the mightiest Julius fell,
The graves stood tenantless and the sheeted dead   115
Did squeak and gibber in the Roman streets;
As stars with trains of fire, and dews of blood,
Disasters in the sun; and the moist star,
Upon whose influence Neptune's empire stands,
Was sick almost to doomsday with eclipse.   120
And even the like precurse of feared events,
As harbingers preceding still the fates
And prologue to the omen coming on,
Have heaven and earth together demonstrated
Unto our climatures and countrymen.]   125

Enter GHOST

But soft, behold, lo where it comes again!
I'll cross it though it blast me. Stay, illusion.
It spreads his arms
If thou hast any sound or use of voice,

127 'In pre-Fechterian days Horatios senselessly *crossed the Ghost's path*, as if such a step
would stay its progress. Not so with Fechter, whose Horatio made the sign of the cross, at
which the Ghost stopped as a Catholic ghost should' (Field, p. 98).

        Speak to me.
        If there be any good thing to be done   130
        That may to thee do ease, and grace to me,
        Speak to me.
        If thou art privy to thy country's fate,
        Which happily foreknowing may avoid,
        Oh speak.   135
        Or if thou hast uphoarded in thy life
        Extorted treasure in the womb of earth,
        For which they say you spirits oft walk in death,   *The cock crows*
        Speak of it. Stay and speak! Stop it Marcellus.
MARCELLUS Shall I strike at it with my partisan?   140
HORATIO Do if it will not stand.
BARNARDO   'Tis here.
HORATIO   'Tis here.
MARCELLUS 'Tis gone.

                           Exit Ghost

        We do it wrong being so majestical
        To offer it the show of violence,
        For it is as the air invulnerable,   145
        And our vain blows malicious mockery.
BARNARDO It was about to speak when the cock crew.
HORATIO And then it started like a guilty thing
        Upon a fearful summons. I have heard,
        The cock, that is the trumpet to the morn,   150
        Doth with his lofty and shrill-sounding throat
        Awake the god of day; and at his warning,
        Whether in sea or fire, in earth or air,
        Th'extravagant and erring spirit hies
        To his confine. And of the truth herein   155
        This present object made probation.
MARCELLUS It faded on the crowing of the cock.
        Some say that ever 'gainst that season comes
        Wherein our Saviour's birth is celebrated,
        This bird of dawning singeth all night long,   160

129ff   The silent beats after Horatio's half-line exhortations in Q2 at 132 and 135 suggest an
        expectant pause. In F's lineation the exhortations are extra-metrical.

141–2a   In the latter part of the nineteenth century multiple ghosts were sometimes used by Irving
        and others to justify the watchers' cries of 'Tis here! Tis here! Tis gone!'

142–4   With Craig, after the Ghost's disappearance, a long pause. The three mortals are at first
        nonplussed ('they think they've suffered a stroke'), then cling together.(Senelick, p. 60).

152b–5a With Burton, Horatio looks to where the spirit has disappeared (Sterne, p. 146).

And then, they say, no spirit dare stir abroad,
The nights are wholesome, then no planets strike,
No fairy takes, nor witch hath power to charm,
So hallowed and so gracious is that time.
HORATIO So have I heard, and do in part believe it.   165
But look, the morn in russet mantle clad
Walks o'er the dew of yon high eastward hill.
Break we our watch up, and by my advice
Let us impart what we have seen tonight
Unto young Hamlet, for upon my life   170
This spirit, dumb to us, will speak to him.
Do you consent we shall acquaint him with it,
As needful in our loves, fitting our duty?
MARCELLUS Let's do't I pray, and I this morning know
Where we shall find him most conveniently.   175

Exeunt

166ff Gielgud comments on the 1929 Alexander Moissi production: Horatio's 'relief and its effect
       upon the other actors made one feel as if a great curtain of darkness which had hung over
       them during a long sleepless night had rolled away at last to let in the fresh air of a cold
       morning and another day' (Gilder, p. 35).
170   On the Caedmon recording Horatio stresses *young* to distinguish the Prince from 'old'
       Hamlet, the former King.
175SD Before they leave the stage Marcellus and Barnardo 'turn, look towards where the Ghost has
       gone off' (Irving promptbook).

1.2 *Flourish. Enter* CLAUDIUS *King of Denmark,* GERTRUDE *the Queen,* HAMLET, POLONIUS, LAERTES, OPHELIA, [VOLTEMAND, CORNE-LIUS,] LORDS *attendant*

CLAUDIUS Though yet of Hamlet our dear brother's death
  The memory be green, and that it us befitted
  To bear our hearts in grief, and our whole kingdom

OSD Edwards conflates Q2 and F. Only Q1 specifically mentions 'the two Ambassadors'; in F they enter after 25. Only F mentions Ophelia. In Q1 and F Hamlet's name comes after the King and Queen; in Q2 his name comes last, perhaps indicating that he entered after the other principals. In all three stage directions, mention of supernumerary lords suggests a meeting of the full court, an effect readily accommodated on the large, platform stage of the Globe, which could then rapidly clear, leaving Hamlet alone for his soliloquy (129ff). Since the thrust-style stage projected into the centre of the theatre, the contrast of public speech followed by private self-revelation could be sharp and immediate.

Subsequent productions have conceived the occasion in very different ways. With Wilson Barrett (1884), the curtain went up on a hall of the tenth and early eleventh centuries full of people shouting 'Long live the King!' and when Hamlet entered 'Long live the Prince!' (Jackson, 'Designer', p. 192). Craig saw the court as a place of pretence: 'in this golden court, this world of show' individualities have melted into a 'single mass': 'Separate faces as in the old masters of painting must be colored with one brush, with one paint'. Accordingly the courtiers, in their golden caps and mantles, were all made up with 'a deathlike pallor'. Craig wished that 'the voices of the courtiers should not sound too definite or sharp. They must be blended as much as possible into one general effect' (Senelick, pp. 64, 157, 68).

To convey the idea of a '*very* LECHEROUS Court' Barrymore instructed the London cast in whispering that grew 'more and more frenzied as the curtain and then the lights went up': it was only after many repeats that 'Finally, lechery triumphed' (Webster, *The Same*, pp. 300–1). Gielgud adds that Barrymore's 'court was discovered lolling in amorous groups' (Gilder, p. 37), thus contrasting with his seated and silently brooding Prince.

The 1930 Gielgud production, directed by Harcourt Williams, 'had the Queen and her ladies sewing and the King entering in cloak and gloves, as if from hunting' (Gilder, p. 37). The 1936 Gielgud production, directed by Guthrie McClintic, placed the scene in a council chamber, with the court leaving the stage at 63: 'the scene thus became a domestic argument between the three principal characters'; questioning this arrangement, Gielgud comments: 'the formality of address used by Hamlet and the flowery tone, half rebuking, half avuncular, of Claudius's speeches have greater point and effect when uttered for the benefit of his admiring and sycophantic courtiers' (Gilder, p. 38).

In 1963 Guthrie at Minneapolis treated the scene as a wedding reception, with bells ringing and Gertrude (Jessica Tandy) in her wedding gown. The Branagh film did the same. The Gibson/Zeffirelli film started the episode with a brief full-court address by the King; it then broke the scene into a series of private interviews of the King with Laertes and Polonius, of the King with Hamlet and the Queen, and finally of the Queen alone with Hamlet.

Hamlet's costume: clearly Burbage wore black. Ophelia's description at 2.1.76–9 confirms that, as was the general custom, he wore the clothing of his own time, as distinguished from 'period costume' of medieval Denmark. In that sense he was the first Hamlet to wear 'modern dress', a practice which was to continue for the next two centuries. After the Restoration illustrators seem to be reflecting stage practice in picturing Hamlet as wearing contemporary attire, and we know that Betterton wore a neckcloth because, by a contemporary account, when he saw the Ghost his ordinarily ruddy face turned 'as pale as his neckcloath' (Anon., *Laureat*, 1740, p. 31). Until the latter part of the eighteenth century, Hamlet's costume continued to be that of 'a modern gentleman in a black suit such as might be seen any day in the Mall' – as John Doran described Charles Macklin (*Annals*, II, p. 421). Accordingly, Garrick changed Hamlet's reference to his 'inky cloak' to 'mourning suit'. Controversially, however, Garrick modified conventional style by following the elegant fashion of the French court (Lichtenberg, *Visits*, p. 21). Other parts of his costume were essential to the effect of his famous 'start' at first seeing the ghost: his hat, to be knocked off with a 'grace and elegance' that successors could only aspire to (Sprague, *Actors*, p. 139), and his wig, whose hairs may well have been wired to stand on end (Roach, 'Ghost').

The next phase in Hamlet costuming was inaugurated by Kemble in the early 1780s. Just as he replaced modernized vocabulary with original readings (restoring 'inky cloak', for example), he was the first of the latter-day Hamlets to wear garb suggestive of Shakespeare's own period, variously referred to as 'Vandyke' or 'Old English' or 'stage Elizabethan'. His basic costume of doublet and short, stuffed breeches with tights, plus a prominent medallion of his father, predominated for the next fifty years. His regalia also included garters, a blue ribbon symbolizing the order of the Elephant, and a baldrick; in the graveyard, as in Thomas Lawrence's famous portrait, he wore a cloak and sable-plumed hat (Pentzell, 'Costume', pp. 81–5). Such trappings were modified by leading Hamlets who followed this style, such as Young and Kean. Dickens satirized it in the garb of Mr. Wopsle, the would-be tragedian in *Great Expectations* (chs. 27 and 31), with his obligatory hat, feathers, ribbon, star, cloak, stocking 'disordered' by a very neat and ironed fold in the top and white napkin (to dust his fingers after handling Yorick's skull).

The third phase accompanied the archeological style of decor and simulated medieval Denmark. In 1838 Charles Kean was the first Hamlet to wear a tunic with hose, soon followed by Macready and most other Hamlets until the mid-1920s. There were of course individual variations. Booth made conspicuous use of the cross-gartering characteristic of the early period, Wilson Barrett was notorious for his plunging neckline, Irving modified the medieval look of the tunic with Renaissance touches, including a jewelled sword-belt and a furred open jacket indoors or a furred cloak outdoors. He drew ridicule by affecting a plumed hat à la Kemble.

The fourth phase has been self-consciously eclectic. There have been a number of 'modern dress' productions. Colin Keith-Johnston not only wore 'plus fours' in the last act of the Birmingham Repertory production of 1925 but had earlier worn Oxford bags and a dinner jacket. Usually Hamlet wears two costumes at most, but in 1938 Alec Guinness was dressed variously as 'a sort of Salvation Army bandmaster, as an undergraduate at Keble, as a lean intellectual in a lounge-suit. In the play scene he is a Guards' officer, and eventually he comes to handle Yorick's skull in the impertinent jersey and jack boots of a fisherman' (*Manchester Guardian*, 12 October). Many twentieth-century Hamlets have worn garb of the Early Modern period, whether on the model of Durer (as with the puffed sleeves, short surcoat, and slashed tights that Gyles Isham wore in the influential 1924 Oxford University Dramatic Society production) or of Van Dyke (as in Gielgud's 1936 costume in New York). More recent Hamlets have worn the clothing of later periods. In 1966, wearing his Regency costume, Richard Pasco was very much the Romantic poet cast upon the thorns of life. In 1948 Paul Scofield wore an early Victorian frock coat, narrow strapped trousers, and fly-away tie that set Kenneth Tynan thinking of Matthew Arnold and his Scholar Gipsy (*He that Plays*, p. 111). In 1992 Kenneth Branagh's formal, upright Prince wore an Edwardian uniform, with a black armband, before being confined in a straitjacket. In 1964 Burton wore contemporary street-clothes – slacks and a V-necked shirt – as if in rehearsal (Russell, 'Costumes'; plus Mander and Mitchenson, 'Correction').

In ways besides their costumes Hamlets have set themselves apart from the others. Rawboned Edwin Forrest was uncharacteristically subtle: he was first 'seen in the rear, as if avoiding notice' in his melancholy (Alger, *Forrest*, 1, p. 751). With Irving, at the end of the opening procession 'came the solitary figure of Hamlet' (Terry, p. 104), who then sat while the others stood, not apart but 'in the midst, in semi-distraction, not obtrusive yet unmistakably the hero of the play' (Russell, p. 22). Paul Scofield, directed by Peter Brook, stood 'alone, framed for a moment in the entrance before the full court appears – the troubled soul of Denmark living, still to be summoned by the majesty of Denmark dead' (*Illustrated London News*, 17 December 1955).

1ff   With Jacobi on BBC-TV, Patrick Stewart was at first all smiles, a gracious and able administrator, considerate husband, concerned stepfather. At the other extreme Craig

To be contracted in one brow of woe,
Yet so far hath discretion fought with nature   5
That we with wisest sorrow think on him,
Together with remembrance of ourselves.
Therefore our sometime sister, now our queen,
Th'imperial jointress to this warlike state,
Have we, as 'twere with a defeated joy,   10
With one auspicious and one dropping eye,

With mirth in funeral and with dirge in marriage,
In equal scale weighing delight and dole,
Taken to wife; nor have we herein barred
Your better wisdoms, which have freely gone   15
With this affair along – for all, our thanks.
Now follows that you know: young Fortinbras,
Holding a weak supposal of our worth,
Or thinking by our late dear brother's death
Our state to be disjoint and out of frame,   20
Colleaguèd with this dream of his advantage,
He hath not failed to pester us with message
Importing the surrender of those lands
Lost by his father, with all bands of law,
To our most valiant brother. So much for him.   25
Now for ourself and for this time of meeting
Thus much the business is: we have here writ
To Norway, uncle of young Fortinbras,
Who, impotent and bed-rid, scarcely hears
Of this his nephew's purpose, to suppress   30
His further gait herein, in that the levies,
The lists, and full proportions, are all made
Out of his subject; and we here dispatch
You, good Cornelius, and you, Voltemand,

wanted the Moscow Art Theatre's Claudius played as he seems to Hamlet, vulgar, false, rough, with a voice 'like falling chains' (Senelick, p. 64). When Macready gave a concert reading of the play, his Claudius was courteous, dignified, persuasive, although 'at moments a little oiliness of tone' raised suspicion (Pollock, *Macready*, p. 41).

8   In the Branagh film the King (Derek Jacobi) gently squeezes the Queen's hand, to which she (Julie Christie) responds with a wifely smile.

14   At Minneapolis Guthrie directed Lee Richardson to 'play the court for their open approval' with Polonius (Robert Pastene) cuing their responses. Here they applauded (Rossi, p. 8). In the Zeffirelli film Ian Holm's Polonius exercised the same kind of unspoken control.

16b   All bow to King (Booth promptbook 112).

29a   Pryce/Eyre: Michael Elphick chuckled (Gilbert, 'Pryce').

For bearers of this greeting to old Norway,   35
Giving to you no further personal power
To business with the king, more than the scope
Of these dilated articles allow.
Farewell, and let your haste commend your duty.
CORNELIUS ⎫ In that and all things will we show our duty.   40
VOLTEMAND ⎭
CLAUDIUS We doubt it nothing, heartily farewell.
                              Exeunt Voltemand and Cornelius
And now Laertes, what's the news with you?
You told us of some suit, what is't Laertes?
You cannot speak of reason to the Dane
And lose your voice. What wouldst thou beg Laertes,   45
That shall not be my offer, not thy asking?
The head is not more native to the heart,
The hand more instrumental to the mouth,
Than is the throne of Denmark to thy father.
What wouldst thou have Laertes?
LAERTES   My dread lord,   50
Your leave and favour to return to France,
From whence though willingly I came to Denmark
To show my duty in your coronation,
Yet now I must confess, that duty done,
My thoughts and wishes bend again toward France,   55
And bow them to your gracious leave and pardon.
CLAUDIUS Have you your father's leave? What says Polonius?
POLONIUS He hath my lord wrung from me my slow leave
By laboursome petition, and at last
Upon his will I sealed my hard consent.   60
I do beseech you give him leave to go.
CLAUDIUS Take thy fair hour Laertes, time be thine,
And thy best graces spend it at thy will.

42–9   Pryce/Eyre: Laertes 'seems too shy to speak' – hence the repeated questions addressed to
       him (Gilbert, 'Pryce'). The BBC-TV Laertes similarly needed prompting.
58–62 William Popple protests the farcing of Polonius by eighteenth-century actors: 'Here is the
       most simple, plain, unstudied, unaffected reply that could be given. Yet how is this spoke
       and acted? The eyes are turned obliquely and dressed up in a foolish leer at the King, the
       words intermittently drawled out with a very strong emphasis, not to express a father's
       concern, which would be right but something ridiculous to excite laughter . . . the voice ton'd
       like the squeak of a bag-pipe'; the emphasized words were "wearisome" (substituted for
       "laboursome") "wrung", "slow leave", and "hard". (*The Prompter*, No. 57, 27 May 1735).

But now my cousin Hamlet, and my son –
HAMLET (*Aside*) A little more than kin, and less than kind. 65
CLAUDIUS How is it that the clouds still hang on you?
HAMLET Not so my lord, I am too much i'th'sun.
GERTRUDE Good Hamlet cast thy nighted colour off,
      And let thine eye look like a friend on Denmark.
      Do not forever with thy vailèd lids 70
      Seek for thy noble father in the dust.
      Thou know'st 'tis common, all that lives must die,
      Passing through nature to eternity.
HAMLET Ay madam, it is common.
GERTRUDE   If it be,
      Why seems it so particular with thee? 75
HAMLET Seems madam? nay it is, I know not seems.
      'Tis not alone my inky cloak, good mother,
      Nor customary suits of solemn black,
      Nor windy suspiration of forced breath,
      No, nor the fruitful river in the eye, 80
      Nor the dejected haviour of the visage,
      Together with all forms, moods, shapes of grief,
      That can denote me truly. These indeed seem,
      For they are actions that a man might play,
      But I have that within which passes show – 85

64   When the King turns to Hamlet, the hostility between the two needs to be projected. At 'my son' Booth 'started slightly and moved away'; his 'scornful' reply was half-whispered (Calhoun, 'Booth', p. 78).

65–7   In 1803 Charles Kemble (John Philip's brother) avoided as 'unseemly' open sarcasm. These lines 'were thrown off with an air of courtly ease and respect' though with a 'touch of causticity' (Marston, *Actors*, pp. 113–14).

66   *You* (Irving's studybook).

67   'Bows a little too low to mean it' (Walter Hampden promptbook).

68–74   Francesca Annis with Ralph Fiennes played Gertrude as a 'majestically self-absorbed woman who does not like problems and gets impatient with anybody who has any'. Here her tone was 'edgy with weariness, almost with annoyance' (*Sunday Times*, 5 March 1995).

69b   Booth: By 'Denmark' Gertrude means Claudius, 'at which Hamlet shows contempt – not, however, to be seen by the court' (studybook).

74a   Gielgud asked Burton to suspend the end of the half-line, not only echoing Gertrude but as though having something more to say (Sterne, p. 73).

79b   Sothern (1906): 'King sighs – Hamlet glowers at King'. His reference to the King's 'windy suspiration' causes the 'surprise of court. King glowers at Hamlet' (promptbook).

84   Booth: 'Meaning his uncle; with a slight glance at him' (studybook).

These but the trappings and the suits of woe.
CLAUDIUS 'Tis sweet and commendable in your nature Hamlet,
  To give these mourning duties to your father;
  But you must know, your father lost a father,
  That father lost, lost his, and the survivor bound   90
  In filial obligation for some term
  To do obsequious sorrow; but to persever
  In obstinate condolement is a course
  Of impious stubbornness, 'tis unmanly grief,
  It shows a will most incorrect to heaven,   95
  A heart unfortified, a mind impatient,
  An understanding simple and unschooled.
  For what we know must be, and is as common
  As any the most vulgar thing to sense,
  Why should we in our peevish opposition   100
  Take it to heart? Fie, 'tis a fault to heaven,
  A fault against the dead, a fault to nature,
  To reason most absurd, whose common theme
  Is death of fathers, and who still hath cried,
  From the first corse till he that died today,   105
  'This must be so.' We pray you throw to earth
  This unprevailing woe, and think of us
  As of a father, for let the world take note
  You are the most immediate to our throne,
  And with no less nobility of love   110
  Than that which dearest father bears his son,
  Do I impart toward you. For your intent

---

86   In the Branagh film, the crowd whispers; here as at 67: 'They're witnessing a scene that
      should take place behind closed doors' (*Screenplay*, p. 15).

94   Irving: Hamlet 'looks at king' (studybook).

94b With Barrymore: 'Growing rather stern', so much so that at 'Tis unmanly grief' the Queen
      touches the King's hand: 'he starts and again becomes smiling' (promptbook 156).
      Pryce/Eyre: 'A dangerous hearty', Claudius clutches Hamlet's knees in an iron grip
      (*Manchester Guardian*, 3 April 1980).

97   Sothern: 'Hamlet rises indignantly' (promptbook).

106b–8a Evans: as the King's anger mounts, Gertrude places a restraining hand on his arm (*G. I.
          Hamlet*, p. 42).

107b Of Booth: 'Hamlet shows contempt at this, merely by the curl of the lip' (studybook). At 108a
      he 'starts and looks at the King, expressing repugnance with his eyes' (Shattuck, pp. 126–7).

112a Evans: at the King's attempt to place a paternal hand on Hamlet's shoulder, the Prince
      moves away; the King represses his anger (*G. I. Hamlet*, p. 42).

In going back to school in Wittenberg,
It is most retrograde to our desire,
And we beseech you bend you to remain   115
Here in the cheer and comfort of our eye,
Our chiefest courtier, cousin, and our son.
GERTRUDE Let not thy mother lose her prayers Hamlet.
I pray thee stay with us, go not to Wittenberg.
HAMLET I shall in all my best obey you madam.   120
CLAUDIUS Why, 'tis a loving and a fair reply.
Be as ourself in Denmark. Madam, come.
This gentle and unforced accord of Hamlet
Sits smiling to my heart, in grace whereof,
No jocund health that Denmark drinks today   125
But the great cannon to the clouds shall tell,
And the king's rouse the heaven shall bruit again,
Re-speaking earthly thunder. Come away.

Flourish. Exeunt all but Hamlet

113   Playing Claudius to Stacy Keach's Hamlet, James Earl Jones, 'bubbling with some roguish
       interior humour' (*Time*, 10 July 1972), made 'a dirty, three-syllable mocking sound of Witt-
       en-berg' (*New York Post*, 30 June 1972).

117   With Macready 'the court salute Hamlet' (promptbook 29).

117b   Fechter 'started' at '*our* son' (Field, p. 98). Booth bowed 'constrainedly' at this (studybook);
       only 'the spasmodic closing' of his hands revealed his inward passion (Calhoun, 'Booth', p.
       78). Evans: Claudius appeals mutely for Gertrude's support (*G. I. Hamlet*, p.43).

118   In a concert reading Fanny Kemble emphasized *her* (Terry, p. 137). In Burton/Gielgud,
       Gertrude (Eileen Herlie) touches Hamlet's cheek; he turns his head away, she withdraws her
       hand, hurt.

120   Fechter accented '*you*, Madam' (Field, p. 98); Barrett did not (*Shakespeariana*, p. 31). When
       Warner (1965) emphasized *you* the audience 'hummed' at his impertinence' (Maher,
       Soliloquies, p. 53). Kingsley (1975) delivered this line 'with so dry an irony that the King's
       hasty "Why, 'tis a loving and a fair reply" became a comically transparent demonstration of
       Claudius' uneasiness in the face of Hamlet's opposition' (David, *Theatre*, p. 70).

128   In the Olivier film, Basil Sydney as King interrupted Herlie's prolonged parting kiss with her
       son with an annoyed 'Come away'.

128SD With Macready as the lords and ladies exited, two by two, they each saluted the prince
       (promptbook 29). Fechter's Hamlet was lost in meditation, accidentally blocking the
       withdrawing procession. Suddenly realizing this, he as a 'well-bred Danish gentleman' with
       a smile and a bow invited the ladies and gentlemen to pass before him (Beckett,
       Recollections, p. 23). As Craig envisaged the transition, 'the whole court fades away and
       becomes lost in a sort of warm darkness' (Senelick, p. 70); as Stanislavsky staged it, a light

HAMLET O that this too too solid flesh would melt,
    Thaw and resolve itself into a dew,   130
    Or that the Everlasting had not fixed
    His canon 'gainst self-slaughter. O God, God,
    How weary, stale, flat and unprofitable
    Seem to me all the uses of this world!
    Fie on't, ah fie, 'tis an unweeded garden   135
    That grows to seed, things rank and gross in nature
    Possess it merely. That it should come to this!
    But two months dead – nay not so much, not two –
    So excellent a king, that was to this
    Hyperion to a satyr, so loving to my mother   140

   black curtain 'came down like quietly falling fog' (Osanai, 'Craig's production', p. 590). It concealed all but Hamlet, who seemed to be awakening from a nightmare.

129–58 Using voice-over in his film, Kozintsev shot the first soliloquy 'in a crush of courtiers, amid the noise of a court reception' because Hamlet's genuine tragedy lies 'in solitude in a crowd' (*Shakespeare*, p. 258).

   Jacobi finds two opposing forces: 'There is the man who cannot hold it in any longer, and it comes bubbling, bubbling, bubbling out. The other force is – "I must hold my tongue – let me not think on't" . . . So that accounts for the structure of broken sentences and incomplete thoughts.' (Maher, *Soliloquies*, p. 101).

129 Mounet Sully, who saw Hamlet as longing to return to nothingness, 'sat for a long time, silent and still, eyes closed as if in sleep, his mouth partly open, before beginning'. He touched 'his arms and body at "flesh"' (*Shakespeare Survey*, 9, 1956, p. 64). 'Kemble lingers for some seconds on the "Oh!" with a strongly tremulous cadence' (T. Martin, 'Eye-Witness', p. 284). With Pryce: 'a sigh escapes his lips and that sound becomes the "Oh"' (Gilbert, 'Pryce'). Irving 'breathed' this line 'as one long yearning' (Terry, p. 106). Richard Risso at Ashland, Oregon in 1961, emphasized *sh* in 'flesh' with revulsion; he explained: 'as flesh of her flesh, my loathing for Gertrude's behavior was directed as much against myself' (Rosenberg, p. 686).

133 Gielgud advised Burton 'to find each of these words out of the other' (Sterne, p. 66).

137 Off-stage laughter prompted Barrett to look in the direction the King and Queen had gone (Phelps, p. 71).

139 Of Garrick, the last of 'So excellent a King,' was inaudible: 'one catches it only from the movement of the mouth, which quivers and shuts tight immediately afterwards', restraining unmanly grief (Lichtenberg, *Visits*, p. 15). At 'this' Booth pointed to where Claudius had exited (promptbook 111).

140–2 When Kean recalled his father's tenderness, 'reproach, sorrow, and indignation spoke together' (*Literary Gazette*, 1 March 1817). Fechter gazed fondly at the miniature of his father he wore around his neck (Cook, *Hours*, p. 262).

That he might not beteem the winds of heaven
Visit her face too roughly – heaven and earth,
Must I remember? why, she would hang on him
As if increase of appetite had grown
By what it fed on, and yet within a month –   145
Let me not think on't; frailty, thy name is woman –
A little month, or ere those shoes were old
With which she followed my poor father's body
Like Niobe, all tears, why she, even she –
O God, a beast that wants discourse of reason   150
Would have mourned longer – married with my uncle,
My father's brother, but no more like my father
Than I to Hercules – within a month,
Ere yet the salt of most unrighteous tears
Had left the flushing in her gallèd eyes,   155
She married. Oh most wicked speed, to post
With such dexterity to incestuous sheets.
It is not, nor it cannot come to good.
But break, my heart, for I must hold my tongue.

Enter HORATIO, MARCELLUS *and* BARNARDO

HORATIO Hail to your lordship.
HAMLET   I am glad to see you well.   160
Horatio – or I do forget myself.
HORATIO The same, my lord, and your poor servant ever.
HAMLET Sir, my good friend, I'll change that name with you.

140–3   Kemble delivered 140b–2a 'in a very low tone (*sotto voce*)', 142b–3a 'with a vehement burst
of indignation and grief' (Austin, *Chironomia*, p. 79).

143   On the Decca (1951) recording Gielgud emphasized *him*, to distinguish his father from his
uncle.

144   Garrick emphasized *grown* (Vickers, *Critical Heritage*, IV, p. 425).

151b   Gielgud's face 'curdled' with distaste (Gilder, p. 95).

152   J. B. Booth paused after 'married with my uncle', then spoke 'my father's brother' in low and
slighting tones (Gould, p. 53).

153a   Looking for a comparison, Irving paused before saying 'Hercules' (*Standard*, 31 December
1878) as did Rylance, whose stature is less than Herculean, ruefully 'making us see the joke'
(Gilbert, 'Rylance').

156–7   Gielgud spat these lines out (Gilder, p. 95). Risso hissed them, emphasizing the sibilants.

159a   Booth: All bow (promptbook 112).

163   Kemble's reading emphasized FRIEND and *that*; Dr Johnson advocated stressing FRIEND
and *change*. They seem to have understood 'change' to mean 'exchange'. Henderson

And what make you from Wittenberg, Horatio?
Marcellus. 165
MARCELLUS My good lord.
HAMLET I am very glad to see you. (*To Barnardo*) Good even sir.
But what in faith make you from Wittenberg.
HORATIO A truant disposition, good my lord.
HAMLET I would not hear your enemy say so, 170
Nor shall you do my ear that violence
To make it truster of your own report
Against yourself. I know you are no truant.
But what is your affair in Elsinore?
We'll teach you to drink deep ere you depart. 175
HORATIO My lord, I came to see your father's funeral.
HAMLET I pray thee do not mock me fellow student,
I think it was to see my mother's wedding.
HORATIO Indeed my lord, it followed hard upon.

HAMLET Thrift, thrift, Horatio. The funeral baked meats 180
Did coldly furnish forth the marriage tables.
Would I had met my dearest foe in heaven
Or ever I had seen that day, Horatio.
My father, methinks I see my father –

evidently understood it to mean 'Change the term servant into that of friend', for he
emphasized *that* and YOU (Boaden, p. 94).

163–7 Fechter's three greetings were given 'three distinct shades of tone' (Field, p. 98). Irving 'lets
you see that in his mind there is some sense of the difference in rank as well as the more
obvious difference in intimacy, in the very pronunciation of the two names, "Horatio" –
"Marcellus"' (*Academy*, 7 November 1874, p. 519).

165–7 In the Branagh film, he greeted Marcellus warmly and with a handshake (*Screenplay*, p. 18).
Kemble addressed 'Good even, sir' to Barnardo. This was thought a novelty (Boaden, p. 95).
Booth addressed it to Barnardo 'as to a stranger' (studybook).

175 Kemble insinuated the King's intemperance, accentuating DRINK *deep* (Boaden, p. 95). With
Tree a 'laugh off' is heard (promptbook). But Booth delivered it 'nodding and looking *rather*
roguish and speaking in a hospitable tone' (Stone, p. 21); Robertson in the silent film gave
Horatio's breast a pat; and in this convivial spirit Maximilian Schell's film Hamlet hugged
him.

177 Charles Kean after a brief escape into feelings of friendship suddenly 'flung back' to his
earlier woe (*Dramatic Essays*, pp. 108–9).

178 Garrick explained to a correspondent in 1762 that he 'suspended' his voice after 'see': 'for
Hamlet's Grief causes ye break & with a Sigh he finishes ye Sentence' (quoted by Stone,
Garrick, p. 543).

184 Fechter with clasped hands tenderly murmured 'My father' (Field, p. 99). Kemble

HORATIO Where my lord?
HAMLET   In my mind's eye, Horatio.   185
HORATIO I saw him once, a was a goodly king.
HAMLET A was a man, take him for all in all.
         I shall not look upon his like again.
HORATIO My lord, I think I saw him yesternight.
HAMLET Saw? Who?   190
HORATIO My lord, the king your father.
HAMLET   The king my father!
HORATIO Season your admiration for a while
         With an attent ear, till I may deliver
         Upon the witness of these gentlemen
         This marvel to you.
HAMLET   For God's love let me hear.   195

emphasized 'see' with 'the fixed eye of a visionary' (H. Martin, *Remarks*, p. 4).

185   With Macready the other three 'bend forward a little, in alarm looking at Hamlet'
      (promptbook 29). With Booth, 'all start' (Sprague, *Actors*, p. 135); his Horatio spoke 'Where,
      my lord?' eagerly, as if he 'thought Hamlet really beheld his father with his bodily eyes' –
      just as he himself had done (Stone, p. 21). As Horatio to Gielgud, Jack Hawkins was
      'staggered' at this: 'a little disappointed to find that his news is no news, and not sorry to
      hear that Hamlet is talking only of his mind's eye' (*Sunday Times*, 18 November 1934).

187–8 Kean repunctuated this passage: 'He was *a man*. Take him for all in all / I shall not look upon
      his like again' (Hawkins, *Kean*, p. 191). Both Q1 and Q2 have punctuation that would
      accommodate this reading; only F, which places a colon at the end of 187, would not. Fechter,
      with his hand on Horatio's shoulder, spoke 187a with 'filial pride' (Field, p. 99). At 188 'a flood
      of tenderness' came over Kemble, and he spoke the line 'with tears' (Boaden, p. 96).

189   In the Branagh film, ever-cautious Horatio (Nicholas Farrell) emphasized *think*.

190–245 Pryce's Hamlet changes slowly 'from surprise, to a kind of challenging suspicion, "Arm'd say
      you?" to impatience when they get off into debating how long the ghost was there and he
      breaks in with "His beard was grizzled, no?" When he says, "I'll speak to it," it is with the
      tone of a decision finally arrived at' (Gilbert, 'Pryce').

190–5 Still carried away by his recollection of his father, Gielgud does not at first heed Horatio's
      revelation. But at 'Who?' he leaps to his feet and cries out 'The king, my father!' (Gilder, pp.
      98–9).

195ff Gielgud used as a guide (Gilder, p. 39) Ellen Terry's account of Irving, whose attention at 'Let
      me hear' became 'as sharp as a needle': his face 'blazed with intelligence. He cross-
      examined the men with keenness and authority' (Terry, p. 106). In contrast to Irving's 'abrupt
      transitions of tone', Robertson put his questions 'in a grave and earnest fashion, but with no
      token of involuntary impulses' (*Graphic*, 18 September 1897).

HORATIO Two nights together had these gentlemen,
　　　　 Marcellus and Barnardo, on their watch
　　　　 In the dead waste and middle of the night,
　　　　 Been thus encountered. A figure like your father,
　　　　 Armèd at point exactly, cap-a-pe,　　　　　　　　200
　　　　 Appears before them, and with solemn march
　　　　 Goes slow and stately by them. Thrice he walked
　　　　 By their oppressed and fear-surprisèd eyes
　　　　 Within his truncheon's length, whilst they, distilled
　　　　 Almost to jelly with the act of fear,　　　　　　205
　　　　 Stand dumb and speak not to him. This to me
　　　　 In dreadful secrecy impart they did,
　　　　 And I with them the third night kept the watch,
　　　　 Where, as they had delivered, both in time,
　　　　 Form of the thing, each word made true and good,　210
　　　　 The apparition comes. I knew your father,
　　　　 These hands are not more like.
HAMLET　　　　　　　　　　　　　 But where was this?
MARCELLUS My lord, upon the platform where we watched.
HAMLET Did you not speak to it?
HORATIO　　　　　　　　　　　 My lord, I did,

196–213　Booth advised the actor of Horatio: 'Now that the "ice is broken" speak with animation . . . as Hamlet's interest becomes intense, speak somewhat rapidly, yet distinctly. Let your *feeling* keep pace with Hamlet's which gradually heightens until the climax – "Where was this?"' (studybook 109). Booth himself, as he listened, showed 'surprise, curiosity, wonder' grow to 'astonishment, alarm, consternation' (Stone, p. 23).

214　Kemble accented *you*, 'emphatically and tenderly', reflecting their special intimacy. When this reading was criticised, Kemble submitted the point to Dr Johnson who said, 'To be sure, sir, – *you* should be strongly marked. I told Garrick so, long since, but Davy never could see it' (Boaden, pp. 96–7). In *The New Rosciad* (1785), Leigh, with a satirist's sharp eye and tongue, recorded the ways in which Kemble drew on the repertoire of formal acting to stress this point:

　　Sudden he starts! each feature turn'd awry,
　　The lips contracted, vacant is the eye;
　　The left hand without motion, wrist half bent,
　　The right *slow* moves, as if he *something* meant;
　　His head and hands affected airs display,
　　Then opes his mouth, says nothing – walks away!
　　Quickly returns – stops short – quite resolute –
　　Exclaims, "*Horatio did not YOU speak to 't?*'

But answer made it none. Yet once methought   215
It lifted up it head and did address
Itself to motion like as it would speak;
But even then the morning cock crew loud,
And at the sound it shrunk in haste away
And vanished from our sight.
HAMLET   'Tis very strange.   220
HORATIO As I do live my honoured lord 'tis true,
          And we did think it writ down in our duty
          To let you know of it.
HAMLET Indeed, indeed sirs, but this troubles me.
          Hold you the watch tonight?
MARCELLUS ⎫
                          We do, my lord.   225
BARNARDO ⎭

HAMLET Armed say you?
MARCELLUS ⎫
               Armed my lord.
BARNARDO ⎭
HAMLET   From top to toe?
MARCELLUS ⎫ My lord, from head to foot.
BARNARDO ⎭
HAMLET Then saw you not his face?
HORATIO Oh yes my lord, he wore his beaver up.
HAMLET What, looked he frowningly?   230
HORATIO A countenance more in sorrow than in anger.
HAMLET Pale, or red?
HORATIO Nay very pale.
HAMLET   And fixed his eyes upon you?
HORATIO Most constantly.
HAMLET   I would I had been there.
HORATIO It would have much amazed you.   235

The satirist altered the quoted line, displacing 'YOU' from before 'not' to after it, causing the accented 'YOU' to go awkwardly against the meter rather than with it, as it does in the original. The line appears in Kemble's acting edition exactly as it does in the present edition (Kemble, *Promptbooks*, p. 13). Barrett stressed *speak* as well as *you*, recalling that the witnesses other than Horatio had 'stood dumb and spake not to him' (*Shakespeariana*, p. 32). Fechter addressed his question to Marcellus, to which Horatio replied, 'My lord, *I* did' (Field, p. 99).

228   In the film, Branagh, incredulous, is trying to 'catch them out' (*Screenplay*, p. 21).

234b   Booth spoke this half-line 'more to himself than to them' (*North American Review*, December 1900, p. 912).

HAMLET Very like, very like. Stayed it long?
HORATIO While one with moderate haste might tell a hundred.
MARCELLUS ⎫
BARNARDO ⎰ Longer, longer.
HORATIO Not when I saw 't.
HAMLET   His beard was grizzled, no?
HORATIO It was as I have seen it in his life,   240
      A sable silvered.
HAMLET   I will watch tonight,
      Perchance 'twill walk again.
HORATIO   I warrant it will.
HAMLET If it assume my noble father's person,
      I'll speak to it though hell itself should gape
      And bid me hold my peace. I pray you all,   245
      If you have hitherto concealed this sight,
      Let it be tenable in your silence still,
      And whatsomever else shall hap tonight,
      Give it an understanding but no tongue.

236   Q1 reads 'Yea very like, very like', with 'yea' strongly connecting Hamlet's response to
      Horatio's preceding remark. Q2's 'very like' seems a more laconic way of making the same
      connection. F's 'very like, very like' invites a more brooding delivery and suggests a wider
      resonance.
         Instead of responding to Horatio, Fechter was still thinking of the Ghost's countenance,
      his murmured words meant 'very like – my father' (Field, p. 101). To Robins Horatio's
      comment at 235 seemed 'officious' and Booth's response 'almost a moody rebuff to one
      who would intrude upon his thought' ('*Hamlet*', p. 912). With Barrett 'Hamlet returns
      casually, "Very like", – and then significantly and slowly, as if at last concluding the whole to
      be most true and probable to his vague suspicions, he adds, "*Very like!*"' (*Shakespeariana*,
      p. 33). Daniel Day Lewis's reading of 'very like' established 'a nice ironic scepticism'
      (*Country Life*, 30 March 1989).
239   Booth puts the first part of the question to Marcellus, then he 'addresses to Horatio the long-
      drawn-out, hesitating "*No?*"' His 'whole body trembles' in dread of the answer (Shattuck, p.
      134). With Branagh this was one last test of their veracity (*Screenplay*, p. 22).
241b–5a Garrick, 'buoyant with hope and paternal love, rushed exultingly forward', speaking the
      lines with electrifying 'ardor and animation' (Phelps, pp. 76–7). Irving here is 'full of rapt,
      nervous excitement' (Russell, p. 27) while the other three 'look at one another' (studybook).
      Barrett speaks 'with dread as well as eagerness' (*Shakespeariana*, p. 33). Branagh takes a
      deep breath at 241b before making 'the unavoidable decision' (*Screenplay*, p. 22).
249   Burton/Gielgud: Hamlet holds a finger to his lips.

HAMLET   I will requite your loves. So fare you well: 250
                      Upon the platform 'twixt eleven and twelve
                      I'll visit you.
ALL   Our duty to your honour.
HAMLET   Your loves, as mine to you. Farewell.

                                                    Exeunt all but Hamlet
                      My father's spirit, in arms! All is not well.
                      I doubt some foul play. Would the night were come.   255
                      Till then sit still my soul. Foul deeds will rise
                      Though all the earth o'erwhelm them to men's eyes.   *Exit*

252b–3 Of Gielgud: the words of the others remind abstracted Hamlet to return and express his
        appreciation of their devotion (Gilder, p. 100).

   254 Garrick put an extra exclamation point after 'spirit', a reading Booth preferred: 'Else it would
        seem that spirits were no uncommon sights' (studybook).

256–7 J. B. Booth said 'Foul deeds will rise' 'as with the voice of fate'. 'Though all the earth
        o'erwhelm them' was given, barnstorming style, 'with a sweeping gesture, as if taking the
        solid earth, and lifting it as a wave of the sea is lifted, and letting it fall' (Gould, p. 54). Less
        flamboyantly, Edwin Booth made 'a comprehensive gesture with outspread hands pointing
        downwards to indicate "all the earth"' (Stone, p. 26). Of Irving: 'After having been very quiet
        and rapid, very discreet, he pronounced these lines in a loud, clear voice, dragged out every
        syllable as if there never could be an end to his horror and his rage' (Terry, p. 106). Terry's
        description helped Gielgud 'to realize how those few short words bind the end of the scene
        together' and lead forward to the revelation of the Ghost and all that follows (Gilder, p. 41).

ACT I, SCENE 3

1.3 *Enter* LAERTES *and* OPHELIA *his sister*

LAERTES My necessaries are embarked, farewell.
   And sister, as the winds give benefit
   And convoy is assistant, do not sleep
   But let me hear from you.
OPHELIA   Do you doubt that?
LAERTES For Hamlet, and the trifling of his favour,   5
   Hold it a fashion, and a toy in blood,
   A violet in the youth of primy nature,
   Forward, not permanent, sweet, not lasting,
   The perfume and suppliance of a minute,
   No more.
OPHELIA   No more but so?
LAERTES   Think it no more.   10
   For nature crescent does not grow alone
   In thews and bulk, but as this temple waxes

1   When Michael Redgrave played Hamlet in 1950, his Laertes (Peter Copley) addressed the line to someone unseen before turning to Yvonne Mitchell's Ophelia (Trewin, *Five & Eighty*, p. 78).

4   Julia Marlowe from her first words revealed Ophelia's loneliness: unmistakably, she made us understand here that Ophelia's mother was dead (C. Russell, *Marlowe*, p. 324).

5   Terry showed a 'slight change of countenance at the first mention of Hamlet's name' (*Standard*, 31 December 1878).

6b   Marlowe 'backs away – slightly fearfully' (promptbook).

10a   With Booth (1889–90) Modjeska spoke 'in a half-playful tone, turning her face from Laertes, dropping her eyes, and smiling' (Mason 106). With Marlowe there was 'a vague wistfulness in the voice, and an undertone of tragic boding' (C. Russell, p. 324).

10b   'Pointedly'. Ophelia 'feels an indefinable pain or dread from Laertes's emphasis on *think* (Walter Hampden promptbook).

10b–44   With Burton Gielgud cut lines 11–14a, 22–8, 38–44 from this long speech. He advised John Cullum as Laertes: 'you mustn't put false stops in your long speech. It makes the audience

The inward service of the mind and soul
Grows wide withal. Perhaps he loves you now,
And now no soil nor cautel doth besmirch   15
The virtue of his will; but you must fear,
His greatness weighed, his will is not his own,
For he himself is subject to his birth.
He may not, as unvalued persons do,
Carve for himself, for on his choice depends   20
The sanctity and health of this whole state,
And therefore must his choice be circumscribed
Unto the voice and yielding of that body
Whereof he is the head. Then if he says he loves you,
It fits your wisdom so far to believe it   25
As he in his peculiar sect and force
May give his saying deed, which is no further
Than the main voice of Denmark goes withal.
Then weigh what loss your honour may sustain

If with too credent ear you list his songs,   30
Or lose your heart, or your chaste treasure open
To his unmastered importunity.
Fear it Ophelia, fear it my dear sister,
And keep you in the rear of your affection,
Out of the shot and danger of desire.   35
The chariest maid is prodigal enough
If she unmask her beauty to the moon.
Virtue itself scapes not calumnious strokes.
The canker galls the infants of the spring
Too oft before their buttons be disclosed,   40
And in the morn and liquid dew of youth
Contagious blastments are most imminent.
Be wary then, best safety lies in fear:
Youth to itself rebels, though none else near.
OPHELIA I shall th'effect of this good lesson keep   45
As watchman to my heart. But good my brother,
Do not as some ungracious pastors do,
Show me the steep and thorny way to heaven,
Whiles like a puffed and reckless libertine

think you've come to the end of it, and then when you go on, it seems long and labored.
Overlap your ideas so that they carry through. Suspend the end of lines to telegraph that
there is more to come. It has to be brash and have all the confidence of youth – like
undergraduates telling each other how to live life' (Sterne, p. 46).

16   In the Branagh film, Ophelia (Kate Winslet) tries unsuccessfully to interrupt her brother's
lecture at 'will' and after 24a (*Screenplay*, p. 24).

Himself the primrose path of dalliance treads,   50
And recks not his own rede.
LAERTES   Oh fear me not.

Enter POLONIUS

I stay too long – But here my father comes.
A double blessing is a double grace;
Occasion smiles upon a second leave.
POLONIUS Yet here Laertes? Aboard, aboard for shame!   55
The wind sits in the shoulder of your sail,
And you are stayed for. There, my blessing with thee,
And these few precepts in thy memory
Look thou character. Give thy thoughts no tongue,
Nor any unproportioned thought his act.   60
Be thou familiar, but by no means vulgar.
Those friends thou hast, and their adoption tried,
Grapple them unto thy soul with hoops of steel,
But do not dull thy palm with entertainment
Of each new-hatched, unfledged courage. Beware   65
Of entrance to a quarrel, but being in,
Bear't that th'opposèd may beware of thee.
Give every man thy ear, but few thy voice;
Take each man's censure, but reserve thy judgement.
Costly thy habit as thy purse can buy,   70
But not expressed in fancy: rich, not gaudy.
For the apparel oft proclaims the man,
And they in France of the best rank and station
Are of a most select and generous chief in that.

50   In the Branagh film Laertes (Michael Maloney) 'knows he's been caught. A big smile and a
     kiss on the lips' for his sister (*Screenplay*, p. 25). Their physical closeness in this scene hints
     at an incestuous intimacy (p. 23).

52a Harcourt Williams, who directed Gielgud in 1930, saw Laertes like his father as 'a born talker
     and giver of fatuous advice who, when Ophelia slyly tries to turn the tables, retorts "I stay
     too long"' (Williams, *Years*, p. 157).

57   With H. B. Irving, Lyall Swete 'gives his advice to Laertes exactly as if each axiom occurred to
     him on the spur of the moment' (Beerbohm, *Last Theatres*, p. 149).

57a In Olivier's stage version, Cherry Cottrell humorously seems resigned to a paternal lecture,
     as if she were thinking 'Father's off again' (Crosse, *Playgoing*, p. 123).

65–7 Terry gives a 'little frightened start when the old man suggests the possibility of a duel'
     (*Montreal Star*, 4 October 1884).

70–4 Of Modjeska: 'Ophelia looks critically at Laertes; she raises his cloak and drops it again with
     a look of approbation' (Mason 106).

Neither a borrower nor a lender be,   75
For loan oft loses both itself and friend,
And borrowing dulls the edge of husbandry.
This above all, to thine own self be true,
And it must follow, as the night the day,
Thou canst not then be false to any man.   80
Farewell, my blessing season this in thee.
LAERTES Most humbly do I take my leave, my lord.
POLONIUS The time invites you. Go, your servants tend.
LAERTES Farewell Ophelia, and remember well
    What I have said to you.
OPHELIA   'Tis in my memory locked,   85
    And you yourself shall keep the key of it.
LAERTES Farewell.   *Exit Laertes*
POLONIUS What is't Ophelia he hath said to you?
OPHELIA So please you, something touching the Lord Hamlet.

78-80   When Redgrave played Laertes with Olivier he exchanged the usual glances and giggles with Ophelia during most of their father's few precepts, but here he turned suddenly serious and with 'boyish warmth' touched his father's hand with a gesture of affection (*Daily Telegraph*, 6 January 1937). When Redgrave himself played Hamlet in 1950, Ophelia and Laertes silently mouthed these lines, 'an injunction that would have bored them since childhood' (Trewin, *Five & Eighty*, p. 78). Tony Church has contrasted his 1965 machiavellian Polonius with his fatherly portrayal in 1980: 'In the 1965 production I had delivered those lines as a direct appeal to naked self-interest; in 1980 I spoke them as a simple moral truth which I knew my son would share with me' (Church, 'Polonius', p. 109).

84-8   As in his 1965 Polonius (*Shakespeare Quarterly*, 16, Autumn, 1965, p. 322), Church in 1980 at first seemed preoccupied and appeared not to overhear 84-7. Working at some state papers (87), the loving father whistled along as Ophelia hummed the tune for 'How should I your true love know?': 'the world stood still for a moment, and father and daughter were in harmony'. Only at 88 did the amused audience realize that 'the sly old man was not so relaxed as he seemed, and Ophelia was not to escape without an explanation' (Church, 'Polonius', pp. 109-10). With Day Lewis, Michael Bryant was 'inordinately fond' of his son (*Time-Out*, 22 March 1989) while blasting his daughter with 'angry love and stern admonition' (*Plays and Players*, May 1989).

88-9   Modjeska 'droops her head, lowers her eyes, and replies in a low tone, and with a hesitating and troubled manner' (Mason 106). Of Terry: 'The swift shade of pain and anxiety that passes over her features at the first token of her father's displeasure is very beautiful; as is her meek embarrassment and momentary pause at the word "touching"; her reluctance to add the name of "the Lord Hamlet"' (*Academy*, 7 November 1874, p. 19).

POLONIUS Marry, well bethought. 90
         'Tis told me he hath very oft of late
         Given private time to you, and you yourself
         Have of your audience been most free and bounteous.
         If it be so, as so 'tis put on me,
         And that in way of caution, I must tell you 95
         You do not understand yourself so clearly
         As it behooves my daughter, and your honour.
         What is between you? Give me up the truth.
OPHELIA He hath my lord of late made many tenders
         Of his affection to me. 100
POLONIUS Affection? Puh! You speak like a green girl,
         Unsifted in such perilous circumstance.
         Do you believe his tenders as you call them?
OPHELIA I do not know my lord what I should think.
POLONIUS Marry I'll teach you. Think yourself a baby 105
         That you have tane these tenders for true pay,
         Which are not sterling. Tender yourself more dearly,
         Or – not to crack the wind of the poor phrase,
         Roaming it thus – you'll tender me a fool.
OPHELIA My lord, he hath importuned me with love 110
         In honourable fashion.
POLONIUS Ay, fashion you may call it. Go to, go to.
OPHELIA And hath given countenance to his speech, my lord,
         With almost all the holy vows of heaven.
POLONIUS Ay, springes to catch woodcocks. I do know, 115
         When the blood burns, how prodigal the soul

104   Isabella Pateman, another of Booth's later Ophelias, spoke while 'twisting her hands nervously together and looking down' (Stone, p. 29).

109   Modjeska 'draws herself up in a dignified protest' (Mason 106).

110–11   Pateman: 'very earnestly and with an undertone of appeal to her father'' emphasizing *honourable*. With Gielgud Lillian Gish's 'Ophelia leaps to her feet in protest' and exclaims these lines 'indignantly' (Gilder, p. 103).

113–14   Pateman spoke 'very solemnly with eyes upraised to Heaven and clasped hands' (Stone, p. 29). Modjeska spoke 114 with 'a happy smile, as if recalling past scenes, and rejoicing in the memory of them' (Mason 106).

116ff   With Burton in 1964, Hume Cronyn at first smiles at Ophelia in mentioning Hamlet's attraction to her, becomes gradually sterner up to his harsh pronouncement at 132–4. He then softens a bit at the end, holding his hand out to her at 135b. His shadow towards the end suggests the Ghost's shadow in the first scene.

Lends the tongue vows. These blazes daughter,
Giving more light than heat, extinct in both
Even in their promise as it is a-making,
You must not take for fire. From this time   120
Be something scanter of your maiden presence.
Set your entreatments at a higher rate
Than a command to parley. For Lord Hamlet,
Believe so much in him, that he is young
And with a larger tedder may he walk   125
Than may be given you. In few Ophelia,
Do not believe his vows, for they are brokers,
Not of that dye which their investments show,
But mere implorators of unholy suits,
Breathing like sanctified and pious bonds,   130
The better to beguile. This is for all:
I would not in plain terms from this time forth
Have you so slander any moment leisure
As to give words or talk with the Lord Hamlet.
Look to't I charge you. Come your ways.   135
OPHELIA I shall obey, my lord.

Exeunt

---

117 Marlowe 'cowers in horror'. At 123b she 'removes hands from eyes'. She delivers 136
    'tearfully' (promptbook 143).

126 Ophelia's refusal to give immediate agreement 'renders Polonius very stern' (Walter
    Hampden promptbook).

135b Modjeska 'pauses a moment, and then goes quickly to him, kisses his head, lays her head
    upon his breast' (Mason 106).

136 In her 'affectionate submission' Terry's Ophelia also conveyed 'the deep dejection of her
    spirit when her maiden dream of love suddenly vanishes and leaves her in the presence of
    misery and despair' (*Academy*, 7 November 1874, p. 19). With Gielgud in 1945 Peggy
    Ashcroft threw her arms around Miles Malleson's neck with a smile, 'as tolerantly accepting
    a fussy parent's rebuke' (Crosse, *Playgoing*, p. 141). In the Rees/Daniels production (1984),
    Frances Barber's 'final acquiescence came only after several attempted interruptions', one
    of which provoked her father's 'Look to't I charge you' ('Ophelia', p. 141).
        Benson's Polonius, G. F. Black, who was in general more affectionate toward his daughter
    than most, turned from her in anger after warning her about Hamlet, but then showed a
    'father's anxiety to comfort Ophelia' (*Saturday Review*, 15 March 1890). In the
    Branagh/Noble production Joanne Pearce was 'wrapped up in (and weighed down by)
    Polonius's topcoat – paternal over-protectiveness and infantilising domination registered
    sartorially' (*Independent*, 21 December 1992). Compare the similar business by earlier Royal
    Shakespeare Company productions at 2.1.118.

ACT I, SCENE 4

[1.4] *Enter* HAMLET, HORATIO *and* MARCELLUS

HAMLET The air bites shrewdly, it is very cold.
HORATIO It is a nipping and an eager air.
HAMLET What hour now?
HORATIO   I think it lacks of twelve.
MARCELLUS No, it is struck.
HORATIO Indeed? I heard it not. It then draws near the season   5
          Wherein the spirit held his wont to walk.
               A flourish of trumpets and two pieces goes off
          What does this mean, my lord?

OSD Macready had Hamlet enter first, alone, then joined by the other two (promptbook 29).
      Fechter had Hamlet enter from one side, the others from the opposite (Field, p. 100). Hamlet
      had said 'Upon the platform 'twixt eleven and twelve / I'll visit you' (1.2.251–2), suggesting
      separate arrivals; yet the absence of greetings makes these blockings seem forced.

  1   With Kemble 'expectation, doubt, awe, were all blended – his step was unquiet – he stirred
      in anxiety – yet his words were composed' (H. Martin, *Remarks*, p. 4). Forrest 'finely
      indicated by his absent and preoccupied manner that he was not thinking about the cold,
      but was full of the solemn expectation of something else' (Alger, *Forrest*, p. 753). Wilkie
      Collins, who thought Fechter's Hamlet the best he had seen, may well have been thinking of
      it when in his 1872 novel *Poor Miss Finch* (ch. 23) cocksure Nugent Dubourg observes that
      Hamlet here is nervous and feels the cold: 'Let him show it naturally; let him speak as any
      other man would speak . . . Quick and quiet – like this. "The air bites shrewdly" – there
      Hamlet stops and shivers – pur-rer-rer! "It is very cold"' (Catherine Peters, *The King of
      Inventors*, Princeton University Press: 1993, pp. 288–9). Irving's Hamlet spoke 'pacing the
      stage as if to fight off the cold' but in fact 'to conceal his agitation' (*Belgravia*, December
      1874, p. 187). Forbes-Robertson, Beerbohm observed, did not speak 'ruminantly' in the
      traditional way but to 'make conversation' and 'with a peevish emphasis on the "very"' – as
      if he feels the cold excessive for that time of year. 'We feel that the remark is a real remark
      made by a real man' (*More Theatres*, p. 486).

  2   Pause after 'air' (Macready promptbook).

HAMLET The king doth wake tonight and takes his rouse,
        Keeps wassail, and the swaggering up-spring reels,
        And as he drains his draughts of Rhenish down,   10
        The kettle-drum and trumpet thus bray out
        The triumph of his pledge.
HORATIO   Is it a custom?
HAMLET Ay marry is't,
        But to my mind, though I am native here
        And to the manner born, it is a custom   15
        More honoured in the breach than the observance.
        [This heavy-headed revel east and west

        Makes us traduced and taxed of other nations.
        They clepe us drunkards, and with swinish phrase
        Soil our addition; and indeed it takes   20
        From our achievements, though performed at height,
        The pith and marrow of our attribute.
        So, oft it chances in particular men,
        That for some vicious mole of nature in them,
        As in their birth, wherein they are not guilty,   25
        Since nature cannot choose his origin,
        By their o'ergrowth of some complexion,
        Oft breaking down the pales and forts of reason,
        Or by some habit that too much o'erleavens
        The form of plausive manners – that these men,   30
        Carrying I say the stamp of one defect,
        Being nature's livery or fortune's star,
        His virtues else be they as pure as grace,
        As infinite as man may undergo,
        Shall in the general censure take corruption   35
        From that particular fault. The dram of eale
        Doth all the noble substance of a doubt
        To his own scandal.]

Enter GHOST

HORATIO   Look my lord, it comes!

13ff   Warner/Hall: Hamlet 'was very much the student still learning, more interested in chewing
       over an intellectual question with Horatio than in watching for his father's ghost' (*Peace
       News*, 1965).
17–38 Not in Q1 or F. Olivier used this passage as the epigraph for his film.
   22 Guthrie in Minneapolis: Hamlet 'starts as if hearing something'; also at 30a (Rossi, p. 25).
  38b With Gielgud, Horatio is the first to see the Ghost: 'There is an instant of immobility ... Then
       Hamlet turns slowly, slowly, toward the thing at which Horatio is staring' (Gilder, p. 107).

HAMLET Angels and ministers of grace defend us!
Be thou a spirit of health, or goblin damned, 40
Bring with thee airs from heaven or blasts from hell,
Be thy intents wicked or charitable,
Thou com'st in such a questionable shape
That I will speak to thee. I'll call thee Hamlet,

39 The long-prepared-for encounter of Prince with Ghost presents a special problem for the actor of Hamlet since, as Michael Redgrave remarks, he must 'meet his father's ghost for the first time after several of the other characters have already met the ghost twice' ('Shakespeare', p. 136). Early-eighteenth-century Hamlets were oddly combative, perhaps prompted by Hamlet's opening challenge to the 'goblin damned'. Of one such Addison dryly inquired of Colley Cibber 'if I thought Hamlet should be in so violent a passion with the Ghost, which, though it might have astonished, it had not provoked him' (Cibber, *Apology*, p. 61). At the Ghost's first appearance, Robert Wilks had to be restrained by his companions as he attempted to advance upon it; Aaron Hill protested: 'He threw out, from the Beginning, all the *Sharps* of a *precipitate Clamour*, without Pause, without Terror, without *Rub*, *Rest*, or *Marking*.' At the end of the scene, he cried 'I say, away!' to the Ghost 'in a high rage, and with a flourish of his drawn sword' (*Prompter*, 24 October 1735). James Quin was another (*Reformer*, March 1748). Charles Macklin's approach made more sense. After conquering his initial terror, he spoke 'calmly, but respectfully, and with a firm voice, as from one who had subdued his timidity and apprehension' (Phelps, 78–9). It is Garrick's famous 'start', however, that stands out among all responses to the Ghost, before or since: he 'staggers back two or three paces with his knees giving way under him; his hat falls to the ground and both his arms, especially the left, are stretched out nearly to their full length, with the hands as high as his head, the right arm more bent and the hand lower, and the fingers apart; his mouth is open: thus he stands rooted to the spot, with legs apart, but no loss of dignity, supported by his friends . . . At last he speaks, not at the beginning, but at the end of a breath, with a trembling voice' (Lichtenberg, *Visits*, pp. 9–10). Boswell: 'Do you think, Sir, if you saw a ghost, you would start as Garrick does in Hamlet?' Dr Johnson: 'No, Sir. If I did, I should frighten the Ghost' (Boswell, *Tour*, p. 22).

Charles Kean 'throws himself into no convulsive attitude but sinking slowly to his knees – as over-awed by the solemn presence – addresses it with touching and affectionate adjuration' (Merchant, *Shakespeare*, p. 111). Booth shivers 'as if the cold of the grave were upon him' (Calhoun, 'Booth', p. 79).

Redgrave praised Alec Guinness's 1951 Hamlet for 'doing precisely nothing, which, after the elaborate starts . . . of the other characters, was signally effective' ('Shakespeare', pp. 136–7). Redgrave's own solution, was also 'to do nothing' – in the confidence that the audience will see in the actor 'all that they want and need to see' (*Mind's I*, p. 190).

44a Burton emphasized *will*.

King, father, royal Dane. Oh answer me. 45
Let me not burst in ignorance, but tell
Why thy canonised bones, hearsèd in death,
Have burst their cerements; why the sepulchre,
Wherein we saw thee quietly enurned,
Hath oped his ponderous and marble jaws 50
To cast thee up again. What may this mean,
That thou, dead corse, again in complete steel
Revisits thus the glimpses of the moon,
Making night hideous, and we fools of nature
So horridly to shake our disposition 55
With thoughts beyond the reaches of our souls?
Say, why is this? wherefore? What should we do?
    Ghost beckons Hamlet
HORATIO It beckons you to go away with it,
As if it some impartment did desire
To you alone.
MARCELLUS   Look with what courteous action 60
It wafts you to a more removèd ground.
But do not go with it.
HORATIO   No, by no means.
HAMLET It will not speak. Then I will follow it.
HORATIO Do not my lord.

---

45 J. B. Booth placed his primary pause after 'father'; when the ghost remained silent, he went
  on to exhort: 'Royal Dane, O answer me' (Gould, p. 55). (The punctuation in the early
  editions gives no encouragement to thus breaking up the series of titles.) Kean's heartfelt
  intonation of 'father' was famous for 'its mixture of duty and affection, love and reverence'
  (Finlay, *Miscellanies*, p. 221). Booth followed his father's punctuation here (Furness,
  Variorum, I, p. 90); his harshest critic, Nym Crinkle, had to admire his delivery: 'The
  "Hamlet" is an articulate sigh of loyalty; that of "father" is the yearning of filial affection; and
  "royal Dane" swells roundly and grandly into the pride of lineage and pomp of power'
  (*World*, 9 January 1870); his 'O answer me' was 'imploring and persuasive' (Calhoun,
  'Booth', p. 79). In his studybook Barrymore noted of this invocation 'wait between words'.

57 In 1953 Burton did not turn to face the Ghost until it started to leave, at which Hamlet 'very
  deliberately, did turn' followed by 'a wild burst of recognition' (Trewin, *Five & Eighty*, p. 85).

57ff Garrick wanted to follow 'with eyes fixed on the ghost'. When the Ghost leaves the stage,
  Garrick at first remains motionless, then 'begins slowly to follow him, now standing still and
  then going on, with sword still upon guard, eyes fixed on the ghost' (Lichtenberg, *Visits*, p.
  10).

HAMLET   Why, what should be the fear?
                I do not set my life at a pin's fee,   65
                And for my soul, what can it do to that,
                Being a thing immortal as itself?
                It waves me forth again. I'll follow it.
HORATIO What if it tempt you toward the flood my lord,
                Or to the dreadful summit of the cliff   70
                That beetles o'er his base into the sea,
                And there assume some other horrible form
                Which might deprive your sovereignty of reason,
                And draw you into madness? Think of it.
                [The very place puts toys of desperation,   75
                Without more motive, into every brain
                That looks so many fathoms to the sea
                And hears it roar beneath.]

64-8   Of Kemble: In contrast to his earlier 'pathetic and murmuring trepidation of voice' when
        addressing the Ghost, he here 'breaks out in an elevated and powerful pitch of voice with
        the finest effect, expressive at once of the most fixed resolution, and unshaken firmness of
        mind. This is particularly observable in the first line, and the first word' (Austin, *Chironomia*,
        pp. 79–80).

66   Garrick with great quickness accented THAT; Kemble accented CAN and *that*: 'In Garrick it
        was a truism asserted; in Kemble's, not merely asserted, but enjoyed' (Boaden, p. 97). J. B.
        Booth, who especially emphasized Hamlet's 'strange ties to the invisible world', in this
        speech 'seemed to have digested in his soul the very bitterness of death, to have passed
        beyond, and to speak as one conscious of his immortality' (Gould, pp. 49, 56). George Eliot
        felt that Fechter gave this line 'with perfect simplicity, whereas the herd of English actors
        imagine themselves in a pulpit when they are saying it' (*Letters*, III, p. 442).

72b   In his studybook Booth warned Horatio against stressing *other*; instead he should
        'emphasize *horrible* with a pause after "other" – to distinguish it from "fair and warlike"' (as
        Horatio had referred to the Ghost at 1.1.47).

73-4   Alec Guinness greeted Horatio's warning with a 'sharp look of terror': 'his Hamlet may not
        be mad, but it is a Hamlet who is afraid of madness . . . To this Hamlet, the world is an evil
        place; and the most evil spot upon it is his home' (*Sunday Times*, 20 May 1951).

74a   In addition to the Ghost's beckonings clearly indicated in the text at lines 58 and 61,
        Kemble's promptbook called for further gestures here and at 83b (*Promptbooks*, p. 18).
        Macready did the same (promptbook 29).

78   According to the theatre historian Nikolai Chushkin, Stanislavsky demonstrated in rehearsal
        how Hamlet 'didn't fall back in fright. Just the opposite; his Hamlet is irresistibly drawn to his
        father' (Rosenberg, p. 297).

HAMLET It wafts me still. Go on, I'll follow thee.
MARCELLUS You shall not go my lord.
HAMLET   Hold off your hands.   80
HORATIO Be ruled, you shall not go.
HAMLET   My fate cries out,
    And makes each petty arture in this body
    As hardy as the Nemean lion's nerve.
    Still am I called. Unhand me gentlemen!
    By heaven I'll make a ghost of him that lets me.   85
    I say away! – Go on, I'll follow thee.
                        Exit Ghost and Hamlet
HORATIO He waxes desperate with imagination.
MARCELLUS Let's follow, 'tis not fit thus to obey him.
HORATIO Have after. To what issue will this come?
MARCELLUS Something is rotten in the state of Denmark.   90
HORATIO Heaven will direct it.
MARCELLUS   Nay let's follow him.
                                Exeunt

86b   Salvini here 'stood in rigid stillness for a long pause ... At last he just moved the little finger of his right hand to indicate his decision' and spoke these words. Poel described this effect to his nephew, Reginald Pole, who was playing the Ghost with John Barrymore in New York, and Barrymore adopted it in his own performance' (Speaight, *Poel*, p. 27).

87SD   'Every Hamlet before Kemble presented the point to the phantom, as he followed him to the removed ground' but Kemble, 'drooped the weapon after him' (Phelps, p. 81). Kean did this also (Hazlitt, *Theatre*, p. 13). Fechter held the sword hilt like a cross. So did Booth, who as he follows the ghost shows 'the half doubt and shuddering dread that overtake him,' and then 'the re-resolve that come what may, he will pluck out the heart of this mystery' (Calhoun, 'Booth', p. 79). When Rossi exclaimed 'Away', the others bowed low 'at the command of the Prince' (Phelps, p. 82).

ACT I, SCENE 5

[1.5] *Enter* GHOST *and* HAMLET

HAMLET Whither wilt thou lead me? Speak, I'll go no further.
GHOST Mark me.
HAMLET   I will.

0   Hughes observes that Irving 'was probably the first English Hamlet to speak with the Ghost
    at a distance from the castle' (*Irving*, p. 49). In his 1879 staging, the Ghost stands among a
    number of massive rocks, 'the soft light of the moon falls upon the spectral figure; not a
    sound from below can be heard, and the first faint flushes of the dawn are stealing over the
    immense expanse of water before us', a scene of 'weird grandeur' (*Theatre*, 1 February 1879,
    pp. 46–50). 'Irving advances crouching, as if drawn onwards in terror and against his will by
    a mesmeric spell' (*Examiner*, 7 November 1874). In the Branagh film, the interview takes
    place after a wild race through a wood.
1   Of Kemble: '*Step by step*, slow, trembling, yet eager, he followed; and when he uttered, *I'll
    go no further*! it was because he *could not* proceed – his limbs were all nervous – he had
    hardly power to give voice even to that sentence' (H. Martin, *Remarks*, p. 5).
2   At long last the Ghost speaks. Quin spoke with a 'solemnity of expression' (*Gentleman,
    Censor*, p. 58), Barton Booth with a 'slow, solemn, and under, tone of voice' (Davies, p. 32).
    When Macready gave a concert reading of the play, his Ghost 'neither growled, nor droned,
    nor dragged the time, but his tones seemed to come from another world . . . without
    resonance' (Lady Pollock, *Macready*, p. 41). Half a century later, Courtenay Thorpe, playing
    the Ghost with Ben Greet's company, was admonished for his lack of 'deep sepulchral tones'
    (*Graphic*, 15 May 1897); G. B. Shaw, however, heard something original in his 'spectral wail
    of a soul's bitter wrong crying from one world to another' (*Shakespeare*, p. 89). With
    Barrymore in London Thorpe's voice was 'still seared with purgatorial fires', *Time and Tide*,
    27 February 1925). Desmond MacCarthy compared his tones to 'the wind in a chimney'
    (*Theatre*, p. 25).
        With David Warner Patrick Magee spoke with a 'graveyard voice' (*Sunday Times*, 22
    August 1965), as if 'from another world' (*Tablet*, 11 September 1965). Such stylization has
    often seemed apropos to 'supernatural utterance', especially when the style is that of an

GHOST	My hour is almost come	
	When I to sulph'rous and tormenting flames	
	Must render up myself.	
HAMLET	Alas poor ghost!	
GHOST	Pity me not, but lend thy serious hearing	5
	To what I shall unfold.	
HAMLET	Speak, I am bound to hear.	
GHOST	So art thou to revenge, when thou shalt hear.	
HAMLET	What?	
GHOST	I am thy father's spirit,	
	Doomed for a certain term to walk the night,	10
	And for the day confined to fast in fires,	

earlier era. Hence the assignment of the role to Gielgud with Burton and Richard Chamberlain, to Scofield with Gibson, to Pennington with Stephen Dillane. When Scofield himself played Hamlet (1948), Esmond Knight struggled for breath 'as if he were scouring up the deepest fumes of hell to bear the noxious pain of his message to Hamlet's ears' (Tynan, *He that Plays*, p. 113).

Verbal effects have suggested the modern idea that the Ghost is a projection of Hamlet's own psyche. In Zeffirelli's stage version the Ghost was 'a projection of the Prince's super-ego', in which an epileptic Hamlet mouthed commands whispered from the wings and spoke aloud many of the Ghost's lines himself (*The Times*, 16 September 1964). Nicol Williamson recorded the lines himself and they were played off-stage. Inspired by the film *The Exorcist*, Jonathan Pryce as Hamlet croaked the Ghost's lines from his own solar plexus as if possessed.

3 Booth: 'A shudder at this' (studybook).

4b Gielgud's 'tender tone' expresses his realization that the Ghost is 'a helpless, pitiful thing' (Gilder, p. 111).

5a With Guthrie in Minneapolis George Grizzard played 'a real love and reverence' for the Ghost (Ken Ruta), but Guthrie directed the Ghost to treat his son 'like dirt – like a sniveling weakling' (Rossi, p. 15).

8 Booth 'asks not in the sense of "What do you say?" but "What am I to revenge?"' (Shattuck, p. 149).

9 With Booth, 'Slowly, Hamlet sinks to his knees. There is no longer terror in his countenance. Infinite yearnings, infinite compassion, infinite tenderness, agonized longing to know the truth, look from his face' (Calhoun, 'Booth', p. 79). In the Branagh/Noble production, '"I *am* thy father's spirit," said Clifford Rose's Ghost; that is to say, "I know that the devil hath power/ T'assume a pleasing shape"' (*Shakespeare Bulletin*, Spring 1993, p. 26).

9ff Concerning Garrick, Partridge remarked on 'how his Fear forsook him by Degrees, and he was struck dumb with Sorrow' (*Tom Jones*, bk. XVI, ch. 5).

11 Gielgud's 'left hand comes up as though warding off the words' (Gilder, p. 113).

Till the foul crimes done in my days of nature
Are burnt and purged away. But that I am forbid
To tell the secrets of my prison house,
I could a tale unfold whose lightest word   15
Would harrow up thy soul, freeze thy young blood,
Make thy two eyes like stars start from their spheres,
Thy knotted and combinèd locks to part
And each particular hair to stand an end
Like quills upon the fretful porpentine.   20
But this eternal blazon must not be
To ears of flesh and blood. List, list, oh list!
If thou didst ever thy dear father love –
HAMLET O God!
GHOST Revenge his foul and most unnatural murder.   25
HAMLET Murder?
GHOST Murder most foul, as in the best it is,
But this most foul, strange, and unnatural.
HAMLET Haste me to know't, that I with wings as swift
As meditation or the thoughts of love   30
May sweep to my revenge.
GHOST   I find thee apt,
And duller shouldst thou be than the fat weed
That rots itself in ease on Lethe wharf,
Wouldst thou not stir in this. Now Hamlet, hear.
'Tis given out that, sleeping in my orchard,   35

25–7   With Scofield and Knight, the three echoing shrieks of 'murder' at 'full volume' sent Tynan 'out of my seat for fright' (*He that Plays*, p. 113).

25   When Salvini played the Ghost with Booth, he was 'less piteous and more resentful' than customary: 'He did not supplicate but commanded Hamlet to avenge his murder' (*Philadelphia Evening Bulletin*, 1 May 1886). Pennington observes: 'Everything preceding this moment needs to be held on a tight leash, straining towards it' (*Hamlet*, p. 157).

26   Booth: 'The rising accent of the word conveys at once amazement, fright, and the corroboration of a fearful surmise' (Shattuck, p. 150).

29–31   As Hamlet, Salvini paused for an instant on 'as', seeking the image exactly to correspond with the idea, and then delivers it with all the vivacity of a fresh inspiration' (*Century Magazine*, November 1881, p. 115). Burton in 1964 prolonged 's-w-e-e-p'.

31   David Warner, who stands well over six feet, reached up to the huge Ghost, like a small child, and was folded protectively in its gigantic arms, where he remained through most of their interview, 'looking for the comforts of the nursery' (*The Times*, 20 August 1965).

34   Guthrie at Minneapolis: 'The Ghost, by speaking directly into Hamlet's ear, poisons him with words of revenge' (Rossi, p. 20).

A serpent stung me. So the whole ear of Denmark
Is by a forgèd process of my death
Rankly abused; but know, thou noble youth,
The serpent that did sting thy father's life
Now wears his crown.

HAMLET   O my prophetic soul!   40
My uncle?

GHOST Ay, that incestuous, that adulterate beast,
With witchcraft of his wits, with traitorous gifts –
O wicked wit and gifts that have the power
So to seduce – won to his shameful lust   45
The will of my most seeming virtuous queen.
O Hamlet, what a falling off was there,
From me whose love was of that dignity
That it went hand in hand even with the vow
I made to her in marriage, and to decline   50
Upon a wretch whose natural gifts were poor
To those of mine.
But virtue as it never will be moved,
Though lewdness court it in a shape of heaven,
So lust, though to a radiant angel linked,   55
Will sate itself in a celestial bed,
And prey on garbage.
But soft, methinks I scent the morning air;
Brief let me be. Sleeping within my orchard,
My custom always of the afternoon,   60
Upon my secure hour thy uncle stole,
With juice of cursèd hebenon in a vial,
And in the porches of my ears did pour
The leperous distilment, whose effect
Holds such an enmity with blood of man   65
That swift as quicksilver it courses through
The natural gates and alleys of the body,
And with a sudden vigour it doth posset
And curd, like eager droppings into milk,

39–40   'Hamlet expresses by face and gesture, anticipation of this information' (Booth's studybook).

40   Burton chuckled with 'savage glee . . . at the wild, wicked joke of life' (*New York Herald Tribune*, 10 April 1964).

41   Fechter emphasizes 'my' as he realizes his family relationship to this monster (*Sunday Times*, 24 March 1861).

The thin and wholesome blood. So did it mine, 70
And a most instant tetter barked about,
Most lazar-like, with vile and loathsome crust,
All my smooth body.
Thus was I, sleeping, by a brother's hand,
Of life, of crown, of queen, at once dispatched; 75
Cut off even in the blossoms of my sin,
Unhouseled, disappointed, unaneled;
No reckoning made, but sent to my account
With all my imperfections on my head –
Oh horrible, oh horrible, most horrible! 80
If thou hast nature in thee bear it not;
Let not the royal bed of Denmark be
A couch for luxury and damnèd incest.
But howsomever thou pursues this act
Taint not thy mind, nor let thy soul contrive 85
Against thy mother aught. Leave her to heaven
And to those thorns that in her bosom lodge
To prick and sting her. Fare thee well at once.
The glow-worm shows the matin to be near,
And gins to pale his uneffectual fire. 90
Adieu, adieu, adieu. Remember me. *Exit*

74–9 In Minneapolis Guthrie directed Ken Ruta to increase the volume of his voice and raise its
       pitch, saying the last three lines on a single breath, and elongating the vowels in 77,
       'building to an emotional peak on "head"' (Rossi, p. 14).

80   Since at least as far back as Garrick (Furness, *Variorum*, I, p. 104), Hamlets have often
       appropriated this line, including Gielgud, Olivier in the film, and Kevin Kline. With Irving, 'O
       horrible, O horrible! most horrible!' was a groan (Terry, p. 107). On BBC-TV Jacobi sobbed
       'horrible', the Ghost responded 'most horrible'.

91   Pennington: 'The words can be an appeal, or furiously mandatory . . . All the Ghost's
       qualities jostle behind the four final syllables. If pain isn't in it, you may get a laugh; if
       firmness isn't, it will be sentimental. If it isn't simple, the audience will soon forget it'
       (*Hamlet*, p. 159).

91SD Kemble knelt at the descent of the ghost by trapdoor, as did Henderson, following Kemble
       (Boaden, p. 98). Forrest 'looked as pale and shriveled as the frozen moonlight and the
       wintry landscape around him' (Alger, *Forrest*, p. 754). At Minneapolis Guthrie had the Ghost
       reach towards Hamlet as Hamlet reached towards him; they almost touch before Hamlet
       falls (Rossi, p. 31). In the Zeffirelli film, Scofield's Ghost reached out to his son but Mel
       Gibson's Hamlet did not respond in kind.

HAMLET O all you host of heaven! O earth! what else?
And shall I couple hell? Oh fie! Hold, hold, my heart,
And you my sinews grow not instant old
But bear me stiffly up. Remember thee?   95
Ay thou poor ghost, whiles memory holds a seat
In this distracted globe. Remember thee?

Yea, from the table of my memory
I'll wipe away all trivial fond records,
All saws of books, all forms, all pressures past,   100
That youth and observation copied there,
And thy commandment all alone shall live
Within the book and volume of my brain,
Unmixed with baser matter: yes, by heaven!
O most pernicious woman!   105
O villain, villain, smiling damnèd villain!
My tables – meet it is I set it down
That one may smile, and smile, and be a villain;
At least I'm sure it may be so in Denmark. [*Writing*]
So uncle, there you are. Now to my word: 110
It is 'Adieu, adieu, remember me.'
I have sworn't.

92–3a   Kean gazed 'in awful silence' where the Ghost had descended, then 'came forward with an
         eye of supplication, as if he implored the sacred Deity to aid him in his purpose' (Phippen,
         Kean, pp. 99–100). 'Looking upward, Booth says: "Oh, all you host of heaven!" Then, looking
         down, "Oh, earth!" and then, as though struck by the association: "What else? And shall I
         couple hell?"' (Mason 110). Robertson lay 'exhausted and supine', looking up at the 'host of
         heaven' (*Manchester Guardian*, 24 May 1898). In Branagh's film, he lies prone, giving point
         to his apostrophe to the 'earth' and his image of coupling hell.

93–5a   Of Gielgud: 'little by little, he raises himself on one knee. He is bruised, beaten; only his will
         remains and forces him up' (Gilder, p. 115).

   105   Of Burton: 'By dropping each of the four words a tone at a time . . . he can judge his mother
         so finally that for her Judgement Day will be an entirely superfluous occasion' (Walter Kerr,
         New York Herald Tribune, 10 April 1964).

   106   With Barrett awe 'turns to the staccato of a giddy relief, as with a change of manner and
         great swiftness and lightness of tone' he says this line (*Shakespeariana*, p. 35).

   107   Tree: 'His passion has reached its climax. He has drawn his sword, it falls back into its
         scabbard; physical action, the immediate brutal revenge, is abandoned . . . He turns from
         the sword to the pen' (p. 865).

   112   Burton in 1964 crossed himself, knelt with hands joined in prayer. Rylance cut his hand with
         his sword and smeared the blood on his forehead.

HORATIO (*Within*) My lord, my lord!
MARCELLUS *(Within)*   Lord Hamlet!

Enter HORATIO *and* MARCELLUS

HORATIO   Heavens secure him!
HAMLET So be it.
MARCELLUS Illo, ho, ho, my lord!   115
HAMLET Hillo, ho, ho, boy! Come bird, come.
MARCELLUS How is't, my noble lord?
HORATIO   What news my lord?
HAMLET Oh, wonderful!
HORATIO Good my lord, tell it.
HAMLET   No, you will reveal it.
HORATIO Not I my lord, by heaven.
MARCELLUS   Nor I my lord.   120
HAMLET How say you then, would heart of man once think it –
        But you'll be secret?
HORATIO ⎫
MARCELLUS ⎭   Ay, by heaven, my lord.
HAMLET There's ne'er a villain dwelling in all Denmark
        But he's an arrant knave.

113   Although Horatio was here thinking of Hamlet, Fechter's Hamlet applied the words to the
      Ghost, and 'prayerfully' added 'So be it' (Field, p. 101).
115ff Irving was praised for rendering a scene which is often a jumble 'clear and solemnly
      impressive' (*Belgravia*, December 1874, p. 187). Yet a different critic found him guilty of
      'toning down into seriousness' Hamlet's bizarre behaviour, especially since it entailed
      cutting references to the Ghost as 'boy' and 'old mole' (*Examiner*, 7 November 1874).
116   Booth mopped his brow with a handkerchief, then waved it above his head once or twice at
      this line, prolonging the *o* sounds (Shattuck, p. 154). Compare the handkerchief twirlings of
      Garrick (3.2.248) and Macready (3.2.80). Tree 'had a spotlight by which to see him working
      hysterically up to that astonishing, romantic cry' (*Sunday Times*, 18 November 1934, p. 4).
121   Of Booth: 'he who was frankness itself becomes astute and evasive' (Garland, 'Lecture', p.
      22).
123–4a From Kemble's time many Hamlets were suspicious of Marcellus and therefore deflected
      their disclosure after 'in all Denmark'. Irving spoke it 'all in one key, as though deliberately
      intending from the commencement to baffle interrogation by unmeaning replies'
      (*Belgravia*, December 1874, p. 187). Barrymore 'took each of the men around the shoulder,
      led them up to the footlights, assumed a very conspiratorial air with "But you'll be secret?",
      played up the suspense of what he was about to say, and delivered "But he's an arrant
      knave," as though it were all a great joke'. Gielgud 'bursting with what he has been told' was
      on the verge of disclosing everything yet just in time 'clapped a hand over his mouth to dam

HORATIO There needs no ghost, my lord, come from the grave,   125
    To tell us this.
HAMLET   Why right, you are i'th'right,
    And so without more circumstance at all
    I hold it fit that we shake hands and part –
    You as your business and desire shall point you,
    For every man hath business and desire,   130
    Such as it is, and for my own poor part,
    Look you, I'll go pray.
HORATIO These are but wild and whirling words, my lord.
HAMLET I'm sorry they offend you, heartily,
    Yes faith, heartily.
HORATIO   There's no offence my lord.   135
HAMLET Yes by Saint Patrick but there is Horatio,
    And much offence too. Touching this vision here,
    It is an honest ghost, that let me tell you.
    For your desire to know what is between us,
    O'ermaster't as you may. And now good friends,   140
    As you are friends, scholars, and soldiers,
    Give me one poor request.
HORATIO What is't my lord? we will.
HAMLET Never make known what you have seen tonight.
HORATIO ⎫
MARCELLUS ⎰   My lord we will not.
HAMLET   Nay but swear't.
HORATIO   In faith   145
    My lord not I.

       the current, and staggered away almost drunkenly, while muttering "But he's an arrant
       knave"' (Grebanier, *Actor*, pp. 143–4).

130–1a 'Forbes-Robertson made Hamlet suddenly perceive that he is a doomed man', now excluded
       from pursuing business and desire (*Sunday Times*, 18 November 1934, p. 4).

133–4a Of Irving: 'His thoughts are not in the chance phrase of regret. But before anybody else he
       would have veiled their absence with a more careful civility of manner' (*Academy*, 7
       November 1874, p. 519).

   136 Both Kemble and Henderson started to confide to Horatio, emphasizing *is* but stopped when
       Marcellus pressed forward to hear (Boaden, p. 98). With Booth, 'again and again he came
       near the point, standing with hands on the shoulders of Horatio, peering eagerly as if to read
       his soul in his face, then turns away with some senseless jest' unwilling 'to unveil the horror
       of the tale' (Garland, 'Lecture', p. 19).

137–40 Fechter addressed the first lines to Horatio; at 'for *your* desire' he looked at Marcellus (Field,
       p. 101).

MARCELLUS   Nor I my lord in faith.
HAMLET Upon my sword.
MARCELLUS   We have sworn my lord already.
HAMLET Indeed, upon my sword, indeed.
GHOST Swear.   *Ghost cries under the stage*
HAMLET Ha, ha, boy, sayst thou so? art thou there truepenny?   150
        Come on, you hear this fellow in the cellarage,
        Consent to swear.
HORATIO   Propose the oath my lord.
HAMLET Never to speak of this that you have seen,
        Swear by my sword.
GHOST Swear.   155
HAMLET *Hic et ubique?* then we'll shift our ground.
        Come hither gentlemen,
        And lay your hands again upon my sword.
        Never to speak of this that you have heard,
        Swear by my sword.   160
GHOST Swear.
HAMLET Well said old mole, canst work i'th'earth so fast?
        A worthy pioneer. Once more remove, good friends.
HORATIO O day and night, but this is wondrous strange.
HAMLET And therefore as a stranger give it welcome.   165
        There are more things in heaven and earth, Horatio,
        Than are dreamt of in your philosophy.
        But come –
        Here as before, never so help you mercy,
        How strange or odd some'er I bear myself,   170

147   J. B. Booth held out the hilt of his sword, the cross and not the blade for the others to swear
      by (Gould, p. 56). Edwin Booth held 'the crossed hilt upright between the two, his head
      thrown back and lit with high resolve' (*Atlantic Monthly*, May, 1866).

150b Booth: 'This is not unfeeling levity but the very intensity of mental excitement' (studybook).
      Burton: 'one half of him would be humorously inclined to believe that the Ghost is a devil
      and is making fun of him, and the other half will say, "No, it is true" . . . Hamlet is continually
      making fun of himself at the moment of high pity and terror and great passion' (Sterne, p.
      287).

167   Following the Folio, Kean substituted *our* for *your* (the readings in Q1 and Q2). Not wanting
      to insult Horatio, Fechter accented *philosophy* rather than *your* (Field, p. 102). Forbes-
      Robertson similarly 'relieved the sentence of the somewhat discourteous tone which it might
      otherwise bear' (Crosse, *Diaries*, II, 1898). Burton in 1964 touched his cheek with a winning
      smile and look.

As I perchance hereafter shall think meet
To put an antic disposition on –
That you at such times seeing me never shall,
With arms encumbered thus, or this head-shake,
Or by pronouncing of some doubtful phrase, 175
As 'Well, well, we know,' or 'We could and if we would,'
Or 'If we list to speak,' or 'There be and if they might,'
Or such ambiguous giving out, to note
That you know aught of me: this not to do,
So grace and mercy at your most need help you, 180
Swear.

GHOST Swear.

HAMLET Rest, rest, perturbèd spirit. So gentlemen,
With all my love I do commend me to you,
And what so poor a man as Hamlet is 185
May do t'express his love and friending to you,
God willing shall not lack. Let us go in together,
And still your fingers on your lips I pray. –
The time is out of joint: O cursèd spite,
That ever I was born to set it right. – 190
Nay come, let's go together.

Exeunt

171–2   Burton rumpled his hair forward slightly.

174   'Irving takes the arm of one of his companions, as he supposes they may take each others' hereafter, and assumes a confidential air, as if the two were comparing their past recollections' (Russell, p. 33).

182–3a   Booth: 'Swear' 'should be given as a long-drawn, far off sigh' until it fades into Hamlet's 'rest, rest, perturbed spirit', 'which should be spoken in the same key' (studybook).
     Caressingly at 183a Salvini 'extended his hands and murmured, in a tenderly imploring tone of voice' (*Boston Globe*, 3 October 1873).

189b–90   Booth: 'to himself. 'Tis the groan of his over-burthened soul' (studybook).

190   With Fechter, Marcellus 'again makes a movement of curiosity' and – ever suspicious of him – Hamlet 'motions him away and goes up with Horatio – Marcellus following' (promptbook).
     Leslie Howard emphasized *I* because 'he knows so clearly that it is his business not to do things but to consider them curiously' (*The Nation*, 21 November 1936). Very young and fragile, Guinness in 1938 looked at his sword with a 'curiously impotent expression' (Williamson, *Old Vic*, p. 107).

191   Hamlets have frequently reached out to the others for companionship here. Macready did so (*Morning Post*, 2 November 1874) as did Irving (*Belgravia*, December 1874, p. 188); so did Barrett, emphasizing *together* (*Shakespeariana*, p. 46). With Gielgud: seeing Hamlet shiver

Horatio wraps his own cloak around him. Suddenly realizing Horatio is cloakless, Hamlet's 'right arm with the cloak sweeps over Horatio's shoulders in an enveloping gesture of trust and affection' (Gilder, p. 120). As Booth left the stage he showed 'head-resolve but heart-doubt, despair, aching memory, and gloomy self-reliance' (Shattuck, p. 159). Irving spoke the very last line with a 'pensively bowed head' (Russell, pp. 31–2) and a 'down-hearted accent' (*Belgravia*, December 1874, p. 188). As the curtain came down, he turned his head to where the Ghost had been (promptbook).

ACT 2, SCENE I

2.1 *Enter* POLONIUS *and* REYNALDO

POLONIUS Give him this money, and these notes, Reynaldo.
REYNALDO I will my lord.
POLONIUS You shall do marvellous wisely, good Reynaldo,
       Before you visit him, to make inquire
       Of his behaviour.
REYNALDO   My lord, I did intend it.   5

OSD Q2: 'Enter old Polonius, with his man or two'. In the Branagh/Noble production, 'David Bradley's grey-faced Polonius sits behind a vast desk, a grey hatstand on one side, a ten-foot-high pile of grey filing cabinets on the other, a Kafkaesque clerk greyly hovering in front of a grey cyclorama' (*The Times*, 21 December 1992); he is 'a razor-faced, upright senior civil servant, self-important, capable, imperious and narrow, always economical with the *actualité* and just beginning to lose his grip' (*Sunday Times*, 27 December 1992).

2 From his 1937 production with Olivier, Tyrone Guthrie remembered the very young Alec Guinness as Reynaldo – 'a gentleman's gentleman whose extravagant primness did not prevent one seeing that he was a snake in the grass' (*Shakespeare*, p. 188). Directing Dillon Evans for the Burton production, Gielgud told him to 'make Reynaldo a civil servant, foreign office, enormously condescending. The bored feeling of someone who knows everything' (Sterne, p. 57). He is at first superciliously 'indulgent' at 5; at 24 he is not above helpfully contributing a suggestion to Polonius's plan; but then he is eager to be on his way. He starts putting on his gloves at 35, 'giving a final tug on his gloves, hoping to end the conversation' at 48. His 'My lord, I have' at 67 is 'long-suffering', and he starts to exit at each of his next two lines only to be interrupted by Polonius's after-thoughts. At 72 he 'whisks out' before Polonius can deliver his final farewell (Sterne, pp. 174–6).

3–6 In the Branagh film Reynaldo (Gerard Depardieu) is played as a pimp (a prostitute is in the background), Polonius (Richard Briers) as his client, is still tidying his clothes. The politesse of this exchange is heavily ironic on both sides, part of their 'low-life sparring match' (*Screenplay*, p. 43).

5 In the Kingsley/Goodbody production (1975), Charles Dance in general submitted to

POLONIUS Marry well said, very well said. Look you sir,
        Inquire me first what Danskers are in Paris,
        And how, and who, what means, and where they keep,
        What company, at what expense; and finding
        By this encompassment and drift of question   10
        That they do know my son, come you more nearer
        Than your particular demands will touch it.
        Take you as 'twere some distant knowledge of him,
        As thus, 'I know his father and his friends,
        And in part him' – do you mark this Reynaldo?   15
REYNALDO Ay, very well, my lord.
POLONIUS 'And in part him, but' – you may say – 'not well,
        But if't be he I mean, he's very wild,
        Addicted so and so' – and there put on him
        What forgeries you please; marry, none so rank   20
        As may dishonour him, take heed of that,
        But sir, such wanton, wild, and usual slips
        As are companions noted and most known
        To youth and liberty.
REYNALDO   As gaming my lord?
POLONIUS Ay, or drinking, fencing, swearing,   25
        Quarrelling, drabbing – you may go so far.
REYNALDO My lord, that would dishonour him.
POLONIUS Faith no, as you may season it in the charge.
        You must not put another scandal on him,
        That he is open to incontinency,   30
        That's not my meaning. But breathe his faults so quaintly
        That they may seem the taints of liberty,
        The flash and outbreak of a fiery mind,
        A savageness in unreclaimèd blood,
        Of general assault.
REYNALDO   But my good lord –   35
POLONIUS Wherefore should you do this?

Polonius's instruction 'with obsequious contempt' (*The Times*, 5 February 1976). He
delivered this line with 'a deprecatory, cocky little half-sneer, as if to say, "Don't tell me how
to suck eggs. I've learned all I can from you about the business. Why don't you retire and let
me take over?" He is a thrusting junior executive' (*Times Higher Education Supplement*, 13
February 1976). The exchange contributed to 'a climate of suspicion and intrigue' (*Observer*,
8 February 1976).

26   In the Branagh film, Polonius at 'drabbing' signals the prostitute to go; that Reynaldo 'enjoys
     the irony of the situation' (*Screenplay*, p. 44) is shown by Depardieu's grin at 58–9.

REYNALDO   Ay my lord,
    I would know that.
POLONIUS   Marry sir, here's my drift,
    And I believe it is a fetch of warrant.
    You laying these slight sullies on my son,
    As 'twere a thing a little soiled i'th'working,   40
    Mark you,
    Your party in converse, him you would sound,
    Having ever seen in the prenominate crimes
    The youth you breathe of guilty, be assured
    He closes with you in this consequence,   45
    'Good sir', or so, or 'friend', or 'gentleman',
    According to the phrase and the addition
    Of man and country.
REYNALDO   Very good my lord.
POLONIUS And then sir does a this – a does – what was I about to say?
    By the mass I was about to say something. Where did I leave?   50
REYNALDO At 'closes in the consequence', at 'friend, or so', and
    'gentleman'.
POLONIUS At 'closes in the consequence' – ay marry,
    He closes with you thus: 'I know the gentleman,
    I saw him yesterday, or th'other day,   55
    Or then, or then, with such or such, and as you say,
    There was a gaming, there o'ertook in's rouse,
    There falling out at tennis', or perchance,
    'I saw him enter such a house of sale' –
    Videlicet, a brothel – or so forth. See you now,   60
    Your bait of falsehood takes this carp of truth,
    And thus do we of wisdom and of reach,
    With windlasses and with assays of bias,
    By indirections find directions out.
    So, by my former lecture and advice,   65
    Shall you my son. You have me, have you not?

51   Q1 and Q2 do not include F's 'At friend, or so, and Gentleman'. Especially as originally
    punctuated, F allows for more comic by-play. At Minneapolis Guthrie's Reynaldo has been
    taking notes, reads back from them.

53   In the Branagh film Polonius tries to regain the upper hand by treating this phrase as the
    'correct' answer to his question amid Reynaldo's scatter-shot recollections.

59–60   With Warner, Tony Church emphasized a streak of 'prurient sexuality' in Polonius that
    prompted his desire for details about Laertes's escapades (Church, 'Polonius', p. 107).

REYNALDO My lord, I have.
POLONIUS   God buy ye, fare ye well.
REYNALDO Good my lord.
POLONIUS Observe his inclination in yourself.
REYNALDO I shall my lord.
POLONIUS And let him ply his music.   70
REYNALDO   Well my lord.
POLONIUS Farewell.

                                                    Exit Reynaldo

                    Enter OPHELIA

                    How now Ophelia, what's the matter?
OPHELIA Oh my lord, my lord, I have been so affrighted.
POLONIUS With what, i'th'name of God?
OPHELIA My lord, as I was sewing in my closet,   75
          Lord Hamlet with his doublet all unbraced,
          No hat upon his head, his stockings fouled,
          Ungartered, and down-gyvèd to his ankle,
          Pale as his shirt, his knees knocking each other,
          And with a look so piteous in purport   80
          As if he had been loosèd out of hell
          To speak of horrors – he comes before me.
POLONIUS Mad for thy love?
OPHELIA   My lord I do not know,
          But truly I do fear it.
POLONIUS   What said he?
OPHELIA He took me by the wrist, and held me hard;   85
          Then goes he to the length of all his arm,
          And with his other hand thus o'er his brow
          He falls to such perusal of my face
          As a would draw it. Long stayed he so;
          At last, a little shaking of mine arm,   90
          And thrice his head thus waving up and down,

---

67   As Reynaldo Guinness here 'listened with a discreet, hooded smile to his master's haverings
     and found a gentle emphasis for his reply . . . "My lord, I *have*"' (Trewin, *Five & Eighty*, pp.
     176, 47).

83   In the 1964 Burton, director Gielgud 'felt it should be a statement, though [Hume] Cronyn
     preferred to keep it a question so that his later line, "That hath made him mad," could be
     delivered as a concluding statement' (Sterne, p. 26).

85ff Marlowe reenacted the encounter, doing herself what Hamlet did as if Polonius were herself
     (promptbook).

He raised a sigh so piteous and profound
As it did seem to shatter all his bulk,
And end his being. That done, he lets me go,
And with his head over his shoulder turned   95
He seemed to find his way without his eyes,
For out-a-doors he went without their helps
And to the last bended their light on me.
POLONIUS Come, go with me, I will go seek the king.
This is the very ecstasy of love,   100
Whose violent property fordoes itself,
And leads the will to desperate undertakings
As oft as any passion under heaven
That does afflict our natures. I am sorry.
What, have you given him any hard words of late?   105
OPHELIA No my good lord; but as you did command,
I did repel his letters, and denied
His access to me.
POLONIUS   That hath made him mad.
I am sorry that with better heed and judgement
I had not quoted him. I feared he did but trifle,   110
And meant to wrack thee, but beshrew my jealousy.
By heaven, it is as proper to our age
To cast beyond ourselves in our opinions
As it is common for the younger sort

To lack discretion. Come, go we to the king.   115
This must be known, which being kept close, might move
More grief to hide than hate to utter love.
Come.

                                                        Exeunt

99ff   Here and at 118 'come' does not appear in F as it does in Q2. To Rosenberg (p. 367) this
       suggests a more 'resistant' Ophelia in Q2. Only in Q1, however, does she actually go with
       him to the King at this point.
108a   Marlowe wiped her eyes (promptbook).
115b   Frances Barber, with Roger Rees, was shocked at 'divulging so much information' ('Ophelia',
       p. 142).
118   Church's fatherly 1980 Polonius covered his frightened daughter (Carol Royle) in his robes
       of state and led her protectively from the stage; Glenda Jackson in 1965 had used similar
       business (Church, 'Polonius', p. 110). Compare 4.5.20SD.

ACT 2, SCENE 2

2.2 *Flourish. Enter* KING *and* QUEEN, ROSENCRANTZ *and* GUILDEN-STERN, *with others*

CLAUDIUS Welcome dear Rosencrantz and Guildenstern!
        Moreover that we much did long to see you,
        The need we have to use you did provoke
        Our hasty sending. Something have you heard
        Of Hamlet's transformation – so call it,   5

OSD   Macready blocked this episode as a full court scene (promptbook 29).
    Rosencrantz and Guildenstern are commonly regarded as indistinguishable nonentities. With Garrick, their portrayers were 'two very pliant courtly young men': 'Good clothes, tolerable persons and well-powdered wigs (which is not always the case) are the requisite qualifications for these two young well-bred gentlemen' (*St. James's Chronicle*, 3 March 1772). Olivier cut them out of his film altogether.
    Many productions in the latter part of the twentieth century have had fun with royal confusions about their identities. During rehearsals at Minneapolis Guthrie experimented with various refinements on this mix-up. At first, the King cannot remember their names and bluffs it through with mumbles and hearty handshakes (Rossi, p. 15), next he hesitates but then remembers (p. 23), finally: 'The King remembers the *names* but not the *faces*; Claudius says, "Welcome dear Rosencrantz . . . " but then looks from one to the other for an acknowledgment before extending his hand' (p. 56).
    The most elaborated confusion is in Tom Stoppard's *Rosencrantz and Guildenstern Are Dead*, where the King's initial mix-up causes each of the two to bow when the King thinks he is addressing the other. As they realize that their identities have been mixed, the courtiers do their best to bow accordingly, so that Rosencrantz when half-way up from his previous bow 'bows down again. With his head down, he twists to look at Guildenstern, who is on the way up.' Their contortions alert the King to his mistake and the next time he addresses them (33), he gets their identities right, but they bow as if he still had them confused. The confusion is further compounded when Gertrude, thinking she is correcting the King, again reverses their identities, leaving them at one point 'both bent double, squinting at each other'.

Sith nor th'exterior nor the inward man
Resembles that it was. What it should be,
More than his father's death, that thus hath put him
So much from th'understanding of himself,
I cannot dream of. I entreat you both,   10
That being of so young days brought up with him,
And sith so neighboured to his youth and haviour,
That you vouchsafe your rest here in our court
Some little time, so by your companies
To draw him on to pleasures, and to gather   15
So much as from occasion you may glean,
Whether aught to us unknown afflicts him thus,
That opened lies within our remedy.

GERTRUDE Good gentlemen, he hath much talked of you,
And sure I am, two men there is not living   20
To whom he more adheres. If it will please you
To show us so much gentry and good will
As to expend your time with us a while,
For the supply and profit of our hope,
Your visitation shall receive such thanks   25
As fits a king's remembrance.

ROSENCRANTZ   Both your majesties
Might by the sovereign power you have of us
Put your dread pleasures more into command
Than to entreaty.

GUILDENSTERN   But we both obey,
And here give up ourselves in the full bent   30
To lay our service freely at your feet
To be commanded.

CLAUDIUS Thanks Rosencrantz, and gentle Guildenstern.

GERTRUDE Thanks Guildenstern, and gentle Rosencrantz.
And I beseech you instantly to visit   35
My too much changèd son. Go some of you
And bring these gentlemen where Hamlet is.

34 In Evans's *G. I. Hamlet*, after the Queen thanks Guildenstern 'A look from the King reminds
    her that she has omitted thanking Rosencrantz', which she hastens to do (p. 82). Of the
    Albert Finney/Peter Hall production in 1976, David objects to the 'corny old joke' of making
    the Queen's reversal of the names a correction, contrasting it with the Kingsley/Goodbody
    version in which 'King and Queen were in full agreement as to the identities of their guests,
    and Gertrude's reversal of the names was merely an elegant courtesy to ensure that each
    was accorded equal precedence' (*Theatre*, p. 78). In the BBC-TV version (1980) the Queen
    (Claire Bloom) reverts to correcting the King's mistake by addressing the two properly. So
    does Julie Christie in the Branagh film.

GUILDENSTERN Heavens make our presence and our practices
    Pleasant and helpful to him.
GERTRUDE   Ay, amen.
    Exeunt Rosencrantz and Guildenstern [and some Attendants]

Enter POLONIUS

POLONIUS Th'ambassadors from Norway, my good lord,   40
    Are joyfully returned.
CLAUDIUS Thou still hast been the father of good news.
POLONIUS Have I my lord? Assure you, my good liege,
    I hold my duty, as I hold my soul,
    Both to my God and to my gracious king;   45
    And I do think, or else this brain of mine
    Hunts not the trail of policy so sure
    As it hath used to do, that I have found
    The very cause of Hamlet's lunacy.
CLAUDIUS Oh speak of that, that do I long to hear.   50
POLONIUS Give first admittance to th'ambassadors;
    My news shall be the fruit to that great feast.
CLAUDIUS Thyself do grace to them and bring them in.
                             [Exit Polonius]
    He tells me, my dear Gertrude, he hath found
    The head and source of all your son's distemper.   55
GERTRUDE I doubt it is no other but the main:
    His father's death, and our o'erhasty marriage.
CLAUDIUS Well, we shall sift him.

Enter POLONIUS, VOLTEMAND *and* CORNELIUS

                   Welcome my good friends.
    Say Voltemand, what from our brother Norway?
VOLTEMAND Most fair return of greetings and desires.   60
    Upon our first, he sent out to suppress
    His nephew's levies, which to him appeared
    To be a preparation 'gainst the Polack;
    But better looked into, he truly found
    It was against your highness; whereat grieved   65
    That so his sickness, age and impotence
    Was falsely borne in hand, sends out arrests
    On Fortinbras, which he in brief obeys,
    Receives rebuke from Norway, and in fine
    Makes vow before his uncle never more   70
    To give th'assay of arms against your majesty.
    Whereon old Norway, overcome with joy,
    Gives him three thousand crowns in annual fee,

And his commission to employ those soldiers,
So levied as before, against the Polack;   75
With an entreaty, herein further shown,
That it might please you to give quiet pass
Through your dominions for this enterprise,
On such regards of safety and allowance
As therein are set down.

                    [*Gives a document*]

CLAUDIUS   It likes us well,   80
And at our more considered time we'll read,
Answer, and think upon this business.
Meantime, we thank you for your well-took labour.
Go to your rest; at night we'll feast together.
Most welcome home.

                                   Exeunt Ambassadors

POLONIUS   This business is well ended.   85
My liege, and madam, to expostulate
What majesty should be, what duty is,
Why day is day, night night, and time is time,
Were nothing but to waste night, day, and time.
Therefore, since brevity is the soul of wit   90
And tediousness the limbs and outward flourishes,
I will be brief. Your noble son is mad.
Mad call I it, for to define true madness,
What is't but to be nothing else but mad?
But let that go.

GERTRUDE   More matter with less art.   95

76–80   This request drew a reaction from Donald Sinden, Polonius with Stephen Dillane, that was
        'swift and warily disapproving' (*Sunday Times*, 13 November 1994).

85SD   Rylance/Daniels: At the success of the diplomacy with Norway, Clare Higgins threw herself
        into the arms of Claudius (Peter Wight) – a tender moment interrupted by Polonius.

86ff   Evans: Polonius (Thomas Chalmers) is 'basking in his own importance, he speaks as though
        addressing an assembly' (*G. I. Hamlet*, p. 83). Warner/Hall: When Tony Church's Polonius
        proved to be not as funny as hoped, he doubled his speaking-rate, speeding up the
        reactions of the other characters, 'and the laughter started' (Church, 'Polonius', p. 107). On
        BBC-TV Eric Porter delivers Polonius's pedantries, not with a flourish but as a fussiness of
        mind that is out of his own control. As a way of asserting his control, Michael Bryant, with
        Day Lewis, 'paces himself very slowly so that instead of being garrulous, he is ponderous'
        (*Literary Reviews*, March 1989).

92b   Bryant has 'a habit of blurting out blunt truths' (*Manchester Guardian*, 18 March 1989).

POLONIUS Madam, I swear I use no art at all.
That he is mad, 'tis true; 'tis true 'tis pity,
And pity 'tis 'tis true – a foolish figure,
But farewell it, for I will use no art.
Mad let us grant him then, and now remains   100
That we find out the cause of this effect,
Or rather say, the cause of this defect,
For this effect defective comes by cause.
Thus it remains, and the remainder thus.
Perpend.   105
I have a daughter – have while she is mine –
Who in her duty and obedience, mark,
Hath given me this. Now gather and surmise.

Reads the letter

'To the celestial, and my soul's idol, the most beautified Ophelia,' –
That's an ill phrase, a vile phrase, 'beautified' is a vile phrase – but   110
you shall hear. Thus:
'In her excellent white bosom, these, *et cetera*.'
GERTRUDE Came this from Hamlet to her?
POLONIUS Good madam stay awhile, I will be faithful.
'Doubt thou the stars are fire,   115
Doubt that the sun doth move,
Doubt truth to be a liar,
But never doubt I love.
'O dear Ophelia, I am ill at these numbers, I have not art to reckon
my groans; but that I love thee best, O most best, believe it. Adieu.   120
'Thine evermore, most dear lady, whilst this machine is
to him, Hamlet.'
This in obedience hath my daughter shown me,
And, more above, hath his solicitings,
As they fell out, by time, by means, and place,   125
All given to mine ear.

97–8 With Burton in 1964, Hume Cronyn hurried these lines when Gertrude seemed about to
repeat 'less art'. He held his hand up to stop her, conceded 'a foolish figure'. When she tried
to hurry him again at line 113, he had his revenge: 'sta-a-y awhile' (be patient).

105 After 'perpend', the Branagh film has Ophelia (Kate Winslet) come in at her father's
interpolated call for her (Q1 has her on-stage throughout this episode). At 'these' (112), she
breaks down and runs from the room (*Screenplay*, p. 178).

106b Michael Redgrave with Richard Chamberlain on television (1970) crossed himself.

112–14 'With an embarrassed glance at the Queen he clears his throat and mumbles "*et cetera*"'.
Gertrude says 113 while 'reaching for the letter', which Polonius draws back at 114 (*G. I.
Hamlet*, p. 84).

CLAUDIUS   But how hath she
                Received his love?
POLONIUS   What do you think of me?
CLAUDIUS As of a man faithful and honourable.
POLONIUS I would fain prove so. But what might you think,
                When I had seen this hot love on the wing –   130
                As I perceived it, I must tell you that,
                Before my daughter told me – what might you,
                Or my dear majesty your queen here, think,
                If I had played the desk, or table-book,
                Or given my heart a winking, mute and dumb,   135
                Or looked upon this love with idle sight –
                What might you think? No, I went round to work,
                And my young mistress thus I did bespeak:
                'Lord Hamlet is a prince out of thy star.
                This must not be.' And then I prescripts gave her,   140
                That she should lock herself from his resort,
                Admit no messengers, receive no tokens.
                Which done, she took the fruits of my advice,
                And he, repulsed – a short tale to make –
                Fell into a sadness, then into a fast,   145
                Thence to a watch, thence into a weakness,
                Thence to a lightness, and by this declension
                Into the madness wherein now he raves,
                And all we mourn for.
CLAUDIUS   Do you think 'tis this?
GERTRUDE It may be, very like.   150
POLONIUS Hath there been such a time, I'ld fain know that,
                That I have positively said, 'tis so,
                When it proved otherwise?
CLAUDIUS   Not that I know.
POLONIUS Take this from this, if this be otherwise.
                If circumstances lead me, I will find   155
                Where truth is hid, though it were hid indeed
                Within the centre.
CLAUDIUS   How may we try it further?

145–9   With Burton, Cronyn took a step at each phrase of the 'declension'.

149b   Of Michael Pennington, Claudius to Stephen Dillane's Hamlet: 'He likes the idea that
           Hamlet's problem is love – he's a lover himself' (*Times Educational Supplement*, 1994).

151–3   When at 150 the King expresses doubt about his judgement, Bryant's self-important Polonius
           explodes into 'uncourtly indignation' (*Independent*, 18 March 1989).

153   In the Olivier film Basil Sydney sceptically emphasized *know*.

POLONIUS You know sometimes he walks four hours together
  Here in the lobby.
GERTRUDE   So he does indeed.
POLONIUS At such a time I'll loose my daughter to him.   160
  Be you and I behind an arras then.
  Mark the encounter: if he love her not,
  And be not from his reason fallen thereon,
  Let me be no assistant for a state,
  But keep a farm and carters.
CLAUDIUS   We will try it.   165

    Enter HAMLET *reading on a book*

166SD This is the audience's first view of Hamlet since he declared his intention to assume an 'antic disposition' (1.5.172) and Ophelia described his altered attire and behaviour (2.1.75–82). In 1604 Anthony Skoloker refers to how 'mad Hamlet puts off his cloathes, his shirt he only weares' (*Munro, Allusion Book*, 1, p. 133). Of Garrick: 'his thick hair dishevelled and a lock hanging over one shoulder; one of his black stockings has slipped down so as to show his white socks, and a loop of his red garter is hanging down beyond the middle of the calf' (Lichtenberg, *Visits*, p. 16). In the Restoration and eighteenth century, Hamlet's stockings were traditionally 'down-gyved'. The frontispiece to Rowe's 1709 edition, which may well reflect performance in Betterton's time, shows his stocking fallen down. At mid-century *The Connoisseur* observed: 'The players are afraid we should lose sight of Hamlet's pretended madness, if the black stockings, discovering a white one underneath, was not rolled half way down the leg' (19 September 1754). In the late 1790s, prints show Henry Johnston thus attired. In 1838 it was controversial when Charles Kean entered 'without any disorder of dress' (*Dramatic Essays*, p. 45; also Cole, *Charles Kean*, 1, p. 282); perhaps it would have seemed out of keeping with the tunic and hose he was introducing. After that the practice appears to have become much less common, and to Gielgud in 1937 it seemed 'almost impossible, in any costume, to follow Ophelia's detailed account . . . without continually distracting the audience' (Gilder, p. 32). Miming to Ophelia's voice-over account, Olivier wore his 'doublet all unbraced' but did not otherwise follow Ophelia's description of his attire, cutting 77–8. Later Hamlets have felt freer in marking his antic change. Warner wore spectacles and a funny hat. In 1992/3 Branagh donned a straitjacket 'as a prop that goes with his double talk' (*Shakespeare Bulletin*, Fall, 1994, p. 7); later the King would use it as a forcible constraint on his 'mad' nephew.
  In Moscow (1912) Hamlet here silently traversed the stage, his dark figure contrasting with the screens, the gilt of which was made to shimmer by reddish lighting. He was absorbed in a book which to Osanai looked like the 'tables' he used to record the Ghost's words ('Craig's Production', p. 591). At one point he looked around 'suspiciously' (Morgan, *Encounter*, p.

GERTRUDE But look where sadly the poor wretch comes reading.

POLONIUS Away, I do beseech you both, away.

        I'll board him presently.

                    Exeunt Claudius and Gertrude [and Attendants]

                        Oh give me leave.

        How does my good Lord Hamlet?

HAMLET Well, God-a-mercy. 170

POLONIUS Do you know me, my lord?

HAMLET Excellent well, y'are a fishmonger.

POLONIUS Not I my lord.

HAMLET Then I would you were so honest a man.

POLONIUS Honest my lord? 175

HAMLET Ay sir. To be honest, as this world goes, is to be one man picked out of ten thousand.

POLONIUS That's very true my lord.

HAMLET For if the sun breed maggots in a dead dog, being a good kissing carrion – Have you a daughter? 180

POLONIUS I have my lord.

HAMLET Let her not walk i'th'sun. Conception is a blessing, but as your daughter may conceive – Friend, look to't.

POLONIUS (*Aside*) How say you by that? Still harping on my daughter. Yet he knew me not at first, a said I was a fishmonger – a is far 185 gone, far gone. And truly, in my youth I suffered much extremity for love, very near this. I'll speak to him again. – What do you read my lord?

106). A reviewer marvelled at the power of the resulting image of Hamlet 'so alone amidst those enormous walls, so dark amidst the gold, so alien to everything' (Senelick, p. 162). This was precisely Craig's point (Senelick, pp. 64, 69).

169 Macready 'convinces the audience by his manner that he suspects [Polonius] of having been sent as a spy' (*Theatrical Journal*, 5 September 1840, p. 312). Repeatedly in this exchange Irving in his studybook has Polonius 'follow after' Hamlet. J. H. Barnes, Polonius to Forbes-Robertson, treated 'what he considers the madness of Hamlet as a thing to be pitied and endured' (*Stage*, 16 September 1897).

170 In Moscow (1912) 'Kachalov, following Craig's and Stanislavsky's instructions, is neither scornful nor vicious; instead, he tries to elude his unwished-for interlocutor, to turn the conversation into a joke, warn him with a laugh away from his dishonorable games' (Senelick, p. 163).

180 Irving: After 'carrion' Polonius tries to look at Hamlet's book; he closes it (promptbook).

180ff Barrymore 'made you feel that Polonius for Hamlet stood for the kind of thing in life that had taken Ophelia from him' (*New Republic*, 6 December 1922, p. 45).

HAMLET Words, words, words.

POLONIUS What is the matter, my lord? 190

HAMLET Between who?

POLONIUS I mean the matter that you read, my lord.

HAMLET Slanders sir, for the satirical rogue says here that old men have
grey beards, that their faces are wrinkled, their eyes purging thick
amber and plumtree gum, and that they have a plentiful lack of wit, 195
together with most weak hams. All which sir, though I most
powerfully and potently believe, yet I hold it not honesty to have
it thus set down. For yourself sir shall grow old as I am, if like a
crab you could go backward.

POLONIUS (*Aside*) Though this be madness, yet there is method 200
in't. – Will you walk out of the air, my lord?

HAMLET Into my grave?

POLONIUS Indeed that's out of the air. (*Aside*) How pregnant sometimes
his replies are! a happiness that often madness hits on, which reason
and sanity could not so prosperously be delivered of. I will leave 205

189 Hamlets have frequently repeated 'words' in different tones. Fechter changed from listless
to excited (Phelps, p. 95), Rossi from irritation to regret to resignation (*Academy*, 13 May
1870, p. 445), Bernhardt from indifference to sighing acknowledgement that 'all books and
everything else in life and in the whole world are only "words, words, words, words"'
(Marius Baring, quoted by MacCarthy, *Theatre*, p. 154). With Gielgud: '"Words," the answer
is instantaneous, mechanical, then a pause, looking out. "Words, words." He speaks with a
sombre emphasis. A quick straightening of the body, the shadow of a gesture of futility,
unveils the depths of weariness within' (Gilder, p. 131). With Kingsley: '"Words", curt;
"Worrds" as, seated back to the audience, he flips over the pages of his book under the old
man's peering nose; a pause, and then "Words", sharp and rudely dismissive' (David,
Theatre, p. 70).

190–2 Warner/Hall: Tony Church's crafty 1965 Polonius knowingly acts stupid 'as a mask to hide his
real thoughts and to flatter the intelligence of his hearers'. Here he realizes that Hamlet is
deliberately misunderstanding him and delivers his reply 'laughing as if to say, "I know you
are mocking me"' (Church, 'Polonius', pp. 106, 108).

193 At 'Slanders': Kemble tore a page out of the book. Booth would wonder why (studybook).
Boaden thought it was 'to give the stronger impression of his wildness' (pp. 98–9).

198–9 Wearing a straitjacket as an emblem of the 'antic disposition' he was assuming, Branagh in
1992/3 waved the straitjacket's flapping arms as he walked backwards away from Polonius;
his interviewer remarks that 'it got a huge laugh' (*Shakespeare Bulletin*, Fall, 1994, p. 7).

202 Macready said 'grave' 'interrogatively' (Hackett, *Notes*, p. 148). F has a question-mark, the
Quartos do not.

203–4 With Burton, Cronyn was genuinely amused. He shook his head and shared his admiration
with the audience.

him, and suddenly contrive the means of meeting between him and
my daughter. – My honourable lord, I will most humbly take my
leave of you.

HAMLET You cannot sir take from me anything that I will more
willingly part withal; except my life, except my life, except my life. 210

POLONIUS Fare you well my lord.

HAMLET These tedious old fools!

Enter GUILDENSTERN *and* ROSENCRANTZ

POLONIUS You go to seek the Lord Hamlet, there he is.

ROSENCRANTZ God save you sir.

[*Exit Polonius*]

GUILDENSTERN My honoured lord! 215

ROSENCRANTZ My most dear lord!

HAMLET My excellent good friends! How dost thou Guildenstern? Ah,
Rosencrantz. Good lads, how do you both?

210 William Dean Howells, the American man of letters, recalled that Fechter 'put such divine
despair into the words . . . that the heartbreak of them . . . lingered with me for thirty years'
(*Literature*, p. 135).

212 Fechter was indulgent with Polonius, spoke here 'more with a shrug of patient pity, than in
petulance' (*Orchestra*, 28 May 1864).

212SD In Moscow (1912) 'Rosencrantz and Guildenstern enter timorously, shoulder to shoulder,
eyeing each other askance, suspicious of one another' and everyone else. After greeting
them warmly, Kachalov soon divines their designs: 'the palms of his hands, softly lying on
his sword's hilt, gradually squeezed it to prevent his scorn from erupting outwardly, a
shadow of a smile said that the cunning of his companions was revealed'. When he asked
them to be frank with him, his inner stress caused a 'lightning-charged quaver' to run from
his shoulder through his palm to his sword-hilt (Senelick, pp. 163–4). Kachalov thus
combined and internalized the conflicting views held by Craig, who saw Hamlet as friendly
and trusting towards his former schoolmates, and Stanislavsky, who saw him as cold and
suspicious towards them from the outset (Senelick, p. 75).

In the 1964 Burton/Gielgud production, William Redfield at first portrayed Guildenstern
'as a man who curries favor, complete with bowing, scraping, and smiling' (*Letters*, p. 219).
After Gielgud suggested that Guildenstern 'should not be just a booby – he should be a
cunning booby' (Sterne, p. 113), Redfield overdid 'the sinister quality' until Gielgud objected
that he had become a 'thug' (Sterne, p. 140). In subsequent Guildensterns, a sinister quality
has often been emphasized.

217ff 'Macready happily kept up the quiet demeanour of conscious detection, of cool observance
yet friendly familiarity' (*Dramatic Essays*, p. 9). With Gielgud, the banter about fortune 'is
the small talk of the Renaissance gentleman. His wit, so acrid in his recent encounter with

ROSENCRANTZ As the indifferent children of the earth.

GUILDENSTERN Happy in that we are not over-happy; on Fortune's   220
cap we are not the very button.

HAMLET Nor the soles of her shoe?

ROSENCRANTZ Neither, my lord.

HAMLET Then you live about her waist, or in the middle of her favours?

GUILDENSTERN Faith, her privates we.   225

HAMLET In the secret parts of Fortune? Oh most true, she is a
strumpet. What news?

ROSENCRANTZ None my lord, but that the world's grown honest.

HAMLET Then is doomsday near – but your news is not true. Let me
question more in particular. What have you, my good friends,   230
deserved at the hands of Fortune, that she sends you to prison
hither?

GUILDENSTERN Prison, my lord?

HAMLET Denmark's a prison.

ROSENCRANTZ Then is the world one.   235

HAMLET A goodly one, in which there are many confines, wards, and
dungeons; Denmark being one o'th'worst.

ROSENCRANTZ We think not so my lord.

HAMLET Why then 'tis none to you, for there is nothing either good
or bad but thinking makes it so. To me it is a prison.   240

ROSENCRANTZ Why then your ambition makes it one; 'tis too narrow
for your mind.

HAMLET O God, I could be bounded in a nutshell, and count myself
a king of infinite space, were it not that I have bad dreams.

GUILDENSTERN Which dreams indeed are ambition, for the very   245
substance of the ambitious is merely the shadow of a dream.

HAMLET A dream itself is but a shadow.

ROSENCRANTZ Truly, and I hold ambition of so airy and light a quality
that it is but a shadow's shadow.

HAMLET Then are our beggars bodies, and our monarchs and out-   250
stretched heroes the beggars' shadows. Shall we to th'court? for by
my fay I cannot reason.

BOTH We'll wait upon you.

Polonius, is for the moment light and superficial. But he notices the forced note in the gaiety
of the other two' (Gilder, p. 133).

229–56   Not in Q1 or Q2. The passage in F, where Rosencrantz and Guildenstern both dwell on
'ambition', signpost for Hamlet their ulterior purposes. By arriving much sooner at his
surmise that they were sent for, the Prince of the Quartos may seem more discerning and
intuitive. Or perhaps the toadying of the pair was more overt than in the Folio version.

239   In his studybook, Irving wrote 'sighing' before 'Why 'tis none to you'.

HAMLET No such matter. I will not sort you with the rest of my
    servants; for to speak to you like an honest man, I am most   255
    dreadfully attended. But in the beaten way of friendship, what make
    you at Elsinore?
ROSENCRANTZ To visit you my lord, no other occasion.
HAMLET Beggar that I am, I am even poor in thanks, but I thank
    you – and sure, dear friends, my thanks are too dear a halfpenny.   260
    Were you not sent for? Is it your own inclining? Is it a free
    visitation? Come, deal justly with me. Come, come. Nay, speak.
GUILDENSTERN What should we say my lord?
HAMLET Why, anything but to the purpose. You were sent for – and
    there is a kind of confession in your looks which your modesties   265
    have not craft enough to colour. I know the good king and queen
    have sent for you.
ROSENCRANTZ To what end my lord?
HAMLET That you must teach me. But let me conjure you, by the rights
    of our fellowship, by the consonancy of our youth, by the obligation   270
    of our ever-preserved love, and by what more dear a better proposer
    can charge you withal, be even and direct with me, whether you
    were sent for or no.
ROSENCRANTZ (*To Guildenstern*) What say you?
HAMLET (*Aside*) Nay then I have an eye of you. – If you love me, hold   275
    not off.
GUILDENSTERN My lord, we were sent for.
HAMLET I will tell you why. So shall my anticipation prevent your
    discovery, and your secrecy to the king and queen moult no feather.

255   Peter Hall: 'Important findings at rehearsal': Hamlet (Albert Finney) knows at once that
    Rosencrantz and Guildenstern are spies; what he is concerned about is 'the honesty of the
    characters in their replies when he charges them with duplicity' (*Diaries*, p. 188).
264   In his studybook, Irving underlined '*sent* for' and wrote 'great disgust'. Stephen Dillane
    made the same emphasis 'with an utter despair at the betrayal of friendship' (*Country Life*,
    17 November 1994).
269–77 When Gielgud's final appeal for candour to Rosencrantz is met by a 'shallow, closed face',
    he wearily opens a big book: 'The two men start to consult each other with a glance and
    murmured word, but are instantly interrupted by a bang as Hamlet slams the book shut and
    flashes around on them, intercepting their exchange' (Gilder, p. 137).
278   Maximilian Schell in the film put his finger to his lips when Guildenstern seemed about to
    continue. Gielgud advised Burton: 'You mustn't be too sharp with Rosencrantz and
    Guildenstern in their first scene or else the recorder scene will be anticipated' (Sterne,
    p. 29).

I have of late, but wherefore I know not, lost all my mirth, forgone   280
all custom of exercises; and indeed it goes so heavily with my
disposition that this goodly frame, the earth, seems to me a sterile
promontory; this most excellent canopy the air, look you, this brave
o'erhanging firmament, this majestical roof fretted with golden
fire – why, it appeareth no other thing to me but a foul and pestilent   285
congregation of vapours. What a piece of work is a man! How noble
in reason, how infinite in faculties, in form and moving how express
and admirable, in action how like an angel, in apprehension how
like a god! The beauty of the world, the paragon of animals – and
yet to me, what is this quintessence of dust? Man delights not   290
me – no, nor woman neither, though by your smiling you seem to
say so.

ROSENCRANTZ My lord, there was no such stuff in my thoughts.

286 Macready adopted Kemble's omission of the definite article 'a' before 'man' (Hackett, *Notes*, p. 148).

286–9 Edwards largely follows the Folio punctuation, as have most actors. Q2 reads: ' . . . how noble in reason, how infinit in faculties, in forme and moouing, how expresse and admirable in action, how like an Angell in apprehension, how like a God'. Q2's punctuation points up differences in rhetorical patterning (from phrases beginning 'how . . . ' F shifts to 'in . . . ', Q2 to 'how like . . . ') and meaning (the quality attributed to angels in F is action, in Q2 apprehension). Most important for performance, Q2 also differs from F in tone. Beyond the marks of exclamation that Edwards uses, F employs such marks after 'reason', 'faculty', 'admirable', 'angel'. As Dover Wilson observes, F suggests a declamatory delivery where Q2, 'without an exclamation of any kind', seems 'brooding' (*Hamlet*, p. 175).

289–90 Fechter's 'pause at the end of the phrase "The paragon of animals", followed by the impatient wretchedness of the exclamation "And yet to me", was something thrilling' (*Sunday Times*, 24 March 1861).

290b 'For a time Barrymore used to laugh quite gaily at this point – and balance himself on the back of the chair' but soon stopped doing it (promptbook 156). In 1964 Burton spontaneously arrived at similar business during the whole of 280–90. As Sterne tells it, during the Boston tryout he climbed over a chair, in New York he started bouncing on the chair and towards the end of the run would sometimes walk on a table. Burton explained that he kept these bizarre acts to counteract his tendency to deliver the speech – his personal favourite – too lyrically and thus lose the audience's attention (pp. 190, 289). To Gary Wills, however, it made Burton's Prince seem 'not a tragic character playing a clown, but simply one too trivial to know how serious his situation is' (*National Review*, 2 June 1964).

HAMLET Why did ye laugh then, when I said man delights not me?

ROSENCRANTZ To think, my lord, if you delight not in man, what 295
lenten entertainment the players shall receive from you. We coted
them on the way, and hither are they coming to offer you service.

HAMLET He that plays the king shall be welcome, his majesty shall have
tribute of me; the adventurous knight shall use his foil and target,
the lover shall not sigh gratis, the humorous man shall end his part 300
in peace, the clown shall make those laugh whose lungs are tickle
o'th'sere, and the lady shall say her mind freely – or the blank verse
shall halt for't. What players are they?

ROSENCRANTZ Even those you were wont to take such delight in, the
tragedians of the city. 305

HAMLET How chances it they travel? their residence, both in reputation
and profit, was better both ways.

ROSENCRANTZ I think their inhibition comes by the means of the late
innovation.

HAMLET Do they hold the same estimation they did when I was in the 310
city? Are they so followed?

ROSENCRANTZ No indeed are they not.

HAMLET How comes it? Do they grow rusty?

ROSENCRANTZ Nay, their endeavour keeps in the wonted pace, but
there is sir an eyrie of children, little eyases, that cry out on the 315
top of question and are most tyrannically clapped for't. These are
now the fashion, and so be-rattle the common stages (so they call
them) that many wearing rapiers are afraid of goose-quills, and dare
scarce come thither.

HAMLET What, are they children? Who maintains 'em? How are they 320
escoted? Will they pursue the quality no longer than they can sing?

294   Kemble 'chid their puny jest' with his 'dignified' tone (H. Martin, *Remarks*, p. 6). At first his
greeting had been 'not only familiar, but gay and smiling' (*Public Advertiser*, 7 October
1783), but his manner had changed after he realized the two 'were sent to sound him'
(Boaden, p. 99).

298   In his studybook Barrymore called for 'he that plays the king' to be delivered in a 'dreamlike
voice'.

313–33   Not in Q2. The passage is topical, alluding to the rise in popularity of the boys' acting
companies that for a time threatened the adult companies, Shakespeare's in particular (the
sign of the Globe Theatre depicted Hercules bearing the world). As at 229–56 there is more
camaraderie between Hamlet and Rosencrantz and Guildenstern in F than in the Quartos.
This gossip helps to establish the Folio Hamlet as a devotee of the theatre. In the Branagh
film, Rosencrantz (Timothy Spall) is 'very pleased with his inside knowledge' (*Screenplay*, p.
63).

Will they not say afterwards, if they should grow themselves to common players – as it is most like if their means are no better, their writers do them wrong to make them exclaim against their own succession?   325

ROSENCRANTZ Faith, there has been much to do on both sides, and the nation holds it no sin to tar them to controversy. There was for a while no money bid for argument unless the poet and the player went to cuffs in the question.

HAMLET Is't possible?   330

GUILDENSTERN Oh there has been much throwing about of brains.

HAMLET Do the boys carry it away?

ROSENCRANTZ Ay that they do my lord, Hercules and his load too.

HAMLET It is not very strange, for my uncle is king of Denmark, and those that would make mouths at him while my father lived give   335 twenty, forty, fifty, a hundred ducats apiece for his picture in little. 'Sblood, there is something in this more than natural, if philosophy could find it out.

A flourish

GUILDENSTERN There are the players.

HAMLET Gentlemen, you are welcome to Elsinore. Your hands, come   340 then. Th'appurtenance of welcome is fashion and ceremony. Let me comply with you in this garb, lest my extent to the players, which I tell you must show fairly outwards, should more appear like entertainment than yours. You are welcome – but my uncle-father and aunt-mother are deceived.   345

GUILDENSTERN In what my dear lord?

HAMLET I am but mad north-north-west. When the wind is southerly, I know a hawk from a handsaw.

Enter POLONIUS

POLONIUS Well be with you gentlemen.

HAMLET Hark you Guildenstern, and you too – at each ear a hearer.   350 That great baby you see there is not yet out of his swaddling clouts.

---

336 Fechter illustrated his meaning by handling the medallion worn by Guildenstern (Cook, *Hours*, p. 262).

339 In Moscow, Craig had wished that the Players might fly in through windows (he had seen Chinese jugglers make their entrance by sliding down a tightrope); Stanislavsky had them enter in swaggering procession, to the sound of flutes, cymbals, hautboys, and drums, carrying banners, masks, and ancient musical instruments.

344–6 Kean took Rosencrantz and Guildenstern 'under each arm, under pretence of communicating his secret to them, when he only means to trifle with them' (Hazlitt, *Theatre*, p. 13).

ROSENCRANTZ Happily he's the second time come to them, for they
    say an old man is twice a child.
HAMLET I will prophesy: he comes to tell me of the players, mark
    it. – You say right sir, a Monday morning, 'twas then indeed.   355
POLONIUS My lord, I have news to tell you.
HAMLET My lord, I have news to tell you. When Roscius was an actor
    in Rome –
POLONIUS The actors are come hither my lord.
HAMLET Buzz, buzz!   360
POLONIUS Upon my honour.
HAMLET Then came each actor on his ass –
POLONIUS The best actors in the world, either for tragedy, comedy,
    history, pastoral, pastoral-comical, historical-pastoral, tragical-
    historical, tragical-comical-historical-pastoral, scene individable or   365
    poem unlimited. Seneca cannot be too heavy, nor Plautus too light.
    For the law of writ and the liberty, these are the only men.
HAMLET O Jephtha judge of Israel, what a treasure hadst thou!
POLONIUS What a treasure had he my lord?
HAMLET Why –   370
    'One fair daughter and no more,
    The which he lovèd passing well.'
POLONIUS Still on my daughter.
HAMLET Am I not i'th'right, old Jephtha?

360   Booth gave the 'zzs' a humming sound, waved his hand 'to and fro before his face'
      (Shattuck, p. 171). The actress Elizabeth Robins described how Bernhardt made this 'a
      prolonged piece of comic business, affecting to follow a fly about, which ultimately she
      pretends to catch, herself buzzing vigorously all through Polonius' speech' (*North American
      Review*, 171, December 1900, p. 914). She then opened her hand to show Polonius what she
      had 'caught' (Taranow, *Bernhardt Hamlet*, p. 146). To Robins there was in general something
      'almost childlike' in Bernhardt's Prince (p. 908).
363–5   Q1 reads 'Comedy, Tragedy, History, Pastoral,/ Pastoral, Historical, Historical, Comical,/
      Comical historical, Pastoral, Tragedy historical'. The humour here is broad, of a muddled
      mind at sea amid generic categories. Q2 reads 'Tragedy, Comedy, History, Pastoral, Pastoral
      Comical, Historical Pastoral'. This need not be thought humorous at all; at most there may
      be some mild amusement at Polonius's thoroughness, yet it can be seen as a knowledgeable
      survey of the actors' specialties by one who fancies himself a connoisseur. It is F, as in this
      edition, that reveals a mind comically carried away by its own propensity to categorize,
      especially in the four-part hybrid 'Tragical-Comical-Historical-Pastoral'.
368   'Bowing with affection' (Irving's studybook).
371–2   Barrymore sang these lines 'to a plaintive little tune' (promptbook 156).

POLONIUS If you call me Jephtha my lord, I have a daughter that I   375
    love passing well.
HAMLET Nay, that follows not.
POLONIUS What follows then my lord?
HAMLET Why –
    'As by lot God wot,'   380
    And then you know –
    'It came to pass, as most like it was,' –
    the first row of the pious chanson will show you more, for look where
    my abridgement comes.

Enter the PLAYERS

Y'are welcome masters, welcome all. I am glad to see thee well.   385
Welcome good friends. Oh, my old friend! why, thy face is valanced
since I saw thee last; com'st thou to beard me in Denmark? What,
my young lady and mistress – byrlady, your ladyship is nearer to
heaven than when I saw you last by the altitude of a chopine. Pray
God your voice like a piece of uncurrent gold be not cracked within   390
the ring. Masters, you are all welcome. We'll e'en to't like French
falconers, fly at anything we see: we'll have a speech straight. Come
give us a taste of your quality: come, a passionate speech.
I PLAYER What speech, my good lord?
HAMLET I heard thee speak me a speech once, but it was never acted,   395
    or if it was, not above once, for the play I remember pleased not
    the million: 'twas caviary to the general. But it was, as I received
    it, and others whose judgements in such matters cried in the top
    of mine, an excellent play, well digested in the scenes, set down with
    as much modesty as cunning. I remember one said there were no   400
    sallets in the lines to make the matter savoury, nor no matter in
    the phrase that might indict the author of affectation, but called it
    an honest method, as wholesome as sweet and by very much more
    handsome than fine. One speech in't I chiefly loved, 'twas Aeneas'
    tale to Dido, and thereabout of it especially where he speaks of   405
    Priam's slaughter. If it live in your memory, begin at this line, let
    me see, let me see –
    'The rugged Pyrrhus, like th'Hyrcanian beast' –

385a   'All the actors bow' (Macready promptbook 40). 'Getting very cheerful' (Irving's studybook).
388–9   Fechter was the first since Shakespeare's time to introduce a boy wearing chopins instead of
     an actress (Field, p. 106).
406–7   'Very courteously' (Irving's studybook).
  408   'Kean hesitates in repeating the first line of the speech ... and then, after several ineffectual
     attempts to recollect, suddenly hurries on with it' (Hazlitt, *Theatre*, p. 13).

'Tis not so, it begins with Pyrrhus –
    'The rugged Pyrrhus, he whose sable arms,   410
    Black as his purpose, did the night resemble
    When he lay couchèd in the ominous horse,
    Hath now this dread and black complexion smeared
    With heraldy more dismal. Head to foot
    Now is he total gules, horridly tricked   415
    With blood of fathers, mothers, daughters, sons,
    Baked and impasted with the parching streets,
    That lend a tyrannous and a damnèd light
    To their lord's murder. Roasted in wrath and fire,
    And thus o'er-sizèd with coagulate gore,   420
    With eyes like carbuncles, the hellish Pyrrhus
    Old grandsire Priam seeks –'
So, proceed you.
POLONIUS 'Fore God my lord, well spoken, with good accent and good
discretion.   425
I PLAYER   'Anon he finds him,
    Striking too short at Greeks; his antique sword,
    Rebellious to his arm, lies where it falls,
    Repugnant to command. Unequal matched,
    Pyrrhus at Priam drives, in rage strikes wide,   430
    But with the whiff and wind of his fell sword
    Th'unnervèd father falls. Then senseless Ilium,
    Seeming to feel this blow, with flaming top
    Stoops to his base, and with a hideous crash
    Takes prisoner Pyrrhus' ear; for lo, his sword,   435
    Which was declining on the milky head
    Of reverend Priam, seemed i'th'air to stick.
    So, as a painted tyrant, Pyrrhus stood,
    And like a neutral to his will and matter,
    Did nothing.   440
    But as we often see against some storm,
    A silence in the heavens, the rack stand still,
    The bold winds speechless, and the orb below
    As hush as death, anon the dreadful thunder
    Doth rend the region; so after Pyrrhus' pause,   445
    A rousèd vengeance sets him new a-work,

426ff   Like Garrick, Fechter silently mouthed the words of the speech (Field, p. 104). As Irving
        listens to the First Player, 'the scheme which he afterwards evolves for striking to the soul of
        the king seems suddenly to dawn upon his mind' (*Evening Standard*, 2 November 1874).

435a   In Minneapolis, George Grizzard's Hamlet reacted physically here and at 446 (Rossi, p. 52).

And never did the Cyclops' hammers fall
On Mars's armour, forged for proof eterne,
With less remorse than Pyrrhus' bleeding sword
Now falls on Priam.   450
Out, out, thou strumpet Fortune! All you gods,
In general synod take away her power,
Break all the spokes and fellies from her wheel,
And bowl the round nave down the hill of heaven
As low as to the fiends.'   455
POLONIUS This is too long.
HAMLET It shall to th' barber's with your beard. Prithee say on.
     He's for a jig or a tale of bawdry, or he sleeps. Say on, come to
     Hecuba.
I PLAYER 'But who – ah woe! – had seen the mobled queen –'   460
HAMLET The mobled queen?
POLONIUS That's good, 'mobled queen' is good.
I PLAYER 'Run barefoot up and down, threat'ning the flames
          With bisson rheum, a clout upon that head
          Where late the diadem stood, and, for a robe,   465
          About her lank and all o'er-teemèd loins
          A blanket, in th'alarm of fear caught up –
          Who this had seen, with tongue in venom steeped
          'Gainst Fortune's state would treason have pronounced.
          But if the gods themselves did see her then,   470
          When she saw Pyrrhus make malicious sport
          In mincing with his sword her husband's limbs,
          The instant burst of clamour that she made,
          Unless things mortal move them not at all,

456   'Stroking his beard' (Barrett promptbook). With Evans Polonius 'has almost dozed' (*G. I.
       Hamlet*, p. 97).
456–9 With Burton Gielgud told Hume Cronyn as Polonius to whisper 456 to Hamlet 'like those
       awful people who whisper in theatres'. He suggested to Burton that he make separate
       thoughts of 'He's for a jig. Or a tale of bawdry. Or he sleeps' (Sterne, p. 37).
459b 'Tenderly' (Irving's studybook).
461   'Garrick repeated this after the player, as in doubt: Kemble, as in sympathy' (Boaden, p.
       100). Q1 and F use a question mark; Q2, a period.
471–5 Gielgud praised the gifted and physically imposing First Player in the Alexander Moissi
       production: 'He played the part as high tragedy and at the end of the speech on Hecuba he
       veiled his face with his cloak thrown over his forearm and fell headlong on the stage . . . If
       the Player has done his work well, Hamlet's comments need only echo the audience's
       thoughts' (Gilder, p. 53).

> Would have made milch the burning eyes of heaven, 475
> And passion in the gods.

POLONIUS Look where he has not turned his colour, and has tears in's
eyes. Prithee no more.

HAMLET 'Tis well, I'll have thee speak out the rest of this soon. – Good
my lord, will you see the players well bestowed? Do you hear, let 480
them be well used, for they are the abstract and brief chronicles
of the time. After your death you were better have a bad epitaph
than their ill report while you live.

POLONIUS My lord, I will use them according to their desert.

HAMLET God's bodkin man, much better. Use every man after his 485
desert, and who shall scape whipping? Use them after your own
honour and dignity; the less they deserve, the more merit is in your
bounty. Take them in.

POLONIUS Come sirs. *Exit Polonius*

---

475 Forbes-Robertson quietly, as if unobserved, brushed away a tear (*Stage*, 16 September 1897,
p. 14). In Minneapolis Grizzard fondly puts his hand on the First Player's shoulder (Rossi, p.
21). On BBC-TV Jacobi goes to comfort the weeping First Player, who uncovers his face to
show a wide smile.

476–7 Bryant 'checks his philistine jeer at the tears of the First Player, hastily joining in the round of
applause that the moment has solicited' (*Country Life*, 30 March 1989).

489 With Burton, Cronyn emphasized '*sirs*' mockingly, pretending to obey Hamlet's order to
treat them with respect.

489–500 Edwards conflates the stage directions of Q2 and F. Q2 shows Polonius exiting with the
players after 499 rather than separately at 489 as here and in F; F shows the players and
Rosencrantz and Guildenstern exiting together at 500 rather than separately as here and in
Q2. The Q2 stage directions suggest that characters linger even after the Prince has bade
them farewell. From 488–90 it would seem that Hamlet means for Polonius and all the
players except the First Player to be on their way at that point. But their actual exeunt is not
shown in Q2 until after 499. Similarly, Hamlet says farewell to Rosencrantz and Guildenstern
at 499. But in Q2 Rosencrantz does not say his last words and, with Guildenstern, exeunt
until Polonius and the Players have left. Are the King's emissaries rightly suspicious that the
Prince is up to something as he huddles with the First Player and are they trying to keep him
under surveillance? Certainly in recent performances they have tended to linger. With
Burton, Rosencrantz was 'trying to talk to him' with 'Good my lord . . . ' (Sterne, p. 198). In
contrast Hamlet has sought to hurry them off. Rosenberg recalls: 'Pennington in effect
ordered the two out; McKellen physically, anticly, shooed them. Jacobi suddenly drew the
prop sword he had kept, and mockingly menaced them' (p. 439). Burton said 'Aye, so God
. . . be . . . with . . . you' 'vituperously' and then 'I am alone' 'with great relief' (Sterne, p. 198).

HAMLET Follow him friends, we'll hear a play tomorrow. – Dost thou   490
    hear me old friend, can you play *The Murder of Gonzago?*
I PLAYER Ay my lord.
HAMLET We'll ha't tomorrow night. You could for a need study a
    speech of some dozen or sixteen lines, which I would set down and
    insert in't, could you not?   495
I PLAYER Ay my lord.
HAMLET Very well. Follow that lord, and look you mock him not.
                                                  Exeunt Players
    My good friends, I'll leave you till night. You are welcome to
    Elsinore.
ROSENCRANTZ Good my lord.   500
                          Exeunt Rosencrantz and Guildenstern
HAMLET Ay so, God bye to you. Now I am alone.
    O what a rogue and peasant slave am I!
    Is it not monstrous that this player here,
    But in a fiction, in a dream of passion,
    Could force his soul so to his own conceit   505
    That from her working all his visage wanned,
    Tears in his eyes, distraction in's aspect,
    A broken voice, and his whole function suiting   .
    With forms to his conceit? And all for nothing?
    For Hecuba!   510
    What's Hecuba to him, or he to Hecuba,
    That he should weep for her? What would he do,
    Had he the motive and the cue for passion
    That I have? He would drown the stage with tears,
    And cleave the general ear with horrid speech,   515

497 Macready rearranged the sequence of exits so that the First Player is the last of the players
    to leave; Hamlet detains him with 'old friend'. He then turns to say farewell to Rosencrantz
    and Guildenstern and sees them out, before beckoning the First Player forward for their talk
    of *The Murder of Gonzago* (promptbook 29). He emphasized *you* (*Boston Semi-Weekly
    Advertiser*, 29 November 1843), as did Booth: 'You have just heard me do so, but do not *you*
    presume to play your play-house tricks with him. Spoken playfully. My father emphasized
    "mock"' (studybook).
501 Forbes-Robertson led into the soliloquy by conning a promptbook of the play handed him
    by the First Player (*World*, 15 September 1897, p. 26).
502 'Shaking head' (Irving's studybook).
510–12 Of Peter O'Toole: 'The first player's concern for Hecuba seems to him such a joke that he can
    hardly speak for guffaws' (*Sunday Telegraph*, 27 October 1963).
514 Irving dwelt heavily on *drown* (*Academy*, 4 January 1879, p. 19).

Make mad the guilty and appal the free,
Confound the ignorant, and amaze indeed
The very faculties of eyes and ears. Yet I,
A dull and muddy-mettled rascal, peak
Like John-a-dreams, unpregnant of my cause, 520
And can say nothing – no, not for a king,
Upon whose property and most dear life
A damned defeat was made. Am I a coward?
Who calls me villain, breaks my pate across,
Plucks off my beard and blows it in my face, 525
Tweaks me by th'nose, gives me the lie i'th'throat
As deep as to the lungs? Who does me this?
Ha, 'swounds, I should take it, for it cannot be
But I am pigeon-livered, and lack gall

517b–41 Gielgud's delivery is structured around a rising series of climaxes, each followed by an extreme falling off. The first crests at 'amaze indeed'; the next builds 'in swift, staccato exclamations until "Who does me this?" brings him to his feet with a cry'. When he builds to his final climax and hisses 'treacherous, lecherous, kindless villain': 'Hamlet is trembling with fury, his body shaking, his voice high. With "Vengeance!" he snatches his dagger from its sheath and rushes to the doorway right, throwing himself against it as the wave of his futile fury crashes to its height and dies. His raised arm falls, the dagger rolls on the ground, his body sways against the door and he sinks . . . his voice is broken with a sob of humiliation.' A silence follows, then he slowly raises his head: 'About my brain . . . ' (Gilder, pp. 147–8).

523b After 'coward?' a heckler of David Warner called out 'Yes'. Warner responded by delivering the lines that follow (524–7), leading to the question 'Who does me this?' – at which a name was shouted out from the audience. Excited (Warner remembered this as one of the most exhilarating nights of his acting career), he responded with some vehemence 'Hah, 'swounds, I should take it'. Warner 'was stunned with the rightness of feeling and the naturalness of speaking these soliloquy lines directly to the theatre audience', especially 'I should take it', 'which played with an absolute logic after the dialogue with the audience member' (Maher, *Soliloquies*, pp. 41, 55).

527–8a Fechter's 'pauses of thought followed by a change of tone' were praised by Clement Scott, especially in this passage (*Drama*, I, p. 461). He 'worked himself into a phrenzy by the elaboration of every conceivable insult and degradation, suddenly lapses back again into self-consciousness' (*Sunday Times*, 24 March 1861). After 'Who does me this?' he came forward, stopped suddenly at 'Ha', then, dropping his arms in despair, said, 'I should take it' (promptbook). Those last words were 'electrifying' (*Morning Chronicle*, 23 March 1861).

529 Irving emphasized *am*, 'as if he were quoting the observation of some impertinent person which had long been rankling in his mind' (*Academy*, 4 January 1879, p. 19). So did Jonathan Pryce (Gilbert, 'Pryce', p. 6).

To make oppression bitter, or ere this   530
I should ha' fatted all the region kites
With this slave's offal. Bloody, bawdy villain!
Remorseless, treacherous, lecherous, kindless villain!
Oh, vengeance!
Why, what an ass am I! This is most brave,   535
That I, the son of the dear murderèd,
Prompted to my revenge by heaven and hell,
Must like a whore unpack my heart with words,
And fall a-cursing like a very drab,
A scullion!   540
Fie upon't, foh! About, my brains. Hum, I have heard
That guilty creatures sitting at a play
Have by the very cunning of the scene
Been struck so to the soul, that presently
They have proclaimed their malefactions;   545
For murder, though it have no tongue, will speak
With most miraculous organ. I'll have these players
Play something like the murder of my father
Before mine uncle. I'll observe his looks,
I'll tent him to the quick. If a do blench,   550
I know my course. The spirit that I have seen
May be a devil – and the devil hath power
T'assume a pleasing shape. Yea, and perhaps,
Out of my weakness and my melancholy,
As he is very potent with such spirits,   555

532   Tree made 'sword-thrusts at the empty throne' ('Hamlet', p. 868).

533   Macready ejaculated 'kindless' in 'a passionate burst of tears' as he recalled the irreparable loss he had sustained. The other terms were given 'in a tone breathing the deepest hatred against his uncle' (*Theatrical Journal*, 5 September 1840, p. 312). Ralph Fiennes 'knocked his own forehead with his fist, as if to shake the adjectives out one by one' (*New Yorker*, 17 April 1995, p. 88).

534   This half-line is only in F. On the Ashland, Oregon, Elizabethan-style stage, Richard Risso in 1961 ran across its length and swung around a pillar. Michael Redgrave in 1949 held the Player's sword in both hands and 'did a forward fall as if stabbing Claudius' (*Mind's I*, p. 191).

541a Face in hands, Barrymore rocked his body back and forth (promptbook 156).

551–6 Booth 'caught eagerly at the hope that the command to kill might be from hell and not from heaven. Always the shrinking of the delicate nature, of the religious soul, from the murder' (Calhoun, 'Booth', p. 80).

Abuses me to damn me. I'll have grounds
More relative than this. The play's the thing
Wherein I'll catch the conscience of the king.   *Exit*

556   On BBC-TV Jacobi emphasizes each *me*.

558   J. B. Booth emphasized *catch* as well as *conscience* (Gould, p. 59). Edwin Booth made a
gesture as if encompassing his victim with a net (*Morning Post*, 8 November 1880). As the
curtain came down, Irving 'was seen to be writing madly on his tablets against one of the
pillars'. To Terry this was the 'one moment when his intensity concentrated itself in a
straightforward unmistakable emotion, without side-current or back-water' (Terry, p. 104).
With Tree, 'the scene now has gradually darkened, and the only light comes from the huge
wood fire' (Scott, *Hamlets*, p. 106); when he 'writes upon his tablets, he crouches in the red
glare of a fire in the attitude of a Bedlamite' (*Academy*, 18 September 1897, p. 224). Gielgud
ended the scene 'writing frantically' (Gilder, p. 148). Redgrave in 1949 held the Player's
crown at arm's length above his head and swirling his red cloak 'gave a joyous shout, as if,
for the first time, Hamlet knew what to do' (*Mind's I*, p. 191). With Burton in 1964: 'the play's
the thing' (plotting) 'wherein I'll catch the conscience' (smile) 'of the king' (lowered voice,
looking offstage as if to say to Claudius: 'I'll get *you*').

The first interval usually comes at this point. Arguing against a 'strong curtain' here,
however, Guinness held that, if uninterrupted, the audience gets 'the greater part of
Hamlet's character stripped bare before them . . . all in the space of about fifteen minutes'
(*Spectator*, 6 July 1951). He put his views into practice in his 1951 production. With Burton
Gielgud placed the interval after 3.1. Here he directed Burton to see the King coming, point
to him, 'and that's why you exit'. The King also sees Hamlet as he leaves and looks puzzled,
thus leading into the question that begins 3.1 (Sterne, pp. 31, 200). In the Branagh film, the
Prince releases the trapdoor of his toy theatre with a 'snap', sending the toy King to hell, at
which the doors of the state hall open to reveal the real Claudius and 3.1 begins.

ACT 3, SCENE 1

[3.1] *Enter* KING, QUEEN, POLONIUS, OPHELIA, ROSENCRANTZ, GUILDENSTERN, LORDS

CLAUDIUS And can you by no drift of circumstance
      Get from him why he puts on this confusion,
      Grating so harshly all his days of quiet
      With turbulent and dangerous lunacy?
ROSENCRANTZ He does confess he feels himself distracted,   5
      But from what cause a will by no means speak.
GUILDENSTERN Nor do we find him forward to be sounded,
      But with a crafty madness keeps aloof
      When we would bring him on to some confession
      Of his true state.
GERTRUDE   Did he receive you well?   10
ROSENCRANTZ Most like a gentleman.
GUILDENSTERN But with much forcing of his disposition.
ROSENCRANTZ Niggard of question, but of our demands
      Most free in his reply.

0 At Minneapolis Guthrie began the scene offstage with Claudius ad-libbing shouts at Rosencrantz and Guildenstern, furious at their failure to find out the cause of Hamlet's 'confusion'. Taken at a fast pace, the high-energy scene followed the first interval; Guthrie said, 'This will wake 'em up after the break' (Rossi, pp. 17–18).

7 In rehearsals for the Burton production, Gielgud urged Redfield as Guildenstern, to be 'smug with achievement'. Reading the scene much as Guthrie had, Redfield at first resisted this note because Guildenstern's report was one of failure (*Letters*, p. 85). Since the King concludes by urging the two to continue their surveillance, Guildenstern might in the course of the scene *become* confident of being in the King's good graces.

10 In the Branagh film Gertrude here and at 14b–15a seems a bit insistent about drawing them out, although she is less overtly impatient than Claudius.

12 Redfield saw Guildenstern as an 'honest reporter' whereas Rosencrantz was deviously trying 'to put a good face on things' (*Letters*, p. 85).

13 Evans: 'Modifying this' (*G. I. Hamlet*, p. 104).

GERTRUDE   Did you assay him
    To any pastime?   15
ROSENCRANTZ Madam, it so fell out that certain players
    We o'er-raught on the way; of these we told him,
    And there did seem in him a kind of joy
    To hear of it. They are about the court,
    And as I think, they have already order   20
    This night to play before him.
POLONIUS   'Tis most true,
    And he beseeched me to entreat your majesties
    To hear and see the matter.
CLAUDIUS With all my heart, and it doth much content me
    To hear him so inclined.   25
    Good gentlemen, give him a further edge,
    And drive his purpose on to these delights.
ROSENCRANTZ We shall my lord.
               Exeunt Rosencrantz and Guildenstern
CLAUDIUS   Sweet Gertrude, leave us too,
    For we have closely sent for Hamlet hither,
    That he, as 'twere by accident, may here   30
    Affront Ophelia. Her father and myself,
    Lawful espials,
    Will so bestow ourselves, that seeing unseen,
    We may of their encounter frankly judge,
    And gather by him, as he is behaved,   35
    If't be th'affliction of his love or no
    That thus he suffers for.

21b–3   Evans: 'Claiming the credit for himself' (*G. I. Hamlet*, p. 104). 'Philistine' Michael Bryant, with Day Lewis, was 'at first all middle-brow assurance that the drama – not something adults take seriously – will be pleasantly innocuous' (*Independent*, 18 March 1989).

28–49   Irving excused Ophelia from complicity in the plot since much of what is said might have been spoken apart from her. At 43–9, Irving accordingly pictured Polonius as turning back and forth between Ophelia and the King, as he alternates between directing her where to walk and proposing to him, as an aside, that they 'bestow' themselves, then telling her to read upon a book and returning to him to moralize about hypocrisy ('Notes . . . no. 2', p. 525). A problem with this interpretation is that 45–6a, which Irving did not cut, seems to presuppose some knowing participation on Ophelia's part.

31a   Unwilling to join in the plot (*Daily Telegraph*, 2 May 1907), and struggling with herself (C. Russell, *Marlowe*, p. 322), Marlowe here has a 'shocked expression' and at 36b 'shows pain' (promptbook).

37b   Evans: 'Kissing him' (*G. I. Hamlet*, p. 105).

GERTRUDE   I shall obey you.
            And for your part Ophelia, I do wish
            That your good beauties be the happy cause
            Of Hamlet's wildness. So shall I hope your virtues   40
            Will bring him to his wonted way again,
            To both your honours.
OPHELIA   Madam, I wish it may.
                                  [*Exit Gertrude with Lords*]
POLONIUS Ophelia walk you here. – Gracious, so please you,
            We will bestow ourselves. – Read on this book,
            That show of such an exercise may colour   45
            Your loneliness. – We are oft to blame in this:
            'Tis too much proved, that with devotion's visage,
            And pious action, we do sugar o'er
            The devil himself.
CLAUDIUS (*Aside*)   Oh, 'tis too true.
            How smart a lash that speech doth give my conscience!   50
            The harlot's cheek, beautied with plastering art,
            Is not more ugly to the thing that helps it
            Than is my deed to my most painted word.
            O heavy burden!
POLONIUS I hear him coming. Let's withdraw, my lord.   55
                                  Exeunt Claudius and Polonius

                            Enter HAMLET

HAMLET To be, or not to be, that is the question –
            Whether 'tis nobler in the mind to suffer

38–42   Defending Ophelia's 'half willing' complicity, Helena Faucit points out the Queen's hope at
        40b–1 that her 'virtues/Will bring him to his wonted way again' (*Female Characters*, p. 13).
54   Q2 has Hamlet enter before Polonius's last line rather than after it as in F. In Q1 he enters still
        earlier, before Ophelia is instructed to 'read on this book'. Calling attention to these early
        entrances, Irving felt that Hamlet here had 'a half-awakened sense' of the eavesdropping but
        this awareness only 'faintly lingered in his mind'. Not until 126 does he remember that he is
        watched ('Notes ... no. 2', p. 524).
55   With Macready, Ophelia turns the leaves of her missal, 'her back being turned towards
        Hamlet' (promptbook 29). Left alone, Marlowe shows 'great distress': 'extends hand
        tenderly toward Hamlet, hurried exit, glancing back left [where Hamlet enters]'
        (promptbook). Tree: 'From her coign of vantage [a small arbor] Ophelia listens to the self-
        torturings of Hamlet ... and she falls upon her knees praying over her lover' ('Hamlet', p.
        869). Jacobi, Pryce, and Branagh addressed the speech directly to Ophelia.
56–88   From the beginning this soliloquy has been regarded as special. It was frequently referred to
        by Shakespeare's contemporaries. It is the one speech from the play that Samuel Pepys

The slings and arrows of outrageous fortune,
Or to take arms against a sea of troubles,
And by opposing end them. To die, to sleep –   60
No more; and by a sleep to say we end
The heart-ache and the thousand natural shocks
That flesh is heir to – 'tis a consummation
Devoutly to be wished. To die, to sleep –
To sleep, perchance to dream. Ay, there's the rub,   65
For in that sleep of death what dreams may come,

chose to memorize. Its first line may well be the best-known single line in Shakespeare and indeed in world drama. Actors have sought to make it seem fresh (and to discourage auditors from reciting it with them). Mochalov, for example, 'did not enter slowly, sunk in deep meditation, but came in almost running in a state of extreme nervous excitement, and then, stopping, cried: "To be or not to be" – and after several minutes of contemplation threw himself into an armchair, and uttered despairingly – "that is the question"' (Speaight, *Stage*, p. 113).

With Garrick, 'Hamlet, who is in mourning . . . comes on to the stage sunk in contemplation, his chin resting on his right hand, and his right elbow on his left, and gazes solemnly downwards. And then, removing his right hand from his chin, but, if I remember right, still supporting it with his left hand, he speaks' (Lichtenberg, *Visits*, p. 16). Joshua Steele in 1775 contrasted Garrick's delivery of this speech with 'the stile of a ranting actor'. The volume of the latter 'swelled with *forte* and softened with *piano*' whereas Garrick's delivery was 'nearly uniform, something below the ordinary force, or, as a musician would say, *sotto voce*' (*Essay*, p. 47). Steele recorded in his own system of notation (which I have translated into modern musical symbols) the ponderous rhythm – perhaps influenced by Quin (p. 14) – in which he himself spoke the first line (p. 40):

With this, Steele contrasted Garrick's lighter and more conversational delivery:

Garrick used a downward intonation for 'to be' in 'or not to be' and for 'question'. His rhythm for 60–1 was:

When we have shuffled off this mortal coil,
Must give us pause. There's the respect
That makes calamity of so long life,
For who would bear the whips and scorns of time, 70
Th'oppressor's wrong, the proud man's contumely,
The pangs of disprized love, the law's delay,
The insolence of office, and the spurns
That patient merit of th'unworthy takes,
When he himself might his quietus make 75

At 63 Garrick spoke 'heir to' with an upward intonation in such a way as to 'give the idea of the sense being suspended, for the thought which immediately follows' (pp. 47–8).

Kean was not 'a grim debater of the pro and con of suicide: he was the man of misery driven by his loathing of life and the villany of those about him to escape all further ills by death' (*Examiner*, 20 March 1814). Macready entered: 'his hands behind him, the right hand clasping the left wrist like a vice, the eyes fixed in a gaze of concentrated abstraction' (Kirk, 'Tragedies', p. 614). His delivery 'in its disjointed reasoning and restless inner manner, conveys the idea of a man whose mind is but ill at rest' (*Theatrical Journal*, 29 August 1840, p. 301). Fechter brought on an unsheathed sword as though contemplating suicide (Field, p. 105). Booth entered with his right hand on the back of his head. He sat, clasped his hands, and began to speak. At 'by opposing' he struck his breast; at 'there's the rub' he rose; at 'cowards of us all' he crossed right; at 'enterprises' he turned left (promptbook 111). Richard Burton, playing Booth in the film *The Prince of Players*, largely follows this choreography. Gielgud sought to place the speech in a line of progression: 'the effect of despondency in "to be, or not to be" is a natural and brilliant psychological reaction from the violent and hopeless rage of the earlier speech [2.2.501–58]' (Gilder, p. 55). Gielgud explained to Burton: 'First he lashes himself for his own stupidity and then he becomes despondent and feels that he doesn't care one way or another and tries to determine if everything is worth it' (Sterne, p. 68). Radovan Lukavsky, who played Hamlet in Prague in 1959, described the progression in his diary: 'Either the King is a murderer or the Ghost is a damned soul . . . Hamlet's will to action is struggling. – And suddenly the desire simply to get away from it all, the longing for peace, to sleep, and never wake up' (quoted in Rosenberg, p. 482).

In Q1 there is no such difficulty since in it this soliloquy precedes the 'play's the thing' soliloquy. Often the first interval comes just before this scene, lessening the abruptness of Hamlet's changing moods.

65 'Kemble prolonged the word dream "meditatingly"' (Boaden, p. 101). Kevin Kline said 'to sleep' with a smile and sigh of satisfaction, then a change to a tone of concern at 'perchance to dream'.

67 Burton made a downward sweep of his hands and a sway of his body to suggest 'shuffling'.

72a Irving saw here a reference to 'the poor girl to whom he has been compelled to appear heartless' ('Notes . . . no. 2', p. 526).

With a bare bodkin? Who would fardels bear,
To grunt and sweat under a weary life,
But that the dread of something after death,
The undiscovered country from whose bourn
No traveller returns, puzzles the will,   80
And makes us rather bear those ills we have
Then fly to others that we know not of?
Thus conscience does make cowards of us all,
And thus the native hue of resolution
Is sicklied o'er with the pale cast of thought,   85
And enterprises of great pitch and moment
With this regard their currents turn awry
And lose the name of action. Soft you now,
The fair Ophelia. – Nymph, in thy orisons
Be all my sins remembered.

OPHELIA   Good my lord,   90
How does your honour for this many a day?
HAMLET I humbly thank you, well, well, well.

76–82   Burton delivered this section almost as a lecture to the audience. Having whipped out a
        dagger after 'bare bodkin', Branagh in the film unknowingly for a moment points it right at
        Claudius, who is hiding behind a two-way mirror.

   79   Salvini slowly pointed a finger downward – 'Hamlets traditionally cast their eyes
        heavenward at this line instead of pointing in the direction of the grave' (Carlson,
        Shakespearians, p. 84).

   80   J. B. Booth emphasized *returns* (Gould, p. 60).

   83   Stephen Dillane 'gives a weary shrug of resignation, as if admitting that even the suicide
        option is closed down' (*Country Life*, 17 November 1994).

   88   Charles Kemble emphasized Hamlet's 'mingled anguish'. His daughter Fanny, who acted
        Ophelia with him, was moved to tears by his tenderness, compassion, and 'self-scorning'.
        (*Journal*, I, pp. 148–9).

        At the Moscow Art Theatre 'Kachalov's subtext in his encounter with Ophelia is "They are
        poisoning you. I should reveal to you what monstrous thing is tormenting me, but I cannot
        and will not. If you are like them, it means there is nothing holy in the world." So, he imbues
        his voice with pity and understanding, not revulsion and contempt. His subtext for "Are you
        honest?" is "I want to show her to her face that I know all"' (Senelick, p. 165).

  88b   Irving spoke these words as if about to develop a further thought which was interrupted
        when he saw Ophelia (Winter, *Shakespeare*, p. 358).

  90a   Barrett emphasized *my* (*Shakespeariana*, p. 37).

   92   Hamlet's realization that he is being spied upon may well have originated around 1820 with
        J. B. Booth, the earliest instance so far discovered (Sprague, *Actors*, pp. 153–4). Clearly
        Kemble did not practice it. His promptbook does not indicate a 'call' for the King and

OPHELIA My lord, I have remembrances of yours
    That I have longèd long to re-deliver.
    I pray you now receive them.
HAMLET   No, not I,   95
    I never gave you aught.
OPHELIA My honoured lord, you know right well you did,
    And with them words of so sweet breath composed
    As made the things more rich. Their perfume lost,
    Take these again, for to the noble mind   100
    Rich gifts wax poor when givers prove unkind.
    There my lord.
HAMLET Ha, ha, are you honest?
OPHELIA My lord?
HAMLET Are you fair?   105
OPHELIA What means your lordship?
HAMLET That if you be honest and fair, your honesty should admit no
    discourse to your beauty.

Polonius until 119 (*Promptbooks*, p. 39). At this point Edwin Booth like his father sees the King and Polonius as they hide behind the hangings (Shattuck, p. 190).

92b   When he spoke the third 'well', Maurice Evans's 'voice broke and he turned quickly from Ophelia and the audience, as if suddenly shaken by the irony of his own reply. It was a revealing flash of anguish and in the contracted shoulders and instinctive lift of the hand to the face one had the impression of tears rising to the surface and with an effort suppressed' (Williamson, *Old Vic*, p. 28). Kevin Kline, touched by Ophelia's 'many a day', spoke the three words tenderly, reaching towards her (televised 1990). In the Branagh film, Hamlet and Ophelia (Kate Winslet) kiss at this point, 'a moment of bliss' (*Screenplay*, p. 78) 'but then she breaks away'.

93   With Walter Hampden Hamlet starts to go; Ophelia stops him, 'forcing herself' to begin 'My lord' (promptbook).

93–4   Of Terry, *The Academy* found 'her lingering over the love- gifts' to be 'true, direct, and tender' (7 November 1874, p. 19).

95   While Ophelia was returning his remembrances Forrest caught a glimpse of the eavesdroppers (promptbook).

101   Of Irving: Terry recalled 'With what passionate longing his hands hovered over Ophelia' (p. 104).

101b   Kate Terry with Fechter: 'Ophelia raises packet [of letters] to her lips, is about to kiss them, when she seems to remember she is watched. She drops her arms slowly and offers them to him' (promptbook). In the Branagh film 'he lashes out at the letters, sending them flying' (*Screenplay*, p. 79).

103–17   Irving saw behind Hamlet's lines his consciousness of his mother's contaminating guilt. He realizes that Ophelia 'is lost to him for ever' ('Notes . . . no.2', pp. 528, 527).

OPHELIA Could beauty, my lord, have better commerce than with
honesty? 110

HAMLET Ay truly, for the power of beauty will sooner transform
honesty from what it is to a bawd, than the force of honesty can
translate beauty into his likeness. This was sometime a paradox, but
now the time gives it proof. I did love you once.

OPHELIA Indeed my lord you made me believe so. 115

HAMLET You should not have believed me, for virtue cannot so
inoculate our old stock but we shall relish of it. I loved you not.

OPHELIA I was the more deceived.

HAMLET Get thee to a nunnery – why wouldst thou be a breeder of
sinners? I am myself indifferent honest, but yet I could accuse me 120
of such things, that it were better my mother had not borne me.
I am very proud, revengeful, ambitious, with more offences at my
beck than I have thoughts to put them in, imagination to give them
shape, or time to act them in. What should such fellows as I do
crawling between earth and heaven? We are arrant knaves all, 125
believe none of us. Go thy ways to a nunnery. Where's your father?

112 Marlowe 'shrinks' at 'bawd' (promptbook).

113b–14a After 'paradox' Fechter 'paused, looked sadly at the letters in his hand returned by the
woman Hamlet loved', and then continued, emphasizing *now* (Field, p. 105).

114b Pryce emphasized *did* (*Observer*, 6 April 1980). Branagh in 1992 underscored his last
sentence by picking up one of the love-letters Ophelia had returned (*Shakespeare Bulletin*,
Fall, 1994, p. 7).

115–118 'Those who ever heard Mrs. Siddons read the play of *Hamlet*, cannot forget the world of
meaning, of love, of sorrow, of despair, conveyed in these two simple phrases' (Jameson,
Characteristics, p. 204).

118 *Vanity Fair* praised the 'pathos and regret' of Terry's delivery of this line (18 January 1879, p.
33). Marlowe: 'despairingly' (promptbook).

118b Kate Terry with Fechter: 'As Ophelia turns away dejectedly, Hamlet suddenly takes her hand
affectionately. She turns to him joyously. Hamlet drops her hand and says "Get thee to a
nunnery"' (promptbook).

120ff Booth 'stands looking partly down at her, partly out from her, scowling a little as if in self-
condemnation; he seems to be reaching ahead in his thought and only partially conscious of
the words he is actually speaking' (Shattuck, p. 192).

Marlowe protests Hamlet's self-accusations, placing her hand on his shoulder after 121,
124a, and 126a. The first two times he 'retreats' from her; the third, he throws her away from
him (promptbook).

122 Barrett darted 'revengeful' at the arras (*Shakespeariana*, p. 37).

125 Of Booth, Robins wonders: 'Did any one, before or since, ever make meanness the reptile
that he showed it, with his slight, dragging emphasis on "crawling"?' ('Hamlet', p. 916).

OPHELIA At home my lord.

HAMLET Let the doors be shut upon him, that he may play the fool
    nowhere but in's own house. Farewell.

OPHELIA Oh help him you sweet heavens!   130

HAMLET If thou dost marry, I'll give thee this plague for thy dowry:
    be thou as chaste as ice, as pure as snow, thou shalt not escape
    calumny. Get thee to a nunnery, go. Farewell. Or if thou wilt needs
    marry, marry a fool, for wise men know well enough what monsters
    you make of them. To a nunnery go, and quickly too. Farewell.   135

Barrymore 'paused after the word "earth", and, by surrounding Ophelia's face with his hands and lowering his voice to a tone of longing tenderness, conveyed that *she* was "Heaven"' (MacCarthy, *Theatre*, p. 59).

125b–6 Of Lillian Gish with Gielgud: Hamlet's 'words are harsh but his tone is tender. He is not thinking of what they mean – not thinking at all. Their bodies sway toward each other – for a moment it seems as though their natural affection would break the nightmare spell, but "Go thy ways to a nunnery" cuts Ophelia to the quick and she walks away' (Gilder, p. 155).

126 To the *Daily Telegraph* reviewer, it was solely the expression on Marlowe's face that told Hamlet they were being spied upon (2 May 1907).

      With Barrymore, after 'Go thy ways to a nunnery', 'Hamlet abruptly turned away from the weeping Ophelia and began to leave the stage . . . Polonius had intermittently been peeking out from behind his column to see what was going on . . . This time Hamlet's sudden move to leave caught Polonius unprepared . . . In a flash, Hamlet looked to Ophelia (who was unaware of what had passed), back to the column, back to Ophelia again, and in perfect fury shouted, "Where's your father?"' (Grebanier, *Actor*, pp. 220–1).

127 Faucit thought that Ophelia 'fears to tell the truth, lest, in this too terrible paroxysm of madness which now possesses him, Hamlet might possibly kill her father' (*Female Characters*, p. 15), a fear that of course proves premonitory. Oscar Wilde thought he detected an expression of 'quick remorse' on Terry's face at this point (quoted by Wingate, *Heroines*, p. 305), but the reviewer who found that 'the innocence of her reply . . . leaves no doubt that this Ophelia is an unconscious agent' (*Standard*, 31 December 1878) seems closer to the mark since Irving goes to elaborate lengths to place the best possible construction on her apparent lie ('Notes . . . no. 2', p. 525). Of Booth's silent response to Ophelia's words: 'no reproach could be so terrible as . . . the pain of the face he turns from her' (Calhoun, 'Booth', p. 81). Alec Guinness at the Old Vic responded with a 'sorrowful shake of the head with a half smile' (Crosse, *Diaries*, XVII).

128–9 Barrett hurled this speech at the arras (*Shakespeariana*, p. 37).

133 Marlowe: Here and each time hereafter, Hamlet's 'get thee to a nunnery' (at 135 and 142) comes after Marlowe has extended her arms to him 'appealingly' (promptbook).

134b 'Indicates with a gesture the cuckold's horns' (Booth's studybook). Burton also made the gesture.

OPHELIA O heavenly powers, restore him!

HAMLET I have heard of your paintings too, well enough. God hath
given you one face and you make yourselves another. You jig, you
amble, and you lisp, you nickname God's creatures, and make your
wantonness your ignorance. Go to, I'll no more on't, it hath made   140
me mad. I say we will have no mo marriages. Those that are married
already, all but one shall live, the rest shall keep as they are. To
a nunnery, go.   *Exit*

OPHELIA Oh what a noble mind is here o'erthrown!
    The courtier's, soldier's, scholar's, eye, tongue, sword,   145
    Th'expectancy and rose of the fair state,
    The glass of fashion and the mould of form,
    Th'observed of all observers, quite, quite down,

136 Marlowe: 'desperately' (promptbook). The line 'seemed torn out of a stricken soul and from that time her disaster was foreshadowed upon us not as the weakness of a commonplace intellect overthrown, but as the inevitable and only possible ending of a great and shattered life' (C. Russell, *Marlowe*, p. 323).

138-9 Booth: '"You *jig*, you *amble*, and you *lisp*" (he is holding his right hand before him palm upward, and on each of these stressed words he gives it a little outward jerk such as card-players do when dealing' (Shattuck, p. 194).

139-40 Jonathan Pryce kissed Harriet Walter brutally, then, 'starts pushing her up against the wall, his hand to her breast, then down to her crotch – she and he finally wind up on the floor – he, reeling away in disgust and anger – wiping his mouth in self-disgust' (Gilbert, 'Pryce').

140-1 Branagh emphasized *hath* (*Country Life*, 14 July 1988), as did Jacobi, who directed Branagh, in his BBC-TV portrayal.

142 Macready made Hamlet 'walk up close to the King's place of concealment, and there *vociferate* his parting speech' (Hackett, *Notes*, p. 157).

143 Following Kean's famous return to kiss Ophelia's hand, subsequent Hamlets have rung their own changes on the business. Fechter turned mutely with outstretched arms and Ophelia advanced 'as if to embrace him' but 'suspicion again hardens him, and he waves her off' (*Orchestra*, 28 May 1864). To Tree 'the tragedy of the situation lay in the fact that Ophelia goes to her death ignorant of Hamlet's love'. As she sobs, he returns unobserved, 'tenderly kisses one of the tresses of her hair, silently steals from the room' ('Hamlet', p. 871).

144ff As Ophelia Mrs. Siddons was praised for 'her expression of grief mixed with terror at the behaviour of Hamlet' (*St. James Chronicle*, 3-5 March 1772). Terry spoke these lines as 'the epitaph, not of her lost love, but of Hamlet's shattered reason' (*Punch*, 11 January 1870, p. 10). With Pryce, Harriet Walter's 'perplexed and guilt-ridden sense of responsibility . . . provides a fully understandable transition to Ophelia's subsequent madness, which for once seems a perfectly logical development' (*Plays and Players*, May, 1980).

148 Glenda Jackson shouted here 'as if to the spying king and father' (*Shakespeare Survey*, 19 (1966), p. 115).

And I of ladies most deject and wretched,
That sucked the honey of his music vows, 150
Now see that noble and most sovereign reason,
Like sweet bells jangled, out of time and harsh;
That unmatched form and feature of blown youth
Blasted with ecstasy. Oh woe is me
T'have seen what I have seen, see what I see. 155

Enter KING *and* POLONIUS

CLAUDIUS Love? His affections do not that way tend;
    Nor what he spake, though it lacked form a little,
    Was not like madness. There's something in his soul
    O'er which his melancholy sits on brood,
    And I do doubt the hatch and the disclose 160
    Will be some danger; which for to prevent,
    I have in quick determination
    Thus set it down: he shall with speed to England
    For the demand of our neglected tribute.
    Haply the seas, and countries different, 165
    With variable objects, shall expel
    This something-settled matter in his heart,
    Whereon his brains still beating puts him thus
    From fashion of himself. What think you on't?
POLONIUS It shall do well. But yet do I believe 170
    The origin and commencement of his grief
    Sprung from neglected love. How now Ophelia?
    You need not tell us what Lord Hamlet said,
    We heard it all. My lord, do as you please,
    But if you hold it fit, after the play, 175
    Let his queen mother all alone entreat him
    To show his grief. Let her be round with him,
    And I'll be placed, so please you, in the ear
    Of all their conference. If she find him not,
    To England send him; or confine him where 180
    Your wisdom best shall think.
CLAUDIUS   It shall be so.
    Madness in great ones must not unwatched go.

Exeunt

156–69   In the Branagh film, Polonius (Richard Briers) comforts Ophelia, cradling her in his arms,
           stroking her head.

163b–4   E. S. Willard as Barrett's King added the explanation in the fear 'that the old courtier may
           suspect the scheme he has formed' (*Evening Standard*, 17 October 1884, p. 3).

180b–1a   In the Richard Chamberlain TV version (1970), Michael Redgrave's hitherto genial Polonius
           here turned ruthless.

ACT 3, SCENE 2

[3.2] *Enter* HAMLET *and two or three of the* PLAYERS

HAMLET Speak the speech I pray you as I pronounced it to you,
trippingly on the tongue; but if you mouth it as many of our players
do, I had as lief the town-crier spoke my lines. Nor do not saw the
air too much with your hand thus, but use all gently; for in the
very torrent, tempest, and, as I may say, whirlwind of your passion,   5
you must acquire and beget a temperance that may give it
smoothness. Oh, it offends me to the soul to hear a robustious
periwig-pated fellow tear a passion to totters, to very rags, to split
the ears of the groundlings, who for the most part are capable of
nothing but inexplicable dumb-shows and noise. I would have such   10
a fellow whipped for o'erdoing Termagant – it out-Herods Herod.
Pray you avoid it.
I PLAYER I warrant your honour.
HAMLET Be not too tame neither, but let your own discretion be your
tutor. Suit the action to the word, the word to the action, with this   15
special observance, that you o'erstep not the modesty of nature. For
anything so o'erdone is from the purpose of playing, whose end both
at the first and now, was and is, to hold as 'twere the mirror up
to nature; to show virtue her own feature, scorn her own image,

0   Kean 'enters with the players at his heels', as if continuing 'an easy mannered conversation'
(Finlay, *Miscellanies*, p. 223). Booth at the Winter Garden entered 'reading a paper
(presumably the speech which he had written for insertion in the play); this he rolled up as
he began the "advice," using it in gesticulations, and handing it to the First Player when he
dismissed him' (Mason 110).

1ff   Irving did not 'advise' the players; he gave a royal 'order' (Terry, p. 104). Burton in 1964
spoke these lines not as reflections on the nature of dramatic art but as a set of rapidly
delivered commands for the ambush of the King.

3–4   Irving here mimicked a gesture of the First Player in 2.2 (Towse, 'Irving', p. 666).

18–19   Irving paused, seeking the right word, then at 'nature' raised his hand in triumph over his

and the very age and body of the time his form and pressure. Now   20
this overdone, or come tardy off, though it makes the unskilful
laugh, cannot but make the judicious grieve, the censure of the
which one must in your allowance o'erweigh a whole theatre of
others. Oh, there be players that I have seen play, and heard others
praise and that highly, not to speak it profanely, that neither having   25
th'accent of Christians, nor the gait of Christian, pagan, nor man,
have so strutted and bellowed that I have thought some of nature's
journeymen had made men, and not made them well, they imitated
humanity so abominably.

I PLAYER I hope we have reformed that indifferently with us, sir.   30

HAMLET Oh reform it altogether. And let those that play your clowns
speak no more than is set down for them, for there be of them that
will themselves laugh, to set on some quantity of barren spectators
to laugh too, though in the meantime some necessary question of
the play be then to be considered. That's villainous, and shows   35
a most pitiful ambition in the fool that uses it. Go make you ready.

Exeunt Players

Enter POLONIUS, ROSENCRANTZ *and* GUILDENSTERN

How now my lord, will the king hear this piece of work?

POLONIUS And the queen too, and that presently.

HAMLET Bid the players make haste.

Exit Polonius

Will you two help to hasten them?   40

ROSENCRANTZ Ay my lord.

Exeunt Rosencrantz and Guildenstern

HAMLET What ho, Horatio!

Enter HORATIO

HORATIO Here sweet lord, at your service.

HAMLET Horatio, thou art e'en as just a man
As e'er my conversation coped withal.   45

---

head (Terry, pp. 104–5). Gielgud paused before 'mirror', seeking the clearest simile, then
seemed to hold one in his hand (Gilder, p. 161).

36   Following 'uses it' Q1 uniquely specifies some interpolations by which a clown might try to
get a laugh, from familiar catch-phrases and punch-lines from jests attributed to Richard
Tarlton, the famous Elizabethan clown, to 'blabbering with his lips'. The Q1 Prince seems to
relish enumerating them. Does, he, in mimicry, blabber with his own lips? For the complete
passage see *The Three-Text Hamlet*.

44ff   Booth 'takes him by both hands and bends upon him a look of love and trust . . . It is
beautiful to see how he relies upon Horatio, keeps him near him in his trials, turns his eyes

HORATIO Oh my dear lord.
HAMLET   Nay, do not think I flatter,
For what advancement may I hope from thee,
That no revenue hast but thy good spirits
To feed and clothe thee? Why should the poor be flattered?
No, let the candied tongue lick absurd pomp   50
And crook the pregnant hinges of the knee
Where thrift may follow fawning. Dost thou hear?
Since my dear soul was mistress of her choice,
And could of men distinguish her election,
Sh'ath sealed thee for herself, for thou hast been   55
As one in suffering all that suffers nothing,
A man that Fortune's buffets and rewards
Hast tane with equal thanks. And blest are those
Whose blood and judgement are so well commeddled
That they are not a pipe for Fortune's finger   60
To sound what stop she please. Give me that man
That is not passion's slave, and I will wear him
In my heart's core, ay in my heart of heart,
As I do thee. Something too much of this.
There is a play tonight before the king: 65
One scene of it comes near the circumstance
Which I have told thee of my father's death.
I prithee when thou seest that act afoot,
Even with the very comment of thy soul

upon him often. He loved to clasp his hand, to exchange glances with him' (Garland,
'Lecture', p. 29).

   Supporting Henry Ainley in an all-star production in 1930, Godfrey Tearle as Horatio was
variously praised as 'manly', 'loyal', 'burly-tender' – his 'quiet distinction', 'muted integrity'
and 'grave and commanding' demeanour contrasting with Ainley's outbursts (*Empire News*,
27 April 1930). Agate also saw in him the 'unalloyed spirit which Hamlet might so easily have
been' (*Sunday Times*, 27 April 1930).

   In 1953 Burton gave this speech 'with a gentle warmth and a touch of self-consciousness'
(*Shakespeare at the Old Vic*, London: Black, 1954, p. 54).

59–61 Irving was felt to be referring to himself (*Academy*, 7 November 1874, p. 519).

61–2 Of Gielgud: Hamlet's 'words describe not only what Horatio is, but what he himself is not'
       (Gilder, p. 163).

64a 'As I *do* thee' (Barrymore's studybook).

64b 'With a gentle reserve' (Tree, 'Hamlet', p. 873). Barrymore broke off his effusion to Horatio
     'with half-reluctant shyness' (MacCarthy, *Theatre*, p. 57). With Burton in 1964 the half-line,
     prompted by a laugh off-stage of the court, meant: 'we must not dally, must hurry'.

> Observe my uncle. If his occulted guilt   70
> Do not itself unkennel in one speech,
> It is a damnèd ghost that we have seen,
> And my imaginations are as foul
> As Vulcan's stithy. Give him heedful note,
> For I mine eyes will rivet to his face,   75
> And after we will both our judgements join
> In censure of his seeming.

HORATIO   Well my lord.
> If a steal aught the whilst this play is playing
> And scape detecting, I will pay the theft.
>   *Sound a flourish*

HAMLET They are coming to the play. I must be idle.   80
> Get you a place.

Danish march (trumpets and kettle-drums). Enter KING, QUEEN, POLONIUS, OPHELIA, ROSENCRANTZ, GUILDENSTERN *and other* LORDS *attendant, with his* GUARD *carrying torches*

80   Macready 'assumed the manner of an idiot, or of a silly and active and impertinent booby, by tossing his head right and left, and walking rapidly across the stage five or six times before the foot-lights and switching his hankerchief – held by a corner – over his right and left shoulder alternately, until the whole court have had time to parade and be seated' (Hackett, 'Notes', p. 158). Ian McKellen in 1972 similarly twirled his handkerchief at this point (Trewin, *Five & Eighty*, p. 155).

82SD Both Q2 and F have the stage direction immediately before 80. Q2 reads: *Enter Trumpets and Kettle Drummes, King, Queene, Polonius, Ophelia;* F reads: *Enter King, Queene, Polonius, Ophelia, Rosincrance, Guildensterne, and other Lords attendant, with his Guard carrying Torches. Danish March. Sound a Flourish*. Edwards has moved all but the 'Flourish' to 82. The 'Danish March' almost certainly involved trumpets and kettle drums. In *The Magnificent Entertainment*, Thomas Dekker described the 1603 coronation procession of King James and Queen Anne of Denmark: 'to delight the Queene with her owne country Musicke, nine Trumpets, and a Kettle Drum, did very sprightly & actiuely sound the *Danish March*'. It may be that, as they sometimes did for the playhouses, royal trumpeters themselves played the same march at the Globe (Long, *Music*, pp. 119–20).

      Staging of the play scene involves three centres of attention: the players; the King and Queen (seated), usually with Polonius (standing); and Ophelia (seated), Hamlet (on the floor at her feet), usually with Horatio (standing). The most common arrangement – there are instances in each century, especially the nineteenth – is to perform the playlet upstage centre, with the royal party downstage on one side and the Hamlet group on the other. This is the arrangement shown in two illustrations of eighteenth-century performances

CLAUDIUS How fares our cousin Hamlet?

HAMLET Excellent i'faith, of the chameleon's dish: I eat the air, promise-crammed. You cannot feed capons so.

CLAUDIUS I have nothing with this answer Hamlet, these words are not   85
mine.

(Merchant, *Shakespeare*, pp. 46–7; Burnim, *Garrick*, pp. 164–5). Kemble in 1804 followed it (*Promptbooks*, p. 47). So did Macready (shown in Daniel Maclise's 1842 painting), except that in it Hamlet turned his back to the playlet while scrutinizing the King, a practice followed by Irving as well. The 1925 Birmingham Repertory production varied the pattern by placing the King and Queen on a bench facing the players, with their backs to the real audience.

Sometimes the royals have been placed on a dais or other elevation upstage centre with the players downstage and the Hamlet group on one side or the other. So they are shown in two eighteenth-century depictions (Merchant, *Shakespeare*, pp. 46–7). Commenting on Garrick, *The Theatrical Review* observed of the playlet that it 'has been been usual for the Actors of it, to perform with their backs to the King and Queen' (May, 1763). In Prague in 1927 this placement was used, with the players in silhouette.

Instead of the usual triangle, a twentieth-century pattern has distributed the three centres of attention in a diagonal. For example, in the 1937 Olivier/Guthrie production, the King and Queen are on high, stage left, while the players are in the centre at a middle level, and Hamlet and Ophelia, downstage right. For pictures of many of these arrangements, plus others, see Mander and Mitchenson, *Hamlet*, pp. 70–87.

What all these stagings have in common is the prominence given the Prince. At the beginning of the play he is invariably physically below the King and Queen, usually because he is downstage but always because he is sitting on the floor. The choreography of the scene shows his rise, literally as well as figuratively. Also Hamlet stands out because where the other characters are fixed in their assigned places, he has more and more been free to move about. First it was Kean and his famous 'crawl', emulated by some of his nineteenth-century successors. By 1935 Gielgud was much more active. As the King and Queen sat on thrones at the upper landing watching the players on the main stage, Hamlet roamed by way of the throne-area from one middle-landing vantage-point to the other, focusing first on the Queen, then on the King.

Many of these features were pushed to exciting extremes in the 1912 Moscow Art Theatre production. The King and Queen are high and remote, the players are on the narrow apron with their backs to the real audience. Kachalov's Hamlet is especially identified with the deep trap which runs the width of centre stage; he places Horatio on the edge of the apron from where he can observe the King from behind a pillar. Hamlet darts around the whole stage (in rehearsal Craig had told him that 'Hamlet's movement must be like lightning cutting across the stage'). From his place at Ophelia's feet upstage, he leaps up and rushes

HAMLET No, nor mine now. – My lord, you played once i'th'university, you say.

POLONIUS That did I my lord, and was accounted a good actor.

HAMLET And what did you enact? 90

POLONIUS I did enact Julius Caesar. I was killed i'th'Capitol. Brutus killed me.

HAMLET It was a brute part of him to kill so capital a calf there. – Be the players ready?

ROSENCRANTZ Ay my lord, they stay upon your patience. 95

GERTRUDE Come hither my dear Hamlet, sit by me.

HAMLET No good mother, here's metal more attractive.

POLONIUS Oh ho, do you mark that?

HAMLET Lady, shall I lie in your lap?

OPHELIA No my lord. 100

HAMLET I mean, my head upon your lap?

OPHELIA Ay my lord.

HAMLET Do you think I meant country matters?

OPHELIA I think nothing my lord.

HAMLET That's a fair thought to lie between maids' legs. 105

OPHELIA What is, my lord?

HAMLET Nothing.

OPHELIA You are merry my lord.

HAMLET Who, I?

OPHELIA Ay my lord. 110

HAMLET O God, your only jig-maker. What should a man do but be merry? for look you how cheerfully my mother looks, and my father died within's two hours.

into the trap to watch the dumb show, with his back to the King and with only his upper body visible, blindingly spotlighted. Later he returns to Ophelia, then the Queen, then back to the trap. Kachalov found the scene exhausting to play, not only because of these moves but because of the need to project his voice from the extremes of the stage, which had been opened to its full length and breadth.

82–120 Stanislavsky advised Kachalov that in this passage Hamlet 'wants to slap the king in the face, but without revealing that it is a slap in the face; ditto to Polonius, ditto to Ophelia' (Senelick, p. 142).

87a Fechter waved his hand, showing that those words 'had passed into the air for all time' (Field, p. 107).

87b–93a In the Branagh film, the two play this passage as if it were patter in a double-act, warming up the audience (*Screenplay*, p. 87).

94 To take off the rudeness of this line, Charles Kemble 'tells Polonius "it was a brute part," and then walks away, chuckling to himself over the remainder of the joke – "to kill so capital a calf there"' (*New York Evening Post*, 18 September 1832).

OPHELIA Nay, 'tis twice two months my lord.

HAMLET So long? Nay then let the devil wear black, for I'll have a suit 115
of sables. O heavens! die two months ago, and not forgotten yet?
Then there's hope a great man's memory may outlive his life half
a year, but byrlady a must build churches then, or else shall a suffer
not thinking on, with the hobby-horse, whose epitaph is, 'For O,
for O, the hobby-horse is forgot.' 120

Hoboys play. The dumb-show enters

Enter a KING *and a* QUEEN, *very lovingly, the Queen embracing him. She
kneels and makes show of protestation unto him. He takes her up, and declines
his head upon her neck. He lies him down upon a bank of flowers. She, seeing
him asleep, leaves him. Anon comes in another man, takes off his crown, kisses
it, pours poison in the sleeper's ears, and leaves him. The Queen returns,
finds the King dead, and makes passionate action. The poisoner, with some
two or three mutes, comes in again, seeming to condole with her. The dead
body is carried away. The poisoner woos the Queen with gifts. She seems
harsh awhile, but in the end accepts his love.* Exeunt

115 Pryce's Hamlet 'does a huge double-take on "So long?"' (Gilbert, 'Pryce').

121SD Edwards amalgamates Q2 and F. Among other differences Q2 stipulates 'trumpets' rather
than F's 'hoboys'. Q2's Queen is less demonstratively loving to her husband (Q2 does not
include F's 'very lovingly' or 'She kneels and makes show of protestation unto him') while
Q2's King is more demonstrative towards her (where F has simply 'Queen embracing him',
Q2 continues 'and he her'). Q2's Queen is initially more resistant to the poisoner ('harsh'
rather than F's 'loath and unwilling'). The Q1 stage direction is much shorter than the other
two; its Queen shows no affection at all.

The dumb show has customarily been cut in performance, thereby avoiding the risk of
diminishing by repetition the impact of the climactic Mousetrap while obviating the question
of why Claudius's conscience is able to resist the miming of his crime yet succumbs to the
spoken version. Even when the dumb show is performed, this question is commonly side-
stepped by freely adapting the scenario in such a way as to make it inexplicable and thus
unthreatening, even ludicrous – as in the Williamson film, which features acrobats with
funny noses and a maypole (bewilderingly, in this version it is the player Queen, not her
lover, who uses one of its streamers to strangle the player King). Or Claudius may simply be
inattentive. For the 1930 Gielgud production, its director saw the King as 'enjoying his liquor;
thus in the manner of our own late-comers to the stalls, he misses the point of the dumb
show' (Williams, *Years*, p. 162). For Burton Gielgud had the King at first preoccupied by
'socializing with the Courtiers who regard the play as quaint and amusing' (Sterne, p. 214).
Even though Burton then takes away Claudius's goblet and forces him to watch, the King
betrays no sign of guilt. Why not here but later? Presumably because Gielgud has omitted

OPHELIA What means this my lord?

HAMLET Marry this is miching mallecho, it means mischief.

OPHELIA Belike this show imports the argument of the play?

Enter PROLOGUE

HAMLET We shall know by this fellow; the players cannot keep counsel,
    they'll tell all. 125

OPHELIA Will a tell us what this show meant?

HAMLET Ay, or any show that you'll show him. Be not you ashamed
    to show, he'll not shame to tell you what it means.

OPHELIA You are naught, you are naught. I'll mark the play.

> *PROLOGUE* For us and for our tragedy, 130
> Here stooping to your clemency,
> We beg your hearing patiently.

HAMLET Is this a prologue, or the posy of a ring?

OPHELIA 'Tis brief my lord.

HAMLET As woman's love. 135

Enter the PLAYER KING *and* QUEEN

> *PLAYER KING* Full thirty times hath Phoebus' cart gone round
> Neptune's salt wash and Tellus' orbèd ground,
> And thirty dozen moons with borrowed sheen
> About the world have times twelve thirties been,
> Since love our hearts, and Hymen did our hands, 140
> Unite commutual in most sacred bands.

from his dumb show the reenactment of the poisoning. Yet allowing the King to witness the full dumb show as written can provide what Granville-Barker called 'the first round of the war of nerves between Prince and King' (*Prefaces*, p. 88). So a self-possessed King, like Patrick Stewart in the BBC-TV production, can help to build suspense by winning this opening round, appearing imperturbed, indeed vastly amused, when first confronted by the reenactment of his crime.

    In the Olivier film the dumb show (which follows the originals closely) is substituted for the spoken version. The drawback is that although the King winces at the poisoning he does not break until after the whole dumb show is over, thus lessening Shakespeare's emphasis on the 'talk of the poisoning'.

127–8 Gielgud directed Burton to 'emphasize the alliteration in "Be not you ashamed to show," so that the line sounds very bitter and bawdy. The court is shocked, but let's have one lady laugh lewdly at that' (Sterne, p. 117).

134–5 'Most Hamlets insult Ophelia by hurling this reply at her. Fechter gave it as if communing with his own thoughts, and looked the while toward his mother' (Field, p. 107).

PLAYER QUEEN So many journeys may the sun and moon
　　　　　　　Make us again count o'er ere love be done.
　　　　　　　But woe is me, you are so sick of late,
　　　　　　　So far from cheer and from your former state,　　　145
　　　　　　　That I distrust you. Yet though I distrust,
　　　　　　　Discomfort you my lord it nothing must.
　　　　　　　For women's fear and love hold quantity,
　　　　　　　In neither aught, or in extremity.
　　　　　　　Now what my love is, proof hath made you know;　　150
　　　　　　　And as my love is sized, my fear is so.
　　　　　　　[Where love is great, the littlest doubts are fear;
　　　　　　　Where little fears grow great, great love grows there.]
PLAYER KING Faith, I must leave thee love, and shortly too:
　　　　　　　My operant powers their functions leave to do;　　　155
　　　　　　　And thou shalt live in this fair world behind,
　　　　　　　Honoured, beloved; and haply one as kind
　　　　　　　For husband shalt thou –
PLAYER QUEEN　　　　　　　　Oh confound the rest!
　　　　　　　Such love must needs be treason in my breast.
　　　　　　　In second husband let me be accurst:　　　　　　160
　　　　　　　None wed the second but who killed the first.

HAMLET That's wormwood, wormwood.

PLAYER QUEEN The instances that second marriage move
　　　　　　　Are base respects of thrift, but none of love.
　　　　　　　A second time I kill my husband dead　　　　　　165
　　　　　　　When second husband kisses me in bed.
PLAYER KING I do believe you think what now you speak,
　　　　　　　But what we do determine oft we break.
　　　　　　　Purpose is but the slave to memory,
　　　　　　　Of violent birth but poor validity,　　　　　　　170
　　　　　　　Which now like fruit unripe sticks on the tree,

160ff Guthrie at Minneapolis directed the scandalized Court to begin whispering here, growing
　　　more intense at 165–6, and – undaunted by the Player King's attempt to silence them –
　　　building to 204. All the while they are drawing apart from the King so that by the end of the
　　　playlet, they are all huddled together in back of Hamlet, leaving 'the lone figure of the King'
　　　(Rossi, pp. 48–9). At 237SD Claudius gasps uncontrollably, abruptly cutting off the
　　　whispering, and in this silence Hamlet can very softly say: 'He poisons him i' the garden for
　　　his estate' while Claudius registers a series of fearful reactions after each phrase (Rossi, pp.
　　　28–9).
162　Macready addressed 'That's wormwood' to Horatio (promptbook 37) as did Fechter (Field,
　　　p. 107).

But fall unshaken when they mellow be.
Most necessary 'tis that we forget
To pay ourselves what to ourselves is debt.
What to ourselves in passion we propose,   175
The passion ending, doth the purpose lose.
The violence of either grief or joy
Their own enactures with themselves destroy.
Where joy most revels, grief doth most lament;
Grief joys, joy grieves, on slender accident.   180
This world is not for aye, nor 'tis not strange
That even our loves should with our fortunes change,
For 'tis a question left us yet to prove,
Whether love lead fortune, or else fortune love.
The great man down, you mark his favourite flies;   185
The poor advanced makes friends of enemies,
And hitherto doth love on fortune tend;
For who not needs shall never lack a friend,
And who in want a hollow friend doth try
Directly seasons him his enemy.   190
But orderly to end where I begun,
Our wills and fates do so contrary run
That our devices still are overthrown;
Our thoughts are ours, their ends none of our own.
So think thou wilt no second husband wed,   195
But die thy thoughts when thy first lord is dead.
PLAYER QUEEN Nor earth to me give food, nor heaven light,
Sport and repose lock from me day and night,
[To desperation turn my trust and hope,
An anchor's cheer in prison be my scope,]   200
Each opposite that blanks the face of joy
Meet what I would have well, and it destroy;
Both here and hence pursue me lasting strife,
If once a widow, ever I be wife.

HAMLET If she should break it now!   205

PLAYER KING 'Tis deeply sworn. Sweet, leave me here awhile;
My spirits grow dull, and fain I would beguile
The tedious day with sleep.
                              Sleeps
PLAYER QUEEN   Sleep rock thy brain,
And never come mischance between us twain.   *Exit*

---

205 Fechter: 'to King and Queen' (Field, p. 107). Irving spoke this line to Ophelia: he 'looks at her
and grows sad' (Terry's rehearsal book).

HAMLET Madam, how like you this play? 210
GERTRUDE The lady doth protest too much methinks.
HAMLET Oh but she'll keep her word.
CLAUDIUS Have you heard the argument? Is there no offence in't?
HAMLET No, no, they do but jest, poison in jest, no offence i'th'world.
CLAUDIUS What do you call the play? 215
HAMLET The Mousetrap. Marry how? Tropically. This play is the
    image of a murder done in Vienna. Gonzago is the duke's name,
    his wife Baptista. You shall see anon. 'Tis a knavish piece of work,
    but what o' that? Your majesty, and we that have free souls, it
    touches us not. Let the galled jade winch, our withers are unwrung. 220

Enter LUCIANUS

    This is one Lucianus, nephew to the king.
OPHELIA You are as good as a chorus my lord.
HAMLET I could interpret between you and your love if I could see the
    puppets dallying.
OPHELIA You are keen my lord, you are keen. 225
HAMLET It would cost you a groaning to take off mine edge.
OPHELIA Still better and worse.
HAMLET So you mistake your husbands. Begin, murderer. Pox, leave
    thy damnable faces and begin. Come, the croaking raven doth
    bellow for revenge. 230

---

212   On BBC-TV Jacobi emphasizes *her*.

213b   With Frank Benson, Claudius addressed this question to Polonius (*World*, 7 March 1900).

216   Wilks was praised for 'The *Gayety*, the unforc'd, soft, becoming NEGLIGENCE, with which,
    reclining at the Feet of *Ophelia* and toying with her Fan as if *genteely Insignificant*, He kept a
    Guard upon his *Uncle*'s EYE and *watch'd* (unnotic'd) the *Effect* of his *Play*'s *Influence*'
    (*Prompter*, 24 October 1735). Kemble used the same business (H. Martin, *Remarks*, pp.
    6–7). Finlay adds that Kemble 'answered the questions as to the name and plot of the play
    carelessly, as if they were interrupting his situation, and as if he took no interest in the play
    farther than that he had casually seen it'. In contrast, Finlay faulted Kean for dividing his
    attention between the play (which Hamlet already knew) and the King to the neglect of
    Ophelia (*Miscellanies*, p. 227). Fechter carries the manuscript pages of *The Murder of*
    Gonzago when giving his advice to the players and during the playlet uses it as a screen
    while he watches the King (*Morning Chronicle*, 23 March 1861).

216a   Barrymore paused before and after saying 'The Mousetrap' (promptbook 156).

229ff   Kachalov brought his face closer and closer to the King's, hypnotizing him with his eyes and
    voice, his tone rising to a shout for the first time in the performance until the King in panic
    calls for 'light!' As the King flees 'in a series of ludicrous leaps' along with the Court, the

LUCIANUS Thoughts black, hands apt, drugs fit, and time agreeing,
          Confederate season, else no creature seeing.
          Thou mixture rank, of midnight weeds collected,
          With Hecat's ban thrice blasted, thrice infected,
          Thy natural magic and dire property   235
          On whoiesome life usurp immediately.
          Pours the poison in his ears

HAMLET A poisons him i'th'garden for's estate. His name's Gonzago.
         The story is extant, and written in very choice Italian. You shall
         see anon how the murderer gets the love of Gonzago's wife.
OPHELIA The king rises.   240
HAMLET What, frighted with false fire?
GERTRUDE How fares my lord?

Prince wraps himself in the Player King's cloak: 'capering and electrifying the house with . . . a kind of antic mummery whose hysteria concealed horror' (Senelick, p. 167).

231–6 When J. B. Booth delivered these lines, playing Lucianus to Charles Kean's Hamlet, 'each word dropped poison' (Gould, p. 64). Here as earlier in the playlet, Gielgud beat 'the measure of Lucianus' lines as though he would whip them forward to their desperate goal' (Gilder, p. 169). Branagh in 1992/3 took the vial from Lucianus and himself poured the poison in the Player King's ear (*Cahiers Elisabethains*, October, 1993, pp. 72, 78); in the film he turns on Claudius with the phial (*Screenplay*, p. 93).

233a–9 With Macready, when the poisoner produces a phial, the King starts; when the poison is poured (237), he covers his face with both hands; at 'murderer' (239) he rises (promptbook 129). Reviewers commented on the 'strange fire' in Macready's eyes, which were 'fixed with serpent-fascination on the king' (*New Monthly Magazine*, 1 July 1821, p. 333). He seemed to 'read the thoughts that moved within his guilty uncle's breast; and when he starts up, and with a cry of exultation follows the craven and flying murderer to the door, the audience seemed relieved from a spell' (*Theatrical Journal*, 5 September 1840).

237b–9 Barrymore 'leans closely over King, speaking in his ear. King becomes terror-stricken, gives shriek' (promptbook 156).

240–3 With Barrymore these lines were 'all spoken simultaneously, characters all moving at the same time' (promptbook 156).

240 With Irving, after the king rises, the *Academy* explains: 'it is not so much by his rising, nor by Ophelia's words of surprise, as by the actor's [Irving's] seething excitement, that you perceive the enterprise has succeeded' (7 November 1874). In the end 'he leaps in momentary wildness' upon the vacant throne, 'with an hysterical yell of triumph' (Scott, *Hamlets*, p. 40).

241 Of Gielgud: 'the house was really excited, and with that genuine excitement of a crowd when a goal is scored in a Cup final' (*Sunday Times*, 11 May 1930, p. 6).

POLONIUS Give o'er the play.
CLAUDIUS Give me some light. Away!
LORDS Lights, lights, lights!   245

                    Exeunt all but Hamlet and Horatio

HAMLET Why, let the strucken deer go weep,
              The hart ungallèd play,
        For some must watch while some must sleep,
              Thus runs the world away.

        Would not this, sir, and a forest of feathers, if the rest of my fortunes   250
        turn Turk with me, with two provincial roses on my razed shoes,
        get me a fellowship in a cry of players, sir?
HORATIO Half a share.
HAMLET A whole one I.
              For thou dost know, O Damon dear,   255
              This realm dismantled was

244   Playing opposite Derek Jacobi in the BBC-TV production, Patrick Stewart here coolly called
       for light, then held the torch to Hamlet's face, which Jacobi covered with his hands. When
       (like the First Player at 2.2.475) Jacobi then revealed his grinning, antic face, Stewart glanced
       around and shook his head as if to say 'You see how impossible my nephew is . . . ' At the
       talk of the poisoning, his hand had gone up and down several times as if he wanted to shield
       his eyes but was restraining the impulse. Except for this momentary break, however, he kept
       his self-control.

245   'The Quarto [Q2] gives the line "Lights, lights, lights!" to Polonius only, while the Folio has
       "All." It is very evident that in practice the cry for lights might well be started by Polonius but
       must be taken up by "All"' (Webster, *Shakespeare*, p. 131).

245SD With Booth 'the Players on the platform stage . . . stare in amazement and retire in doubt
       and chagrin' (Shattuck, p. 217).

246   Gielgud 'tears the "dozen or sixteen lines" into a thousand pieces and scatters them abroad'
       (Gilder, p. 169).

246–58 Of Irving: 'his body swaying the while from side to side in irrepressible excitement' he
       recites the doggerel stanzas; at 258 he referred to Ophelia's peacock-feathered fan, which
       he still retained (Towse, 'Irving', p. 666).

248–9 Garrick always 'wound up his burst of exultation . . . by three flourishes of his pocket-
       handkerchief over his head, as he paced the stage backwards and forwards. It was once
       remarked, as an extraordinary deviation, that he added a fourth flourish' (Cole, *Charles
       Kean*, I, p. 283). Davies wished he would vary the practice (III, pp. 93–4). Describing
       Macready, Forster caught the irony of the aftermath: 'As he stands there, in the flushed
       excitement of a triumph, we feel that he is satisfied with the discovery alone . . . and that to
       act upon it was as far from his thoughts as ever' (*Dramatic Essays*, p. 11).

> Of Jove himself, and now reigns here
> A very, very – pajock.

HORATIO You might have rhymed.

HAMLET O good Horatio, I'll take the ghost's word for a thousand   260
    pound. Didst perceive?

HORATIO Very well my lord.

HAMLET Upon the talk of the poisoning?

HORATIO I did very well note him.

> *Enter* ROSENCRANTZ *and* GUILDENSTERN

HAMLET Ah ha! – Come, some music! Come, the recorders!   265
    For if the king like not the comedy,
      Why then – belike he likes it not, perdy.
  Come, some music!

GUILDENSTERN Good my lord, vouchsafe me a word with you.

HAMLET Sir, a whole history.   270

GUILDENSTERN The king, sir –

HAMLET Ay sir, what of him?

GUILDENSTERN Is in his retirement marvellous distempered.

HAMLET With drink sir?

264SD So F and Q1. Q2 has Rosencrantz and Guildenstern enter later, at 269. The earlier entrance
     allows for unspoken interaction. Edwards suggests that Hamlet 'pointedly ignores' them. Or,
     if unobserved, they may have a chance to appraise the situation and exchange looks. Or
     perhaps the earlier entry simply gave them more time to cross the large Elizabethan stage.

265 'Fechter tore the leaves from his play-book and scattered them in the air . . . he put his hand
     to his throat as if choking. "Ah, ha!" became a gasp; he leaned upon Horatio and, for relief,
     for solace, called for music' (Field, p. 108). Of Booth: 'the "ah" is an indrawn sound like a
     moan, the "ha" an expulsion of breath like a low, sorrowful, but triumphant laugh'
     (Shattuck, p. 209).

268 Of Macready: as usual after his 'highest flights of passion' he subsided into his natural
     gentleness; 'he drooped his head upon Horatio's shoulder, and asked in the tone of a sick
     man for some music' (Lady Pollock, *Macready*, p. 107).

269 In the 1964 Burton production, Gielgud directed Redfield, who had been exaggeratedly
     servile and alarmed, to: 'bully Hamlet now! You must tell him off! He's behaved disgracefully
     – let him have it! . . . You've got the King on your side now. You're not afraid of Hamlet any
     more' (Redfield, *Letters*, p. 90).

270–8 Irving delivers 270 'with choler' and through 278 'he is apparently full of high spirits –
     blazing away all the while' (Terry's rehearsal book – the notes for this scene are not in
     Terry's hand).

274 Macready said these words rapidly, not as a question but as an 'exclamation denoting an
     unquestionable conclusion' (Hackett, *Notes*, p. 159).

GUILDENSTERN No my lord, rather with choler.   275

HAMLET Your wisdom should show itself more richer to signify this
to his doctor, for, for me to put him to his purgation would perhaps
plunge him into far more choler.

GUILDENSTERN Good my lord, put your discourse into some frame,
and start not so wildly from my affair.   280

HAMLET I am tame sir, pronounce.

GUILDENSTERN The queen your mother, in most great affliction of
spirit, hath sent me to you.

HAMLET You are welcome.

GUILDENSTERN Nay good my lord, this courtesy is not of the right   285
breed. If it shall please you to make me a wholesome answer, I will
do your mother's commandment. If not, your pardon and my return
shall be the end of my business.

HAMLET Sir, I cannot.

ROSENCRANTZ What, my lord?   290

HAMLET Make you a wholesome answer; my wit's diseased. But, sir,
such answer as I can make, you shall command, or rather, as you
say, my mother. Therefore no more, but to the matter. My mother,
you say.

ROSENCRANTZ Then thus she says. Your behaviour hath struck her   295
into amazement and admiration.

HAMLET O wonderful son that can so stonish a mother! But is there
no sequel at the heels of this mother's admiration? Impart.

ROSENCRANTZ She desires to speak with you in her closet ere you go
to bed.   300

HAMLET We shall obey, were she ten times our mother. Have you any
further trade with us?

ROSENCRANTZ My lord, you once did love me.

HAMLET And do still, by these pickers and stealers.

282   Redfield with Burton in 1964: 'the que-e-en, your mo-o-ther', as if to say: 'surely you'll pay
      attention to *her*'.

297   Forbes-Robertson spoke 'O wonderful son . . . ' with 'tender melancholy' (*Daily News*, 13
      September 1897, p. 6).

301a–2 Macready gave a 'long pause' after 'mother' (promptbook 37). Booth: 'This is [Hamlet's] first
      use of the royal plural. He is resolved now to assume his rights' (studybook). He spoke
      'trade' with a 'hard, sarcastic tone, implying in the word a reproach for their conspiracy
      against him' (Shattuck, p. 211).

303–8 With Forbes-Robertson 'Rosencrantz and Guildenstern are sharply differentiated, the former
      being the more sympathetic of the two. When (after the play) he appeals to Hamlet by their
      mutual friendship the Prince appears to be about to make some confidence to him when he
      catches the sinister look of Guildenstern fixed upon him and turns it off with an obviously

ROSENCRANTZ Good my lord, what is your cause of distemper? You 305
do surely bar the door upon your own liberty if you deny your griefs
to your friend.

HAMLET Sir, I lack advancement.

ROSENCRANTZ How can that be, when you have the voice of the king
himself for your succession in Denmark? 310

HAMLET Ay sir, but while the grass grows – the proverb is something
musty.

Enter the PLAYERS *with recorders*

Oh, the recorders. Let me see one. To withdraw with you – Why
do you go about to recover the wind of me, as if you would drive
me into a toil? 315

GUILDENSTERN O my lord, if my duty be too bold, my love is too
unmannerly.

HAMLET I do not well understand that. Will you play upon this pipe?

GUILDENSTERN My lord, I cannot.

HAMLET I pray you. 320

GUILDENSTERN Believe me I cannot.

HAMLET I do beseech you.

GUILDENSTERN I know no touch of it my lord.

HAMLET 'Tis as easy as lying. Govern these ventages with your fingers
and thumb, give it breath with your mouth, and it will discourse 325
most eloquent music. Look you, these are the stops.

GUILDENSTERN But these cannot I command to any utterance of
harmony. I have not the skill.

HAMLET Why look you now how unworthy a thing you make of me.
You would play upon me, you would seem to know my stops, you 330
would pluck out the heart of my mystery, you would sound me from
my lowest note to the top of my compass – and there is much music,
excellent voice, in this little organ, yet cannot you make it speak.

affected "I lack advancement", and his indignation in the "recorders" passage which
immediately follows is directed only against Guildenstern' (Crosse, *Diaries*, II, 1898).

308 With Gielgud this line 'is not merely a statement, but a proclamation of his thwarted right to
power' (Gilder, p. 171).

313 In rehearsal with Rosencrantz and Guildenstern, Stanislavsky 'moved back and forth, forcing
them to chase him like foxhounds. He led this "chase" at a hectic tempo and then suddenly
stopped short, tossing them a line, so that Rosencrantz and Guildenstern with no time to halt
crashed into him' (Senelick, p. 143).

325 Burton rolled the 'r' in 'brrreath' up the scale.

330 Irving: 'dropping all humorous banter and blazing out' (Terry's rehearsal book).

'Sblood, do you think I am easier to be played on than a pipe? Call
me what instrument you will, though you can fret me, you cannot   335
play upon me.

Enter POLONIUS

God bless you sir.
POLONIUS My lord, the queen would speak with you, and presently.
HAMLET Do you see yonder cloud that's almost in shape of a camel?
POLONIUS By th'mass, and 'tis like a camel indeed.   340
HAMLET Methinks it is like a weasel.
POLONIUS It is backed like a weasel.
HAMLET Or like a whale?
POLONIUS Very like a whale.
HAMLET Then I will come to my mother by and by. – They fool me   345
to the top of my bent. – I will come by and by.
POLONIUS I will say so.   *Exit*
HAMLET By and by is easily said. – Leave me, friends.
                              Exeunt all but Hamlet

334a   Irving: 'breaking a pipe across his knee' (Terry's rehearsal book). Of Forbes-Robertson:
       'Unlike Irving he does not smash the recorder on his knee.' Instead of rage he projected 'a
       quiet sense of superiority over the two courtiers who foolishly fancied that it would be easy
       to play on him' (*Graphic*, 18 September 1897, p. 374).
336   At this point Irving threw away the two pieces of his pipe (Terry's rehearsal book). Then he
       interpolated the sponge passage from 4.2.11–19, with Rosencrantz 'angry' at 'Take you me
       for a sponge?' and Hamlet emphasizing '*Sponge*, you shall be dry again' with an added 'you
       shall!' At 337, he, in backing up, came upon Polonius. He turned and spoke the line, bowing
       low (Terry's rehearsal book).
337   With Booth, in these four words, 'there is such weariness, there is such scorn of this
       miserable, dishonest, luxurious court, there is such despair of a noble nature set upon by
       ignoble natures, there is such impatience of this last crafty, unscrupulous, lying courtier, that
       the grace of speech is more bitter than a curse' (Calhoun, 'Booth', p. 81).
339ff 'Ion Swinley [as Hamlet] watched the camel-backed cloud through all the changes Hamlet
       suggests while Ernest Milton, with mocking attention, 'never looked away from the old
       man's foolish, assenting face' (*Queen*, 2 July 1924). In the Branagh film Polonius's manner
       towards 'cold-eyed' Hamlet moves from 'barely civil' to 'vicious' (*Screenplay*, p. 98).
343   Forrest paused after 'or' 'as if rummaging for a simile' (promptbook).
348b   Irving spoke the word 'friends' with sarcasm. He wishes Horatio goodnight 'very tenderly,
       though rather absently and wearily – extending his hand which Horatio kisses' (Terry's
       rehearsal book). With Barrymore, too, Hamlet and Horatio exchanged goodnights
       (promptbook 156).

'Tis now the very witching time of night,
When churchyards yawn, and hell itself breathes out   350
Contagion to this world. Now could I drink hot blood,
And do such bitter business as the day
Would quake to look on. Soft, now to my mother.
O heart, lose not thy nature; let not ever
The soul of Nero enter this firm bosom.   355
Let me be cruel, not unnatural:
I will speak daggers to her but use none.
My tongue and soul in this be hypocrites,
How in my words somever she be shent,
To give them seals never my soul consent.   *Exit*   360

349ff Irving: Large bell strikes 12 (promptbook). After the ironic comedy of the 'clouds' exchange, Kingsley meant to shock the audience by abruptly floating 'that black-magic, terrifying Halloween thing on this sea of laughter' (Maher, *Soliloquies*, p. 84). Pennington sees Hamlet's 'melodramatic rhetoric' here as a retreat from action, 'making himself an actor whose deeds are only gestures'; accordingly, he spoke it wearing a Player's cloak, as – he points out – Dillane would wear the Player King's crown and Fiennes a Player's mask (*Hamlet*, p. 92n).

351–6 Kevin Kline spoke 351–3a in a 'spooky stage-whisper'; at 'soft' the 'elation and energy' of the first lines was checked by his straining resolve not to harm his mother: 'Let me be cruuu-elll, not unnaturrrrell' (Maher, *Soliloquies*, p. 193).

353a George Grizzard makes 'an underhand stabbing motion' then checks it (Rossi, p. 85).

357 Warner unbuckled his sword belt (Maher, *Soliloquies*, p. 57).

ACT 3, SCENE 3

[3.3] *Enter* CLAUDIUS, ROSENCRANTZ *and* GUILDENSTERN

CLAUDIUS I like him not, nor stands it safe with us
        To let his madness range. Therefore prepare you:
        I your commission will forthwith dispatch,
        And he to England shall along with you.
        The terms of our estate may not endure   5
        Hazard so near us as doth hourly grow
        Out of his brows.
GUILDENSTERN   We will ourselves provide.
        Most holy and religious fear it is
        To keep those many many bodies safe
        That live and feed upon your majesty.   10
ROSENCRANTZ The single and peculiar life is bound
        With all the strength and armour of the mind
        To keep itself from noyance; but much more
        That spirit upon whose weal depends and rests
        The lives of many. The cess of majesty   15

1–27   Rossi, who played Rosencrantz, reports that Guthrie at Minneapolis had Rosencrantz and
        Guildenstern help the King out of his public garb of office, including a ribbon and medal,
        into a dressing gown. Guthrie saw the two as 'just opportunistic climbers . . . Royalists – loyal
        to the King and The Establishment . . . who really don't know what the King's designs are' (p.
        16). As he staged this scene they are at first sincerely deferential. At 10, Guildenstern is
        kneeling (to tie the King's belt) and at 11 Rosencrantz is buttoning him into his robe (pp.
        85–6). Yet in the course of rehearsing this exchange, 'Rosencrantz became a bit sadistic'. At
        'the cess of majesty' Guthrie had him 'slowly advance behind the seated King and speak
        from behind his right ear, reaching a soft, insinuating climax on "falls," at which point
        Claudius winced and made a half-gesture to his ear' (p. 23). Compare the business Guthrie
        introduced at 1.5.34.
  15   In the Branagh film, trying to soothe the King's choler, Rosencrantz after 'lives of many'
        seems to run dry, looks in vain for help from Guildenstern, then continues to elaborate in
        the same vein.

Dies not alone, but like a gulf doth draw
What's near it with it. It is a massy wheel
Fixed on the summit of the highest mount,
To whose huge spokes ten thousand lesser things
Are mortised and adjoined, which when it falls, 20
Each small annexment, petty consequence,
Attends the boisterous ruin. Never alone
Did the king sigh, but with a general groan.

CLAUDIUS Arm you I pray you to this speedy voyage,
For we will fetters put about this fear 25
Which now goes too free-footed.

ROSENCRANTZ We will haste us.
Exeunt Rosencrantz and Guildenstern

Enter POLONIUS

POLONIUS My lord, he's going to his mother's closet.
Behind the arras I'll convey myself
To hear the process. I'll warrant she'll tax him home,
And as you said, and wisely was it said, 30
'Tis meet that some more audience than a mother,
Since nature makes them partial, should o'erhear
The speech of vantage. Fare you well my liege,
I'll call upon you ere you go to bed
And tell you what I know.

CLAUDIUS Thanks, dear my lord. 35
Exit Polonius

Oh my offence is rank, it smells to heaven;
It hath the primal eldest curse upon't,
A brother's murder. Pray can I not,
Though inclination be as sharp as will.

27–35 Patrick Stewart on BBC-TV had been able to sustain his self-possession through his interview with Rosencrantz and Guildenstern, in which he was warmly confidential with them, putting his arm around Guildenstern at one point. But when Polonius came in, the King was plainly preoccupied, so much so that he did not express his thanks to Polonius until after he had gone. Finally, his guilty conscience could be contained no longer and he virtually vomited before attempting to pray.

36ff Q1's Claudius wept at the beginning of his soliloquy: 'O that this wet that falles upon my face / Would wash the crime cleere from my conscience!'
To Morris Carnovsky, who played Claudius at Stratford, Connecticut in 1958, this soliloquy is 'the revelation of an extremely sensitive and conscience-ridden man', his final couplet (97–8) 'a wrenching confession' (*Actor's Eye*, pp. 69, 170). Playing opposite Jacobi on stage, Timothy West gave this speech as 'a dog-tired worrying-away at an old, incurable obsession,

My stronger guilt defeats my strong intent,   40
And like a man to double business bound,
I stand in pause where I shall first begin,
And both neglect. What if this cursèd hand
Were thicker than itself with brother's blood,
Is there not rain enough in the sweet heavens   45
To wash it white as snow? Whereto serves mercy
But to confront the visage of offence?
And what's in prayer but this two-fold force,
To be forestallèd ere we come to fall,
Or pardoned being down? Then I'll look up,   50
My fault is past. But oh, what form of prayer
Can serve my turn? 'Forgive me my foul murder'?
That cannot be, since I am still possessed
Of those effects for which I did the murder,
My crown, mine own ambition, and my queen.   55
May one be pardoned and retain th'offence?
In the corrupted currents of this world
Offence's gilded hand may shove by justice,
And oft 'tis seen the wicked prize itself
Buys out the law. But 'tis not so above;   60
There is no shuffling, there the action lies
In his true nature, and we ourselves compelled
Even to the teeth and forehead of our faults
To give in evidence. What then? What rests?
Try what repentance can. What can it not?   65
Yet what can it when one cannot repent?
Oh wretched state! Oh bosom black as death!
Oh limèd soul that struggling to be free
Art more engaged! Help, angels! – Make assay:
Bow stubborn knees, and heart with strings of steel   70
Be soft as sinews of the new-born babe.
All may be well.

[*He kneels*]

Enter HAMLET

packed with self-mockery and self-contempt, the last testament of a man who has already
evolved from despair to a deadly cynicism' (*New Statesman*, 3 June 1977).

40–4a   Michael Pennington, Claudius with Stephen Dillane, shows 'a touch of Hamlet's own
         irresolution' (*Country Life*, 17 November 1994); 'like Hamlet he is precariously balanced
         between guilt, terror and self-control' (*Sunday Times*, 13 November 1994).

HAMLET Now might I do it pat, now a is a-praying,
         And now I'll do't – and so a goes to heaven,
         And so am I revenged. That would be scanned.   75
         A villain kills my father, and for that,
         I his sole son do this same villain send
         To heaven.
         Why, this is hire and salary, not revenge.
         A took my father grossly, full of bread,   80
         With all his crimes broad blown, as flush as May,
         And how his audit stands who knows save heaven?
         But in our circumstance and course of thought
         'Tis heavy with him. And am I then revenged
         To take him in the purging of his soul,   85
         When he is fit and seasoned for his passage?
         No.
         Up sword, and know thou a more horrid hent,
         When he is drunk asleep, or in his rage,
         Or in th'incestuous pleasure of his bed,   90
         At game a-swearing, or about some act
         That has no relish of salvation in't –

73ff Davies praised Garrick as the first to reject 'this horrid soliloquy' (p. 101); since then it has
      often been cut. When included, its vengefulness has commonly been mitigated by treating it
      as a rationalization. In 1763, Thomas Sheridan, a rival of Garrick's in the role, told Boswell
      that this speech 'if really from the heart, would make Hamlet the most black, revengeful
      man. But it coincides better with his character to suppose him here endeavouring to make
      an excuse to himself for his delay' (Boswell, *London Journal*, pp. 234–5). Of Fechter:
      'restrained by reasonable doubt, not vacillation of purpose . . . he did not kill the King at
      prayers, because of that Catholic faith which would send this same villain to heaven'. Field
      adds that Hamlet had feared meeting 'my dearest foe in heaven' at 1.2.182 (p. 93). To Tree
      the speech 'clearly reveals that tenderer side of Hamlet's nature, which makes him seek for
      any excuse which may postpone the shedding of blood' ('Hamlet', p. 875).
         Of the simplicity of Barrymore's staging: 'One man is here, one is there. Here are the
      uplifted hands, there the sword drawn. Here, sick conscience, power, and tormented
      ambition; there, the torture of conflicting thoughts, the irony, the resolution. Two bodies and
      their relation to each other, the words, the essential drama, the eternal content of the scene.
      No tricks, no plausible business' (*New Republic*, 6 December 1922, p. 46). Peter Hall: this
      soliloquy 'is time suspended, a close-up with voice-over that lasts a few seconds. The speech
      rushes out while the sword is poised' (*Diaries*, p. 191).

Then trip him that his heels may kick at heaven,
And that his soul may be as damned and black
As hell whereto it goes. My mother stays.   95
This physic but prolongs thy sickly days.   *Exit*
CLAUDIUS My words fly up, my thoughts remain below.
Words without thoughts never to heaven go.   *Exit*

93–5   Booth's 'eyes, naturally jet black, were almost white with light' (Shattuck, p. 222).

97–8   Pennington comments that this couplet allows an actor playing the King 'to correct his
       performance': 'If he's veered to self-pity in the main speech, he can toughen these lines up;
       if he's been too emphatic they can be simple and direct; if too armoured, he is now
       vulnerable' (*Hamlet*, p. 97n).

ACT 3, SCENE 4

[3.4] *Enter* GERTRUDE *and* POLONIUS

POLONIUS A will come straight. Look you lay home to him.
        Tell him his pranks have been too broad to bear with,
        And that your grace hath screened and stood between
        Much heat and him. I'll silence me e'en here.
        Pray you be round with him.   5
HAMLET (*Within*) Mother, mother, mother!
GERTRUDE I'll warrant you, fear me not. Withdraw, I hear him coming.
        [*Polonius hides himself behind the arras*]

            Enter HAMLET

HAMLET Now mother, what's the matter?
GERTRUDE Hamlet, thou hast thy father much offended.
HAMLET Mother, you have my father much offended.   10
GERTRUDE Come, come, you answer with an idle tongue.
HAMLET Go, go, you question with a wicked tongue.
GERTRUDE Why, how now Hamlet?

Until the twentieth century this was known as the 'closet scene' (see 3.2.299). Since Barrymore in 1922 gave it an oedipal reading, the episode has come to be called the 'bedroom scene'. And Gertrude's bed has more and more become the site for the encounter between mother and son; especially on film and television, many of their exchanges in recent decades have taken place as they lie together on the bed. (Although an illustration of the scene in Rowe's 1714 edition shows a double bed, royal closets did not ordinarily include a bed.)

OSD Michael Redgrave (1949) had a maidservant place the Queen's chestnut-red wig on a block, revealing that Gertrude had grey hair, business borrowed from Poel's production of *Fratricide Punished* (Redgrave, *Mind's I*, pp. 190–1).

1–5 With Burton Gielgud directed Cronyn: 'Hamlet might come at any moment' (Sterne, p. 39).

8 Q1's Hamlet voices his suspicion: 'I'le tell you, but first weele make all safe'.

10 J. B. Booth emphasized *you* and *my father* (Gould, p. 65).

HAMLET   What's the matter now?

GERTRUDE Have you forgot me?

HAMLET   No by the rood, not so.
    You are the queen, your husband's brother's wife,   15
    And, would it were not so, you are my mother.

GERTRUDE Nay, then I'll set those to you that can speak.

HAMLET Come, come and sit you down, you shall not budge.
    You go not till I set you up a glass
    Where you may see the inmost part of you.   20

GERTRUDE What wilt thou do? thou wilt not murder me?
    Help, help, ho!

POLONIUS (*Behind*) What ho! Help, help, help!

HAMLET (*Draws*) How now, a rat? Dead for a ducat, dead.
                    Kills Polonius

POLONIUS (*Behind*) Oh, I am slain!

GERTRUDE   Oh me, what hast thou done?   25

HAMLET Nay I know not, is it the king?

GERTRUDE Oh what a rash and bloody deed is this!

HAMLET A bloody deed? Almost as bad, good mother,
    As kill a king and marry with his brother.

GERTRUDE As kill a king?

HAMLET   Ay lady, 'twas my word.   30
    [*Lifts up the arras and reveals the body of Polonius*]
    Thou wretched, rash, intruding fool, farewell.

14a   Clare Higgins, with Rylance, paused before 'me', as if to mean 'How could you?' (Gilbert, 'Rylance').

15   On BBC-TV Claire Bloom slapped Jacobi's face.

17   Irving caught the arm of the Queen (Georgina Pauncefort), as she crossed the stage (Terry's rehearsal book). After slapping Mel Gibson's face, Glenn Close started to exit but was stopped by a great roar by Gibson.

20   When J. B. Booth said '*in*-most' its sound 'greatly prolonged on the first syllable, was like a searching probe of steel' (Gould, p. 65).

21b   Robert Helpmann gave a 'glance at his sword' in 1944 – 'bewildered, frightened, half-realising how dangerously near he might have been to this' (Williamson, *Old Vic*, p. 170).

27   'Quick' (Terry's rehearsal book).

29   Claire Bloom, playing the Queen opposite Derek Jacobi, holds that she here for the first time realizes that Claudius committed the crime (*BBC-TV Hamlet*, p. 25).

31   J. B. Booth gave each word of this line separately, with ascending emphasis, 'in tones of mingled grief and anger' (Gould, pp. 65–6). Fechter used 'a tone of almost affectionate pity' (*Examiner*, 20 April 1861).

I took thee for thy better. Take thy fortune.
Thou find'st to be too busy is some danger. –
Leave wringing of your hands. Peace! Sit you down
And let me wring your heart, for so I shall 35
If it be made of penetrable stuff,
If damnèd custom have not brazed it so,
That it be proof and bulwark against sense.
GERTRUDE What have I done, that thou dar'st wag thy tongue
In noise so rude against me?
HAMLET   Such an act 40
That blurs the grace and blush of modesty,
Calls virtue hypocrite, takes off the rose
From the fair forehead of an innocent love
And sets a blister there, makes marriage vows
As false as dicers' oaths. Oh such a deed 45
As from the body of contraction plucks
The very soul, and sweet religion makes
A rhapsody of words. Heaven's face doth glow;
Yea, this solidity and compound mass,
With tristful visage as against the doom, 50
Is thought-sick at the act.
GERTRUDE   Ay me, what act,
That roars so loud and thunders in the index?

33 On BBC-TV Jacobi spoke very loudly, as if Polonius were deaf.

53 If the frontispiece to Rowe's 1709 edition reflects stage practice, the 'presentments' at that time may have been portraits on the wall. However, Davies states that 'It has been the constant practice of the stage, ever since the Restoration, for Hamlet, in this scene, to produce from his pocket two pictures in little, of his father and uncle, not much bigger than two large coins or medallions' (p. 106). Kean was the first to have the Queen wear a miniature of her second husband around her neck; Finlay wished that Kean too wore a miniature of his father (*Miscellanies*, p. 228). Fechter did just that, from his first appearance giving prominence to the medallion of King Hamlet that he wore on a chain; here he 'placed his miniature of his father side by side with his mother's miniature of Claudius' (Cook, *Hours*, p. 262). Macready introduced full length paintings not only of King Hamlet and Claudius but of the Queen and the Prince; he had the Ghost enter suddenly, 'gliding through the arras of his own picture as if the warrior of the canvas had stepped from his frame' (*Examiner*, 22 March 1840). As all concerned imagine the pictures, Irving 'points straight out before him in audience' (Terry's rehearsal book). For fuller details about earlier treatments of the pictures, see Sprague, *Actors*, pp. 166–9; for later treatments, see Rosenberg, pp. 676–7.

HAMLET Look here upon this picture, and on this,
    The counterfeit presentment of two brothers.
    See what a grace was seated on this brow; 55
    Hyperion's curls, the front of Jove himself,
    An eye like Mars, to threaten and command;
    A station like the herald Mercury,
    New-lighted on a heaven-kissing hill;
    A combination and a form indeed, 60
    Where every god did seem to set his seal
    To give the world assurance of a man.
    This was your husband. Look you now what follows.
    Here is your husband, like a mildewed ear
    Blasting his wholesome brother. Have you eyes? 65
    Could you on this fair mountain leave to feed
    And batten on this moor? Ha! have you eyes?
    You cannot call it love, for at your age
    The heyday in the blood is tame, it's humble,
    And waits upon the judgement; and what judgement 70
    Would step from this to this? [Sense sure you have,
    Else could you not have motion, but sure that sense
    Is apoplexed, for madness would not err,
    Nor sense to ecstasy was ne'er so thralled,
    But it reserved some quantity of choice 75
    To serve in such a difference.] What devil was't
    That thus hath cozened you at hoodman-blind?
    [Eyes without feeling, feeling without sight,
    Ears without hands or eyes, smelling sans all,
    Or but a sickly part of one true sense 80
    Could not so mope.]
    O shame, where is thy blush? Rebellious hell,

55–63a Jacobi directed Branagh in 1988 to slow the pace of this passage, lose himself in admiration of his remembered father, and thus vary the general 'hectoring' tone (Branagh interview on US National Public Radio, January, 1997).

61 J. B. Booth emphasized *every* (Gould, p. 66).

64 As he showed the picture Alec Guinness 'shrank as though his hand had touched foulness' (*Sunday Times*, 20 May 1951).

65 Michael Redgrave had produced from his pocket a coin with Claudius's head on it which he contrasted with the miniature of his father, which he wore in a locket. He here 'thrust them at the Queen, almost ramming them in her face' (*Mind's I*, p. 191).

71 Gielgud directed Burton to 'inflect the first "this" favorably to indicate your father and color the final "this" repulsively to indicate Claudius' (Sterne, p. 39).

If thou canst mutine in a matron's bones,
To flaming youth let virtue be as wax
And melt in her own fire. Proclaim no shame   85
When the compulsive ardour gives the charge,
Since frost itself as actively doth burn,
And reason panders will.
GERTRUDE   O Hamlet, speak no more.
Thou turn'st my eyes into my very soul,
And there I see such black and grainèd spots   90
As will not leave their tinct.
HAMLET   Nay, but to live
In the rank sweat of an enseamèd bed,
Stewed in corruption, honeying and making love
Over the nasty sty.
GERTRUDE   Oh speak to me no more.
These words like daggers enter in my ears.   95
No more sweet Hamlet.
HAMLET   A murderer and a villain,
A slave that is not twentieth part the tithe
Of your precedent lord, a vice of kings,
A cutpurse of the empire and the rule,
That from a shelf the precious diadem stole   100
And put it in his pocket.
GERTRUDE   No more!

Enter GHOST

86   Garrick emphasized *compulsive* (Vickers, *Critical Heritage*, IV, p. 426).
91–103   Irving delivers this passage 'working it up tremendously – excitedly; "*The laws of Climax*"';
         then, with a tremendous pause, he speaks 'whisperingly, "Save me . . . "' (Terry's rehearsal
         book).
92   Stephen Dillane, with Gwen Taylor as Gertrude, 'actually makes her smell "the rank sweat"'
     (*Daily Telegraph*, 7 November 1994). Recent Hamlets (Jacobi, Gibson, Fiennes among them)
     have here simulated one form or another of sexual intercourse.
101   Of Fechter: 'One moment more and the passion that made a corpse of Polonius might have
      wreaked vengeance on the guilty Queen' (Field, p. 95).
101SD   Q1: 'Enter the ghost in his night gowne'.
102   Large bell strikes One (Irving promptbook). In the Zeffirelli film, Glenn Close here gave Mel
      Gibson a long kiss, whether from passion or from the need to stop his hurtful words.
102–4   Of Betterton: 'This is spoke with arms and hands extended, and expressing his concern, as
        well as his eyes, and whole face' (Gildon, *Betterton*, p. 74). Macready 'broke from the most
        intense and passionate indignation to the lost and bewildered air, and with a face of

HAMLET A king of shreds and patches –
    Save me and hover o'er me with your wings,
    You heavenly guards! – What would your gracious figure?
GERTRUDE Alas he's mad!   105
HAMLET Do you not come your tardy son to chide,
    That lapsed in time and passion lets go by
    Th'important acting of your dread command? Oh say!
GHOST Do not forget. This visitation
    Is but to whet thy almost blunted purpose.   110
    But look, amazement on thy mother sits.
    Oh step between her and her fighting soul:
    Conceit in weakest bodies strongest works.

unearthly horror and tones of strange awe, tremblingly addressed the spirit, or pointed towards him with silent finger' (*New Monthly Magazine*, 1 July 1821, p. 333). For Bernhardt (1899), by means of a transparent painted gauze and a change of lighting, the Ghost in the closet scene materialized from the portrait of King Hamlet on the wall; when it disappeared and only the painting remained, the Prince passed his hands over it, seeking to bring his father back. On Barrymore's American tour during the closet scene a white light enveloped the Prince and a picture of Reginald Pole as the Ghost was projected onto Hamlet 'to convey the effect of the Ghost taking possession of Barrymore' (promptbook 156): 'He went rigid, his voice hoarse like the voice of the Ghost. When the light left him, he dropped to his knees, as though released from the grip of the spirit' (Kobler, *Damned*, p. 179). In the 1976 Albert Finney/Peter Hall production, the Ghost's ascent by the trap was masked from the audience by the prince and queen; as Richard David describes the complex effect when the Ghost thus, unexpectedly, appears:

> Hamlet, by now kneeling at his mother's knee, looks at the Ghost over her shoulder; she, all tenderness for her son suddenly seized in this paroxysm of madness, has no consciousness of his father's presence. The three reactions, Hamlet's intense, Gertrude's all maternal solicitude, the Ghost in painful hope against hope that sufficient memory of their bond may linger in his wife to make her aware of him, built up a strange chord . . . (*Theatre*, pp. 81–2).

104 Emma Lazarus praised Salvini for 'the sudden break in his voice as he appeals to the "heavenly guards" to save and shield him, the attitude of awe and adoration which he instantaneously assumes' (*Century Magazine*, November 1881, p. 116).

106 Irving spoke this line 'most tenderly, never taking his eyes off the Ghost' (Terry's rehearsal book).

111ff With Barrymore, 'the relation of Hamlet to his mother and through her to the ghost was achieved by his moving toward the ghost on his knees and being caught in his mother's arms' (*New Republic*, 6 December 1922, p. 46). With Branagh (1992) Gertrude stands

               Speak to her, Hamlet.

HAMLET   How is it with you lady?

GERTRUDE Alas, how is't with you,   115

       That you do bend your eye on vacancy,

       And with th'incorporal air do hold discourse?

       Forth at your eyes your spirits wildly peep,

       And, as the sleeping soldiers in th'alarm,

       Your bedded hair, like life in excrements,   120

       Start up and stand an end. O gentle son,

       Upon the heat and flame of thy distemper

       Sprinkle cool patience. Whereon do you look?

HAMLET On him, on him! Look you how pale he glares.

       His form and cause conjoined, preaching to stones,   125

       Would make them capable. – Do not look upon me,

       Lest with this piteous action you convert

       My stern effects. Then what I have to do

       Will want true colour: tears perchance for blood.

GERTRUDE To whom do you speak this?   130

behind Hamlet stroking his hair while he reaches across the bed to hold the Ghost's arm, which he has held out to his son: 'the portrait of the ruined family' (*Shakespeare Bulletin*, Fall, 1994, p. 6).

114   Serjeant John Adams remembered that 'Kemble's hand was always on his mother's arm – her eyes fixed on him – his own on the Ghost; and when the Ghost desired him to address her, he did so mechanically, without looking at her or moving a muscle' (Cole, *Charles Kean*, I, p. 276). J. B. Booth also kept his eyes on the Ghost (Gould, p. 68).

121–3   'Wiping [his] brow' (Irving's studybook).

124   J. B. Booth spoke '*On* him, *on* him' 'as if she must see the figure also' (Gould, p. 68). Booth's Queen, Fanny Morant, 'turns so slowly and with such anxious hesitancy, and seeing nothing is so startled and overcome that a sympathetic thrill of terror runs through the audience' (*World*, 9 January 1870). With Irving in 1874 Georgina Pauncefort gave 'a terrific shriek' as if she had caught a glimpse of the Ghost; the business was soon discarded (*Graphic*, 7 November 1874, p. 443). In the Pennington/Barton production, Hamlet grabbed the Queen's head and forced her to look 'On him' (Pennington, *Hamlet*, p. 102n), at which Barbara Leigh-Hunt to her horror actually saw the Ghost, but then repressed the experience (*Daily Mail*, 18 September 1981). Rosenberg adds that she put her hands over her ears when the Ghost spoke and that Leigh-Hunt supported this interpretation to him by citing Gertrude's reference at 4.1.5 to 'what have I seen tonight', which she delivered 'with a shudder' (p. 698). Playing the Ghost in 1994 Pennington almost succeeded in touching the Queen's hand 'until she recoiled as if at an electric shock' (*Hamlet*, p. 102n).

126   Irving spoke 'imploringly' (Terry's rehearsal book).

HAMLET Do you see nothing there?

GERTRUDE Nothing at all, yet all that is I see.

HAMLET Nor did you nothing hear?

GERTRUDE No, nothing but ourselves.

HAMLET Why, look you there – look how it steals away –   135
    My father in his habit as he lived –
    Look where he goes, even now out at the portal.

                                          Exit Ghost

GERTRUDE This is the very coinage of your brain.
    This bodiless creation ecstasy
    Is very cunning in.

HAMLET   Ecstasy?   140
    My pulse as yours doth temperately keep time,
    And makes as healthful music. It is not madness
    That I have uttered. Bring me to the test,
    And I the matter will reword, which madness
    Would gambol from. Mother, for love of grace,   145
    Lay not that flattering unction to your soul,
    That not your trespass but my madness speaks;
    It will but skin and film the ulcerous place,
    Whiles rank corruption, mining all within,

---

131   Booth paused after 'nothing' then 'pointing slowly toward the Ghost, "there?"' (promptbook 111). Irving's delivery was very much the same (*Graphic*, 7 November 1874, p. 443). With Irving in 1878 Pouncefort spoke this line as she was 'turning – and looking straight at the Ghost' (Terry's rehearsal book).

134–5   While Booth stares at his mother's face, he does not notice that the Ghost has crossed the stage. When at 135a he looks at the spot where the Ghost has been and sees nothing, he gasps and starts backward, his hand flies to his forehead and his eyes are full of terror. He turns about, drawing the Queen with him, until he sees the Ghost' (Shattuck, p. 233).

137   Kemble 'threw himself passionately, yet fondly forward, as if to catch and detain the form so revered, so lamented' (H. Martin, *Remarks*, p. 7).

140   F only.

141–2   Booth as if taking his own pulse holds his wrist out to her (Shattuck, p. 234). Burton is less assured: 'Fearful for a moment that she may be right, he feels his pulse, convincing himself of his own sanity' (Sterne, p. 233).

145ff   On the verge of tears throughout the scene, Nicol Williamson at last weeps uncontrollably and at 172–3 is joined in weeping by his mother.

145b–7   'Kemble *knelt* in the fine adjuration to his mother ... As an affectionate son, he is endeavouring to awake all the feelings of the mother in her, to combat the delusion of her guilty attachment' (Boaden, pp. 102–3). Irving 'casts his head upon his mother's lap' (Russell, p. 49). He spoke 145b 'imploringly' (Terry's rehearsal book).

Infects unseen. Confess yourself to heaven,   150
Repent what's past, avoid what is to come,
And do not spread the compost on the weeds
To make them ranker. Forgive me this my virtue,
For in the fatness of these pursy times
Virtue itself of vice must pardon beg,   155
Yea, curb and woo for leave to do him good.
GERTRUDE Oh Hamlet, thou hast cleft my heart in twain.
HAMLET Oh throw away the worser part of it
And live the purer with the other half.
Good night – but go not to my uncle's bed;   160
Assume a virtue if you have it not.
[That monster custom, who all sense doth eat,
Of habits devil, is angel yet in this,
That to the use of actions fair and good
He likewise gives a frock or livery   165
That aptly is put on.] Refrain tonight,
And that shall lend a kind of easiness
To the next abstinence, [the next more easy,
For use almost can change the stamp of nature,
And either...the devil, or throw him out,   170
With wondrous potency.] Once more good night,
And when you are desirous to be blessed,
I'll blessing beg of you. For this same lord,
I do repent; but heaven hath pleased it so,

157   'Breaking down and weeping bitterly' (Terry's rehearsal book).
158–60a Forrest 'compressed into his utterance, in one indescribable mixture a world of entreaty,
         command, disgust, grief, deference, love, and mournfulness' (Alger, *Forrest*, p. 756). Of
         Irving: 'An *ocean* of tenderness to her. Eyes – voice – breaking' (Terry's rehearsal book).
         Forbes-Robertson, 'resting his mother's head on his breast, tenderly kisses her' (*Stage*, 16
         September 1897, p. 14–15). Olivier in the film kissed Gertrude (Eileen Herlie) tenderly on the
         temple.
172–3a   Kemble accented *be* and *beg*, Henderson *blest* and the second *you* (Boaden, p. 103). When
         Fanny Morant with Booth, 'raises both hands as if in benediction, he pushes her hands away
         as if preventing a sacrilege. He rises slowly and with dignity: "When YOU (prolonged) are
         desirous to be *blessed*, I'll *blessing beg* of *you*" (Shattuck, p. 235). In the Olivier film the
         Queen kissed Hamlet on the cheek and lightly on the lips. On BBC-TV Jacobi's inflection of
         these lines acknowledged that Claire Bloom, although troubled, was not persuaded to
         refrain from sex with the King and thus was not yet ready to be blessed.
173b–4a Macready wept (Pollock, *Macready*, p. 107). Irving emphasized *do* (*Academy*, 12 December
         1874).

To punish me with this, and this with me, 175
That I must be their scourge and minister.
I will bestow him, and will answer well
The death I gave him. So again, good night.
I must be cruel only to be kind;
Thus bad begins, and worse remains behind. 180
One word more good lady.
GERTRUDE   What shall I do?
HAMLET Not this by no means that I bid you do:
Let the bloat king tempt you again to bed,
Pinch wanton on your cheek, call you his mouse,
And let him for a pair of reechy kisses, 185
Or paddling in your neck with his damned fingers,
Make you to ravel all this matter out,
That I essentially am not in madness,
But mad in craft. 'Twere good you let him know,
For who that's but a queen, fair, sober, wise, 190
Would from a paddock, from a bat, a gib,
Such dear concernings hide? Who would do so?
No, in despite of sense and secrecy,
Unpeg the basket on the house's top,

179   Stage tradition ended the scene here. Of Macready: when Gertrude starts to leave but returns for a last embrace, Macready motions her to stop: 'the memory of his dead parent was a sacred thought, and would not allow him to enfold in his embrace her who, *even now*, held communication with his murderer' (*Theatrical Journal*, 29 August 1840, p. 313). At this line, Booth tenderly takes his mother in his arms and says the words in such as way as to make clear that his earlier harshness has 'cut his heart and feelings no less than hers' (Shattuck, p. 237). Olivier in the film pressed the side of his head to his mother's bosom, then rested it in her lap as she cradled him with her hands.

181ff   Of Gielgud, seeing the Queen move towards the door and thus to the King: 'His anger rises in a sudden tide, stirring once more the dregs of deep-rooted loathing. His words, again, sting and slash' (Gilder, p. 189).

181b   Judi Dench, with Day Lewis, addressed this line to herself, 'acknowledging the discovery within herself of unsuspected depths she could not fathom'. During the preceding speech her 'climactic kiss' with Hamlet had been 'a naked and mutual acknowledgement of desire that shocked her' (*Shakespeare Survey 43*, 1991, p. 196). Julie Christie in the Branagh film is here utterly vulnerable, all her society-matron defences down, 'on the edge of a breakdown' (*Screenplay*, p. 111).

189–200   With Guthrie in Minneapolis, George Grizzard delivers his lines 'jokingly, and the Queen [Jessica Tandy] begins to laugh in a strange way. She continues the laughter during her speech . . . both are on the verge of hysteria' (Rossi, p. 41).

Let the birds fly, and like the famous ape, 195
To try conclusions, in the basket creep
And break your own neck down.
GERTRUDE Be thou assured, if words be made of breath,
And breath of life, I have no life to breathe
What thou hast said to me. 200
HAMLET I must to England, you know that?
GERTRUDE Alack,
I had forgot. 'Tis so concluded on.
HAMLET [There's letters sealed, and my two schoolfellows,
Whom I will trust as I will adders fanged,
They bear the mandate. They must sweep my way 205
And marshal me to knavery. Let it work,
For 'tis the sport to have the engineer
Hoist with his own petar, an't shall go hard
But I will delve one yard below their mines
And blow them at the moon. Oh 'tis most sweet 210
When in one line two crafts directly meet.]
This man shall set me packing.
I'll lug the guts into the neighbour room.
Mother, good night. Indeed, this counsellor
Is now most still, most secret, and most grave, 215
Who was in life a foolish prating knave.
Come sir, to draw toward an end with you.
Good night mother.
Exit Hamlet tugging in Polonius; [Gertrude remains]

200 After this declaration of loyalty by Clare Higgins with Rylance, there was a long silence as he kisses her, passionately (Gilbert, 'Rylance', p. 13).

213 After this line and before he walks apart Olivier and his mother kiss one another fully on the lips.

218 Barrymore paused between 'good night' and 'mother' – with a suggestion of 'please forgive me' (*Spectator*, 28 February 1925, p. 319). With Gielgud, as his mother flees the room 'his braggadoccio drops from him like the false mask that it is. He sways against the wall, his head and shoulders sink. For a moment he looks after her and then, with repressed anguish, the one word "Mother" – the cry of a child left in the dark' (Gilder, p. 187). As Rylance jauntily dragged off dead Polonius, he bid his mother a final 'good night' through teeth clenched on his dagger.

ACT 4, SCENE I

[4.1] *Enter* CLAUDIUS *with* ROSENCRANTZ *and* GUILDENSTERN

CLAUDIUS There's matter in these sighs, these profound heaves.
You must translate, 'tis fit we understand them.
Where is your son?
GERTRUDE [Bestow this place on us a little while.]
                                    [*Exeunt Rosencrantz and Guildenstern*]
Ah mine own lord, what have I seen tonight!   5
CLAUDIUS What, Gertrude? How does Hamlet?
GERTRUDE Mad as the sea and wind, when both contend
Which is the mightier. In his lawless fit,
Behind the arras hearing something stir,
Whips out his rapier, cries 'A rat, a rat!',   10
And in this brainish apprehension kills
The unseen good old man.
CLAUDIUS   Oh heavy deed!
It had been so with us had we been there.
His liberty is full of threats to all,
To you yourself, to us, to everyone.   15
Alas, how shall this bloody deed be answered?

OSD   In F this scene flows from the one before. The Queen remains on stage, where the King joins
       her, alone. In Q1 he is accompanied by 'Lords'. Q2 reads: 'Enter King, and Queene, with
       Rosencraus and Guyldensterne'. To Stanley Wells and Gary Taylor, the fact that Q2 includes
       Gertrude among those entering suggests a change of location (*Textual Companion*, p. 407);
       this would be consistent with 35. To John Kerrigan, Q2's inclusion of Rosencrantz and
       Guildenstern with the King supports Hamlet's intuition (at 3.4.203 ff) of their betrayal
       ('Reviser', p. 259).

7–12   Q1's Queen tells of how her son 'throwes and tosses me about'. This may reflect how 3.4 was
        performed; or is she – now explicitly allied with Hamlet in this version – deceiving the King?
           Claire Bloom, opposite Patrick Stewart's King in the BBC-TV version, plays the Queen's
        ambivalence, torn between her son and her new husband: 'she withholds information from
        Claudius . . . she *doesn't* say he said "Is it the King?"' (*BBC-TV Hamlet*, p. 27).

It will be laid to us, whose providence
Should have kept short, restrained, and out of haunt,
This mad young man. But so much was our love,
We would not understand what was most fit,   20
But like the owner of a foul disease,
To keep it from divulging, let it feed
Even on the pith of life. Where is he gone?
GERTRUDE To draw apart the body he hath killed,
    O'er whom his very madness, like some ore   25
    Among a mineral of metals base,
    Shows itself pure; a weeps for what is done.
CLAUDIUS Oh Gertrude, come away!
    The sun no sooner shall the mountains touch
    But we will ship him hence, and this vile deed   30
    We must with all our majesty and skill
    Both countenance and excuse. Ho, Guildenstern!

Enter Rosencrantz and Guildenstern

Friends both, go join you with some further aid.
Hamlet in madness hath Polonius slain,
And from his mother's closet hath he dragged him.   35
Go seek him out, speak fair, and bring the body
Into the chapel. I pray you haste in this.
                Exeunt Rosencrantz and Guildenstern
Come Gertrude, we'll call up our wisest friends
And let them know both what we mean to do
And what's untimely done.   40
[Whose whisper o'er the world's diameter,
As level as the cannon to his blank,
Transports his poisoned shot, may miss our name
And hit the woundless air.] Oh come away,
My soul is full of discord and dismay.   45
                          Exeunt

38–45 Evans: The Queen 'shrinks from his touch and, after a momentary look of disgust, rushes
from the room', leaving the King standing alone (*G. I. Hamlet*, p. 142). Bloom's resistance is
more subtle. Although in the previous scene she had been unable to reassure Hamlet that
she would refrain from marital intercourse, she here remains seated and silent even though
Claudius twice tells her to 'come'; Bloom: 'For the moment she doesn't go with him, but the
next day she does . . . there isn't a complete withdrawal' (*BBC-TV Hamlet*, pp. 25–6). After all
Gertrude here calls him 'mine own lord' (5) and will place herself between Claudius and
threatening Laertes in 4.5. In the Branagh film the two end the episode comforting each
other (*Screenplay*, p. 114).

ACT 4, SCENE 2

[4.2] *Enter* HAMLET

HAMLET Safely stowed.
GENTLEMEN (*Within*) Hamlet! Lord Hamlet!
HAMLET But soft, what noise? Who calls on Hamlet? Oh here they
come.

Enter ROSENCRANTZ *and* GUILDENSTERN

ROSENCRANTZ What have you done my lord with the dead body?   5
HAMLET Compounded it with dust whereto 'tis kin.
ROSENCRANTZ Tell us where 'tis, that we may take it thence and bear
it to the chapel.
HAMLET Do not believe it.
ROSENCRANTZ Believe what?   10
HAMLET That I can keep your counsel and not mine own. Besides, to
be demanded of a sponge, what replication should be made by the
son of a king?
ROSENCRANTZ Take you me for a sponge my lord?

---

1   Burton (1964) briskly rubs his hands together. Stephen Dillane played the scene for its black
     comedy: 'smeared with Polonius's blood, he proceeds calmly to remove all his soiled clothes
     until he sits in his nakedness, unruffled and crazy' (*Standard*, 7 November 1994). At the end
     of the scene, he streaked off the stage, wearing nothing but the Player King's crown.
5ff With Paul Scofield in 1948, director Michael Benthall made Rosencrantz and Guildenstern
     'prickly with menace. The two spies, immaculate in evening dress, advance on Hamlet with
     swords lazily at guard; he hysterically jests with them, edging toward escape', only to find
     that he is trapped and 'the whole palace soldiery is joining in the man-hunt' (Tynan, *He that
     Plays*, p. 113). In his modern-dress production in Minneapolis, Guthrie planned to be even
     more menacing, bringing Rosencrantz and Guildenstern on 'with revolvers drawn'; as
     Hamlet ran off, a wild shot was to be fired (Rossi, p. 25). Later he abandoned the revolvers
     and encircled Hamlet with the King's guards training flashlights on his face in the dark (p.
     56).

HAMLET Ay sir, that soaks up the king's countenance, his rewards, his 15
authorities. But such officers do the king best service in the end:
he keeps them like an ape in the corner of his jaw, first mouthed
to be last swallowed. When he needs what you have gleaned, it is
but squeezing you, and, sponge, you shall be dry again.

ROSENCRANTZ I understand you not my lord. 20

HAMLET I am glad of it, a knavish speech sleeps in a foolish ear.

ROSENCRANTZ My lord, you must tell us where the body is, and go
with us to the king.

HAMLET The body is with the king, but the king is not with the body.
The king is a thing – 25

GUILDENSTERN A thing my lord?

HAMLET Of nothing. Bring me to him. Hide fox, and all after!

Exeunt

15–19   Undaunted by Rosencrantz and Guildenstern, who were threatening him with their drawn
swords, Burton was impudently chipper throughout this scene. Here he paused and 'gulped'
before 'swallowed' at 18, then prolonged 'sponnnnge' with a rising and falling pitch (Sterne,
p. 238). Still carrying Polonius's green scarf, Gielgud used it as the sponge to be squeezed,
then tossed aside (Gilder, p. 191). Kevin Kline squeezed in his fist the handkerchief with
which he had wiped his hands, stained with Polonius's blood.

27   Kemble always instructed Guildenstern to attempt to exit before him: 'this breach of
etiquette he checked by a severe look, and then walked off with much dignity' (Cole, *Charles
Kean*, I, p. 113). Kemble's promptbook shows, by numerals above their names, that
Rosencrantz leaves first, Hamlet second, and Guildenstern third (*Promptbooks*, p. 57).
Perhaps at 'Bring me to him' Kemble's Guildenstern understandably assumed that the
Prince meant for him to join his partner in leading the way, only to be given a 'severe look'
when he started to do so. Kemble follows Q2 in ending the scene with 'Bring me to him'; F's
'Hide fox, and all after' would not have made for a dignified exit! Sprague quotes similar
business at this point from a 1788–97 Dublin promptbook (*Actors*, p. 170). Gielgud suddenly
blew out 'the candle which he had been carrying about since the Play scene, leaving
Rosencrantz and Guildenstern terribly scared in the dark' (Crosse, *Diaries*, XII). Burton said
'no . . . thing' with a laugh; like many Hamlets before and since, he concluded the scene by
starting off in one direction, then suddenly making his escape by running off in the other.

ACT 4, SCENE 3

[4.3] *Enter* CLAUDIUS, *and two or three*

CLAUDIUS I have sent to seek him, and to find the body.
How dangerous is it that this man goes loose,
Yet must not we put the strong law on him;
He's loved of the distracted multitude,
Who like not in their judgement, but their eyes;   5
And where 'tis so, th'offender's scourge is weighed,
But never the offence. To bear all smooth and even,
This sudden sending him away must seem
Deliberate pause. Diseases desperate grown
By desperate appliance are relieved,   10
Or not at all.

Enter ROSENCRANTZ

How now, what hath befallen?
ROSENCRANTZ Where the dead body is bestowed, my lord,
We cannot get from him.
CLAUDIUS   But where is he?
ROSENCRANTZ Without, my lord, guarded, to know your pleasure.
CLAUDIUS Bring him before us.
ROSENCRANTZ   Ho! bring in my lord.   15

Enter HAMLET *and* GUILDENSTERN

CLAUDIUS Now Hamlet, where's Polonius?
HAMLET At supper.
CLAUDIUS At supper? Where?
HAMLET Not where he eats, but where a is eaten. A certain convocation
of politic worms are e'en at him. Your worm is your only emperor   20
for diet: we fat all creatures else to fat us, and we fat ourselves for

OSD   F's Claudius enters alone. 1–11 may be read either as a soliloquy or in Q2 as the King's
thinking aloud among 'two or three' confidants.

maggots. Your fat king and your lean beggar is but variable service, two dishes, but to one table; that's the end.

CLAUDIUS Alas, alas.

HAMLET A man may fish with the worm that hath eat of a king, and   25
eat of the fish that hath fed of that worm.

CLAUDIUS What dost thou mean by this?

HAMLET Nothing but to show you how a king may go a progress through the guts of a beggar.

CLAUDIUS Where is Polonius?   30

HAMLET In heaven, send thither to see. If your messenger find him not there, seek him i'th'other place yourself. But if indeed you find him not within this month, you shall nose him as you go up the stairs into the lobby.

CLAUDIUS Go seek him there.   35

HAMLET A will stay till you come.

                                                    [*Exeunt Attendants*]

CLAUDIUS Hamlet, this deed, for thine especial safety,
            Which we do tender, as we dearly grieve
            For that which thou hast done, must send thee hence
            With fiery quickness. Therefore prepare thyself.   40
            The bark is ready and the wind at help,
            Th'associates tend, and everything is bent
            For England.

HAMLET   For England?

CLAUDIUS   Ay Hamlet.

HAMLET   Good.

CLAUDIUS So is it if thou knew'st our purposes.

HAMLET I see a cherub that sees them. But come, for England! Farewell   45
dear mother.

22   Gielgud suggested to Burton that he point 'at Claudius when you say "fat King" and at Guildenstern when you say "lean beggar"' (Sterne, p. 69). He had done the same when playing Hamlet (Gilder, p. 191).

27   In the Olivier film Claudius and Hamlet do not face each other until this question, Claudius having been seated and Hamlet standing behind him, leaning insouciantly against a wall. Hamlet delivers 36 with mock pleasantness; then it is Claudius's turn to speak 37–43 to Hamlet's back until at 'Good' (43) the brooding Prince slowly turns his head, then his body towards the King.

45   Booth spoke 'for England' 'in a loud, swinging voice, as if he were elated at the prospect of going thither' (Stone, p. 113). In his studybook Booth writes: 'I think I was the first to kneel and address the King as *mother*. The traditional method was to speak as to [Hamlet's] absent parent without reference to the King.' Booth took 'the King's hand in both of his own,

CLAUDIUS Thy loving father, Hamlet.
HAMLET My mother. Father and mother is man and wife, man and wife
    is one flesh, and so, my mother. Come, for England. *Exit*
CLAUDIUS Follow him at foot, tempt him with speed aboard. 50
    Delay it not, I'll have him hence tonight.
    Away, for everything is sealed and done
    That else leans on th'affair. Pray you make haste.
        [*Exeunt Rosencrantz and Guildenstern*]
    And England, if my love thou hold'st at aught,
    As my great power thereof may give thee sense, 55
    Since yet thy cicatrice looks raw and red
    After the Danish sword, and thy free awe
    Pays homage to us – thou mayst not coldly set
    Our sovereign process, which imports at full,
    By letters congruing to that effect, 60
    The present death of Hamlet. Do it England,
    For like the hectic in my blood he rages,
    And thou must cure me. Till I know 'tis done,
    Howe'er my haps, my joys were ne'er begun. *Exit*

bending over it, as if to kiss it' (promptbook 111). With Gielgud: '"Farewell, dear mother" is flung full in the King's face, both hands blowing a mocking kiss' (Gilder, p. 193). In 1953 Burton gave the farewell with 'a sardonic smirk and half curtsey' that 'concentrated all his loathing of his uncle into one brilliant gesture' (Williamson, *Old Vic*, p. 54). Directing Burton in 1964, 'Gielgud suggested that Hamlet run up and kiss the King on the cheek just before saying "Farewell, dear Mother." (This became one of Burton's favorite bits of business)' (Sterne, p. 36).

48–9   In the Olivier film Hamlet spoke these lines slowly, abstractedly, shaking his head once or twice as though working out in his own mind their deepest implications for his own plight, his closed eyes wincing at the thought of his uncle and mother being one flesh. Richard Risso at Ashland, Oregon, in 1961 prolonged the 'sh' in 'flesh' with a repugnance that recalled his earlier pronunciation of the word at 1.2.129.

61b   Brian Murray, with Kevin Kline, spoke 'Do it England' regretfully.

ACT 4, SCENE 4

[4.4] *Enter* FORTINBRAS *with his army over the stage*

FORTINBRAS Go captain, from me greet the Danish king.
    Tell him that by his licence, Fortinbras
    Craves the conveyance of a promised march
    Over his kingdom. You know the rendezvous.
    If that his majesty would aught with us,   5
    We shall express our duty in his eye,
    And let him know so.
CAPTAIN   I will do't, my lord.
FORTINBRAS Go softly on.

        [*Exit Fortinbras, with the army*]

     [*Enter* HAMLET, ROSENCRANTZ, *etc.*

HAMLET Good sir, whose powers are these?
CAPTAIN They are of Norway sir.   10
HAMLET How purposed sir I pray you?
CAPTAIN Against some part of Poland.
HAMLET Who commands them sir?
CAPTAIN The nephew to old Norway, Fortinbras.

This scene was regularly omitted from Betterton's time until the twentieth century and often then. Indeed, Hamlet's entry and the lines that follow do not appear in Q1 or F.

OSD In Q1 Fortinbras is accompanied by 'Drumme and Souldiers'; in F, 'with an Armie'. The present edition follows Q2. 'Over the stage' may have indicated in Shakespeare's time that Fortinbras and his troops entered through the yard, crossed over the platform stage, and then left through the yard. See Nicoll, 'Passing over'. Although Nicoll does not cite this instance, it resembles other processions he gives that illustrate the practice.

In the 1944 Guthrie, 'the virile and capable figure of Fortinbras, a high immobile Napoleon on the side parapet, was balanced against a cloaked and seated Hamlet, with scholar's forehead and slender physique, far below' (Williamson, *Old Vic*, p. 167). Guthrie staged the scene similarly at Minneapolis in 1963 (Rossi, p. 41).

HAMLET Goes it against the main of Poland sir,   15
　　　　Or for some frontier?
CAPTAIN Truly to speak, and with no addition,
　　　　We go to gain a little patch of ground
　　　　That hath in it no profit but the name.
　　　　To pay five ducats, five, I would not farm it,   20
　　　　Nor will it yield to Norway or the Pole
　　　　A ranker rate, should it be sold in fee.
HAMLET Why then the Polack never will defend it.
CAPTAIN Yes, it is already garrisoned.
HAMLET Two thousand souls and twenty thousand ducats   25
　　　　Will not debate the question of this straw.
　　　　This is th'impostume of much wealth and peace,
　　　　That inward breaks, and shows no cause without
　　　　Why the man dies. I humbly thank you sir.
CAPTAIN God buy you sir.   [*Exit*]
ROSENCRANTZ   Will't please you go my lord?   30
HAMLET I'll be with you straight; go a little before.
　　　　　　　　　　　　　　　　[*Exeunt all but Hamlet*]
　　　　How all occasions do inform against me,
　　　　And spur my dull revenge! What is a man
　　　　If his chief good and market of his time
　　　　Be but to sleep and feed? A beast, no more.   35
　　　　Sure he that made us with such large discourse,
　　　　Looking before and after, gave us not
　　　　That capability and god-like reason
　　　　To fust in us unused. Now whether it be
　　　　Bestial oblivion, or some craven scruple   40
　　　　Of thinking too precisely on th'event –
　　　　A thought which quartered hath but one part wisdom
　　　　And ever three parts coward – I do not know
　　　　Why yet I live to say this thing's to do,

31b Drawing a contrast with Hamlet's first soliloquy, where he panicked when left alone and
　　　wanted to melt away, Ben Kingsley observed, 'It is a very great journey from being terrified
　　　of being left alone to saying, I want to be left alone.' In general he played the speech that
　　　follows as the Prince's final step into manhood: 'Hamlet leaves home' (Maher, *Soliloquies*,
　　　p. 88).

32 Gielgud accented *me* (Gilder, p. 195).

43b–4 In Olivier's stage version, Trewin finds 'definitive' the 'mounting desperation' of his delivery
　　　of these lines: 'half-wailed, half-proclaimed' (*Five & Eighty*, p. 47). For Pennington these
　　　lines and the rest of the sentence, with their 'monosyllabic, self-inflicted hammer blows',
　　　'form a climax in the part, absolutely concentrating the man's problem' (*Hamlet*, p. 113).

Sith I have cause, and will, and strength, and means   45
To do't. Examples gross as earth exhort me.
Witness this army of such mass and charge,
Led by a delicate and tender prince,
Whose spirit with divine ambition puffed
Makes mouths at the invisible event,   50
Exposing what is mortal and unsure
To all that fortune, death and danger dare,
Even for an egg-shell. Rightly to be great
Is not to stir without great argument,
But greatly to find quarrel in a straw   55
When honour's at the stake. How stand I then,
That have a father killed, a mother stained,
Excitements of my reason and my blood,
And let all sleep, while to my shame I see
The imminent death of twenty thousand men,   60
That for a fantasy and trick of fame
Go to their graves like beds, fight for a plot
Whereon the numbers cannot try the cause,
Which is not tomb enough and continent
To hide the slain. Oh from this time forth,   65
My thoughts be bloody or be nothing worth.   *Exit*]

59–66   Gielgud 'moves into a world greater than his own' and 'dedicates himself anew to his own
         mission . . . his whole movement vigorous' (Gilder, p. 197).

66   Jacobi: 'Hamlet no longer needs to think, to analyze, to question, to ask, to ruminate.' This is
         the moment when he begins to harden. As he demonstrates by sending Rosencrantz and
         Guildenstern to their deaths, he is 'filled with cold resolution' and 'can kill now without
         hesitation and without compunction' (Maher, *Soliloquies*, p. 111). Roger Rees here 'stirs his
         weakening resolve' yet then pauses with a look of 'wan despair, as if acknowledging that
         revenge is pointless and death certain' (*Daily Mail*, 7 September 1984).

ACT 4, SCENE 5

[4.5] *Enter* HORATIO, GERTRUDE *and a* GENTLEMAN

GERTRUDE I will not speak with her.
GENTLEMAN She is importunate, indeed distract;
    Her mood will needs be pitied.
GERTRUDE   What would she have?
GENTLEMAN She speaks much of her father, says she hears
    There's tricks i'th'world, and hems, and beats her heart,   5
    Spurns enviously at straws, speaks things in doubt
    That carry but half sense. Her speech is nothing,
    Yet the unshapèd use of it doth move
    The hearers to collection. They yawn at it,
    And botch the words up fit to their own thoughts,   10
    Which, as her winks and nods and gestures yield them,
    Indeed would make one think there might be thought,
    Though nothing sure, yet much unhappily.
HORATIO 'Twere good she were spoken with, for she may strew
    Dangerous conjectures in ill-breeding minds.   15
GERTRUDE Let her come in.
                             [Exit Gentleman]
    (*Aside*) To my sick soul, as sin's true nature is,
    Each toy seems prologue to some great amiss.

1–20   The Folio Queen is both stronger and more prominent than in Q2. In Q2 14–16 is given to
    Horatio; in F it is given to the Queen, making her authority stronger than that of the Queen
    in Q2. In Q2 Ophelia enters before the Queen's aside (16–20); in F she enters after the aside,
    giving the Folio Queen more of the audience's attention during the aside. This is all the more
    true if, as seems likely, Horatio at the Queen's bidding has exited to admit Ophelia. In that
    case, since F does not include Q2's Gentleman, the Folio Queen would have the stage
    completely to herself for her aside (Urkowitz, 'Five women', p. 302).
  1   Barbara Leigh-Hunt, in the Pennington/Barton production, stressed 'not', 'as if this is clearly
    not her first refusal' (Rosenberg, p. 759).

> So full of artless jealousy is guilt,
> It spills itself in fearing to be spilt.   20

Enter OPHELIA *distracted*

20SD Q2 reads simply 'Enter Ophelia'. Like the F reading, which Edwards follows, Q1 emphasizes her alteration in appearance and manner: 'Enter Ofelia playing on a Lute, and her haire downe singing'.

Ophelias traditionally wore white in the mad scenes. Ellen Terry entertainingly tells of, quite innocently, proposing to wear black. Irving after much diplomatic hemming and hawing over a period of days at last sent an intermediary who expostulated 'My God! Madam, there must be only one black figure in this play, and that's Hamlet!' She wore white (Terry, pp. 123–4). Clement Scott was struck by her first appearance, 'in her clinging white robe, her fair, clustering hair, and a lily branch in her hand' (*Hamlets*, p. 182n). Julia Marlowe's promptbook indicates that she 'carries delicate white scarf over left arm, holds lute in right hand' (she accompanied her singing on the lute). In contrast, Forbes-Robertson's mad Ophelias did wear black: Mrs Patrick Campbell wore a black veil over a white dress and his wife Gertrude Elliott wore complete black (Mander and Mitchenson, *Hamlet*, p. 111). Modjeska wore 'a colored silk gown' (Phelps, p. 97). Lillian Gish, with Gielgud in 1936, wore an orange stocking, like an opera-glove, over her left hand and arm (Gilder, p. 199); the idea came from seeing a 'bag lady' wearing nylon stockings for gloves (Rosenberg, p. 774). The attire worn by later Ophelias has made her strangeness still more graphic. By 1964 Gielgud was taking exception to 'the wild indecency' in recent productions, 'with Ophelia tearing off her clothes and clutching all the gentlemen'; nonetheless, later in rehearsal he urged Linda Marsh to 'wear your blouse right open'; he went on to wonder delicately if she might be willing 'just to wear the brassiere and the skirt' before rejecting the idea: 'You might look like the Playboy Bunny of Elsinore' (Sterne, pp. 16–17, 92–3). In 1965 Glenda Jackson playing opposite Tony Church's authoritarian Polonius wore her dead father's robe, signifying his suffocating influence; in 1980 Carol Royle with Church this time playing a much kindlier Polonius also wore his robe, recalling the business at 1.3.136 and signifying that she had been overpowered by too much paternal love (Church, 'Polonius', p. 110). Elaborating on the Royal Shakespeare Company pattern, Joanne Pearce in the Branagh/Noble production does not wear her father's topcoat as she did at the end of 1.2 but his bloodstained evening suit.

In her appearance and manner, Lily Brayton with H. B. Irving revealed something uncanny as well as pitiful about Ophelia's madness: from a 'healthy pink and white' her complexion has changed to 'an ashy paleness', her voice is now 'strangled, uncertain, quavering' (*King*, 15 April 1905). Tara FitzGerald with Fiennes in 1995 had hacked her hair. In the Branagh film, Kate Winslet is first shown in a straitjacket, banging herself on the walls of her padded cell.

OPHELIA Where is the beauteous majesty of Denmark?
GERTRUDE How now Ophelia?
OPHELIA   *She sings*

> How should I your true love know
>   From another one?
> By his cockle hat and staff   25
>   And his sandal shoon.

GERTRUDE Alas sweet lady, what imports this song?
OPHELIA Say you? Nay, pray you mark.

> He is dead and gone lady,   *Song*
>   He is dead and gone;   30
> At his head a grass-green turf,
>   At his heels a stone.

   Oho!
GERTRUDE Nay but Ophelia –
OPHELIA Pray you mark.   35

> White his shroud as the mountain snow –   *Song*

     Enter CLAUDIUS

GERTRUDE Alas, look here my lord.
OPHELIA   Larded all with sweet flowers,

>   Which bewept to the grave did not go
>   With true-love showers.   40

CLAUDIUS How do you, pretty lady?

21 Writing of his 1953–4 stage production, Kozintsev observed, Nina Mamaeva must 'be convinced that madness is happiness for Ophelia' (Kozintsev, *Shakespeare*, p. 215). Stella Gonet, Ophelia in the Day Lewis/Eyre production, similarly writes of her madness: 'I feel it's an absolute freedom for her for the first time' (quoted in Rosenberg, p. 762).

22 Terry promptbook: 'soothingly'.

23–40 In stage practice for at least the past two centuries, most of the tunes for Ophelia's principal songs have been those given in Chappell, *Ballad Literature*, i; the Variorum *Hamlet* uses Chappell's versions. They in turn derive from those sung at Drury Lane toward the end of the eighteenth century. After the theatre burnt down in 1812, destroying the music library, the melodies were transcribed from renditions by actresses who had played the role at Drury Lane, chiefly Mrs Forster (Miss Field) who appeared as Ophelia in 1785. How far back the melodies go beyond that is problematical. See Seng, *Vocal Songs*.

    Chappell's music for 'How should I your true love know' is as follows:

OPHELIA Well good dild you. They say the owl was a baker's daughter.
Lord, we know what we are, but know not what we may be. God
be at your table.

CLAUDIUS Conceit upon her father.   45

OPHELIA Pray let's have no words of this, but when they ask you what
it means, say you this –

Tomorrow is Saint Valentine's day,   *Song*
All in the morning betime,
And I a maid at your window,   50
To be your Valentine.

Musicologists regard this Drury Lane tune as a version of 'Walsingham', a ballad which was
very popular in Shakespeare's day and which may well have provided the melody for the
first Ophelia:

The ballad contains the line: 'how shold I know yor true loue'. Ophelia's following quatrains
have nothing to do with 'Walsingham', but their words have usually been sung to the stage
version of its melody.

23–37 Terry notes that the first stanza should be 'quick', 24–5 should be delivered 'intelligently',
'cunningly', 'shrewd', '*very* brightly' whereas the second stanza is 'slow', 'sad', with a 'wail'
(rehearsal book).

28ff Marlowe alternated moods even more intensely than did Terry: 'Say you' 'bright, gaily'; the
rest of the line 'very sadly'. After 'Oho!' (33) she 'moans – passes hand over brow' while
'Pray you mark' (35) is given 'brightly'. She 'shudders' at 'know not what we may be' (43)
but at 'God be at your table' she gives a 'courtesy gaily to Queen'. 'Let's have no words of
this' (46) is spoken 'harshly to King' but 'when they ask you what it means' is delivered 'very
gaily' as is the first stanza of the St Valentine song (48–51), which is all of the song that was
included (promptbook).

35 Glenda Jackson shouted the words 'as though she could do murder, drumming a heel on the
floor and lifting her upper lip in a rictus of contempt' (*Observer*, 22 August 1965).

41 Stanislavsky advised his Claudius: 'Concealment of a boorish smile. An Oriental pasha'
(Senelick, p. 143).

43 Terry emphasized *not*.

45–52 Modjeska: 'At the end of the first stanza she breaks into a wordless song, to the music of
which she dances'. Like a 'Bacchante', 'she sways her body, and waves her arms wildly'.
After 51 she 'breaks into a loud laugh, and plucks from her bosom a flower, which she

> Then up he rose and donned his clothes
> And dupped the chamber door;
> Let in the maid that out a maid
> Never departed more. 55

CLAUDIUS Pretty Ophelia!

OPHELIA Indeed la! Without an oath I'll make an end on't.

> By Gis and by Saint Charity,
> Alack and fie for shame,
> Young men will do't if they come to't – 60
> By Cock, they are to blame.

> Quoth she, 'Before you tumbled me,
> You promised me to wed.'

He answers –

> So would I ha' done, by yonder sun, 65
> And thou hadst not come to my bed.

CLAUDIUS How long hath she been thus?

OPHELIA I hope all will be well. We must be patient, but I cannot
choose but weep to think they would lay him i'th' cold ground. My
brother shall know of it, and so I thank you for your good counsel. 70

throws upon the floor. Her eyes follow the flower, and as it falls, her laughter changes to
hysterical weeping' (Mason 106).

48–66   Another Drury Lane tune:

Good mor - row. 'tis St. Valen - tine's day. All in the morn- ing be - time. And I a maid at your win- dow. To be your Val - en - tine.

It was used in several ballad-operas of the first decades of the 18th century, but no earlier
instance has been found.

52–5,   Because of their 'indecency' these lines were customarily cut in performance from the
58–66   Restoration to the early twentieth century.

56–61   In the Pryce/Eyre production, with Michael Elphick as Claudius and Harriet Walter as
Ophelia, at 'Pretty Ophelia' Claudius 'is embarrassed – and he becomes more so, as she
touches his chest [at 58] and then begins to move her hands lower so that she is fumbling
with his belt at "By Cock they are to blame"' (Gilbert, 'Pryce', p. 11). In the Gibson/Zeffirelli
film Helena Bonham Carter at this line stroked the belt of a guard.

69a   Marlowe 'spreads scarf as if it were grave and kneels' and after speaking this line 'sobs
violently' (promptbook).

Come, my coach. Good night ladies, good night sweet ladies, good
night, good night.   *Exit*
CLAUDIUS Follow her close, give her good watch I pray you.
                                                  [*Exit Horatio*]
          Oh this is the poison of deep grief, it springs
          All from her father's death, [and now behold –]   75
          Oh Gertrude, Gertrude,
          When sorrows come, they come not single spies,
          But in battalions. First, her father slain;
          Next, your son gone, and he most violent author
          Of his own just remove; the people muddied,   80
          Thick and unwholesome in their thoughts and whispers
          For good Polonius' death – and we have done but greenly
          In hugger-mugger to inter him; poor Ophelia
          Divided from herself and her fair judgement,
          Without the which we are pictures, or mere beasts;   85
          Last, and as much containing as all these,
          Her brother is in secret come from France,
          Feeds on his wonder, keeps himself in clouds,
          And wants not buzzers to infect his ear
          With pestilent speeches of his father's death,   90
          Wherein necessity, of matter beggared,
          Will nothing stick our person to arraign
          In ear and ear. O my dear Gertrude, this,
          Like to a murdering piece, in many places
          Gives me superfluous death.   95
                    A noise within
GERTRUDE Alack, what noise is this?
CLAUDIUS Attend! Where are my Swissers? Let them guard the door.

70a Isabella Pateman with Booth: 'rising and speaking in a tone as if *then* surely something
    would be done about it; rather a threatening tone' (Stone, p. 114).
 70 Terry emphasized *shall*. When she calls for her coach she should 'fly to Center, clap
    suddenly' (rehearsal book). As fierce when mad as when sane, Glenda Jackson, with
    Warner, called for her coach 'in the rasping tones of an East End harridan' (*London Morning
    Advertiser*, 6 December 1965).
76–8 In the Olivier film Eileen Herlie signalled her withdrawal from the King by turning her back
    on his bid for sympathy and resisting his attempted embrace; in the adapted filmscript the
    scene ended with the arrival of the letters from Hamlet – 'This to your majesty, this to the
    queen' (4.7.37) – and the two going slowly out their separate ways, reading their letters
    privately. More subtly, Alec Clunes, as Claudius with Redgrave gave at this point 'A heart-cry
    made doubly moving by his refusal to overstress it and by Gertrude's rejection of his
    outstretched hand' (*Observer*, 11 December 1955).

Enter a MESSENGER

What is the matter?
MESSENGER   Save yourself my lord.
    The ocean, overpeering of his list,
    Eats not the flats with more impitious haste   100
    Than young Laertes in a riotous head
    O'erbears your officers. The rabble call him lord,
    And, as the world were now but to begin,
    Antiquity forgot, custom not known,
    The ratifiers and props of every word,   105
    They cry 'Choose we! Laertes shall be king.'
    Caps, hands and tongues applaud it to the clouds,
    'Laertes shall be king, Laertes king!'
GERTRUDE How cheerfully on the false trail they cry!
    Oh this is counter, you false Danish dogs!   110
                    A noise within
CLAUDIUS The doors are broke.

Enter LAERTES *with others*

LAERTES Where is this king? – Sirs, stand you all without.
ALL No, let's come in.
LAERTES I pray you give me leave.
ALL We will, we will.   115
LAERTES I thank you. Keep the door.
                            [*Exeunt followers*]
                    O thou vile king,
    Give me my father.
GERTRUDE   Calmly, good Laertes.
LAERTES That drop of blood that's calm proclaims me bastard,
    Cries cuckold to my father, brands the harlot
    Even here, between the chaste unsmirchèd brow   120
    Of my true mother.
CLAUDIUS   What is the cause, Laertes,
    That thy rebellion looks so giant-like? –
    Let him go, Gertrude, do not fear our person.
    There's such divinity doth hedge a king
    That treason can but peep to what it would,   125
    Acts little of his will. – Tell me Laertes,

121 Stanislavsky advised his Claudius: 'This sort of sovereign is told that there's an uprising. In a
    twinkling he's a new man: he does everything confidently, Napoleonically' (Senelick, p. 143).

Why thou art thus incensed. – Let him go Gertrude. –
Speak man.

LAERTES   Where is my father?

CLAUDIUS   Dead.

GERTRUDE   But not by him.

CLAUDIUS Let him demand his fill.

LAERTES How came he dead? I'll not be juggled with.   130
To hell allegiance, vows to the blackest devil,
Conscience and grace to the profoundest pit!
I dare damnation. To this point I stand,
That both the worlds I give to negligence,
Let come what comes, only I'll be revenged   135
Most throughly for my father.

CLAUDIUS   Who shall stay you?

LAERTES My will, not all the world.
And for my means, I'll husband them so well,
They shall go far with little.

CLAUDIUS   Good Laertes,
If you desire to know the certainty   140
Of your dear father, is't writ in your revenge
That, soopstake, you will draw both friend and foe,
Winner and loser?

LAERTES   None but his enemies.

CLAUDIUS Will you know them then?

LAERTES To his good friends thus wide I'll ope my arms,   145
And like the kind life-rendering pelican,
Repast them with my blood.

CLAUDIUS   Why now you speak
Like a good child and a true gentleman.
That I am guiltless of your father's death,
And am most sensibly in grief for it,   150
It shall as level to your judgement pierce
As day does to your eye.

                A noise within: 'Let her come in'

128   In the Branagh film the blunt finality of the King's 'dead' (128) stops Laertes (Michael
      Maloney) in his tracks (*Screenplay*, p. 129).

149   In the Branagh film Jacobi as the King, whom Laertes has held at sword's point through most
      of the episode, here 'slowly pushes the sword away from his throat' (p. 130).

152SD F reads (as a stage direction): 'A noise within. Let her come in'. Q2 gives 'Let her come in' to
      Laertes, Kemble to the King (*Promptbooks*, p. 62), Gielgud (Gilder, p. 202) and Guthrie
      (Rossi, p. 112) to 'Danes (within)'.

LAERTES How now, what noise is that?

Enter OPHELIA

    O heat dry up my brains, tears seven times salt
    Burn out the sense and virtue of mine eye!   155
    By heaven, thy madness shall be paid with weight
    Till our scale turn the beam. O rose of May,
    Dear maid, kind sister, sweet Ophelia –
    O heavens, is't possible a young maid's wits
    Should be as mortal as an old man's life?   160
    Nature is fine in love, and where 'tis fine,
    It sends some precious instance of itself
    After the thing it loves.
OPHELIA   They bore him bare-faced on the bier   *Song*
            Hey non nonny, nonny, hey nonny,   165
            And in his grave rained many a tear –
  Fare you well my dove.
LAERTES Hadst thou thy wits, and didst persuade revenge,
    It could not move thus.
OPHELIA You must sing a-down a-down, and you call him a-down-a.   170
    Oh how the wheel becomes it. It is the false steward that stole his
    master's daughter.
LAERTES This nothing's more than matter.

153   Q1 reads 'Who's this, Ofelia?' Rosenberg suggests that in this version Laertes may possibly
      'not at first even recognize his madness-disguised sister' (p. 799).

154   Terry momentarily seems to recognize her brother, then 'fades into vacancy' (*Pall Mall
      Gazette*, 1 January 1879, pp. 10– 11). In her rehearsal book, Terry wrote after 'sweet Ophelia':
      'Recog[nize] – Yes? – No – No'. With Barrymore 'Ophelia gazes vacantly at Laertes and
      smiles and ogles him in a coquettish manner' (promptbook 156). On BBC-TV Lalla Ward at
      first kisses Laertes lasciviously; when he tries to get through to her she hits him away.

157-8 Otis Skinner, who played Laertes to Modjeska's Ophelia, recalled : 'Her madness was so real
      that it sent a shudder through me when I looked into her eyes' at 'O rose of May!', to which
      'she replied, singing' (*Footlights*, p. 203). With Marlowe, Laertes fails at 157b and 158b to get
      Ophelia to recognize him (promptbook).

164-6 This has been sung on stage either to the tune of 'How should I your true love know' or of
      'And will a not come again?'

164-73 Terry addressed 'false steward' to the King 'mysteriously', 'with "becks and nods and
      wreathed smiles"'.

171b With Fechter, Kate Terry's Ophelia before 'It is the false steward . . . ' 'looks up, encounters
      the King – she shrinks back into Laertes' arms' (promptbook).

OPHELIA There's rosemary, that's for remembrance – pray you, love,
　　　remember – and there is pansies, that's for thoughts.   175
LAERTES A document in madness, thoughts and remembrance fitted.
OPHELIA There's fennel for you, and columbines. There's rue for you,
　　　and here's some for me; we may call it herb of grace a Sundays.
　　　Oh you must wear your rue with a difference. There's a daisy. I
　　　would give you some violets, but they withered all when my father   180
　　　died. They say a made a good end.
　　　　　　　　　　　[*Sings*]
　　　　　　For bonny sweet Robin is all my joy.
LAERTES Thought and affliction, passion, hell itself,
　　　She turns to favour and to prettiness.
OPHELIA　　　　　And will a not come again?   *Song* 185
　　　　　　　And will a not come again?
　　　　　　　No, no, he is dead,
　　　　　　　Go to thy death-bed,
　　　　　　　He never will come again.

174　Modjeska runs to Laertes, 'lays her hands upon his shoulders, and gazes into his face, as if
　　　recognizing him. After a moment . . . her face becomes blank, and she slowly gives him the
　　　rosemary and pansies' (Mason 106). In the Olivier film Jean Simmons addressed 'Pray you,
　　　love, remember' to Hamlet's vacant chair, caressing where his face would have been.

177–9　As was traditional, Terry, Modjeska, and Marlowe all gave the fennel to the King, the rue to
　　　the Queen. Marlowe preferred a more original alternative: 'she had in her scarf of lace only
　　　white rose petals. She gave "rosemary" and "daisies" and "rue" not to the characters on the
　　　stage, but half kneeling she offered the rose leaves to some imaginary person – her father or
　　　Hamlet? – and strewed them about her' (*Chicago Daily Tribune*, 5 October 1904).

182　'Bonny Sweet Robin' was very popular in Shakespeare's time. The surviving versions,
　　　however, do not contain Ophelia's line, although it fits either the first or the last strain of the
　　　complete melody. Chappell gives the beginning portion

My　Ro - bin is to　the　green - wood gone,

185–94　Sung to a Drury Lane tune that Chappell traces to 'The Merry Milkmaids' in *The Dancing
　　　Master* (1650):

And will he not come　a - gain,　　And will he not come　a - gain?　No,

no,　he is　dead,　Gone　to　his deathbed.　He　ne - ver will come　a - gain.

Modjeska 'sings this song seated upon the floor, strewing flowers over an imaginary bier'
(Mason 106). Pateman did the same (Stone, p. 116).

His beard was as white as snow,   190
All flaxen was his poll,
  He is gone, he is gone,
  And we cast away moan,
God-a-mercy on his soul.

   And of all Christian souls, I pray God. God buy you.   *Exit* 195
LAERTES Do you see this, O God?
CLAUDIUS Laertes, I must commune with your grief,
  Or you deny me right. Go but apart,
  Make choice of whom your wisest friends you will,
  And they shall hear and judge 'twixt you and me.   200
  If by direct or by collateral hand
  They find us touched, we will our kingdom give,
  Our crown, our life, and all that we call ours,
  To you in satisfaction. But if not,
  Be you content to lend your patience to us,   205
  And we shall jointly labour with your soul
  To give it due content.
LAERTES   Let this be so.
  His means of death, his obscure funeral,
  No trophy, sword, nor hatchment o'er his bones,
  No noble rite, nor formal ostentation,   210
  Cry to be heard, as 'twere from heaven to earth,
  That I must call't in question.
CLAUDIUS   So you shall.
  And where th'offence is, let the great axe fall.
  I pray you go with me.
                                       Exeunt

195   Ophelias who have not previously come close to recognizing Laertes will often do so here.
     Pateman pulled out all the stops: she 'approaches Laertes and peers into his face, appearing
     almost to be about to recognize him; then suddenly gives a piercing, blood-curdling,
     maniacal shriek. Then she goes out backwards, very slowly, sobbing and holding on to her
     head – an utter lunatic' (Stone, p. 116). Gwen Ffrangcon Davies, with Godfrey Tearle as
     Hamlet, was much more restrained. She 'came down-stage towards Laertes with recognition
     on her face. But before she could take shelter in her brother's arms her mind clouded again
     so that she found herself confronted by a stranger. And it was a stranger to whom she said:
     "God be wi' you"' (*Sunday Times*, 27 April 1930).
195SD Kemble had the Queen exit as well.

ACT 4, SCENE 6

[4.6] *Enter* HORATIO *with an* ATTENDANT

HORATIO What are they that would speak with me?
ATTENDANT Seafaring men sir, they say they have letters for you.
HORATIO Let them come in.

                          [Exit Attendant]
         I do not know from what part of the world
         I should be greeted, if not from Lord Hamlet.   5

               Enter SAILORS

1 SAILOR God bless you sir.
HORATIO Let him bless thee too.
1 SAILOR A shall sir, and please him. There's a letter for you sir, it came
from th'ambassador that was bound for England, if your name be
Horatio, as I am let to know it is.   10
HORATIO (*Reads the letter*) 'Horatio, when thou shalt have overlooked
this, give these fellows some means to the king; they have letters
for him. Ere we were two days old at sea, a pirate of very warlike
appointment gave us chase. Finding ourselves too slow of sail, we
put on a compelled valour, and in the grapple I boarded them. On   15
the instant they got clear of our ship, so I alone became their
prisoner. They have dealt with me like thieves of mercy, but they
knew what they did: I am to do a good turn for them. Let the king
have the letters I have sent, and repair thou to me with as much
speed as thou wouldest fly death. I have words to speak in thine   20
ear will make thee dumb, yet are they much too light for the bore
of the matter. These good fellows will bring thee where I am.
Rosencrantz and Guildenstern hold their course for England. Of
them I have much to tell thee. Farewell.
                 He that thou knowest thine,   25
                     Hamlet.'

0   Of Q2's stage direction 'Enter Horatio and others' Granville-Barker asks: 'What others?'
     Since there is only need for one attendant to fetch the sailors, he speculates that the 'others'
     are agents of the King, keeping 'a polite watch' on Hamlet's friend (*Prefaces*, p. 128).

Come, I will give you way for these your letters,
And do't the speedier that you may direct me
To him from whom you brought them.

Exeunt

ACT 4, SCENE 7

[4.7] *Enter* CLAUDIUS *and* LAERTES

CLAUDIUS Now must your conscience my acquittance seal,
          And you must put me in your heart for friend,
          Sith you have heard, and with a knowing ear,
          That he which hath your noble father slain
          Pursued my life.
LAERTES   It well appears. But tell me   5
          Why you proceeded not against these feats,
          So crimeful and so capital in nature,
          As by your safety, wisdom, all things else,
          You mainly were stirred up.
CLAUDIUS   Oh for two special reasons,
          Which may to you perhaps seem much unsinewed,   10
          But yet to me they're strong. The queen his mother
          Lives almost by his looks, and for myself,
          My virtue or my plague, be it either which,
          She's so conjunctive to my life and soul,
          That as the star moves not but in his sphere,   15
          I could not but by her. The other motive,
          Why to a public count I might not go,
          Is the great love the general gender bear him,
          Who, dipping all his faults in their affection,
          Work like the spring that turneth wood to stone, 20

4.7

0   Directing Burton's 1953 production, Michael Benthall put this scene after Ophelia's funeral,
    as did Guthrie at Minneapolis in 1963. In their films Kozintsev and Zeffirelli did the same,
    thereby making Laertes's treachery more understandable.

1ff Gielgud (Gilder, p. 66) and Guthrie (*Shakespeare*, p. 289) stress the difficulty of holding the
    attention of a tired audience with this 'slow and quiet scene'. To Pennington, however, who
    played Laertes with Williamson and Claudius with Dillane, this 'is one of Shakespeare's great
    temptation scenes': 'the intimacy of the two of them weighing up, venturing, withdrawing,
    defying, deferring, demurring and finally coming together in an unholy alliance brings us, in
    its realistic tones, close to modern theatre and indeed television or film' (*Hamlet*, p. 123).

Convert his gyves to graces, so that my arrows,
Too slightly timbered for so loud a wind,
Would have reverted to my bow again,
And not where I had aimed them.

LAERTES And so have I a noble father lost,   25
A sister driven into desperate terms,
Whose worth, if praises may go back again,
Stood challenger on mount of all the age
For her perfections. But my revenge will come.

CLAUDIUS Break not your sleeps for that. You must not think   30
That we are made of stuff so flat and dull
That we can let our beard be shook with danger
And think it pastime. You shortly shall hear more.
I loved your father, and we love ourself,
And that I hope will teach you to imagine –   35

Enter a MESSENGER *with letters*

How now? What news?
MESSENGER   Letters my lord from Hamlet.
This to your majesty, this to the queen.
CLAUDIUS From Hamlet? Who brought them?
MESSENGER Sailors my lord they say, I saw them not;
They were given me by Claudio – he received them   40
Of him that brought them.
CLAUDIUS   Laertes, you shall hear them. –
Leave us.

Exit Messenger

[*Reads*] 'High and mighty, you shall know I am set naked on your
kingdom. Tomorrow shall I beg leave to see your kingly eyes, when
I shall, first asking your pardon thereunto, recount th'occasion of   45
my sudden and more strange return.

Hamlet.'

What should this mean? Are all the rest come back?
Or is it some abuse, and no such thing?

---

36   Not in Q2. Q2's King seems somewhat less in charge than F's, more taken by surprise by this
      unexpected development. In F the King's questions 'How now? What news?' give him more
      control of the situation than in Q2, where the Messenger abruptly breaks in with the letters
      (Werstine, 'Mystery', p. 22). Rosenberg suggests that by not identifying Hamlet as the sender
      in advance Q2 makes 'Claudius feel the full shock of opening the paper and discovering his
      nemesis' (p. 816).

46   In the Daniels/Rylance production, Peter Wight as Claudius responded to Hamlet's letter
      'with a howl of exasperation and beating the wall' (*The Times*, 27 April 1989).

LAERTES Know you the hand?

CLAUDIUS   'Tis Hamlet's character. Naked?   50
      And in a postscript here he says alone.
      Can you devise me?

LAERTES I'm lost in it my lord. But let him come –
      It warms the very sickness in my heart
      That I shall live and tell him to his teeth   55
      'Thus didest thou!'

CLAUDIUS   If it be so, Laertes –
      As how should it be so? – how otherwise? –
      Will you be ruled by me?

LAERTES   Ay my lord,
      So you will not o'errule me to a peace.

CLAUDIUS To thine own peace. If he be now returned,   60
      As checking at his voyage, and that he means
      No more to undertake it, I will work him
      To an exploit, now ripe in my device,
      Under the which he shall not choose but fall,
      And for his death no wind of blame shall breathe,   65
      But even his mother shall uncharge the practice
      And call it accident.

[LAERTES   My lord, I will be ruled,
      The rather if you could devise it so
      That I might be the organ.

CLAUDIUS   It falls right.
      You have been talked of since your travel much,   70
      And that in Hamlet's hearing, for a quality
      Wherein they say you shine. Your sum of parts
      Did not together pluck such envy from him
      As did that one, and that in my regard
      Of the unworthiest siege.

LAERTES   What part is that my lord?   75

CLAUDIUS A very riband in the cap of youth,
      Yet needful too, for youth no less becomes
      The light and careless livery that it wears
      Than settled age his sables and his weeds
      Importing health and graveness.] Two months since   80
      Here was a gentleman of Normandy.
      I've seen myself, and served against, the French,
      And they can well on horseback, but this gallant
      Had witchcraft in't. He grew unto his seat,

67b–80a   Not in F. Werstine finds Q2's Laertes more submissive than in F and more subject to Claudius's 'hollow' flattery ('Mystery', pp. 9–10).

And to such wondrous doing brought his horse   85
As had he been incorpsed and demi-natured
With the brave beast. So far he topped my thought,
That I in forgery of shapes and tricks
Come short of what he did.
LAERTES   A Norman was't?
CLAUDIUS A Norman.   90
LAERTES Upon my life Lamord.
CLAUDIUS   The very same.
LAERTES I know him well, he is the brooch indeed
    And gem of all the nation.
CLAUDIUS He made confession of you,
    And gave you such a masterly report   95
    For art and exercise in your defence,
    And for your rapier most especial,
    That he cried out 'twould be a sight indeed
    If one could match you. [Th'escrimers of their nation
    He swore had neither motion, guard, nor eye,   100
    If you opposed them.] Sir, this report of his
    Did Hamlet so envenom with his envy
    That he could nothing do but wish and beg
    Your sudden coming o'er to play with you.
    Now out of this –
LAERTES   What out of this, my lord?   105
CLAUDIUS Laertes, was your father dear to you?
    Or are you like the painting of a sorrow,
    A face without a heart?
LAERTES   Why ask you this?
CLAUDIUS Not that I think you did not love your father,
    But that I know love is begun by time,   110
    And that I see, in passages of proof,
    Time qualifies the spark and fire of it.
    [There lives within the very flame of love
    A kind of wick or snuff that will abate it,
    And nothing is at a like goodness still,   115
    For goodness, growing to a plurisy,
    Dies in his own too much. That we would do,
    We should do when we would, for this 'would' changes,
    And hath abatements and delays as many
    As there are tongues, are hands, are accidents;   120
    And then this 'should' is like a spendthrift sigh,

99b–101a Not in F.

113–22 Not in F. Werstine points out that Q2's Claudius here prolongs the time before he discloses
his plan to Laertes ('Mystery', p. 10).

That hurts by easing. But to the quick of th'ulcer –]
Hamlet comes back; what would you undertake
To show yourself in deed your father's son
More than in words?
LAERTES   To cut his throat i'th'church.   125
CLAUDIUS No place indeed should murder sanctuarize;
Revenge should have no bounds. But, good Laertes,
Will you do this, keep close within your chamber;
Hamlet, returned, shall know you are come home;
We'll put on those shall praise your excellence,   130
And set a double varnish on the fame
The Frenchman gave you; bring you in fine together,
And wager on your heads. He being remiss,
Most generous, and free from all contriving,
Will not peruse the foils, so that with ease,   135
Or with a little shuffling, you may choose
A sword unbated, and in a pass of practice
Requite him for your father.
LAERTES   I will do't,
And for that purpose I'll anoint my sword.
I bought an unction of a mountebank,   140
So mortal that but dip a knife in it,
Where it draws blood no cataplasm so rare,
Collected from all simples that have virtue
Under the moon, can save the thing from death
That is but scratched withal. I'll touch my point   145
With this contagion, that if I gall him slightly,
It may be death.
CLAUDIUS   Let's further think of this,
Weigh what convenience both of time and means
May fit us to our shape. If this should fail,

125ff In the Olivier film, the camera punctuates the three aspects of the conspiracy (the unbaited
foil, the poisoned ointment, and the poisoned drink) by three times withdrawing up and
back from a close-up.

140ff With Burton Gielgud directed Alfred Drake as Claudius to delight in the talk of poisoning:
'Claudius is a professional poisoner, and as soon as Laertes mentions it, we should see him
already planning to go one better' (Sterne, p. 71). Gielgud may well have been influenced by
Granville-Barker, who repeatedly remarks upon the fascination of poison for Claudius
(*Prefaces*, p. 222): 'Interesting to watch him first play with the notion, a little reluctantly;
then, with that feline "Soft! let me see" yield – once more! – to its fascination. For even so
must he have looked when he pictured to himself his brother sleeping in the orchard' (pp.
132–3).

And that our drift look through our bad performance, 150
'Twere better not assayed. Therefore this project
Should have a back or second, that might hold
If this did blast in proof. Soft, let me see.
We'll make a solemn wager on your cunnings –
I ha't! 155
When in your motion you are hot and dry,
As make your bouts more violent to that end,
And that he calls for drink, I'll have preferred him
A chalice for the nonce, whereon but sipping,
If he by chance escape your venomed stuck, 160
Our purpose may hold there. But stay, what noise?

Enter GERTRUDE

How, sweet queen!
GERTRUDE One woe doth tread upon another's heel,
So fast they follow. Your sister's drowned, Laertes.
LAERTES Drowned! Oh where? 165
GERTRUDE There is a willow grows askant a brook,
That shows his hoar leaves in the glassy stream.
Therewith fantastic garlands did she make,
Of crow-flowers, nettles, daisies, and long purples,
That liberal shepherds give a grosser name, 170
But our cold maids do dead men's fingers call them.
There on the pendant boughs her cronet weeds

154 In the Branagh film Jacobi speaks this line as if to prime the pump of his invention as his mind hatches a fall-back plan.

161–2 Edwards conflates Q2 and F. In Q1 Laertes announces 'Here comes the Queen' and the King asks, 'How now, Gertrude, why look you heavily?'; in Q2 the only lead-in to Gertrude's arrival is the King's 'but stay what noise?'; in F the King says only 'how sweet Queen?'. Urkowitz summarizes: 'Q1 stresses the King's concern for his distressed wife, Q2 stresses the King's guilty alarm, and F stresses the King's chameleon alacrity of change . . . in one instant [in F] the King leaps from embellishing his repertoire of fail-safe murderous devices into expressing his real concern for the doting mother of his intended victim' ('"Well-sayd"', pp. 58–9).

165 Pryce/Eyre: Laertes was shocked and surprised at 'Drowned!'; then after a pause 'Oh where?' (Gilbert, 'Pryce', p. 13).

166ff Judi Dench, with Day Lewis, 'does not treat the speech as an isolated set-piece. Instead she gives it new point by addressing her words to Laertes, as if still breaking the news, explaining the details of what happened and where' (*Literary Reviews*, March 1989). Clare Higgins in the Rylance/Daniels production comforted Laertes, he on his knees with his head at her breast, she stroking his head.

Clamb'ring to hang, an envious sliver broke,
When down her weedy trophies and herself
Fell in the weeping brook. Her clothes spread wide,   175
And mermaid-like awhile they bore her up,
Which time she chanted snatches of old lauds
As one incapable of her own distress,
Or like a creature native and indued
Unto that element. But long it could not be   180
Till that her garments, heavy with their drink,
Pulled the poor wretch from her melodious lay
To muddy death.

LAERTES   Alas, then she is drowned?

GERTRUDE Drowned, drowned.

LAERTES Too much of water hast thou, poor Ophelia,   185
And therefore I forbid my tears. But yet
It is our trick; nature her custom holds,
Let shame say what it will. When these are gone,
The woman will be out. Adieu my lord,
I have a speech of fire that fain would blaze,   190
But that this folly douts it.   *Exit*

CLAUDIUS   Let's follow, Gertrude.
How much I had to do to calm his rage!
Now fear I this will give it start again.
Therefore let's follow.

                                    Exeunt

175a Pateman with Booth: 'The drowned and dead Ophelia is borne in upon a litter, her garlands
      hanging about her, her face slightly disfigured. The drapery around Ophelia, if not her
      gown, ought to be wet as if taken from the water' (Stone, p. 117). As Sprague records,
      Benson, Forbes-Robertson, Sothern were among those who made such pictorial displays
      around the beginning of the twentieth century (*Actors*, p. 173).

195SD In the Branagh film this is the decisive breaking point between Gertrude and Claudius; she
      'will not follow. Never again' (*Screenplay*, p. 141).

ACT 5, SCENE I

[5.1] *Enter two* CLOWNS

CLOWN Is she to be buried in Christian burial, when she wilfully seeks
 her own salvation?
OTHER I tell thee she is, therefore make her grave straight. The crowner
 hath sat on her, and finds it Christian burial.
CLOWN How can that be, unless she drowned herself in her own   5
 defence?

     In their speech headings Q1, Q2, and F all call them 'clowns', but they are generally
referred to as the First and Second Gravediggers. A perennial favourite, the 'Gravedigger
episode' (preceding the arrival of the funeral procession) has often been trimmed in
performance. But Garrick's 1772 adaptation is exceptional in omitting it altogether. He
realized that the gravediggers were 'favourites of the people' yet was influenced by
Voltaire's strictures on their 'string of miserable jests', an indecorous intrusion of the 'low,
mean, and detestable' upon 'every thing sublime and great' (Introduction to *Semiramis*).
Initially, the adaptation was well received both in England and in France (Voltaire himself
commented in 1776 on its success in removing the gravediggers). Yet it did not survive
Garrick's retirement (Vickers, *Critical Heritage*, v, pp. 10–11).

OSD   In 1870 at his own theatre Booth's set depicted an idealized country churchyard. Amid many
picturesque details what chiefly brought the scene to life was the lighting, as the moonlight
flooded the church and made streaks through the tree branches and 'flickered off' a split
gravestone (Shattuck, pp. 250–1).

1ff   In the eighteenth century 'B. Jonson, the comedian, for above forty years, gave a true
picture of an arch clown in the Grave-digger. His jokes and repartees had a strong effect
from his seeming insensibility of their force. His large speaking blue eyes he fixed steadily
on the person to whom he spoke' (Davies, p. 135).

     From roughly 1780 to 1830, First Gravediggers sought laughs by doffing one waistcoat
after another, folding each 'with great deliberation and nicety', as a way of postponing
getting to work. Sprague gives a full account of this custom, which started in the provinces
then came to London before dying out (*Actors*, pp. 175–6). Rosenberg records a revival of

OTHER Why, 'tis found so.

CLOWN It must be *se offendendo*, it cannot be else. For here lies the point: if I drown myself wittingly, it argues an act, and an act hath three branches – it is to act, to do, to perform. Argal, she drowned herself wittingly. 10

OTHER Nay, but hear you goodman delver –

CLOWN Give me leave. Here lies the water – good. Here stands the man – good. If the man go to this water and drown himself, it is will he, nill he, he goes – mark you that. But if the water come to him, and drown him, he drowns not himself. Argal, he that is not guilty of his own death shortens not his own life. 15

OTHER But is this law?

CLOWN Ay marry is't, crowner's quest law.

OTHER Will you ha' the truth on't? If this had not been a gentlewoman, she should have been buried out o' Christian burial. 20

CLOWN Why, there thou sayst – and the more pity that great folk should have countenance in this world to drown or hang themselves more than their even-Christen. Come, my spade; there is no ancient gentlemen but gardeners, ditchers, and gravemakers; they hold up Adam's profession. 25

OTHER Was he a gentleman?

CLOWN A was the first that ever bore arms.

OTHER Why, he had none.

CLOWN What, art a heathen? How dost thou understand the scripture? The scripture says Adam digged. Could he dig without arms? I'll put another question to thee. If thou answerest me not to the purpose, confess thyself – 30

OTHER Go to!

the business in a 1985 Toronto production; the gravedigger kept searching the pockets of successive waistcoats until in the seventh 'he found what he had been looking for – a stub of cigar to smoke' (p. 832).

13 With Booth, the First Gravedigger here climbs out of the grave he has been digging, lays his spade on the ground to signify the water, and takes the Second Gravedigger's pickaxe and puts his cap on the top of its handle for 'the man' (Shattuck, p. 252–3). With Redgrave (1950), George Benson propped his own hat on the skull of Yorick (Trewin, *Five & Eighty*, p. 78).

16 In the Burton/Gielgud production, George Rose after 'drowns not himself' was 'greatly pleased with his own logic' (Sterne, p. 259); he did not descend into the grave and prepare to dig until after 17.

24 In the Day-Lewis/Eyre production, at 'Come, my spade' the Gravedigger 'spoke friendlily *to* the shovel itself' as he reached for it (Rosenberg, p. 830).

CLOWN What is he that builds stronger than either the mason, the   35
    shipwright, or the carpenter?

OTHER The gallows-maker, for that frame outlives a thousand tenants.

CLOWN I like thy wit well in good faith. The gallows does well, but
    how does it well? It does well to those that do ill. Now, thou dost
    ill to say the gallows is built stronger than the church; argal, the   40
    gallows may do well to thee. To't again, come.

OTHER Who builds stronger than a mason, a shipwright, or a carpenter?

CLOWN Ay, tell me that, and unyoke.

OTHER Marry, now I can tell.

CLOWN To't.   45

OTHER Mass, I cannot tell.

            Enter HAMLET *and* HORATIO *afar off*

CLOWN Cudgel thy brains no more about it, for your dull ass will not
    mend his pace with beating; and when you are asked this question
    next, say a grave-maker. The houses he makes lasts till doomsday.
    Go, get thee to Yaughan, fetch me a stoup of liquor.   50
                             [Exit Second Clown]
        In youth when I did love, did love,   *Song*
        Methought it was very sweet

37   In the Branagh film, Simon Russell Beale is himself surprised and pleased by the aptness of
       his answer.

37–41 In the Burton/Gielgud production both gravediggers laughed after 37. Rose then pointed his
       rebuttal directly at his companion by emphasizing *thou* and *thee* (Sterne, p. 260).

47SD Granville-Barker sees 'dramatic intention' in the fact that the Folio stage direction brings
       Hamlet and Horatio on eight lines before Q2 does and leaves them there, *'afarre off'*,
       listening. Since Hamlet's letters suggest that he is primed for revenge, the audience must be
       surprised that he should 'stand there so indifferent and detached. He is spiritually far off too'
       (*Prefaces*, p. 135). Booth had taken much the same approach. According to Clarke, he paid
       no attention to his surroundings. He and Horatio had evidently been discussing his return
       but Horatio's expectant manner suggested that there was more to be discussed. The
       Gravedigger served to pass the time until Hamlet felt ready to divulge further confidences
       (Shattuck, pp. 264–5).

       Hamlets, who have been off the stage since 4.4, have sometimes found it hard to get back
       into the role. Albert Finney's solution was not to relax or rest during this break but shower
       vigorously, thinking of Hamlet's fight with the pirates, so that he then 'came on again as
       keyed up as possible' (Hall, *Diaries*, p. 200).

51–63 Chappell records that by 'the traditions of the stage' of his time these words were sung to
       the tune of 'The Children of the Wood'.

> To contract-o the time for-a my behove,
>   Oh methought there-a was nothing-a meet.

HAMLET Has this fellow no feeling of his business? A sings in   55
    grave-making.

HORATIO Custom hath made it in him a property of easiness.

This is the melody most commonly used today. In garbled form the words derive from a poem by Thomas Lord Vaux that begins 'I loathe that I did love' and was first printed in Tottel's *Songs and Sonettes*, 1557. Vaux's first stanza reads:

I loathe that I did love,
    In youth that I thought sweet:
As time required for my behove:
    Methink they are not meet.

The Gravedigger then skips the second stanza and sings his version of Vaux's third stanza, including a third line substituted from Vaux's thirteenth stanza. The rest of the Gravedigger's song (79–82, 101–2) is a fairly close rendering of Vaux's eighth stanza.

Two different tunes for 'I loathe that I did love' have survived from Shakespeare's time, either of which may have been sung at the Globe.

53ff   With Burton Gielgud had Hamlet and Horatio enter at 53. Traditionally, the Gravedigger does not see Hamlet until 99b. Gielgud began their encounter at 59, with the Gravedigger performing the second verse of his song directly to Hamlet and then enjoying Hamlet's

HAMLET 'Tis e'en so, the hand of little employment hath the daintier
sense.

CLOWN But age with his stealing steps *Song* 60
    Hath clawed me in his clutch,
    And hath shipped me intil the land,
    As if I had never been such.
      [*Throws up a skull*]

HAMLET That skull had a tongue in it, and could sing once. How the
knave jowls it to th' ground, as if 'twere Cain's jawbone, that did 65
the first murder. This might be the pate of a politician which this
ass now o'erreaches, one that would circumvent God, might it not?

HORATIO It might my lord.

HAMLET Or of a courtier, which could say 'Good morrow sweet lord,
how dost thou sweet lord?' This might be my Lord Such-a-one, 70
that praised my Lord Such-a-one's horse when a meant to beg it,
might it not?

HORATIO Ay my lord.

HAMLET Why, e'en so, and now my Lady Worm's, chopless, and
knocked about the mazard with a sexton's spade. Here's fine 75
revolution, and we had the trick to see't. Did these bones cost no
more the breeding but to play at loggets with 'em? Mine ache to
think on't.

CLOWN A pickaxe and a spade, a spade, *Song*
    For and a shrowding sheet, 80
    Oh a pit of clay for to be made,
    For such a guest is meet.
      [*Throws up another skull*]

HAMLET There's another. Why may not that be the skull of a lawyer?
Where be his quiddities now, his quillets, his cases, his tenures, and
his tricks? Why does he suffer this rude knave now to knock him 85
about the sconce with a dirty shovel, and will not tell him of his

comments on the skulls. Hamlet addresses 76–7 to the Gravedigger, who 'laughs and nods'.
Lines 83–99a were cut. Burton found this earlier recognition 'a great help': 'It's usually so
awkward for me to wait while he sings, and for him to wait while I speak' (Sterne, pp. 41,
260–1).

64ff While previewing, Hall missed the rapport with the audience that Finney's delivery of
Hamlet's soliloquies had earlier created. He then realized that 'If Hamlet addresses a good
deal of his graveyard humour to the audience – so that the lawyer, the politician, and my
lady painted an inch thick are out there, in the audience, then the contact continues'
(*Diaries*, p. 197).

77 Booth would not permit his Gravedigger to shovel out the bones but made him throw them
by hand and hit the shovel, in order to suggest the game of loggets (Shattuck, p. 254n).

action of battery? Hum, this fellow might be in's time a great buyer
of land, with his statutes, his recognizances, his fines, his double
vouchers, his recoveries. Is this the fine of his fines and the recovery
of his recoveries, to have his fine pate full of fine dirt? Will his   90
vouchers vouch him no more of his purchases, and double ones too,
than the length and breadth of a pair of indentures? The very
conveyances of his lands will scarcely lie in this box, and must
th'inheritor himself have no more, ha?

HORATIO Not a jot more my lord.   95

HAMLET Is not parchment made of sheepskins?

HORATIO Ay my lord, and of calves' skins too.

HAMLET They are sheep and calves which seek out assurance in that.
I will speak to this fellow. Whose grave's this sirrah?

CLOWN Mine sir.   100

(Sings)
Oh a pit of clay for to be made
For such a guest is meet.

HAMLET I think it be thine indeed, for thou liest in't.

CLOWN You lie out on't sir, and therefore 'tis not yours. For my part,
I do not lie in't, yet it is mine.   105

HAMLET Thou dost lie in't, to be in't and say 'tis thine. 'Tis for the
dead, not for the quick, therefore thou liest.

CLOWN 'Tis a quick lie sir, 'twill away again from me to you.

HAMLET What man dost thou dig it for?

CLOWN For no man sir.   110

HAMLET What woman then?

CLOWN For none neither.

HAMLET Who is to be buried in't?

CLOWN One that was a woman sir, but rest her soul she's dead.

HAMLET How absolute the knave is! We must speak by the card, or   115
equivocation will undo us. By the lord, Horatio, this three years
I have took note of it: the age is grown so picked, that the toe of
the peasant comes so near the heel of the courtier, he galls his kibe.
How long hast thou been grave-maker?

CLOWN Of all the days i'th'year, I came to't that day that our last King   120
Hamlet o'ercame Fortinbras.

---

99   Irving's tone was of 'gentle and philosophic melancholy, lightened by a tinge of amusement'
(Towse, 'Irving', p. 666).

103–8   In the Branagh film the Gravedigger (Billy Crystal) plays on the Prince's elision ('in't') to
which the Prince responds in kind' (*Screenplay*, p. 146).

119   Having finished his work, Kevin Kline's Gravedigger (MacIntyre Dixon) perched at the top of
the grave and enjoyed a bottle of beer and a sandwich while continuing his chat.

HAMLET How long is that since?

CLOWN Cannot you tell that? Every fool can tell that. It was the very
    day that young Hamlet was born, he that is mad and sent into
    England.   125

HAMLET Ay marry, why was he sent into England?

CLOWN Why, because a was mad. A shall recover his wits there, or if
    a do not, 'tis no great matter there.

HAMLET Why?

CLOWN 'Twill not be seen in him there. There the men are as mad as   130
    he.

HAMLET How came he mad?

CLOWN Very strangely they say.

HAMLET How, strangely?

CLOWN Faith, e'en with losing his wits.   135

HAMLET Upon what ground?

CLOWN Why, here in Denmark. I have been sexton here man and boy
    thirty years.

HAMLET How long will a man lie i'th'earth ere he rot?

CLOWN Faith, if a be not rotten before a die, as we have many pocky   140
    corses nowadays that will scarce hold the laying in, a will last you
    some eight year, or nine year. A tanner will last you nine year.

HAMLET Why he more than another?

CLOWN Why sir, his hide is so tanned with his trade, that a will keep
    out water a great while, and your water is a sore decayer of your   145
    whoreson dead body. Here's a skull now: this skull hath lien you
    i'th'earth three and twenty years.

HAMLET Whose was it?

CLOWN A whoreson mad fellow's it was. Whose do you think it was?

HAMLET Nay I know not.   150

CLOWN A pestilence on him for a mad rogue, a poured a flagon of
    Rhenish on my head once. This same skull sir, was Yorick's skull,
    the king's jester.

130b   Only here did Stanley Holloway in the Olivier film permit himself to appreciate his own wit,
    with a smile and beaming glance at Horatio as well as Hamlet.

137a   In the Branagh film Crystal for the first time breaks the straight face he has assumed for his
    repartee with the Prince. They all enjoy the badness of his joke.

139   'Hamlet is playing with the soil with his foot' (Fechter promptbook).

147   Q1 reads 'this dozen year', a reading that Wilson Barrett used when he played Hamlet as an
    eighteen year-old. Q1 does not give the other indications of Hamlet's age to be found in Q2
    and F (see 5.1.119–25, 137–8).

152–5   Q2's version of 152–3 is more elaborate than Q1 and F more elaborate than Q2; Q1: 'this was
    one Yorick's skull'; Q2: 'this same skull sir, was sir Yoricks skull, the Kings Jester'; F: 'This

HAMLET This?

CLOWN E'en that. 155

HAMLET Let me see. [*Takes the skull.*] Alas poor Yorick! I knew him Horatio, a fellow of infinite jest, of most excellent fancy, he hath borne me on his back a thousand times – and now how abhorred in my imagination it is! My gorge rises at it. Here hung those lips that I have kissed I know not how oft. Where be your gibes now? 160 your gambols, your songs, your flashes of merriment that were wont to set the table on a roar? Not one now, to mock your own grinning? Quite chop-fallen? Now get you to my lady's chamber, and tell her, let her paint an inch thick, to this favour she must come. Make her laugh at that. – Prithee Horatio, tell me one thing. 165

HORATIO What's that my lord?

HAMLET Dost thou think Alexander looked o' this fashion i'th'earth?

HORATIO E'en so.

HAMLET And smelt so? Pah! [*Puts down the skull*]

HORATIO E'en so my lord. 170

HAMLET To what base uses we may return, Horatio! Why may not imagination trace the noble dust of Alexander, till a find it stopping a bunghole?

HORATIO 'Twere to consider too curiously to consider so.

HAMLET No faith, not a jot, but to follow him thither with modesty 175 enough, and likelihood to lead it, as thus: Alexander died, Alexander was buried, Alexander returneth to dust, the dust is earth, of earth we make loam, and why of that loam whereto he was converted might they not stop a beer-barrel?

Imperious Caesar, dead and turned to clay, 180
Might stop a hole, to keep the wind away.
Oh that that earth which kept the world in awe

same scull Sir, this same Scull sir, was Yoricks Scull, the Kings Jester'. Urkowitz observes how the shift in pronouns from Hamlet's 'This' to the Gravedigger's 'E'en that' marks the exact moment the skull changes hands ('"Well-sayd"', pp. 61–2).

156 Irving: 'stroked Yorick's skull gently with his hand' (*Daily Chronicle*, 31 December 1878, p. 6).

159b–60a 'Fechter carried the skull almost to his lips, when he put it away with a shiver' (Field, p. 110). Only here in the whole Zeffirelli film did Mel Gibson smile with his eyes. When Ralph Fiennes 'plants his lips on Yorick's mucky skull, as if curious about the taste of mortal soil, you can taste the rot yourself' (*New Yorker*, 17 April 1995, p. 86).

163 Sothern 'indicates absence of lower jaw. Horatio nods' (Marlowe promptbook).

163–5 In the Olivier film Hamlet touches the skull's cheekbone at 'inch thick' and whispers 'make her laugh at that' in its ear.

180 Bell tolls after 'clay' and at 180, 189, 202, 213, 225, 249, 259 (Irving promptbook).

Should patch a wall t'expel the winter's flaw!
But soft, but soft! Aside – here comes the king,
The queen, the courtiers.

Enter CLAUDIUS, GERTRUDE, LAERTES, *and a coffin,* [*with* PRIEST]
and LORDS *attendant*

                        Who is this they follow? 185
And with such maimèd rites? This doth betoken
The corse they follow did with desperate hand
Fordo it own life. 'Twas of some estate.
Couch we awhile and mark.   [*Retiring with Horatio*]

LAERTES What ceremony else? 190

HAMLET That is Laertes, a very noble youth. Mark.

LAERTES What ceremony else?

PRIEST Her obsequies have been as far enlarged
As we have warranty. Her death was doubtful,
And but that great command o'ersways the order, 195
She should in ground unsanctified have lodged
Till the last trumpet. For charitable prayers,
Shards, flints, and pebbles should be thrown on her.
Yet here she is allowed her virgin crants,
Her maiden strewments, and the bringing home 200
Of bell and burial.

LAERTES Must there no more be done?

PRIEST   No more be done.
We should profane the service of the dead
To sing sage requiem and such rest to her
As to peace-parted souls.

LAERTES   Lay her i'th'earth, 205
And from her fair and unpolluted flesh
May violets spring. I tell thee, churlish priest,
A ministering angel shall my sister be
When thou liest howling.

HAMLET   What, the fair Ophelia!

GERTRUDE Sweets to the sweet, farewell.   [*Scattering flowers*] 210

---

184 With Irving 'Ophelia is buried at nightfall, first because that used to be the custom in the
case of suicide, and secondly because of Hamlet's allusion to the "wandering stars"'
(*Theatre*, 1 February 1879, p. 48).

185SD Q2 reads 'corse' rather than 'coffin' as in Q1 and F, suggesting differing stagings.

186b–8a In the Olivier film these lines are given to Norman Wooland as Horatio, who realizes with
horror that the funeral must be for Ophelia.

195 In the Branagh film, the priest (Michael Bryant) glances towards the King.

I hoped thou shouldst have been my Hamlet's wife.
I thought thy bride-bed to have decked, sweet maid,
And not t'have strewed thy grave.
LAERTES   Oh treble woe
Fall ten times treble on that cursèd head
Whose wicked deed thy most ingenious sense   215
Deprived thee of. Hold off the earth awhile
Till I have caught her once more in mine arms.
                    Leaps in the grave
Now pile your dust upon the quick and dead
Till of this flat a mountain you have made
T'o'ertop old Pelion or the skyish head   220
Of blue Olympus.
HAMLET [*Advancing*]   What is he whose grief
Bears such an emphasis? whose phrase of sorrow
Conjures the wandering stars, and makes them stand
Like wonder-wounded hearers? This is I,
Hamlet the Dane.
                [Laertes climbs out of the grave]
LAERTES   The devil take thy soul. [*Grappling with him*]   225·
HAMLET Thou pray'st not well.
            I prithee take thy fingers from my throat,
            For though I am not splenitive and rash,
            Yet have I in me something dangerous
            Which let thy wisdom fear. Hold off thy hand.   230
CLAUDIUS Pluck them asunder.
GERTRUDE   Hamlet, Hamlet!
ALL   Gentlemen!
HORATIO Good my lord, be quiet.
                [The Attendants part them].
HAMLET Why, I will fight with him upon this theme
            Until my eyelids will no longer wag.
GERTRUDE O my son, what theme?   235
HAMLET I loved Ophelia; forty thousand brothers
            Could not with all their quantity of love
            Make up my sum. What wilt thou do for her?
CLAUDIUS Oh he is mad Laertes.
GERTRUDE For love of God forbear him.   240

224b–5a Q1SD: 'Hamlet leaps in [the grave] after Leartes'. Kingsley spoke 'not as rant but as quiet
         assertion' (*Observer*, 8 February 1976).

236–8   With Irving less than usual is made of the struggle with Laertes and far more of the
         confession, 'I loved Ophelia', as Hamlet 'throws himself into his mother's arms' (*Daily
         Chronicle*, 31 December 1878, p. 6).

HAMLET 'Swounds, show me what thou't do.
Woo't weep, woo't fight, woo't fast, woo't tear thyself?
Woo't drink up eisel, eat a crocodile?
I'll do't. Dost thou come here to whine,
To outface me with leaping in her grave? 245
Be buried quick with her, and so will I.
And if thou prate of mountains, let them throw
Millions of acres on us, till our ground,
Singeing his pate against the burning zone,
Make Ossa like a wart. Nay, and thou'lt mouth, 250
I'll rant as well as thou.
GERTRUDE   This is mere madness,
And thus awhile the fit will work on him;
Anon, as patient as the female dove
When that her golden couplets are disclosed,
His silence will sit drooping.
HAMLET   Hear you sir, 255
What is the reason that you use me thus?
I loved you ever – but it is no matter.
Let Hercules himself do what he may,
The cat will mew, and dog will have his day.   *Exit*
CLAUDIUS I pray thee good Horatio wait upon him. 260
                                        Exit Horatio
(*To Laertes*) Strengthen your patience in our last night's
          speech;
We'll put the matter to the present push. –
Good Gertrude, set some watch over your son. –
This grave shall have a living monument.
An hour of quiet shortly shall we see, 265
Till then in patience our proceeding be.
                                        Exeunt

251   Barrymore spoke with 'an aspirate tone, hoarse, broken with grief and with the
       consciousness of his words' excess' (*New Republic*, 6 December 1922, p. 46).
251b–5a   As here Q2 assigns the speech to the Queen while F assigns it to the King, as does Q1 in
       briefer form. Spoken by the Queen, the lines straightforwardly express maternal solicitude
       (cf. 5.2.180–1, also unique to Q2). Spoken by the King, they reveal him both interceding to
       calm his accomplice Laertes and, hypocritically, making a show of concern for the Prince. As
       at 4.7.36, 161–2, Cladius in F at this point seems very much in charge.
259   Wilson Knight: '"Cat" is spoken to Laertes, his grief a mewing only; "dog" as Hamlet passes
       opposite and pauses in front of the King' (*Production*, p. 117).
259b   Barrymore 'stands looking down into grave – his lips move vaguely – he seems dazed – after
       about 5 seconds he turns slowly – goes out Right quietly – all look after him. Silence for
       about 3 sec' (promptbook 156).

ACT 5, SCENE 2

[5.2] *Enter* HAMLET *and* HORATIO

HAMLET So much for this sir, now shall you see the other.
    You do remember all the circumstance?
HORATIO Remember it my lord!
HAMLET Sir, in my heart there was a kind of fighting
    That would not let me sleep. Methought I lay   5
    Worse than the mutines in the bilboes. Rashly,
    And praised be rashness for it – let us know,
    Our indiscretion sometime serves us well
    When our deep plots do pall, and that should learn us
    There's a divinity that shapes our ends,   10
    Rough-hew them how we will –
HORATIO   That is most certain.
HAMLET Up from my cabin,
    My sea-gown scarfed about me, in the dark
    Groped I to find out them, had my desire,
    Fingered their packet, and in fine withdrew   15
    To mine own room again, making so bold,
    My fears forgetting manners, to unseal
    Their grand commission; where I found, Horatio –
    O royal knavery! – an exact command,
    Larded with many several sorts of reasons,   20
    Importing Denmark's health, and England's too,
    With ho! such bugs and goblins in my life,
    That on the supervise, no leisure bated,
    No, not to stay the grinding of the axe,
    My head should be struck off.
HORATIO   Is't possible?   25
HAMLET Here's the commission, read it at more leisure.
    But wilt thou hear now how I did proceed?
HORATIO I beseech you.
HAMLET Being thus benetted round with villainies,
    Or I could make a prologue to my brains,   30

They had begun the play. I sat me down,
Devised a new commission, wrote it fair.
I once did hold it, as our statists do,
A baseness to write fair, and laboured much
How to forget that learning; but sir, now   35
It did me yeoman's service. Wilt thou know
Th'effect of what I wrote?
HORATIO   Ay good my lord.
HAMLET An earnest conjuration from the king,
  As England was his faithful tributary,
  As love between them like the palm might flourish,   40
  As peace should still her wheaten garland wear,
  And stand a comma 'tween their amities,
  And many suchlike as-es of great charge,
  That on the view and knowing of these contents,
  Without debatement further, more, or less,   45
  He should those bearers put to sudden death,
  Not shriving time allowed.
HORATIO   How was this sealed?
HAMLET Why, even in that was heaven ordinant.
  I had my father's signet in my purse,
  Which was the model of that Danish seal;   50
  Folded the writ up in the form of th'other,
  Subscribed it, gave't th'impression, placed it safely,
  The changeling never known. Now, the next day
  Was our sea-fight, and what to this was sequent
  Thou know'st already.   55
HORATIO So Guildenstern and Rosencrantz go to't.
HAMLET Why man, they did make love to this employment.
  They are not near my conscience. Their defeat
  Does by their own insinuation grow.
  'Tis dangerous when the baser nature comes   60

56 In the Branagh film Nicholas Farrell made this a question, implicitly challenging the severity
 of Hamlet's retaliation.
57 This line appears only in the F. Kerrigan finds a defensiveness in the Folio Hamlet here and
 in 68–70, also unique to F. He links these passages with earlier Folio-unique indications that
 make it questionable whether Rosencrantz and Guildenstern were as knowingly complicit in
 the King's plot as Hamlet alleges ('Reviser', pp. 259–60). Pennington remarks that he
 sometimes spoke this line and the next 'with some self-doubt' (*Hamlet*, p. 140). Kingsley said
 them 'with that guarded look and slight overemphasis that imply that some sense of guilt is
 indeed present' (David, *Theatre*, p. 73).

Between the pass and fell incensèd points
Of mighty opposites.
HORATIO   Why, what a king is this!
HAMLET Does it not, think thee, stand me now upon –
He that hath killed my king, and whored my mother,
Popped in between th'election and my hopes,   65
Thrown out his angle for my proper life,
And with such cozenage – is't not perfect conscience
To quit him with this arm? And is't not to be damned
To let this canker of our nature come
In further evil?   70
HORATIO It must be shortly known to him from England
What is the issue of the business there.
HAMLET It will be short. The interim's mine,
And a man's life's no more than to say 'one'.
But I am very sorry, good Horatio,   75
That to Laertes I forgot myself,
For by the image of my cause, I see
The portraiture of his. I'll court his favours.
But sure the bravery of his grief did put me
Into a towering passion.
HORATIO   Peace, who comes here?   80

Enter young OSRIC

OSRIC Your lordship is right welcome back to Denmark.
HAMLET I humbly thank you sir. – Dost know this water-fly?
HORATIO No my good lord.

68–80   Only in F. Lines 71–4 make explicit the pressure of time and prepare for the impression that
the Prince is dawdling dangerously with Osric. One of the functions of Q2's inclusion of
100–125 (not in F) may be to imply this impression.

71–4   In the Branagh film, Horatio at 71–2 evades giving Hamlet the reassurance he seeks, changes
the subject (*Screenplay*, p. 156).

74   In 1964 Burton snapped his fingers before 'one'.

81SD   Q1: 'Enter a Bragart Gentleman'; Q2: 'Enter a Courtier'; F: 'Enter young Osricke'. These
designations may well reflect differing interpretive emphases.

81ff   With Forbes-Robertson, John Martin Harvey was praised by Shaw because 'he plays Osric
from Osric's own point of view, which is, that Osric is a gallant and distinguished courtier,
and not, as usual, from Hamlet's, which is that Osric is "a waterfly"' (*Shakespeare*, p. 90).
When Alec Guinness first played Osric, to Gielgud in 1934, he was by his own description
'very water-fly' (*Blessings*, p. 69), but with Olivier he was 'an admirable popinjay and wisely
not effeminate' (*Observer*, 10 January 1937). Beneath his 'pretentious elegance' was 'a

HAMLET Thy state is the more gracious, for 'tis a vice to know him.
He hath much land and fertile; let a beast be lord of beasts, and   85
his crib shall stand at the king's mess. 'Tis a chough, but as I say,
spacious in the possession of dirt.

OSRIC Sweet lord, if your lordship were at leisure, I should impart a
thing to you from his majesty.

HAMLET I will receive it sir with all diligence of spirit. Put your bonnet   90
to his right use, 'tis for the head.

OSRIC I thank your lordship, it is very hot.

HAMLET No believe me, 'tis very cold, the wind is northerly.

OSRIC It is indifferent cold my lord, indeed.

HAMLET But yet methinks it is very sultry and hot for my complexion.   95

OSRIC Exceedingly my lord, it is very sultry, as 'twere – I cannot tell
how. But my lord, his majesty bade me signify to you that a has
laid a great wager on your head. Sir, this is the matter –

HAMLET I beseech you remember.

[Hamlet moves him to put on his hat]

OSRIC Nay good my lord, for my ease in good faith. Sir, [here is newly   100
come to court Laertes; believe me an absolute gentleman, full of
most excellent differences, of very soft society and great showing.
Indeed, to speak feelingly of him, he is the card or calendar of
gentry, for you shall find in him the continent of what part a
gentleman would see.   105

HAMLET Sir, his definement suffers no perdition in you, though I know
to divide him inventorially would dozy th'arithmetic of memory,
and yet but yaw neither in respect of his quick sail. But in the verity
of extolment, I take him to be a soul of great article, and his infusion
of such dearth and rareness as, to make true diction of him, his   110
semblable is his mirror, and who else would trace him, his umbrage,
nothing more.

pathetic insecurity' (Guthrie, *Shakespeare*, p. 288) and 'the hint of a courtier's craft'
(Williamson, *Old Vic*, p. 85). Directing Burton, Gielgud 'conceived of Osric as a spy sent by
the King, and . . . his affected manner was only assumed as a trick' (Sterne, p. 49).

96   In his studybook, Booth advised Osric to emphasize *I*: 'It is whatever your lordship would
have it – as *you* say it is, *I* cannot tell how'.

100–25,   Not in F.
127–30

100   In the Gielgud/Burton production Osric 'almost lets his anger show' in his protest, which he
follows with a 'covering laugh' (Sterne, p. 271).

101   Booth: 'At the mention of Laertes, Hamlet suspects some danger is brewing'. At 119 he asks
about Laertes 'slowly and impressively and with a searching gaze of Osrick' (studybook).

106–12   On BBC-TV Jacobi mocked Osric's affectedly French pronunciation of 'continent' (104) by
Frenchifying perdition, infusion, diction, semblable, umbrage.

OSRIC Your lordship speaks most infallibly of him.

HAMLET The concernancy, sir? Why do we wrap the gentleman in our
more rawer breath? 115

OSRIC Sir?

HORATIO Is't not possible to understand in another tongue? You will
to't sir, really.

HAMLET What imports the nomination of this gentleman?

OSRIC Of Laertes? 120

HORATIO His purse is empty already, all's golden words are spent.

HAMLET Of him sir.

OSRIC I know you are not ignorant –

HAMLET I would you did sir, yet in faith if you did, it would not much
approve me. Well sir?] 125

OSRIC You are not ignorant of what excellence Laertes is.

[HAMLET I dare not confess that, lest I should compare with him in
excellence, but to know a man well were to know himself.

OSRIC I mean sir for his weapon; but in the imputation laid on him
by them, in his meed he's unfellowed.] 130

HAMLET What's his weapon?

OSRIC Rapier and dagger.

HAMLET That's two of his weapons, but well.

OSRIC The king sir hath wagered with him six Barbary horses, against
the which he has impawned, as I take it, six French rapiers and 135
poniards, with their assigns, as girdle, hangers, and so. Three of
the carriages in faith are very dear to fancy, very responsive to the
hilts, most delicate carriages, and of very liberal conceit.

HAMLET What call you the carriages?

HORATIO I knew you must be edified by the margent ere you had done. 140

OSRIC The carriages sir are the hangers.

HAMLET The phrase would be more germane to the matter if we could
carry a cannon by our sides; I would it might be hangers till then.
But on, six Barbary horses against six French swords, their assigns,
and three liberal-conceited carriages – that's the French bet against 145
the Danish. Why is this impawned, as you call it?

OSRIC The king sir, hath laid sir, that in a dozen passes between yourself
and him, he shall not exceed you three hits. He hath laid on twelve
for nine. And it would come to immediate trial, if your lordship
would vouchsafe the answer. 150

HAMLET How if I answer no?

OSRIC I mean my lord, the opposition of your person in trial.

137–8 In the Branagh film Robin Williams's beaming Osric Frenchifies 'carr-i-ahj', which the Prince
mimics at 139.

HAMLET Sir, I will walk here in the hall. If it please his majesty, it is
the breathing time of day with me. Let the foils be brought, the
gentleman willing, and the king hold his purpose, I will win for   155
him and I can. If not, I will gain nothing but my shame and the
odd hits.
OSRIC Shall I redeliver you e'en so?
HAMLET To this effect sir, after what flourish your nature will.
OSRIC I commend my duty to your lordship.   160
HAMLET Yours, yours.

                                                    [*Exit Osric*]

He does well to commend it himself, there are no tongues else for's
turn.

151–60 David William, Osric under Nevill Coghill's direction, paraphrases the subtext of this
        passage:

        Hamlet: 'Suppose I say no.' (Brief pause. Osric's mind adjusts swiftly to the disastrous
        consequences – for the King – of this contingency. How best to avoid it. He resolves
        partly to misunderstand what Hamlet has said; to make it clear that all that is being
        canvassed is a courtly occasion, one that a man in Hamlet's position cannot refuse
        without apparent offence being given to all concerned.)
               Osric: (Very charmingly) 'I don't think I can have made myself quite clear, my
        lord. The whole wager depends absolutely on your own participation, in person.'
        (Hamlet now realises to whom he has been talking. He gazes at the elegant preposterous
        figure and sees beyond the smile and the silks and the plumes and the address – one
        more piece of rottenness in the state of Denmark. To refuse the invitation at that moment
        might be to accept membership of that state. However, what does it matter? The
        readiness is all. He decides to accept.) Osric triumphant. That sense of triumph barely
        concealed in the uncharacteristic brevity of 'Shall I redeliver you e'en so?' – hastily
        amended to the final flourish of 'I commend my duty to your lordship.' And then he
        leaves, mission accomplished.   (William, 'Osric', p. 88).

150–2   Only here does Osric (Peter Cushing) in the Olivier film become direct and insistent. Played
        as a fop, he had earlier been obliged to pursue Hamlet and Horatio as they walked away
        from him. In the Gielgud/Burton production he delivers 152 'with a menacing undertone'
        (Sterne, p. 271).

153   Gielgud, whose manner since the voyage has shown 'an inner fatalistic calm', 'glances at
        Horatio who moves toward him as though to protest. But Hamlet stops him before he
        speaks. There is a long pause while Hamlet looks with prescient vision into the future. Then
        with a gesture of acceptance he turns to Osric' (Gilder, p. 223).

161SD   In Olivier's film Osric tumbled down the stairs amid bows and flourishes before scurrying
        off.

HORATIO This lapwing runs away with the shell on his head.

HAMLET A did comply with his dug before a sucked it. Thus has he, 165
and many more of the same bevy that I know the drossy age dotes
on, only got the tune of the time and outward habit of encounter,
a kind of yesty collection, which carries them through and through
the most fanned and winnowed opinions; and do but blow them
to their trial, the bubbles are out. 170

[Enter a LORD

LORD My lord, his majesty commended him to you by young Osric,
who brings back to him that you attend him in the hall. He sends
to know if your pleasure hold to play with Laertes, or that you will
take longer time.

HAMLET I am constant to my purposes, they follow the king's pleasure. 175
If his fitness speaks, mine is ready; now or whensoever, provided
I be so able as now.

LORD The king and queen, and all, are coming down.

HAMLET In happy time.

LORD The queen desires you to use some gentle entertainment to 180
Laertes, before you fall to play.

HAMLET She well instructs me.]

[Exit Lord]

HORATIO You will lose, my lord.

HAMLET I do not think so. Since he went into France, I have been in
continual practice; I shall win at the odds. But thou wouldst not 185
think how ill all's here about my heart – but it is no matter.

HORATIO Nay good my lord –

HAMLET It is but foolery, but it is such a kind of gaingiving as would
perhaps trouble a woman.

185–6 Urkowitz compares the Q1, Q2, and F versions, finding that all three call for the actor of
Hamlet to move his hand to his heart. In Q2, as in this edition, the gesture is followed by an
immediate demurral from his confession: 'but it is no matter'. The F version goes subtly
further in this demurral; it reads: 'but thou wouldest not think how all here about my heart:
but it is no matter.' Urkowitz sees in the absence of a verb in F 'the presence of an
unarticulated feeling'. It is as if Hamlet had been about to confide 'how all here about my
heart *is ill*' (as in Q2) or *is on the sodaine very sore* (as in Q1) but then left the thought
trailing in mid-sentence before adding 'it is no matter' ('"Well-sayd"', pp. 56–7).

188–9 J. B. Booth sometimes paused slightly after 'perhaps', then continued in a lower tone,
emphasizing *woman*, 'meaning, "it ought not to trouble me, a man, yet I feel it does"'. At
other times he emphasized *trouble* and after a slight pause emphasized *woman*, 'meaning,
"but shall not trouble me"' (Gould, p. 70).

HORATIO If your mind dislike anything, obey it. I will forestall their   190
    repair hither, and say you are not fit.
HAMLET Not a whit, we defy augury. There is special providence in
    the fall of a sparrow. If it be now, 'tis not to come; if it be not to
    come, it will be now; if it be not now, yet it will come – the
    readiness is all. Since no man of aught he leaves knows, what is't   195
    to leave betimes? Let be.
A table prepared, with flagons of wine on it. Trumpets, Drums and Officers
with cushions. Enter CLAUDIUS, GERTRUDE, LAERTES *and* LORDS, *with*
other Attendants with foils, daggers and gauntlets
CLAUDIUS Come Hamlet, come and take this hand from me.
        [*Hamlet takes Laertes by the hand*]

191   On BBC-TV Horatio starts to leave.
192–6 Betterton and Garrick gave only 192a, cutting the rest of this speech. With Booth 'a rare,
       spiritual expression comes over his countenance' (Stone, p. 137). Irving combined this
       passage with 5.2.10–11 (Hughes, *Irving*, p. 72). In his film Olivier substituted the latter
       passage for this one.
           Twentieth-century Hamlets have often focused especially on this passage as a
       philosophical epiphany. Of Gielgud: 'with complete prevision he accepts death . . . His pale
       face seems already suspended in eternity' (Gilder, p. 225). With Paul Scofield there was less
       acceptance: 'Pale, haggard, and sleepless, this Hamlet takes a glum view of his destiny; even
       when he declares at the end "The readiness is all" he acknowledges no reconciliation to his
       fate; it is plain that his view that life has led him up a remarkably unweeded garden path
       remains unshaken' (*Sunday Times*, 11 December 1955).
           Harold Hobson contrasted Redgrave, who as a 'spiritual triumph' 'completely accepted
       his fate' with David Warner's 'Hamlet of young despair', speaking 'not, like Redgrave, with
       happiness at the last, but with a sad and hopeless smile; then he turns on his heel and walks
       firmly off the stage, a man without comfort and without hope, going to execution' (*Sydney
       Morning Herald*, 28 May 1966). For Branagh this 'whole speech is an affirmation of life. By
       embracing death Hamlet can get on with living' (*Shakespeare Bulletin*, Fall 1994, p. 7). A
       reviewer celebrated the 'spell-binding moment' when Branagh's 'weary fatalism gives way
       to a spiritual illumination that seems to light up his whole being' (*Daily Telegraph*, 21
       December 1992).
193–4 Branagh emphasized *now* each time (*Shakespeare Bulletin*, Fall, 1994, p. 7).
197SD Q2 reads 'A table prepard, Trumpets, Drums, and officers with Cushions, King, Queene, and
       all the state, Foiles, daggers, and Laertes'; F reads 'Enter King, Queene, Laertes and Lords,
       with other Attendants with Foyles, and Gauntlets, a Table and Flagons of Wine on it'. The
       differences in specified equipment (daggers/gauntlets) may reflect different fencing styles.
       Other differences in detail may reflect different stagings: Q2 suggests preparatory activities
       before the royal party enters.

HAMLET Give me your pardon sir, I've done you wrong;
But pardon't as you are a gentleman.
This presence knows, 200
And you must needs have heard, how I am punished
With a sore distraction. What I have done,
That might your nature, honour and exception
Roughly awake, I here proclaim was madness.
Was't Hamlet wronged Laertes? Never Hamlet. 205
If Hamlet from himself be tane away,
And when he's not himself does wrong Laertes,
Then Hamlet does it not, Hamlet denies it.
Who does it then? His madness. If't be so,
Hamlet is of the faction that is wronged, 210
His madness is poor Hamlet's enemy.
Sir, in this audience,
Let my disclaiming from a purposed evil
Free me so far in your most generous thoughts,
That I have shot my arrow o'er the house 215
And hurt my brother.
LAERTES   I am satisfied in nature,
Whose motive in this case should stir me most
To my revenge; but in my terms of honour
I stand aloof, and will no reconcilement
Till by some elder masters of known honour 220
I have a voice and precedent of peace
To keep my name ungored. But till that time
I do receive your offered love like love,
And will not wrong it.
HAMLET   I embrace it freely,
And will this brother's wager frankly play. 225
Give us the foils, come on.
LAERTES   Come, one for me.
HAMLET I'll be your foil Laertes. In mine ignorance
Your skill shall like a star i'th'darkest night
Stick fiery off indeed.
LAERTES   You mock me sir.
HAMLET No, by this hand. 230
CLAUDIUS Give them the foils, young Osric. Cousin Hamlet,
You know the wager?
HAMLET   Very well my lord.
Your grace has laid the odds a'th'weaker side.
CLAUDIUS I do not fear it, I have seen you both.
But since he is bettered, we have therefore odds. 235
LAERTES This is too heavy, let me see another.

HAMLET This likes me well. These foils have all a length?
OSRIC Ay my good lord.
                              Prepare to play
CLAUDIUS Set me the stoups of wine upon that table.
          If Hamlet give the first or second hit,   240
          Or quit in answer of the third exchange,
          Let all the battlements their ordnance fire.
          The king shall drink to Hamlet's better breath,
          And in the cup an union shall he throw
          Richer than that which four successive kings   245
          In Denmark's crown have worn. Give me the cups,
          And let the kettle to the trumpet speak,
          The trumpet to the cannoneer without,
          The cannons to the heavens, the heaven to earth,
          'Now the king drinks to Hamlet!' Come, begin,   250
          And you the judges bear a wary eye.
                              Trumpets the while
HAMLET Come on sir.
LAERTES Come my lord.
                              They play
HAMLET One.
LAERTES No.   255
HAMLET Judgement.
OSRIC A hit, a very palpable hit.
LAERTES Well, again.
CLAUDIUS Stay, give me drink. Hamlet, this pearl is thine.
          Here's to thy health.
                  Drum, trumpets sound, and shot goes off
                              Give him the cup.   260
HAMLET I'll play this bout first, set it by awhile.
          Come.
                              [*They play*]
                  Another hit. What say you?
LAERTES A touch, a touch, I do confess't.

---

257   Evans: 'The court applauds' (*G. I. Hamlet*, p.180).

260SD To Wilson Knight, who played Hamlet in 1933 and 1935, the 'ominous' cannon shot 'serves to
       make the Prince wary of taking the drink' (Knight, *Production*, pp. 118–19). Edwards's
       placement of the stage direction in this edition encourages such a reading, as does F which
       places the direction after 'Give him the cup'. Q2 puts the direction in the margin opposite
       257–8, presumably celebrating Hamlet's first 'hit', as the King had directed (240–2).

263–74 Evans divided the focus here between Claudius/Laertes and Hamlet/Gertrude, with the
       timing of their exchanges interworked (*G. I. Hamlet*, pp. 181–2).

CLAUDIUS Our son shall win.
GERTRUDE   He's fat and scant of breath.
          Here Hamlet, take my napkin, rub thy brows.   265
          The queen carouses to thy fortune, Hamlet.
HAMLET Good madam.
CLAUDIUS Gertrude, do not drink!
GERTRUDE I will my lord, I pray you pardon me.
                              [Drinks]
CLAUDIUS *[Aside]* It is the poisoned cup. It is too late.   270
HAMLET I dare not drink yet madam, by and by.
GERTRUDE Come, let me wipe thy face.
LAERTES My lord, I'll hit him now.
CLAUDIUS   I do not think't.
LAERTES And yet it is almost against my conscience.
HAMLET Come, for the third, Laertes. You do but dally.   275
          I pray you pass with your best violence.
          I am afeard you make a wanton of me.
LAERTES Say you so? Come on.
                              Play
OSRIC Nothing neither way.
LAERTES Have at you now!   *[Wounds Hamlet]*   280
          In scuffling they change rapiers

266 Jane Lapotaire with Branagh in 1992/3 had developed a drinking problem (*Cahiers Elisabethains*, October 1993, p. 74).

268 Brian Murray, with Kevin Kline, made a real attempt to stop the Queen: 'Do … (long pause) … do not drink'.

269 In the Branagh film the Queen (Julie Christie) delivers this line as a declaration of independence from the King: 'she is her own woman now. And for a moment, all too brief, she and her son are happy' (*Screenplay*, p. 166).

273 With Barrymore, Laertes emphasized 'him' (*John Barrymore Reads Shakespeare*, Audio Rarities 2281, II).

279 Warner/Hall: 'During the fight, when he gets a graze on his hand by accident, he holds his arm away and stares at it as though it were already as unrecognisable as Yorick's skull … attending whey-faced to an idea that had never struck him before – the prospect, not of dying, but of being dead' (*Observer*, 22 August 1965).

280SD Edwards follows F. Q1 reads 'They catch one anothers Rapiers, and both are wounded'. Q2 has no SD.
        Salvini appears to have introduced to English and American audiences the business whereby Hamlet deliberately takes Laertes's weapon and gallantly gives him his own (*Daily News*, 1 June 1875). (In *Shakespearians*, p. 90, Carlson traces the business to Dumas' Theatre Historique production in 1848.) Rossi (Phelps, p. 161) and Irving (*Saturday Review*, 7

CLAUDIUS Part them. They are incensed.
HAMLET Nay, come again.   [*Wounds Laertes*]
                        [*Gertrude falls*]
OSRIC Look to the queen there, ho!
HORATIO They bleed on both sides. How is it my lord?
OSRIC How is't Laertes?   285
LAERTES Why, as a woodcock to mine own springe, Osric.
           I am justly killed with mine own treachery.
HAMLET How does the queen?
CLAUDIUS   She sounds to see them bleed.
GERTRUDE No, no, the drink, the drink – O my dear Hamlet –
           The drink, the drink – I am poisoned.   [*Dies*]   290
HAMLET Oh villainy! – Ho, let the door be locked!
           Treachery! Seek it out!
                        [*Laertes falls*]
LAERTES It is here Hamlet. Hamlet, thou art slain,
           No medicine in the world can do thee good,
           In thee there is not half an hour of life –   295
           The treacherous instrument is in thy hand,
           Unbated and envenomed. The foul practice
           Hath turned itself on me; lo, here I lie,
           Never to rise again. Thy mother's poisoned –
           I can no more – the king, the king's to blame.   300
HAMLET The point envenomed too! Then, venom, to thy work!
                        Hurts the king

November 1874, p. 604) both followed suit in the belief that Hamlet was not aware at this
point of Laertes's treachery. With Tree, however, who sees 'treachery in the face of Laertes',
the change of foils 'is done with ironic, not natural, courtesy' (*Daily Telegraph*, 22 January
1892). Of Barrymore: 'With maniacal energy Hamlet beat the foil from Laertes' hand'
(Grebanier, *Actor*, pp. 243–4). In the Olivier film there is a long pause while Hamlet shows
Horatio the sharpness of Laertes's weapon. Burton 'very quietly and with no struggle' simply
walked up to Laertes and took the weapon from him deliberately (Sterne, p. 52).

282 Booth knocks Laertes's foil from his grasp and, with his left hand, catches it and stabs
     Laertes with it, as if it were a dagger (Furness, *Variorum*, II, p. 258); he then retains both foils
     until he drops his own at 301 and uses the poisoned weapon to kill the King (Shattuck, pp.
     277–8).

289–90 In the Zeffirelli film, Glenn Close here realized with horror the full extent of Claudius's guilt.

290b Gertrude is led off, the courtiers all draw their swords (Macready promptbook 40).

301a Williamson emphasized *too* – 'as if appalled at the limitlessness of treachery' (*Guardian*, 2
      November 1994).

ALL Treason, treason!

CLAUDIUS Oh yet defend me friends, I am but hurt.

HAMLET Here, thou incestuous, murderous, damnèd Dane,
     Drink off this potion. Is thy union here?   305
     Follow my mother.   *King dies*

LAERTES   He is justly served,
     It is a poison tempered by himself.
     Exchange forgiveness with me, noble Hamlet.
     Mine and my father's death come not upon thee,
     Nor thine on me.   *Dies* 310

HAMLET Heaven make thee free of it! I follow thee.
     I am dead, Horatio. Wretched queen adieu.
     You that look pale, and tremble at this chance,
     That are but mutes or audience to this act,
     Had I but time, as this fell sergeant death   315
     Is strict in his arrest, oh I could tell you –
     But let it be. Horatio, I am dead,
     Thou livest; report me and my cause aright
     To the unsatisfied.

HORATIO   Never believe it.
     I am more an antique Roman than a Dane.   320
     Here's yet some liquor left.

HAMLET   As th'art a man,
     Give me the cup. Let go, by heaven I'll ha't.

302 With Macready 'the King draws his sword and endeavours to parry Hamlet's blow. He descends steps of throne, is disarmed and killed on the steps by Hamlet' (promptbook). Booth fights through the courtiers and guards and twice plunges Laertes's poisoned foil through the King's neck (Shattuck, p. 278). Irving flung the King 'down backwards to the earth like a carrion' (Russell, p. 52; *Saturday Review*, 7 November 1874, pp. 604–5).

   Guthrie at Minneapolis directed the court to act as a choric projection of the King's responses. As he moves upstage away from Hamlet so does the court. When he is stabbed, 'the court has a great shocked intake of breath'; when he groans, the court makes a keening sound, each member acting as though stabbed – 'the death of the corporate state' (Rossi, p. 60). Playing opposite Stacy Keach, powerful James Earl Jones 'opened his arms as if to crush Hamlet in a huge embrace' (Rocklin, 'Hamlet').

305a Warner 'in a slow motion pours a giant goblet of poisoned wine over the prostrate body of the King' (*Shakespeare Survey*, 19, 1966, p. 118). Anton Lesser/Jonathan Miller: John Shrapnel as Claudius, accepting his guilt, 'voluntarily swigs the dregs of the poisoned cup' (*New Statesman*, 27 August 1982).

311 Pryce/Eyre: Hamlet's repeated 'I am dead' lines were 'full of disbelief – as if he can't quite believe that this has happened to him' (Gilbert, 'Pryce').

O God, Horatio, what a wounded name,
Things standing thus unknown, shall live behind me!
If thou didst ever hold me in thy heart,   325
Absent thee from felicity awhile,
And in this harsh world draw thy breath in pain
To tell my story.
               March afar off, and shot within
               What warlike noise is this?
OSRIC Young Fortinbras, with conquest come from Poland,
    To the ambassadors of England gives   330
    This warlike volley.
HAMLET   Oh I die, Horatio,
The potent poison quite o'ercrows my spirit.
I cannot live to hear the news from England.
But I do prophesy th'election lights
On Fortinbras; he has my dying voice.   335
So tell him, with th'occurrents more and less
Which have solicited – the rest is silence.   *Dies*

326   J. B. Booth lifted his hand to heaven, indicating the 'felicity' to which he felt Horatio would
    go (Gould, p. 71). Barrymore broke his dying lines to short breaths: 'Absent thee . . . from
    felicity awhile . . . and in this harsh world . . . draw breath in pain . . . to tell my story . . . the
    rest . . . is silence' (*John Barrymore Reads Shakespeare*, Audio Rarities 2281, II).

334–7   Pryce stands facing the audience and falls forward to die. Everything about that last moment
    recalls 'his encounter with the invisible Ghost to whom he has now kept his bargain'
    (Gilbert, 'Pryce').

337   F adds: 'O, o, o, o. Dyes.' About Kean's death throes Leigh Hunt is almost clinical:

> Intense internal pain, wandering vision, swelling veins in the temple . . . his eye dilates
> and then loses lustre; he gnaws his hand in the vain effort to repress emotion; the veins
> thicken in his forehead; his limbs shudder and quiver, and as life grows fainter, and his
> hand drops from between his stiffening lips, he utters a cry of expiring nature, so
> exquisite that I can only compare it to the stifled sob of a fainting woman.
>
>   (Hunt, *Essays*, p. 230)

    Far from Kean's violent death throes, Forbes-Robertson's 'pallor is deathlike' as he
'totters feebly to the empty throne' (Scott, *Hamlets*, p. 132). In the silent film he is helped by
Horatio and an attendant. Early in his final speech he takes up the royal sceptre and towards
the end, with his raised arms and 'startled eyes, and then the smile that is beyond earthly
things' (Kate Gielgud, *Playgoer*, p. 63), he seems divinely inspired in a way that recalled, to a
contemporary observer, his 'expression of beatific recognition' at 'Methinks I see my father'.
'With a quiet, exhausted voice he gives the final line, "The rest is silence," then the hands
relax and fall to the side, and the face becomes composed and fixed' (*Stage*, 16 September

HORATIO Now cracks a noble heart. Good night sweet prince,
 And flights of angels sing thee to thy rest. –
 Why does the drum come hither? 340

Enter FORTINBRAS *and* ENGLISH AMBASSADORS, *with drum, colours and Attendants*

FORTINBRAS Where is this sight?
HORATIO What is it you would see?
 If aught of woe or wonder, cease your search.

1897). With 'the prince dead upon the throne he never filled', Scott observes, 'Horatio places the crown upon his dead companion's knees' (p. 133) 'between Hamlet's lifeless hands' (*Evening Standard*, 13 September 1897). The *Daily Chronicle* concludes: 'The final spectacle at the Lyceum is very imposing, the dead Prince being carried from the scene on the soldiers' shields, whilst a solemn march is played' (13 September 1897).

337SD Martin-Harvey 'goes to the length of embracing his mother and dying on her body at the end' (*Stage*, 25 May 1905, p. 14). Wilson Knight blocked the finale to suggest that 'Hamlet is now King; but king only among the dead. He rises over the group of corpses. The place next in honour is held by the King himself, central, on the steps. This position preserves a correct balance, and prevents Hamlet's new ascendancy being too dominant: to the last we must preserve our see-saw indecisiveness' (Knight, *Production*, pp. 120–1).

338–40 Q2 reads 'cracks . . . rest.' Holderness and Loughrey see F's 'Now cracke a Noble hart' as 'a violent vocative, directly addressed to the dying prince meaning: "Now break, noble heart!"' They see F's comma after 'rest' rather than a period as suggesting 'an *interrupted* elegy', broken off by Fortinbras's arrival ('Text', p. 184).

340SD In the eighteenth and nineteenth century Fortinbras was customarily omitted. William Poel: 'The introduction of Fortinbras at the end is essential. The distant sound of drums, the tramp of soldiers, the gradual filling of the stage with them, the shouts of the crowd outside and the entrance of Fortinbras are materials for a fine stage picture, a strong dramatic contrast. Life in the midst of death' (Speaight, *Poel*, p. 52). In Georges Pitoeff's 1926 production, Fortinbras and his soldiers were dressed in white, symbolizing, he explained, the beauty of all life towards which black-clad Hamlet had struggled and his release through death from a frightening and crushing world: 'the play ends in triumph, not in torturing anguish' (quoted in R. Davril, 'Pitoeff', pp. 194–5). To Wilson Knight, Fortinbras 'should be young, fair, and have a rich voice, wearing a Viking helmet, Mercurially winged, and fine armour': he is 'strong-armed, with the material strength of Claudius and the spiritual strength of Hamlet, a white light on him, the new hope for Denmark' (*Production*, pp. 120–1).

341 In Kingsley/Goodbody: Conscience is 'quite irrelevant to the personal ethics of Charles Dance's menacing young Fortinbras . . . in the battle-dress of an elite officer, smiling as he caresses the poisoned, blood-stained sword which has betrayed both opportunism and idealism' (*Observer*, 6 January 1975).

FORTINBRAS This quarry cries on havoc. O proud death,
        What feast is toward in thine eternal cell
        That thou so many princes at a shot   345
        So bloodily hast struck?
I AMBASSADOR   The sight is dismal,
        And our affairs from England come too late.
        The ears are senseless that should give us hearing,
        To tell him his commandment is fulfilled,
        That Rosencrantz and Guildenstern are dead.   350
        Where should we have our thanks?
HORATIO   Not from his mouth,
        Had it th'ability of life to thank you;
        He never gave commandment for their death.
        But since, so jump upon this bloody question,
        You from the Polack wars, and you from England,   355
        Are here arrived, give order that these bodies
        High on a stage be placèd to the view,
        And let me speak to th'yet unknowing world
        How these things came about. So shall you hear
        Of carnal, bloody, and unnatural acts,   360
        Of accidental judgements, casual slaughters,
        Of deaths put on by cunning and forced cause,
        And in this upshot, purposes mistook
        Fallen on th'inventors' heads. All this can I
        Truly deliver.
FORTINBRAS   Let us haste to hear it,   365
        And call the noblest to the audience.
        For me, with sorrow I embrace my fortune.
        I have some rights of memory in this kingdom,
        Which now to claim my vantage doth invite me.
HORATIO Of that I shall have also cause to speak,   370
        And from his mouth whose voice will draw on more.
        But let this same be presently performed,
        Even while men's minds are wild, lest more mischance
        On plots and errors happen.
FORTINBRAS   Let four captains
        Bear Hamlet like a soldier to the stage,   375
        For he was likely, had he been put on,
        To have proved most royal; and for his passage,

The soldier's music and the rite of war
Speak loudly for him.
Take up the bodies. Such a sight as this   380
Becomes the field, but here shows much amiss.
Go bid the soldiers shoot.
Exeunt marching, after the which a peal of ordnance are shot off

383SD   Warner/Hall: 'The four captains kneel on either side of the body. Awkwardly they hoist it on
         their shoulders, its arms outflung as if in horizontal crucifixion. As they pick their way
         upstage through heaped bodies, pale courtiers and dumbfounded soldiery, its head lolls
         behind them, staring back sightlessly at the audience. The lights dim, the stage darkens, a
         faint spotlight clings with a halo of luminosity to the receding arched throat and hanging
         head . . . [It] deliberately ends with the image which has closed every *Hamlet* you
         remember, formally conventional as a Byzantine icon. Hamlet has become Hamlet, statue,
         legend, the starry Prince' (*New Statesman*, 27 August 1965, p. 295).

BIBLIOGRAPHY

PROMPTBOOKS, STUDYBOOKS, AND RELATED MATERIAL

Barrett, Lawrence, Promptbook (77), Harvard Theatre Collection.

Barrymore, John, Promptbook (154), Folger Shakespeare Library.

    Promptbook (156), Folger Shakespeare Library.

    Studybook (158), Hampden/Booth Library, Players Club.

Booth, Edwin, Studybook (109), Hampden/Booth Library, Players Club.

    Promptbook (111), Hampden/Booth Library, Players Club.

    Promptbook (112), Billy Rose Theatre Collection at Lincoln Center.

Fechter, Charles, Promptbook (72), Folger Shakespeare Library.

Forrest, Edwin, Promptbook (67), Billy Rose Theatre Collection at Lincoln Center.

Hampden, Walter, Promptbook (not listed in Shattuck), Hampden/Booth Library, Players Club.

Irving, Henry, Promptbook (90), Harvard Theatre Collection.

    Studybook (91), Harvard Theatre Collection.

Macready, William Charles, Promptbook (29), Hampden/Booth Library, Players Club.

    Promptbook (40), Billy Rose Theatre Collection at Lincoln Center.

Marlowe, Julia with Edward Sothern, Promptbook (143), Folger Shakespeare Library.

Mason, E. T., Notes on Helen Modjeska's Ophelia (106), Boston Athenaeum Library.

    Notes on Edwin Booth (110), Boston Athenaeum Library.

Roberts, J. B., Studybook (37), Folger Shakespeare Library.

Terry, Ellen, Rehearsal Book (95), Smallhythe Library.

    Promptbook (97), Folger Shakespeare Library.

Tree, Beerbohm H., Promptbook (121), Theatre Museum Library, Covent Garden.

Full bibliographical accounts of these and other *Hamlet* materials up to 1960 are given in Charles H. Shattuck, *The Shakespeare Promptbooks*, and 'The Shakespeare Promptbooks: first supplement', *Theatre Notebook*, 24, 1969, pp. 5–17. Numbers in parentheses above are from Shattuck's listing.

OTHER WORKS

Agate, James. *Brief Chronicles*, London, 1943.

Alger, William R. *Life of Edwin Forrest*, Philadelphia, vol. I, 1877.

Anonymous. *The Laureate or, the Right Side of Colley Cibber, Esq*, London, 1740.

Aronson, Arnold. 'Postmodern Design', *Theatre Journal*, 43, 1991, 1–13.

Austin, Gilbert. *Chironomia*, London, 1806.

Barber, Frances. 'Ophelia', in *Players of Shakespeare 2*, ed. R. Jackson and R. Smallwood, Cambridge, 1988.

Barnes, J. H. *Forty Years on the Stage*, New York, 1915.

Barrymore, John. *Confessions of an Actor*, Indianapolis, 1926.

Bate, Jonathan. 'The Romantic Stage', in *Shakespeare – An Illustrated History*, ed. J. Bate and R. Jackson, Oxford, 1996.

BBC-TV Hamlet. London, 1980.

Beacham, Richard C. *Adolphe Appia: Theatre Artist*, Cambridge, 1987.

Beckett, Arthur W. A. *Green-Room Recollections*, London, 1896.

Beerbohm, Max. *Around Theatres*, New York, 1930.

   Last Theatres, 1904–10, New York, 1970.

   More Theatres, 1898–1903, New York, 1969.

Boswell, James. *Boswell's London Journal 1762–1763*, ed. F. A. Pottle, New York, 1950.

   Journal of a Tour to the Hebrides, ed. F. Pottle and C. Bennett, New York, 1936.

Bragg, Melvyn. *Richard Burton*, Boston, Mass., 1990.

Branagh, Kenneth. *Hamlet Screenplay*, London, 1996.

Branam, George C. *Eighteenth Century Adaptations of Shakespearean Tragedy*, Berkeley, 1956.

Brook, Peter. *Shifting Point*, New York, 1987.

Buell, William Ackerman, *The Hamlets of the Theatre*, New York, 1968.

Burnim, Kalman A. *David Garrick: Director*, Pittsburgh, Penn., 1961.

Burton, Philip. *Richard and Philip*, London, 1992.

Burton, Richard. 'Interview', *Playboy*, September 1963, 51–63.

   'The tragedy of Hamlet', *Introductions to Shakespeare*, London, 1977.

Calhoun, Lucia Gilbert. 'Edwin Booth', *Galaxy*, 7, 1869, 77–87.

Carlisle, Carol Jones. *Shakespeare from the Greenroom*, Chapel Hill, N.C., 1969.

Carlson, Marvin. *The Italian Shakespearians*, Washington D.C., 1985.

Carnovsky, Morris. *The Actor's Eye*, New York, 1984.

Castronovo, David, *The English Gentleman*, New York, 1987.

Chambers, E. K. *William Shakespeare: Facts and Problems*, Oxford, vol. II, 1930.

Chappell, William. *The Ballad Literature and Popular Music of the Olden Time*, New York, vol. I, 1965.

Child, Harold. 'Stage History of *Hamlet*' in *Hamlet*, ed. J. Dover Wilson.

Church, Tony. 'Polonius in *Hamlet*', in *Players of Shakespeare*, ed. P. Brockbank, Cambridge, 1985.

Cibber, Colley. *An Apology for the Life of Colley Cibber*, ed. B. R. S. Fone, Ann Arbor, Mich., 1968.

Clayton, Thomas, ed. *The Hamlet First Published*, Newark, Del., 1992.

Cochrane, Claire. *Shakespeare and the Birmingham Repertory Theatre, 1913–29*, London, 1993.

Cole, John William. *The Life and Theatrical Times of Charles Kean*, London, 2 vols., 1860.

Cole, Toby, ed. *Playwrights on Playwriting*, New York, 1960.

Coleman, John. *Players and Playwrights I Have Known*, London, vol. I, 1888.

Conklin, Paul S. *A History of Hamlet Criticism*, New York, 1947.

Cook, Dutton. *Hours with the Players*, London, vol. II, 1881.

Nights at the Play, London, vol. II, 1883.

On the Stage, London, vol. II, 1883.

Cox, Murray, ed. *Shakespeare Comes to Broadmoor*, Philadelphia, Penn., 1992.

Craig, Edward. *Gordon Craig*, New York, 1968.

Craig, Edward Gordon. *Ellen Terry and her Secret Self*, London, 1931.

Crosse, Gordon. *Diaries* (unpublished: originals in the Shakespeare Collection, Birmingham Central Library; a copy is in the Folger Shakespeare Library).

Shakespearean Playgoing, 1890–1952, London, 1953.

David, Richard. *Shakespeare in the Theatre*, Cambridge, 1978.

Davies, Anthony. *Filming Shakespeare's Plays*, Cambridge, 1988.

Davies, Thomas. *Memoirs of the Life of David Garrick*, London, vol. I, 1780.

Davril, R. 'Les Mises en Scene de Pitoeff', *Etudes Anglais*, 13, 1960, 192–6.

Dobson, Michael. *The Making of the National Poet*, Oxford, 1992.

Donohue, J. W. *Dramatic Character in the English Romantic Age*, Princeton, 1970.

Doran, John. *Annals of the English Stage, from Thomas Betterton to Edmund Kean*, London, vol. II, 1864.

Dort, Bernard. 'Brecht devant Shakespeare', *Revue d'Histoire du Théâtre*, January–March 1965, 69–83.

Douglas, Ann. *The Feminization of American Culture*, New York, 1988.

Downes, John. *Roscius Anglicanus*, London, 1708.

Dramatic Essays by John Forster and George Henry Lewes, ed. W. Archer and
    R. W. Lowe, London, 1894.
Eliot, George. *George Eliot Letters, 1859–61*, ed. G. Haight, New Haven,
    Conn., 1954.
Eyre, Richard. *Utopia and Other Places*, London, 1993.
Falke, Konrad. *Kainz als Hamlet*, 1911.
Farjeon, Herbert. *The Shakespearean Scene*, London, 1949.
Faucit, Helena. *On Some of Shakespeare's Female Characters*, London,
    1893.
Findlater, Richard. *The Player Kings*, New York, 1971.
Finlay, John. *Miscellanies . . . Dramatic Criticism*, Dublin, 1835.
Foakes, R. A. *Hamlet versus Lear*, Cambridge, 1993.
Furness, H. H., ed. *Hamlet: A New Variorum Edition*, Philadelphia, Penn.,
    2 vols., 1877.
Galt, John. *The Lives of the Players*, London, 2 vols., 1831.
Garland, Hamlin. Unpublished lecture on Edwin Booth in Special
    Collections, University of Southern California Library.
Garrick, David. *The Private Correspondence of David Garrick*, London, vol.
    I, 1831.
Gentleman, Francis. *The Dramatic Censor*, London, vol. I, 1770.
Gershkovich, Alexander. *The Theater of Yuri Lyubimov*, trans. M. Yurieff,
    New York, 1989.
Gibson, Mel. Home Box Office Special (TV), 1990.
Gielgud, John. *Acting Shakespeare*, New York, 1992.
    Early Stages, New York, 1939.
    Gielgud – An Actor and his Time, New York, 1980.
    Notes from the Gods, London, 1994.
    Stage Directions, New York, 1963.
Gielgud, Kate Terry. *A Victorian Playgoer*, London, 1980.
Gilbert, Miriam. Unpublished account of the Jonathan Pryce/Richard
    Eyre *Hamlet*.
    Unpublished account of the Mark Rylance/Ron Daniels *Hamlet*.
Gildon, Charles. *The Life of Mr. Thomas Betterton*, London, 1710.
Glick, Claris. '*Hamlet* in the English theater – acting texts from Betterton
    (1676) to Olivier (1963)', *Shakespeare Quarterly*, I, 1969, 17–35.
Goddard, Arthur. *Players of the Period*, London, 1891.
Golub, Spencer. 'Between the curtain and the grave: the Taganka in the
    Hamlet gulag', in *Foreign Shakespeare*, ed. D. Kennedy.
Granville-Barker, Harley. *Prefaces to Shakespeare*, Princeton, New Jersey,
    vol. I, 1952.
Grattan, Thomas Colley. *Beaten Paths*, London, vol. II, 1862.

Grebanier, Bernard. *Then Came Each Actor*, New York, 1975.

Griffith, Hubert. *Iconoclastes*, New York, 1927.

Guinness, Alec. *Blessings in Disguise*, London, 1985.

Guntner, Lawrence. 'Shakespeare on the East German stage', in *Foreign Shakespeare*, ed. D. Kennedy.

Gurr, Andrew. *The Shakespearean Stage, 1574–1642*, Cambridge, 1980.

Guthrie, Tyrone. *A Life in the Theatre*, New York, 1959.

    In Various Directions, New York, 1965.

    Shakespeare – Ten Great Plays, New York, 1862.

Habicht, Werner, D. Palmer, and R. Pringle. *Images of Shakespeare*, Newark, Del., 1988.

Hackett, James Henry, *Notes . . . upon Shakespeare's Plays and Actors*, New York, 1863.

Hall, Peter, *Peter Hall's Diaries*, ed. J. Goodwin, New York, 1984.

    Making an Exhibition of Myself, London, 1993.

Halsted, William P. *Shakespeare as Spoken*, Ann Arbor, Mich., vols. I, XI, XIII, 1977.

Hamburger, Maik. '"Are you a party in this business": Consolidation and subversion in East German productions', *Shakespeare Survey*, 48, 1995, 171–84.

Hattaway, Michael et al., eds. *Shakespeare in the New Europe*, Sheffield, 1994.

Hawkins, F. W. *The Life of Edmund Kean*, London, 1869.

Hayman, Ronald, *John Gielgud*, London, 1971.

    Brecht, Oxford, 1983.

Hazlitt, William. *Hazlitt on Theatre*, ed. W. Archer and R. W. Lowe, New York, n.d.

Holderness, Graham and Bryan Loughrey, 'Text and stage', *New Theatre Quarterly*, May 1993, 179–91.

Howells, William Dean. *Literature and Life Studies*, Port Washington, N.Y., 1968.

Hughes, Alan. *Henry Irving, Shakespearean*, Cambridge, 1981.

Hunt, Leigh. *Dramatic Essays*, ed. William Archer and R. W. Lowe, London, 1894.

Irving, Henry. 'An actor's notes on Shakespeare: No. 2', *Nineteenth Century*, May 1877, 524–30.

    'An actor's notes on Shakespeare: No. 3', *Nineteenth Century*, February 1879, 260–3.

Irving, Laurence. *Henry Irving*, New York, 1952.

Jacobi, Derek, 'Discovering *Hamlet*', video, 1990.

Jackson, Russell. 'Designer and director: E. W. Godwin and Wilson Barrett's *Hamlet* of 1884', *Shakespeare Jahrbuch West*, 1974, 186–200.

Jacquot, Jean. '"Mourir! Dormir! Rêver peut-être?": *Hamlet* de Dumas-Meurice de Rouvière à Mounet-Sully', *Revue d'Histoire du Théâtre*, October-December 1964, 407–445.

James, Henry. *The Scenic Art*, New Brunswick, 1948.

Jameson, Mrs. [Anna]. *Characteristics of Women*, Boston, Mass., 1892.

Jorgens, Jack. *Shakespeare on Film*, Bloomington, Ind., 1977.

Kelley, Hugh. 'Prologue to the Romance of an Hour', *Town and Country Magazine*, December 1774.

Kemble, Fanny [Frances Ann Butler]. *Journal*, Philadelphia, Penn., vol. I, 1835.

Kemble, John Philip. *Promptbooks*, ed. C. Shattuck, Charlottesville, Va., 1974.

Kendal, Madge. *Dame Madge Kendal by Herself*, London, 1933.

Kennedy, Dennis, ed. *Foreign Shakespeare*, Cambridge, 1993.
Looking at Shakespeare, Cambridge, 1993.

Kerrigan, John. 'Shakespeare as reviser', in *English Drama to 1710*, ed. C. Ricks, New York, 1987.

Kirk, John Foster. 'Shakespeare's Tragedies on the Stage: II', *Lippincott's Magazine*, June 1884, 604–16.

Kirkman, Francis. *The Wits, or Sport upon Sport*, London, 1662; ed. J. Elson, Oxford, 1932.

Knight, G. Wilson. *Shakespearean Production*, Evanston, Ill., 1964.
Wheel of Fire, London, 1930.

Knights, L. C. *An Approach to Hamlet*, Stanford, 1960.

Kobler, John. *Damned in Paradise: The Life of John Barrymore*, New York, 1977.

Kozintsev, Grigori. *Shakespeare: Time and Conscience*, trans. J. Vining, New York, 1966.

Lamb, Charles. 'On the artificial comedy of the last century', *Elia*.
The Portable Charles Lamb, ed. J. M. Brown, London, 1980.

Lawrence, William J. *Pre-Restoration Stage Studies*, Cambridge, Mass., 1927.

Le Gallienne, Richard. 'Forbes Robertson, an appreciation', *The Century Magazine*, 1914.

Leiter, Samuel L., ed. *Shakespeare Around the Globe*, Westport, Conn., 1986.

Levine, Lawrence, *Highbrow/Lowbrow*, Cambridge, Mass., 1988.

Levy, Micky. 'David Borovsky designs for Lyubimov', *Theatre Crafts*, 12, November-December 1978, 33–7, 57–61.

Lewes, George Henry. *On Actors and the Art of Acting*, London, 1875; reprint Westport, Conn., 1968.

Lichtenberg, Georg Christoph. *Lichtenberg's Visits to England*, trans. M.
Mare and W. Quarrell, London, 1938.

The London Stage, ed. W. Van Lennep with a critical introduction by E. L.
Avery and A. H. Scouten, Carbondale, Ill., vol I, 1960.

Long, John H. *Shakespeare's Use of Music: The Histories and Tragedies*,
Gainesville, Fla., 1971.

Loughrey, Bryan. 'Q1 in recent performance: an interview', in *The Hamlet
First Published*, ed. T. Clayton.

Lundstrom, Rinda F. *William Poel's Hamlets*, Ann Arbor, Mich., 1984.

MacCarthy, Desmond. *Theatre*, London, 1954.

Mack, Maynard. 'The World of Hamlet', *Yale Review*, 41, 1951–2, 502–23.

Macready, William Charles. *The Diaries of William Charles Macready:
1831–51*, ed. W. Toynbee, New York, vol. I, 1912.

Reminiscences, ed. F. Pollock, London, 1875.

Maher, Mary. *Modern Hamlets and their Soliloquies*, Iowa City, 1992.

Mallarmé, Stéphane. *Selected Prose Poems, Essays, and Letters*, trans. B.
Cook, Baltimore, Md., 1956.

Mander, Raymond and Joe Mitchenson. 'Hamlet costumes: a correction',
Shakespeare Survey, 11, 1958, 123–4.

Hamlet Through the Ages: A Pictorial Record from 1709, London, 1955.

Marowitz, Charles. *The Marowitz Shakespeare*, New York, 1978.

Marston, John Westland. *Our Recent Actors*, London, 2 vols., 1888.

Martin, H. *Remarks on Mr. John Kemble's Performance of Hamlet*, London,
1802.

Martin, Theodore. *Essays on the Drama*, London, 1874.

'An eye-witness of John Kemble', *Nineteenth Century*, 1880, 276–96.

Helena Faucit (Lady Martin), London, 1900.

Martin-Harvey, John. *The Autobiography of Sir John Martin-
Harvey*, London, 1933.

Mason, Philip. *The English Gentleman*, New York, 1982.

McManaway, James G. *Studies in Shakespeare, Bibliography, and Theatre*,
New York, 1969.

Merchant, W. Moelwyn. *Shakespeare and the Artist*, New York, 1959.

Meyerhold, Vsevolod. *Meyerhold on Theatre*, trans. E. Braun, New York,
1969.

Miller, Jonathan. *Subsequent Performances*, New York, 1986.

Mills, John A. 'The modesty of nature: Charles Fechter's
Hamlet', *Theatre Survey*, 15, 1974, 59–78.

Hamlet on Stage, Westport, Conn., 1985.

Mitford, Mary Russell. *The Life of Mary Russell Mitford*, ed. A. L'Estrange,
New York, vol. II, 1870.

More, Hannah. *Letters of Hannah More*, ed. R. B. Johnson, London, 1925.

Morgan, Joyce Vining. *Stanislavski's Encounter with Shakespeare*, Ann Arbor, Mich., 1984.

Morrison, Michael A. *John Barrymore, Shakespearean Actor*, Cambridge, 1997.

Munden, Joseph. *Memoirs of Joseph Shepherd Munden*, London, 1846.

Munro, John. *Shakespere [sic] Allusion-Book*, London, vol. I, 1932.

Murphy, Arthur. *Life of Garrick*, London, 1801.

Nicoll, Allardyce. 'Passing over the stage', *Shakespeare Survey*, 12, 1959, 47–55.

Noble, Adrian. 'Interview', *Shakespeare Bulletin*, Summer, 1993, 5–10.

O'Brien, Ellen J. 'Revision by excision: rewriting Gertrude', *Shakespeare Survey*, 45, 1992, 27–35.

Odell, George C. D. *Shakespeare from Betterton to Irving*, New York, vol. II, 1920.

Olivier, Laurence. *On Acting*, New York, 1986.

Olivier, Tarquin. *My Father Laurence Olivier*, London, 1992.

Orgel, Stephen. 'The authentic Shakespeare', *Representations*, 21, 1988, 1–25.

Osanai, Kaoru. 'Gordon Craig's production of *Hamlet* at the Moscow Art Theatre', *Educational Theatre Journal*, 20, 1968, 586–93.

Palmer, John. 'Hamlet in modern dress', *Fortnightly Review*, 118, November 1925, 675–83.

Papp, Joseph. *'Naked' Hamlet*, London, 1969.

Pasternak, Boris. *Selected Poems*, trans. J. Stallworthy and P. France, New York, 1982.

Payne, Harry. 'Edward Gordon Craig: the revolutionary of the theatre as Hamlet', *biography*, 10, 1987.

Pennington, Michael. 'Hamlet', in *Players of Shakespeare*, ed. Philip Brockbank, Cambridge, 1985.

Hamlet: A User's Guide, New York, 1996.

Pentzell, Raymond J. 'Kemble's Hamlet Costume', *Theatre Survey*, 13, 1972, 81–5.

Peters, Catherine. *The King of Inventors: A Life of Wilkie Collins*, Princeton, N. J., 1991.

Pfister, Manfred. 'Hamlets made in Germany, East and West', in *Shakespeare in the New Europe*, eds. M. Hattaway et al.

Phillpotts, Eden. 'Irving as Hamlet', in *We Saw Him Act: A Symposium on the Art of Sir Henry Irving*, London, 1939.

Phippen, Frances. *Authentic Memoirs of Edmund Kean*, London, 1814.

Pollock, Lady. *Macready as I Knew Him*, London, 1885.

Procter, B. W. (Barry Cornwall). *The Life of Edmund Kean*, London, vol. II, 1935.

Raby, Peter. *'Fair Ophelia': A Life of Harriet Smithson Berlioz*, Cambridge, 1982.

Redfield, William. *Letters from an Actor*, New York, 1966.

Redgrave, Michael. *In My Mind's I*, New York, 1983.
'Shakespeare and the actors', in *Talking of Shakespeare*, ed. J. Garrett, New York, 1954.

Roach, Joseph. 'Garrick, the Ghost and the Machine', *Theatre Journal*, 34, 1982, 431–40.

Robins, Elizabeth. 'On Seeing Madame Bernhardt's *Hamlet*', *North American Review*, 171, December 1900, 908–14.

Rocklin, Edward. 'Hamlet', SHAKSPER Internet, 17 May 1995.

Rowe, Eleanor. *Hamlet: A Window on Russia*, New York, 1976.

Russell, Charles Edward. *Julia Marlowe*, New York, 1926.

Russell, D. A. 'Hamlet Costumes from Garrick to Gielgud', *Shakespeare Survey*, 9, 1956, 54–8.

Scott, Clement. *Drama of Yesterday and Today*, London, vol. I, 1899.
Some Notable Hamlets, London, 1905.

Scott, Walter. 'Life of John Philip Kemble', *Quarterly Review*, 34, June and September 1826, 180–96.

Seng, Peter J. *The Vocal Songs in the Plays of Shakespeare*, Cambridge, Mass., 1967.

Shaftesbury. *Characteristics. Advice to an Author*, London, vol. I, 1710.

Shakespeare at the Old Vic, London, 1954.

Shakespeariana, IV, 1887, 29–40.

Shattuck, Charles H. *The Hamlet of Edwin Booth*, Chicago, 1969.
Shakespeare on the American Stage: From the Hallams to Edwin Booth, Washington, D.C., vol. I, 1976.
Shakespeare on the American Stage: From Booth and Barrett to Sothern and Marlowe, Washington, D.C., vol. II, 1987.
The Shakespeare Promptbooks, Urbana, Ill., 1965.

Shaw, George Bernard. *Shaw on Shakespeare*, ed. E. Wilson, New York, 1961.

Showalter, Elaine. 'Representing Ophelia: women, madness, and the responsibilities of feminist criticism', in *Shakespeare and the Question of Theory*, ed. P. Parker and G. Hartman, London, 1991.

Simmons, Ernest J. *English Literature and Culture in Russia, 1553–1840*, New York, 1961.

Skinner, Otis. *Footlights and Spotlights*, Westport, Conn., 1972.

Smith, Hedrick. *The Russians*, New York, 1976.

Speaight, Robert, *Nature in Shakespearean Tragedy*, New York, 1962.
  *Shakespeare on the Stage: An Illustrated History of Shakespearean
    Performance*, Boston, Mass., 1973.
  William Poel and the Elizabethan Revival, Cambridge, Mass., 1954.
Spoto, Donald. *Laurence Olivier*, New York, 1992.
Sprague, Arthur Colby. *Shakespeare and the Actors*, Cambridge, Mass.,
    1944.
Spurgeon, Caroline. *Shakespeare's Imagery*, London, 1935.
Staël, Madame de. *De l'Allemagne*, Paris, vol. III, 1959.
Stanislavsky, Konstantin. 'Konstantin Stanislavsky on *Hamlet*', in
    Shakespeare in the Soviet Union, Moscow, 1966.
Stedman, E. C. 'Edwin Booth', *Atlantic Monthly*, May 1866.
Steele, Joshua. *An Essay towards Establishing the Melody and Measure of
    Speech*, Menston, 1969.
Stone, George Winchester. 'Garrick's long lost alteration of *Hamlet*',
    PMLA, 49, 1934, 890–921.
Stone, George Winchester and George Kahrl. *David Garrick, a
    Critical Biography*, Carbondale, 1979.
Stříbrný, Zdeněk. 'Shakespearian rates of exchange in Czechoslovakia,
    1945–1989', *Shakespeare Survey*, 48, 1995, 163–70.
Taranow, Gerda. *The Bernhardt Hamlet*, New York, 1996.
Terry, Ellen. *Four Lectures on Shakespeare*, London, 1932.
Thomas, David, ed. *Theatre in Europe, A Documentary History: Restoration
    and Georgian England, 1660–1788*, Cambridge, 1989.
*The Three-Text Hamlet: Parallel Texts of the First and Second Quartos and
    First Folio*, ed. P. Bertram and B. Kliman, New York, 1991.
Towse, J. Ranken. 'Henry Irving', *Century Magazine*, 27, March 1884,
    660–9.
Tree, Herbert, Beerbohm. 'Hamlet from an actor's prompt book',
    Fortnightly Review, December 1895, 863–78.
Trewin, J. C. *Five & Eighty Hamlets*, New York, 1987.
  Shakespeare on the English Stage, 1900–1964, London, 1964.
Tynan, Kenneth. *He that Plays the King*, New York, 1950.
Urkowitz, Steven. 'Back to basics: thinking about the Hamlet First Quarto',
    in *Hamlet First Published*, ed. Thomas Clayton.
  'Five women eleven ways: Changing images of Shakespearean characters
    in the earliest texts', in *Images of Shakespeare*, ed. Habicht, Palmer and
    Pringle.
  '"Well-sayd olde Mole": burying three *Hamlets* in modern editions', in
    Shakespeare Study Today, ed. G. Ziegler, New York, 1986.
Vandenhoff, George. *Leaves from an Actor's Note Book*, New York, 1860.

Vickers, Brian, ed. *Shakespeare: the Critical Heritage*, London, 6 vols.,
    1974–81.
Webster, Margaret. *The Same Only Different*, New York, 1969.
    Shakespeare Today, London, 1957.
Wells, Stanley. *Royal Shakespeare*, Manchester, 1976.
Wells, Stanley and Gary Taylor. *William Shakespeare – A Textual
    Companion*, Oxford, 1987.
Werstine, Paul. 'The textual mystery of *Hamlet*', *Shakespeare Quarterly*, 39,
    1988, 1–26.
Wickham, Glynne. *Early English Stages, 1576–1660*, London, vol. II,
    section ii, 1972.
Wilkes, Thomas. *A General View of the Stage*, London, 1759.
William, David. 'The Osric scene in *Hamlet*', in *To Nevill Coghill from
    Friends*, ed. J. Lawlor and W. H. Auden, London, 1966.
Williams, Harcourt. *Four Years at the Old Vic: 1929–1933*, London, 1935.
Williamson, Audrey. *Old Vic Drama: A Twelve Years' Study of Plays and
    Players*, London, 1948.
Williamson, Claude. *Readings in the Character of Hamlet, 1661–1947*,
    London, 1950.
Wilson, J. Dover. *Hamlet*, Cambridge, 1934.
Wingate, Charles. *Shakespeare's Heroines on the Stage*, Boston, Mass., vol.
    II, 1895.
Winter, William. *Shakespeare on the Stage*, New York, 1911.
Young, Julian Charles. *A Memoir of Charles Mayne Young*, New York, 1871.
Young, Stark. *Glamour*, New York, 1925.

INDEX